9·20·78

Broadcasting
An Introduction to
Radio and Television

Saundra Hybels

LOCK HAVEN STATE COLLEGE

Dana Ulloth

ITHACA COLLEGE

D. Van Nostrand Company

NEW YORK • CINCINNATI • TORONTO • LONDON • MELBOURNE

For our mothers,
Adrienne and Esther

D. Van Nostrand Company Regional Offices:
New York   Cincinnati

D. Van Nostrand Company International Offices:
London   Toronto   Melbourne

ISBN: 0-442-23625-5

Published by D. Van Nostrand Company
135 West 50th Street, New York, N.Y. 10020

10 9 8 7 6 5 4 3 2 1

Preface

2025134

Broadcasting: An Introduction to Radio and Television is designed for both introductory broadcasting and mass media courses. The book will serve the needs of students who seek a career in broadcasting as well as those who are curious about the broadcast industry.

The materials address themselves to how the broadcast industry functions and how it interacts with related organizations, such as rating services, advertisers, government regulatory agencies, researchers, and citizen's groups. The book also discusses in some depth the technology of broadcasting, broadcast history, public broadcasting, cable, satellites, and many of the important issues that are faced by broadcasters. A major focus of the book is centered on the principle that broadcasting is a business and that decisions made in commercial broadcasting can best be understood in regard to business goals.

The text is liberally supplemented with diagrams, tables, and photographs. The diagrams put difficult technological material into understandable terms and the tables give up-to-date facts and figures from the broadcast industry and related organizations. The book also includes many narratives of an anecdotal character.

The book is divided into three main subject areas: Chapters 1–3 are concerned with the technology of broadcasting and broadcast history; Chapters

4–7 explain how the commercial and public broadcasting systems work; and Chapters 8–12 deal with research, regulation, broadcast issues, and new technology. The instructor need not follow this organizational pattern, however, since the chapters are self-contained, crossreferenced, and may be read in any order.

We hope this book will both answer the student's questions and pose new ones. We believe that, because of broadcasting's enormous impact on the American public, the broadcast industry merits study and discussion by all of us. It is for this purpose that we have written this book.

Saundra Hybels
Dana Ulloth

Contents

1. How Broadcasting Works   1

   Oscillation   2
   The Manipulation or Modulation of Radio Waves   9
   Consequences of Engineer Decisions   17
   Television   19
   Engineering Decisions, Economics, and Television   30
   Network Relay Systems   31
   Distribution Systems   35

2. History of Broadcasting to 1927   38

   Invention and Development of Telegraphy   39
   The Telephone   40
   Invention and Development of Wireless   41
   Wireless Inventors and Their Companies   45
   An American Radio Corporation Is Formed   52

Broadcasting Becomes a Reality   55
The Coming of Toll Broadcasting   58
Networking Begins   60

3. History of Broadcasting After 1927   71

Radio Enters its "Golden Age"   71
Radio During the Depression 1928–1937   73
The Evolution of the Disc Jockey   77
Radio During the Second World War 1938–1945   79
The Influence of Networks on Radio Programming   80
The Business of Networks   86
The Emergence of FM Broadcasting   90
The End of Radio's Golden Age 1948–1956   92
The Development of Television   94
Postwar Expansion of Television   98
The Licensing Freeze of 1948–1952   99
The Development of Color Television   103
The Unsteady Growth of UHF   105
The Establishment of National Television Networks   108
Television Programming   109
Fear of Communism Threatens Broadcasting   111
The Invention of Video Tape   112
Television Programming in the 1970s   116

4. Financial Organization and
   Programming Practices   121

Broadcast Ownership   122
Market Areas   122
Broadcast Ownership Patterns   124
The Failure of Diversification of Broadcast Ownership   128
The External Structure of Networks and Stations   129
The Internal Structure of Networks and Stations   133
Broadcast Programming   135
Radio Programming   136
Television Programming   140
Conclusion: Change and the Future   145

5. Broadcast Advertising — 148

The Role of Advertising in the U. S. Economy — 149
Advertising and the Mass Media — 150
Advertising and the Broadcaster — 152
Buying and Selling Advertising Time — 154
Organizations Concerned with Advertising — 157
The Problems of Advertising — 160
Advertising and Program Content — 162

6. Public Broadcasting — 165

The Economics of Public Broadcasting — 171
Program Sources and Funding — 175
The Diversity of Public Broadcast Programming — 180
Problems Facing Public Broadcasting — 181

7. Ratings — 184

The Reasons for Ratings — 185
Conducting Ratings Research — 186
Network and Station Response to Ratings — 200
Monitoring and Ratings Services — 203

8. Broadcasting Research — 207

Research Methods — 208
The Communicators — 210
The Audience — 212
The Message — 215
The Effects — 217
Future Research — 220

9. Broadcasting, Critics, and Public Interest — 225

The Critics: Who Are They? — 226
The Issues — 228

10. Agencies of Regulation 236

The FCC and the Public 236
Creation of the FCC 237
"The Public Interest, Convenience, and Necessity" 239
Structure of Radio Law 240
The FCC as Legislator and Judge 240
Organization of the FCC 245
Operation of the FCC 247
Criticism of the FCC 254
Other Agencies Concerned with Broadcasting 256
Agencies Indirectly Concerned with Broadcasting 263
Self-Regulation 263
Other Forms of Self-Regulation 266

11. Issues in Broadcast Regulation 269

Regulation and the First Amendment 269
History of the Fairness Doctrine 272
Monopoly and Broadcasting 277
Failures of the FCC 282
Proposals for Improving the FCC 286

12. Alternate Technologies, New Directions 290

Cable Television 293
The Future 303

Index 309

How Broadcasting Works

Today we take the complex innovations of radio and television largely for granted. But it took many years and the work of countless people to develop our present system of broadcasting. Perhaps we should stop right here and explain what the term broadcasting means. Broadcasting was originally a farming term that meant spreading seeds all over the field. In radio and television, broadcasting means sending out programs through the air to everyone within reach of a station. Anyone who has the necessary equipment can listen to the programs sent out.

Some of the countless people interested in broadcasting had commercial or military interests, while others experimented with the new medium purely from academic or avocational interests. Without the work of these inventors, radio and television would not have been possible. They discovered ways to transmit coded messages, which was important to ships at sea. It was not until engineers discovered how to impress voices and music on wireless, however, that radio became popular. As industry discovered the economic potential of broadcasting to homes, a great interest in the work of these engineers developed.

This chapter examines how radio and television work and how the broadcast channels are divided among the various services—AM, FM, and television.

OSCILLATION

To understand radio waves clearly we must first understand the electrical impulses that create radio waves and that means exploring the concept of oscillation.

Electricity may exist in at least two forms—direct current (DC) and alternating current (AC). To understand the difference between the two, the system in which electricity flows must be examined. All such systems are closed. This means that one may start at any point and by traveling in one direction eventually return to the point of origin. Figure 1–1 shows a typical circuit. The generator pushes minute, electrically charged particles called electrons through the circuit, much as a pump pushes water through a hose. This generator may be a battery such as one finds in a car, or a giant atomic energy plant used by electric companies. The light bulb uses up the energy of the electrons pushed through the circuit.

If the generator pushes the electricity in only one direction, we call this pattern of electric flow direct current (DC). DC is the kind of electric flow with which batteries, such as those in cars or flashlights, operate. When electricity flows in only one direction, all of the electricity stays in the wire and, therefore, no electrical field is created around the wire. On the other hand, if the electric flow first surges forward—we shall call this the positive direction—and then reverses itself and moves backward—let's call this the negative direction—then the current is oscillating and is often called alternating current (AC). This pattern of electrons first rushing forward and then backward can be compared to the motion of a yo-yo. First the yo-yo races down the string, in what we might

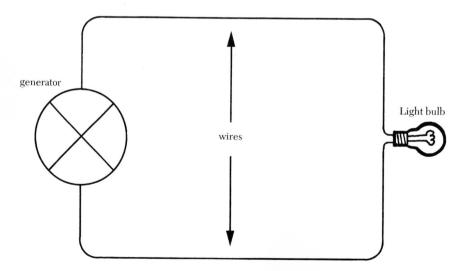

Figure 1–1. Diagram of a simple electrical circuit. The generator pushes the electrons through the wires so that the light bulb can use the resulting energy to produce light.

call a positive direction, only to reverse itself and race back up the string in the negative direction. AC is the type of electric flow found in the wires of one's home.

We can diagram this alternating flow of electricity as shown in Figure 1–2. The horizontal line represents the amount of time that has elapsed and permits us to measure the amount of time required for one cycle, or one forward and one reverse motion. The length of time a cycle requires is sometimes called its period. The segment of the graph above the horizontal line represents the electricity when it is flowing in a positive direction. Then, as the electricity reverses itself and flows backwards, the graph goes below the horizontal line to indicate the negative flow of electricity. One full oscillation has been completed when the forward and reverse surges have ended.

Characteristics of an Oscillating Current

When an alternating current flows through a wire, some of the energy escapes, or radiates, into the area around the wire. With the right instruments, it is possible to pick up this energy. All alternating currents radiate some electrical energy. In fact it is this radiated electrical energy that radio stations transmit that enables us to hear our favorite programs.

Frequency

We call one complete oscillation a cycle. Electricity, like a vibrating reed or violin string, oscillates a certain number of times per second. Ordinary household current oscillates at sixty cycles per second. Radio waves oscillate much faster. We describe the location of a radio station on the radio dial (or on the radio spectrum) by the number of cycles per second at which the radio carrier oscillates. For convenience radio people have chosen to shorten the term "cycles per second" to Hertz (Hz) after the German physicist, Heinrich Hertz, who conducted some of the early radio experiments.

The number of Hertz a station uses is called its frequency. Thus if a certain station operates on a frequency of 980,000 Hz it is possible to determine its location. But if you examine your radio dial, you will discover that no number as large as 980,000 appears on it.

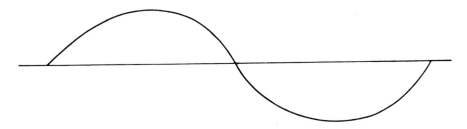

Figure 1–2. Diagram of the flow of alternating current. The top half of this graph represents the positive flow of electricity, while the part below the line represents the negative flow.

Because many radio frequencies are very high, (the highest are near 3,000,000,000,000 Hz) engineers have developed a numerical shorthand to refer to them.[1] The word kilo means 1,000; mega refers to 1 million; and giga means billion. By combining kilo with Hertz to form kiloHertz (kHz), we can now refer to the frequency of the 980,000 Hz station as 980 kHz. Or we could use the prefix megaHertz (mHz) to say that the station has an operating frequency of .98 mHz. When a dial for a new radio is printed, the prefix which makes the numbers on the dial easiest to read is used.

Waves

Although we will discuss radio signals as waves, a modern branch of physics theorizes that radio signals are actually quanta or bursts of energy sent through the air. The wave theory regards radio signals as continuous waves of energy while the quantum theory regards radio signals as bursts. In our discussion we will think of radio as a wave and we will examine this most closely. It is important, however, to remember that both are theories used to explain a concept that we can only partially understand at present.

Radio waves emanate from a transmitting antenna very much as waves radiate from the point at which a rock falls in still water. The waves of water resemble the diagram of a cycle in Figure 1–2. Water waves have hills and valleys that correspond to the high and low points in a radio wave. Further, the water waves radiate from the rock in ever expanding circles. In just such a way radio waves emanate from the radio tower. Of course radio waves travel in all directions—up, down, horizontally—while water waves appear to travel only across the surface of the water.

Just as an ocean wave can be modified or stopped by a rock or beach, so radio waves can be modified or stopped through contact with mountains or buildings. You may have watched a wave encountering a pier or other solid object and then seen the wave reflected by the object back towards its source. Similar things happen when radio waves hit solid objects. This is why we sometimes see two images of a television picture on our screen. The second image is the result of the reflected wave reaching our television set.

Most radio signals radiate out from the radio tower in a circular pattern just as the water waves radiate in a circular pattern. Sometimes stations use several radio towers arranged in a straight line. When this is done radio waves radiate in a figure eight pattern as shown in Figure 1–3.

Wave of different lengths behave differently and can have an important impact on how radio waves travel. Long waves at low frequencies—below the AM broadcast band—tend to travel long distances and will bend around the earth. Medium length waves travel around the earth somewhat but will not travel as far as long waves, and short waves—those above the broadcast band—will not bend around the earth and are dependent upon waves that are reflected back to earth by a band of electrically charged particles, called the ionosphere, that surrounds the earth. However, very short waves are not bent back to earth but

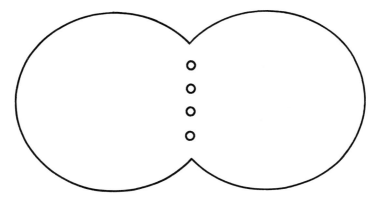

Figure 1–3. Pattern of radiation for directional station. The figure eight pattern of a directional station is the result of the special arrangement of multiple towers and the way radio waves are fed to each tower.

pass through the ionosphere and consequently can be picked up at only short distances from the transmitter.

This behavior of radio waves can be understood by an illustration involving light, which is a radio wave. When a beam of sunlight passes around a sharp surface such as a thin key, the key tends to bend the light waves slightly so that the light waves, which were traveling parallel before reaching the key, are bent slightly and no longer travel parallel. Thus the image of the key on a wall will be somewhat fuzzy. (See Figures 1–4 and 1–5.)So long as the thickness of the key is less than the length of one wave, this bending will occur, but when the thickness of the key becomes greater than the length of a wave, then it is unable to effect any bending.

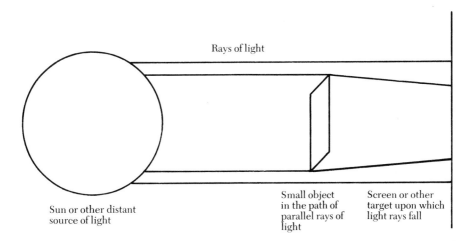

Rays of light

Sun or other distant source of light

Small object in the path of parallel rays of light

Screen or other target upon which light rays fall

Figure 1–4. When rays of light impinge on the edge of a thin object like a sheet of paper or a key, they are bent slightly by the object as is noted by the two lines representing rays of light that touch the object above. Notice how they converge towards each other while the two lines representing rays of light which do not touch the object continue in a straight pa'h. As long as the wavelength of any wave is longer than the thickness of an object with which it comes in contact, the object will bend the wave somewhat.

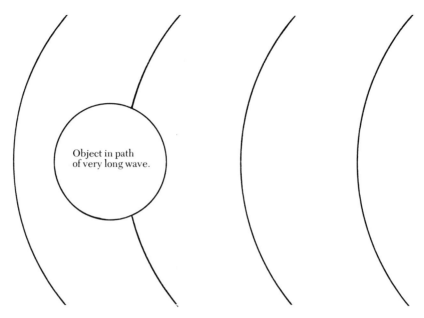

Figure 1–5. Peaks of waves. When one drops a rock in still water waves flow out from the point of impact as shown by the partial circles above. If the waves are much longer than the object is thick, then the waves will flow (or bend) around the object as shown above almost as if the object were invisible to the wave.

Both ocean and radio waves have a length, which is called their wavelength. Wavelength represents the distance from the beginning to the end of one complete cycle. As the frequency of a radio wave increases, the length of the wave decreases. Thus, very high frequencies have short wavelengths and much lower frequencies have long wavelengths.

The reason for this relationship between frequency and wavelength relates to the distance a radio wave travels in a second. All radio waves travel the same distance in one second; that is, about 186,000 miles. As the number of cycles crowded into one second of travel increases, each cycle must become shorter so that all of the cycles can be crowded into one second. The extremely long waves at frequencies below the standard broadcast band are sometimes several miles in length. A building, a tree, a hilltop, or a water tower are all relatively short compared to one wavelength and thus almost anything can cause these waves to bend. As a result, long waves readily travel around the surface of the earth. When a wave clings to the earth it is called a ground wave.

As waves get shorter, the ability of the earth and other objects to bend them becomes less and so shorter waves tend not to follow the contour of the earth as well. This problem becomes pronounced near the middle of the AM broadcast band, with the result that lower frequency AM stations tend to enjoy the benefits of waves bending around the earth while higher frequency stations do not. Thus, some of the AM channels in the higher ranges depend heavily upon being bent back to earth by the ionosphere.

The ionosphere is thinner than most waves up to about 30 mHz and consequently does a pretty good job of bending radio waves back to earth up to that frequency. However, the ionosphere changes thickness from day to night and during different parts of the year, so it is impossible to name an exact upper frequency at which it will no longer bend waves. These radio waves that travel out through space to the ionosphere are called sky waves.

Radio waves above about 30 mHz can neither be bent around the earth by objects on the ground nor back to earth by the ionosphere. Transmitters operating above 30 mHz must depend upon a third type of waves for reaching receivers—line of sight waves. These line of sight waves travel straight from the transmitting antenna to your television or FM radio antenna. This is why television antennas are often placed on top of houses. The higher they are, the greater distance the antenna can be from the transmitter. Of course, tall buildings and other objects prevent these radio waves from reaching your antenna and so in large cities like New York many people complain about television reception problems.

Amplitude

Amplitude and the more popular term volume are the same. When you turn up the volume on your radio set you are increasing the amplitude of the sounds you hear. Amplitude can be understood by thinking of how one might play middle C on a piano. By hitting the key hard, one produces a very loud sound, by only lightly tapping the same middle C, a low sound is produced. The same note has been played, but the volume or amplitude has changed. Just as sound waves have amplitude, radio waves have amplitude and we have diagrammed the difference in amplitudes of two waves in Figure 1–6.

Attenuation

As a radio wave travels through the air some of the signal is absorbed or lost in a process called attenuation. As a result, the radio wave gets weaker and weaker as one gets farther from the station until it is impossible to hear the station. Let's return to our example of striking middle C. If we were to place a piano in

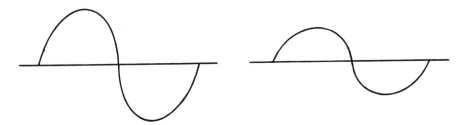

Figure 1–6. Comparison of two waves with different amplitudes. The wave on the left has a much greater amplitude than the wave on the right.

an open field and strike middle C, we could hear the note clearly near the piano. But if we were to stand 300 feet from the piano, we would not hear the note as clearly. Finally, if we were to walk far enough away, we could not hear the note being played at all. This attenuation of sound waves limits the distance we can be from the sound source to still hear it.

All radio frequencies are attenuated as they travel through space; the very highest radio frequencies are absorbed very rapidly in the atmosphere. Of course there are other factors that attenuate radio waves such as rocks, mountains, and buildings. But, in fact, it is this rapid absorption of radio waves at the highest frequencies that limits the usable frequencies.

Electromagnetic Spectrum

Radio waves are only part of a much larger range of waves called electromagnetic waves. Electromagnetic waves include cosmic rays, X-rays, light, and radio waves. Thus, light waves and radio waves are both part of the same spectrum of electromagnetic waves. They differ only in the frequency at which they vibrate. The lower frequencies of the electromagnetic spectrum are occupied by radio waves that can send signals through the air. Just above the radio waves are infrared or heat waves; then come light waves, ultra-violet rays, X-rays, gamma rays, and cosmic rays. Figure 1–7 shows the distribution of the different kinds of waves.

The range of radio waves has been arbitrarily divided into subgroups for convenience. In the early days of radio only the lower frequencies could be used, but as equipment became more sophisticated higher and higher waves became usable. As noted earlier, the highest frequencies are absorbed almost as soon as they leave the transmitter so that, at present, the highest usable frequencies are about 3,000,000,000,000 Hz.

TABLE 1-1.   Division of Radio Spectrum.

Name of Subdivision	FREQUENCY RANGE EXPRESSED IN		
	Kilocycles Per Second (Kilohertz)	Megacycles Per Second (Megahertz)	Gigacycle Per Second (Gigahertz)
Very Low Frequency (VLF)	Below 30	—	—
Low Frequency (LF)	30–300	—	—
Medium Frequency (MF)	300–3,000	—	—
High Frequency (HF)	3,000–30,000	3–30	—
Very High Frequency (VHF)	30,000–300,000	30–300	—
Ultra High Frequency (UHF)	300,000–3,000,000	300–3,000	—
Super High Frequency (SHF)	3,000,000–30,000,000	3,000–30,000	3–30
Extremely High Frequency (EHF)	30,000,000–300,000,000	30,000–300,000	30–300

Source: Frederick Emmons Terman, *Electronic and Radio Engineering*, (New York: McGraw-Hill, 1955), p. 3.

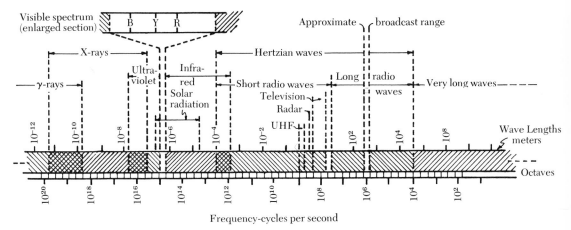

Figure 1–7. Wave distribution. Source: Donald G. Fink and David M. Lutyens, *The Physics of Television*, Garden City, N.Y.: Doubleday and Company, Inc., 1960, p. 30.

THE MANIPULATION OR MODULATION OF RADIO WAVES

No one would be interested in simply sending a radio wave out into the air without sending some information with it. In the earliest days, radio waves were turned on and off to transmit coded information. This on and off keying of a radio signal allowed experimenters to send the Morse code letter "s" across the Atlantic (1901). It allowed ships at sea to communicate with land, but code was of little interest to the general population.

Many wanted to impose voices, music, and pictures on the radio waves. The process of adding sounds and pictures to a radio wave is called modulation. We can draw a rough analogy between modulation and the function of a truck; that

GALLOPING TECHNOLOGY

New innovations seem to be appearing at an increasing rate, for example, optical fibers. These fibers are small filaments similar to wires, but they conduct light rather than electricity. Light holds more promise for carrying many signals than does electricity. While cables and wires carry telephone and telegraph wires, the potential of optical fibers is so much greater than wires that picture phones may be a real possibility. The only problem is that AT & T has such a great investment in wire and cable systems that it is unwilling to adopt the new technology.

TYPES OF ENERGY

Scientists have found only a few different kinds of energy. The first was heat energy derived from burning coal, oil, and wood. Heat powers cars, heats homes, and keeps airplanes in the air. The second form of energy—electricity—lights homes and powers factories. The third form of energy, magnetism, has uses ranging from magnetic toys to powerful industrial machines. Electricity and magnetism often operate together as is the case in radio waves. The fourth source of energy, the atom, provides power for bombs and modern electric plants.

is, our radio wave serves the same function as a truck in that it has no real use unless something is hauled. Indeed radio and television waves are often called carriers because they are used to carry pictures, music, sounds, and speech to the listener and viewer. When one thinks of a radio carrier as a truck and the sound, music, and pictures as the cargo, modulation is the process of loading the cargo onto the carrier. There are several methods for modulating a radio carrier, but three provide the major methods used by commercial broadcasters—amplitude modulation (AM), frequency modulation (FM), and television (TV). The first two provide only sound signals while the third, of course, provides both sound and picture signals.

Amplitude Modulation (AM)

The AM process of modulating a radio carrier is essentially one of varying the amplitude of the radio wave to conform to both the amplitude and frequency of the sounds one wishes to broadcast. This is much like using a water faucet to modulate a stream of water. A trickle of water corresponds to soft sounds, while water flowing fully from a wide open faucet resembles the effect of loud sounds on an AM radio wave. Thus, in AM, the sound wave works as a valve controlling the volume, or amplitude, of the radio wave forcing it to conform to the volume and frequency of the sound wave. The process of amplitude modulation is shown in Figure 1–8.

Size of an AM Channel.   The process of modulating sounds on a radio wave requires a large band of radio frequencies. The actual number of frequencies is dependent upon the quality of sound one wishes to broadcast. The human ear can hear sounds whose frequencies range from a low of about 20 Hz to a high of about 20,000 Hz. If we wanted to modulate all of the sounds we are capable of hearing on a radio wave, our wave would have to carry sounds ranging from 20 Hz to 20,000 Hz. However, AM radio stations can only broadcast frequencies from about 100 Hz to about 5,000 Hz.[2] Although this limited range includes

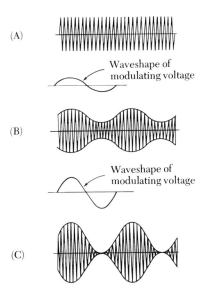

Figure 1–8. Diagram of radio wave modulated by AM. Source: Doug DeMad, ed., *The Radio Amateur's Handbook* (Newington, Conn.: ARRL, 1970), p. 235.

voices and most musical instruments, it does not include many complex nuances of music that make for "high fidelity" reproduction.

To broadcast the sound frequencies between 100 Hz and 5,000 Hz, an AM station must have a band of radio frequencies that is 10 kHz wide. When an announcer tells you that a station is operating on 600 kHz, only the center of the station's channel is being described. It actually extends from 595 kHz to 605 kHz.

The AM Broadcast Band.   Originally, the Federal Radio Commission made the AM broadcast band as small as possible in order to accommodate other services. It extended from 550 kHz to 1,500 kHz.[3] AM broadcast band is a term that refers to the standard broadcast band. Although standard broadcast band is the more technically correct term, we use AM broadcast band since it seems to be more common. The current AM band occupies the frequencies between 540 kHz to 1600 kHz. Since each channel is actually 10 kHz wide, the first channel extends from 535 kHz to 555 kHz. The highest AM channel extends from 1595 to 1605 kHz. There are 107 AM channels. Nationally, nearly 8,000 AM stations occupy those 107 channels. Thus, many of the AM channels have a number of stations on the single band of frequencies.

Factors Affecting the Coverage of AM Stations

Power.   Power is an important factor in determining the size of the area in which a radio station can be heard. Once a radio wave leaves a station's tower no new power can be added. Thus, if the station has a power of 100 watts and if one measures all of the power at any distance from the station, it will not exceed 100 watts. At the antenna all of a station's power is concentrated in a very small area but as the radio wave moves away from the antenna, the station's power spreads over larger and larger circles of area just as a circle of water becomes larger and larger as it radiates from the point at which a rock enters the water. Although the radio wave still contains most of the power it had when it left the radio antenna, the power is spread over larger and larger areas as the wave gets further and further from the antenna. For this reason, there will be less power available as one moves away from the antenna. See Figure 1–9.

For a receiver to pick up a station's signal, a minimum amount of power must reach the receiver from the station. This minimum will vary from receiver to receiver. Eventually, when one gets far enough from a station, the amount of power from the station that reaches the receiver's antenna will become so low that it is impossible to receive the signal. For the same reason the peaks on the

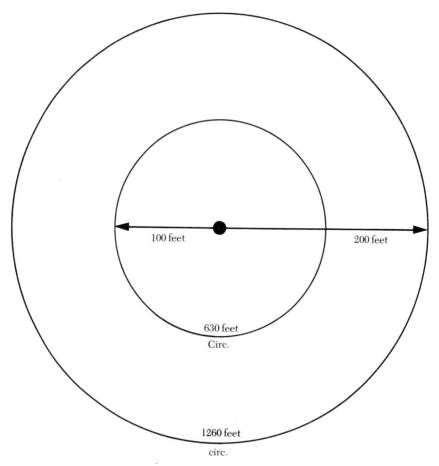

Figure 1–9. Illustration of how power from a radio station must spread over increasing distances as it travels away from the radio tower.

water waves get smaller and smaller as the wave gets farther from the point at which it originated. The wave still has about the same amount of energy, but it is diffused over a larger area.

However, if a station were to increase its power, the amount of power at any distance from the antenna would be increased in direct relation to the increase in the station's power. Therefore, the distance at which a receiver could detect the station's signal would be increased. The higher power stations often reach an entire state or more, while the 250-watt stations rarely reach more than a small city and perhaps the surrounding county.

Clear Channels.   Forty-five of the 107 AM channels have been designated as Class I clear channels. Some of the clear channels are used by stations in the United States, while others are used by Canada and other nations. In the United States, the FCC has authorized one or two high power stations to operate on each Class I channel. It should be noted that international treaties designate which countries have control over various clear channels—and, for that matter, all other radio and television channels.

The FCC intended that the high power stations would serve large cities. In addition, the stations were to broadcast to large rural areas that were unserved by other local or lower power stations. Most of the clear channel stations have a power of 50,000 watts, and none use less than 10,000 watts.

The FCC has designated secondary stations, which share a channel with the class I stations. This secondary category, class II stations, also serve large areas including major cities and often rural areas that are nearly as large as the primary station sharing the channel. When a "secondary" station shares a clear channel with a primary station, the secondary station's signal must not interfere with the primary station so that Class I stations can readily reach large areas.[4] Like the class I stations, class II stations may have up to 50,000 watts of power, but they may have power as low as 250 watts. There are 29 channels designated as class II channels.

Regional Channels.   Regional stations or, as the FCC calls them, class III stations serve a city and its neighboring rural area. The FCC has allocated 41 channels for use by class III stations. Several stations may occupy each of the class III channels, and stations with this classification may have a power ranging from 500 to 5,000 watts.

Local or Class IV Channels.   The FCC set aside six channels for purely local service. The FCC hoped that these stations would supply the needs for local news, sports, and entertainment. On each of these six channels there may be as many as 150 stations. These local stations may not have more than 1,000 watts during the day and 250 watts at night.[5]

Location of Antenna.   The location of an AM station's antenna can be more important to its coverage than its power. One half of an AM station's antenna is the type of tower you sometimes see dotting the landscape. The other half of the antenna is buried in the ground and is extremely important to the distance

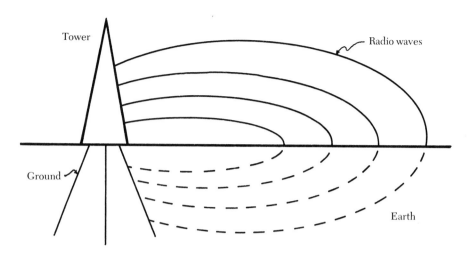

Figure 1–10. The complete AM radio circuit including the ground. Part of an AM wave flows through the air but an important part flows through the ground. The better the ground, the further an AM signal will reach.

the station can cover. To cover the most distance many stations locate their antennas near water. Engineers have found that a 250 watt AM station with its ground wires buried in swampy soil sometimes has greater coverage than a 50,000 watt station with its ground wires buried in dry, sandy terrain.[6]

A grounding system is important to an AM radio signal because, like all circuits, AM radio signals are "closed." As we noted before, closed means that electricity which starts at one point in a circuit can travel around the circuit and return to its point of origin. In the same way radio waves that leave the radio tower above the ground travel through space and then return to the underground wires of the radio station to complete the circuit (see Figure 1–10). As with all circuits, the better the connection, the easier it is for electricity to flow.

Time of Day.   AM stations can cover greater distances during the night hours than during daylight hours. This is because of the unique relationship of "ground," "sky," and "line of sight" radio waves. In Figure 1–11 we can see the relationship of each kind of wave. Ground waves tend to follow the curvature of the earth and, as such, bend around the earth. Line of sight waves are those waves that travel straight from the transmitter to your receiver. Therefore, as soon as you get out of sight of the transmitting station, line of sight waves no longer exist. Sky waves emanate from the transmitter towards the sky at an angle. Some distance above the earth these sky waves are reflected to earth by the ionosphere.

During the day, AM stations depend largely upon line of sight and ground waves because the sky waves penetrate the ionosphere and are not reflected back to earth. Ground waves reach about the same distance during both light and dark hours and provide AM stations with a dependable coverage area. At night the ionosphere becomes more dense than it is during the day. Con-

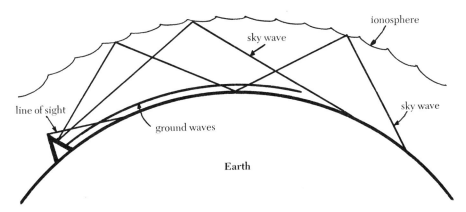

Figure 1–11. Relationship of sky, ground, and line of sight waves.

sequently, it reflects the sky waves back to earth so that people can receive AM stations at night that they would never be able to hear during the day.

Because radio signals cover greater distances at night, the FCC has decreed that some stations must turn off their transmitters at night. Other stations must reduce their power at night so that they will not interfere with the stations that remain on the air.

Noise. AM stations have a major problem that they have never been able to solve—noise. During lightening storms, an AM listener is often plagued by distracting loud pops and crackles. In fact some storms create so much noise that listening to an AM station becomes virtually impossible. This happens because lightening—or for that matter many other sources of electrical noise—can change the amplitude of an AM radio wave. The change in amplitude, of course, introduces undesirable noise onto the AM radio wave. The AM stations have found no solution to the problem of noise picked up from the atmosphere. FM was to provide the answer.

Frequency Modulation. Frequency modulation (FM) broadcasting has the same goal as AM broadcasting—impressing sounds on a radio wave so that the sounds can be heard at great distances from the transmitter. But while AM stations vary the amplitude of the carrier in unison with the sounds to be transmitted, FM varies the frequency of the radio wave. The FM radio wave wobbles up and down the radio spectrum in much the same way as water wobbles out of a hose when you shake it. The sound waves do not change the amplitude of the radio wave in any way when the radio wave is modulated.

Since FM radio does not depend upon the amplitude of the radio wave for modulation, atmospheric noises can not add noise to FM radio waves. Of course, these atmospheric noises do change the amplitude of the FM signal, but your FM radio does not detect the noises. The listener of FM, then, is not bothered by the usual AM static and crackle.

Size of an FM Channel.   To make FM sounds particularly good and to afford opportunity to carry extra programs, the FCC created very wide FM channels. Each channel has a 200 kHz band of frequencies. This is twenty times greater than a single AM channel of 10 kHz. This wide band of frequencies allows for high fidelity broadcasting. In fact, FM stations are required to keep their programming free from distracting noises. In addition, an FM station must be able to broadcast sounds up to 15,000 Hz, which is three times the range of an AM station.

Besides carrying high fidelity programs, FM can also carry second and third channels of programming on its radio wave. For example, many FM stations now broadcast stereophonic programs. Some FM stations also carry a separate music program—for public broadcasting in stores, for example. The commercial music cannot be picked up by your home set without special equipment. Broadcasting background music has saved many FM stations from financial ruin, because the music is sold to stores who wish to subscribe. (See Figure 1–12.)

FM Broadcast Band.   The band of frequencies allocated to FM broadcasters extends from 88 to 108 mHz. This allows for 100 different FM channels. The first twenty channels were specifically set aside for educational users while the other 80 channels were open to anyone who wished to use the channels. FM stations do not generally cover areas as large as the larger AM stations so the FCC was free to place many FM stations on each of the 100 channels. To guide in the placement of FM stations, the FCC drew up a table indicating geographic areas where applicants might build a station.[7]

Factors Affecting the Coverage of FM Stations

Unlike AM broadcasting, FM signals cannot travel far beyond the horizon. Thus there are no "clear channel" stations in the FM broadcast band. The two factors that govern the coverage of an FM station are the height and type of the antenna and the power of the transmitter.

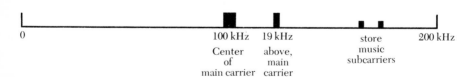

Figure 1–12. Diagram of an FM channel. An FM channel as authorized by the FCC is 200 kHz wide. When the FM carrier is being modulated at full volume (100%) the FM carrier shifts 75 kHz above and below the center frequency. An FM station that programs in stereo has a 19 kHz carrier modulated on to the main carrier. This stereo subcarrier (as it is called) is separated from the main carrier by the equivalent of about two AM channels. In addition, a FM station may add up to two additional subcarriers for carrying music for stores. These subcarriers are more than 60 kHz above the main carrier frequency. This is the equivalent of more than six AM channels. These subcarriers are modulated by AM and the design of FM receivers prevents picking up all subcarriers at once.

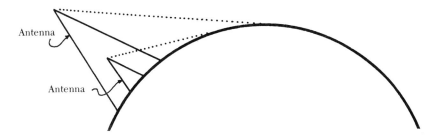

Figure 1–13. Effect of two different antenna heights on FM coverage.

Antenna Height.   More than any other factor, antenna height dictates an FM station's coverage. The very high frequencies (VHF) assigned to FM perform much like light in that they travel in a straight line with FM ground and sky waves of little importance. FM sky waves are not reflected back to earth as are AM waves so they are of no consequence to the listener of a FM station. FM ground waves are also insignificant since they are unable to bend around the earth as are AM waves. For these reasons FM stations are totally dependent upon the waves that travel straight from the FM station to the listener's receiver.

The higher a FM station's antenna is above the average ground level the greater these line of sight waves will travel before the curvature of the earth cuts off reception. Notice in Figure 1–13 how raising the antenna to a greater height causes the waves to reach farther around the curve of the earth. As with AM stations, there are classifications for FM stations and these classifications dictate the height of an FM antenna. Class A stations may erect an antenna that is 300 feet above the average elevation of the land around the station. Class B stations may go to 500 feet and class C stations to 2,000 feet.[8]

Power.   Although FM broadcasting is limited to line of sight reception, the power of a station can improve reception in distant areas. The FCC has adopted maximum power limitations for stations in each of the above three classes: class A—3,000 watts; class B—50,000 watts; and class C—100,000 watts. Therefore the FCC authorizes the combination of high power and tall antenna to some stations and low power and short antenna to other stations.

CONSEQUENCES OF ENGINEERING DECISIONS

The FCC seldom makes an engineering decision on technical considerations alone. When the FCC decided on the location of the AM or FM bands, it did so after considering the conflicting demands of several groups of people and companies. The FCC must consider the economic consequences of different decisions and it must evaluate the effects of a decision on the long range development of radio. When the FCC—and before it the FRC—considers a new engineering rule or regulation, companies with an interest in the decision rally their forces to influence the FCC to rule in their favor. This kind of situation arose first when the FRC considered what to do with AM stations. Later, when the FCC contemplated FM channels, the same types of forces came to bear on the FCC. In both cases the parties with the greatest influence appeared to win.

When the FRC was allocating AM frequencies to different station operators, commercial broadcasters wanted all of the channels. Although there were more than 171 educational AM stations before 1925, only about two dozen are still on the air.[9] Educational institutions did not have sufficient assets to operate their stations and when commercial broadcasters agreed to provide free air time to educational users, most educational stations were sold to commercial operators.

The FRC exhibited no interest in maintaining certain channels for educational use and willingly accepted the solution suggested by commercial radio. Although commercial stations had promised extensive educational programs, very few stations carried out their promise.

Of more severe consequence was the decision to create class I, II, III, and IV stations. The clear channel stations, which are usually located in large markets, have been able to make large amounts of money while many of the class IV stations have had great difficulty in breaking even. Indeed the FCC's classification virtually guaranteed that some stations would become rich while other suffered. The favored status of the class I stations is so great that they have formed an association to protect their position. This clear channel association spends much of its time lobbying before the FCC in the interests of the clear channel stations.

The history of the FCC's handling of FM radio is fraught with what appears now to be some misjudgments. The development of FM came just as large corporations like RCA were trying to exploit the commercial possibilities of television. Consequently, RCA wished to stall the development of FM while it contemplated television. Both FM and television were unable to develop during World War II. Then in 1945, as the war was ending, development of television and FM became an issue again.

Prior to 1945, FM had held the frequencies between 43 and 50 mHz.[10] In 1945 the FCC adopted a rule which ordered the change in FM frequencies to the present 88 to 108 mHz. The FCC declared that its decision was based on a long-range concern for the development of FM. A military engineer who testified before the FCC argued that sunspots might damage performance of FM broadcasting in the 43 to 50 mHz frequencies. Although the engineer's data was classified by the military and thus not open to examination, a group of companies including RCA, Philco, Crosley, and Motorola agreed with the engineer in asking the FCC to change the FM band to higher frequencies. These companies were committed to speedy development of television and thought the lower frequencies would be particularly good for television broadcasting. FM, they thought, should use the higher and less desirable frequencies. The television group thought that the lower frequencies would permit television stations to have greater reach than they would have at higher frequencies.

Moving FM to another channel space damaged its development because it had already become established in its 43 to 50 mHz band with some 47 stations on the air and 500,000 receivers in operation. Moving to new frequencies required the construction of new transmitters and receivers—an expense neither the stations nor the public was willing to incur. Indeed proponents of FM had argued vigorously against the move to higher frequencies, but their arguments went unheard.

The development of FM was effectively stopped until the 1960s by the decision to move FM to higher frequencies. The FCC's own 1949 annual report indicates a leveling off of FM applications and a great increase in television applications. Those with the funds to fight the FCC—in this case the television interests led by RCA—won a substantial victory at the expense of FM.[11]

However, the FCC did decide to allocate twenty channels between 88 and 108 mHz for education, which was fifteen more than had been available in the lower FM frequencies. Even this partial success was largely ineffective because educators did not have the money to buy new transmitters.

TELEVISION

While radio provides only sounds, television adds a picture to those sounds. Although experimenters were trying to develop television before 1900, it did not reach the public until the late 1930s and the early 1940s.

Since television has two channels of information, picture and sound, a television station must duplicate all equipment except the transmitting antenna. There are two transmitters in the station and usually two control rooms. The station generally employs an individual to control the flow of sounds to the transmitter and another person to control the pictures that are broadcast.

The television picture is impressed upon a radio wave by amplitude modulation while the sound is frequency modulated on another radio wave. The process of modulating the sounds, therefore, duplicates the methods discussed under frequency modulation radio. Although the picture uses amplitude modulation, the process of placing a picture on a radio wave is more complex than the process of modulating sounds. We shall examine how television pictures are created and how they reach the radio wave. But first we must discuss some aspects of pictures that affect how television images are created.

Picture Quality

Newspaper pictures, television images, even photographs are comprised of thousands and thousands of microscopic dots of color. To our eyes these dots appear continuous, but if we had microscopes or even good magnifying glasses, we would quickly find that the pictures result from a composite of small dots. No one has yet discovered a method to create a perfectly continuous picture, so pictures are made up of rows and rows of small dots. Since our eyes cannot perceive the many small dots, we see the picture as a continuous whole. But when the dots of the picture become too big, our eyes have difficulty discerning a picture.

The term resolution refers to the picture quality associated with the number of dots used to construct the picture. As the number of dots in the picture increases, the resolution of the picture improves. On the other hand, as the number of dots decreases, the picture becomes unsatisfactory.

A television picture contains about 367,000 dots.[12] These dots are divided into neat rows that run horizontally across the face of the television screen. In fact there are 525 rows of dots in an American television picture. The FCC decided that this number of dots and rows was the best compromise between good resolution and the limits on the amount of channel space that could be allocated to television broadcasting. Each horizontal row of dots in a television picture is often called a line. Thus there are 525 lines of dots on a television picture tube face. This sometimes gives rise to the term "line system" in referring to the system of television scanning. Not all television systems employ 525 lines. In fact, most European nations use a different number of lines such as 625. Therefore, in this chapter when we refer to 525 lines of resolution we are referring to the American system of television.

Television and the Illusion of Motion

Although we see television and motion pictures as moving images, in reality they are a series of stills projected rapidly upon a screen. If you examine a piece of motion picture, you find that it is composed of many still photographs placed in a row on the film. Each photograph is called a frame. When the film is projected, we see not a series of still frames, but a continuous moving image. Although the image of many still pictures reaches our eyes, we are unable to see single frames and because of the phenomenon of persistence of vision, we subconsciously blend the slight jerks together and perceive a continuous and moving image.

Persistence of Vision

We have discussed the fact that the eye tends to blend still photographs, but we still have the problem that the screen has no picture about half of the time while a new frame is moving into place. The projector contains a shutter that interrupts the light while a new frame is pulled into position, leaving the screen dark during this time. Each picture frame remains motionless while it is being projected—the time when the shutter is open.

We do not perceive the screen as being dark because of persistence of vision. Perhaps you have been in a dimly lit room when someone photographed you using a flash attachment. You may remember that the image of that flash was "burned" into your eye for several seconds after the picture was taken. This capacity to retain images on the eye is called persistence of vision and is essential to our viewing of film and television.

Just as you saw the flash for a short time, so you see the projection of a film frame for an instant after it has vanished. This slight delay on the part of the eye can cause the viewer to think that there is always a picture on the screen. Without persistence of vision, television would appear. Without persistence of vision, television would appear to be a long series of disjointed still photographs and it would be impossible for us to enjoy motion pictures or television as they now exist.

Experimenters have found that for the human eye to perceive the projection of a picture as continuous motion about eighteen frames of pictures must be projected each second. However, if only eighteen flashes of light, fall upon the screen, the eye will see a flickering picture. To reduce the flickering each frame of film is projected twice. In television where there are thirty frames projected each second, each frame is scanned twice. In one scanning only the odd lines such as one, three, and five are scanned while in the second scanning only the even lines are scanned.

Mechanics of Television Picture

Aspect Ratio.   Television pictures are always projected in a horizontal shape which is about four units wide and three units high as is shown in Figure 1–14.

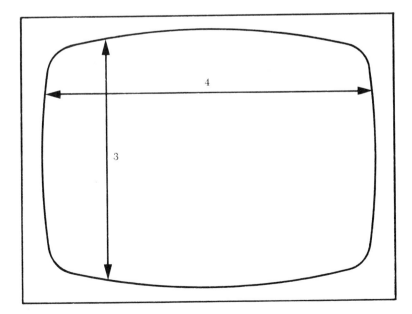

Figure 1–14. Dimensions of a television screen.

This shape conforms to the original shape of motion picture screens and has long been accepted as the most comfortable for the eye to view.

Image Size.   While the rectangular shape of the television picture has been fixed, the dimensions of the border have not. Early sets were very small, with diagonal measures of only six to nine inches. Modern sets have diagonal measures ranging up to 25 inches, and projection television sets may project images up to six or eight feet across. No matter how large or how small the size of a picture, all television pictures contain the same amount of resolution or picture information. There is no way that one can project more than 525 lines of dots onto an American television screen. Thus, large screens will not give better pictures than small screens.

How a Television Camera Works

The television camera is the device that picks up the television picture and converts the picture into electrical signals so that it can be imposed on a radio wave by means of amplitude modulation. The important element in the television camera is a pickup tube that receives light focused upon it through a lens and converts the light into an electrical image. Within the camera tube is a light sensitive plate akin to light sensitive film in a film camera. This plate is composed of about 367,000 small light sensitive dots deposited in orderly rows on the plate. These dots release electrons—electrons are negatively charged particles—when light falls on them. Each dot releases a quantity of electrons corresponding to the amount of light falling on it. A bright spot would release more electrons than a dark spot.

The electrons released from the light sensitive plate travel a short distance to another small glass plate called the target. Like the original light sensitive plate, the target has some 367,000 dots and the electrical charge that reached the target from the light sensitive plate creates a corresponding—but larger—

THE SEVEN FOOT TELEVISION

At least one manufacturer, Advent, is producing a television set that will project a seven foot (diagonal) picture upon a wall screen. The set throws a beam from a control unit eight feet to a screen mounted on a wall. Although the cost is well above that of conventional sets, its manufacturer predicts that large screen television will shortly start coming down in price. The unit, its maker says, requires no more power than a conventional set.

Source: "Wall-Size TV: The Ultimate Idiot Box," by Andrew Tobias, *New York* (August 4, 1975), p. 32.

charge. Thus, on our second plate we have an electrical equivalent of the picture appearing on the original light sensitive plate. Our problem is to lift this image from the target and send it on to the transmitter.

An electron beam is projected from the back of the pickup tube towards the target. This beam wiggles back and forth, up and down so that it can scan (or impinge upon) each of those 367,000 dots. As the beam scans each of the thousands of dots, it picks up the free electrons and carries them back to the rear of the pickup tube. The magnitude of the beam is varied in relationship to the intensity of light falling upon the original plate. When it reaches the bottom of the picture, the scanning beam moves back to the top of the picture and starts the process again. This scanning (sometimes called scansion) of the target is set up in such a way that each dot is scanned thirty times every second and is synchronized with a similar beam of electrons in the television set in your home.

This individual scanning of each dot occurs because a television channel is unable to transmit the output from all of the dots at one time, therefore, each dot must be read in its turn. In this way each dot in your television is illuminated in its turn. In addition to the picture information, synchronizing and blanking impulses are sent.[13]

Let's use a typewriter to illustrate the need for synchronizing and blanking impulses. Suppose two automatic teletypewriters are connected, one generating information and the other typing the information out. You know that it is necessary for the sending and receiving ends to keep in step so that when the end of a line comes at the sending end, it will be matched by the end of a line at the receiving end. In addition it is necessary to cause the carriage to move from left to right and from top to bottom. The same thing is necessary in television, and it is the role of the synchronizing and blanking impulses to control how each of the dots is scanned.

Just as the pickup tube in the television camera has a mosaic (light sensitive plate) and an electron gun, your television picture tube has its own electron gun and something related to the mosaic. Behind the face of a picture tube there are many thousands of dots of phosphorus material—one dot to match each dot on the mosaic in the pick-up tube. These phosphorus dots can be illuminated by electrons—the more electrons hitting the phosphorus material, the brighter the light.

Let's suppose all we are going to see is a picture of a large, black X against white background. The electron beam in the camera will sweep across the mosaic from left to right and top to bottom. While tracing the white area the camera will have a high output, but when it hits the dark X the output will go down.

Now let's consider what happens at the television receiver. When the electron beam is scanning the part of the television screen that corresponds with the white area, many electrons will be hitting the phosphorus dots and they will glow brightly. However, almost no electrons will reach the screen when the electron beam is scanning the area where the X appears. The television set has shown an image of a black X on a white background.

Of course, if the electron beam in the camera doesn't scan its mosaic in just the same way the electron beam in your television set is scanning the screen, then the picture begins to roll or straight lines become curved. When this happens, a readjustment of the set is called for.

Scanning Patterns.   One complete scanning of the mosaic plate in a pickup tube is called a *frame*, and it compares to a single picture or frame of a motion picture. Just as the motion picture frame is really a still photograph, so a single frame of television is only a still picture. The assembling of many still television pictures into a sequence gives the illusion of motion in the same way that the illusion is created by motion picture frames.

The electron beam scans the mosaic thirty times every second, which means that television broadcasts thirty frames per second. But your television set and the camera are so constructed that the electron beam scans only every other line. Thus lines one, three, five, and so on are scanned first. Then when the electron beam has reached the bottom of the picture it returns and scans the lines that were missed the first time. On the second scanning the electron beam covers lines two, four, six, and so on. Although the electron gun scans the entire picture only thirty times per second, it appears that the number of scannings have been doubled to sixty. This apparent scanning frequency of sixty corresponds to the frequency of ordinary house current, which has a frequency of 60 Hz. Engineers found it desirable to relate the number of frames per second to the frequency of house current because they found that when the television frame frequency was different from that of house current the picture would flicker and make television viewing impossible. (See Figure 1–15.)

Camera Pickup Tubes.   Valdimir Zworykin invented the earliest television pickup tube and called it the kinescope (see Figure 1–16). Newer, more sensitive tubes and cameras have since replaced the kinescope. More sophisticated

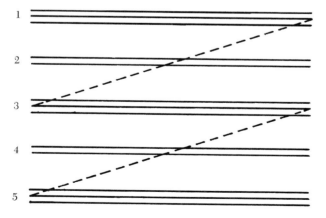

Figure 1–15. Diagram of scanning pattern used in American television. On first scan the odd-numbered lines are eliminated by the electron beam. On a second pass, the even rows are eliminated. This gives the illusion of two frames for each complete scanning.

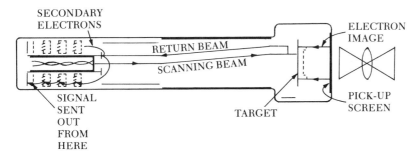

Figure 1–16. Diagram of a television pickup tube.

cameras include the image orthicon camera, the plumbicon camera, and the vidicon camera.

The image orthicon camera which was invented before the vidicon or the plumbicon is the standard television camera in most broadcast operations for two reasons. First, because it requires less light than other cameras, it can be used in very low light situations. The image orthicon derives its sensitivity because as electrons travel from the light sensitive plate to the target, the electrons gain so much speed that they dislodge many electrons in the target, making the tube particularly sensitive. The second advantage of the image orthicon is its excellent picture detail. The small dots of the light sensitive plate and the target tend not to release their electrons to adjacent dots. By keeping the electrons from jumping from dot to dot, smearing of the image is reduced and the picture quality is enhanced. The major drawbacks of the image orthicon camera are its cost and its sensitivity to physical vibration.

More recent was the invention of the vidicon camera which is smaller, cheaper, and less fragile. The combination of low cost and ruggedness made the vidicon camera immediately popular for educational use and for people with limited funds. But the vidicon suffers from inferior picture quality and it lacks the low light sensitivity of the image orthicon camera.

The plumbicon camera improved the vidicon in that it was able to respond to low light situations like the image orthicon while having the ruggedness of the vidicon. The plumbicon camera receives extensive use in portable or mobile applications. Today, these three tubes are the only ones used in educational and broadcast television.

Channels for Television Broadcasting

Like radio, television broadcasting requires a band of frequencies to accommodate all of the information that must be transmitted, but the band of frequencies needed to contain all of the picture and sound information must be quite large. If a high quality picture is to be transmitted, then a wide band of frequencies must be allocated for each television channel. In addition, the quantity of radio frequencies needed for television broadcasting would increase

Vladimir Zworykin is holding a kinescope tube he used for picking up pictures and converting them into electrical images. As you can see, the tube is quite large, but it made possible the kind of television we enjoy today. (Culver Pictures.)

as the number of channels increased. Consequently, the FCC was confronted with the complex tasks of providing an adequate number of channels large enough to transmit pictures with good resolution as well as providing for the needs of radio users. When the FCC first confronted the problem of television channels, the technology for using UHF (ultra high frequencies) had not been fully developed.[14] The FCC was limited to using VHF (very high frequencies) for any television allocations.

From its hearings the FCC decided to allocate thirteen (later reduced to twelve) channels for commercial television broadcasting. This decision rested upon the belief that thirteen channels would satisfy the current needs of television broadcasters. Later, when UHF developed, the FCC expanded the existing channels to include sufficient UHF channels to satisfy any additional demand.

In deciding on the size of a television channel, the FCC settled on a six million Hertz band of frequencies for each television channel. This choice made it possible to broadcast most of the 367,000 dots of picture information that a television camera produces along with the synchronizing, blanking, and sound information.

The use of a television channel is shown graphically in Figure 1–17. The bottom frequency of a television channel is designated by zero and the top by six megaHertz. Note that the carrier frequency for the picture is located 1.25 mHz above the bottom of the channel and the radio wave, which carries the sound, is located .25 mHz below the top of the channel. These are the locations of the two carriers when no picture or sound is being transmitted.

When modulation occurs most of the six million Hertz must carry sound and picture information. As the amount of information that must be carried on a radio wave increases, the number of frequencies used must be correspondingly increased. To conserve channel space all of the picture information that is modulated below the radio wave or carrier is surpressed before the television picture is broadcast. Since the information modulated on each side of the radio carrier is identical, no picture information is lost. Of course the process of

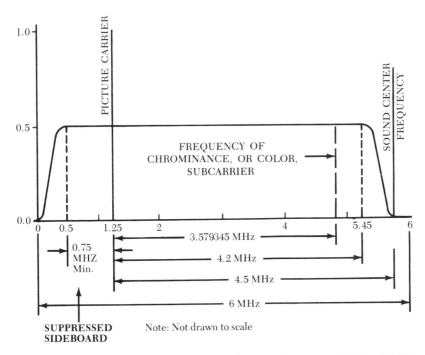

Figure 1–17. Idealized picture transmission amplitude characteristic. Source: FCC § 73,699, Figure 5.

eliminating some information is not perfect, so the FCC left some frequencies between the radio carrier and the bottom of the channel for the remnants of the surpressed waves. A total of 1.25 mHz was set aside for this purpose. Thus the actual picture information uses the frequencies from 1.25 mHz to 5.25 mHz. As you can see, a great many frequencies must be used to transmit a television picture.

Transmitting a Television Program

As we noted earlier, there is separate equipment for sound and picture in both studio and transmitter equipment at a television station. Figure 1–18 shows typical television station equipment. In the audio or sound portion of the station there are microphones, tape recorders, and turntables to provide sources for sound. All of these components come together in a control board that permits the appropriate sources to pass to the transmitter. From the control board the sounds travel to a FM transmitter where they are modulated onto a radio wave.

The picture portion of the television station is more complex. First, there are lights, television cameras, video tape recorders and film projectors, and slide projectors providing pictures—the video tape recorders and film projec-

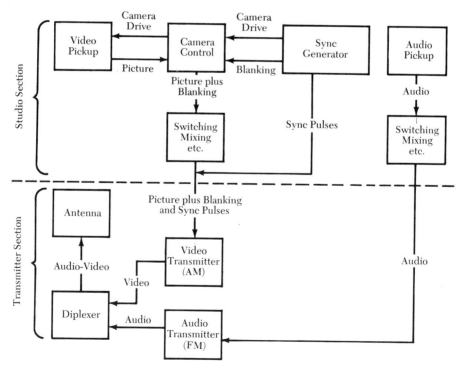

Figure 1–18. Drawing of typical television station. Block diagram of television-system components and signals.

An antenna used by television stations in New York City to send television pictures through the air. This antenna is located on the Empire State Building. (Courtesy Empire State Building.)

tors also provide sound to the audio control board. Obviously, if all of these picture sources were permitted to travel to the transmitter without any control, we would have a jumbled mess of pictures. For this reason a control board, often called a switcher, selects the sources to be transmitted. This switcher may make rapid cuts from one picture source to another, it may fade out of one camera and into another, it may dissolve from picture to picture, or it may create a vast number of complex special effects. The results of the switcher are sent to the visual transmitter.

Color Television

As yet little is known about how people see color, but enough has been discovered to make it possible to transmit color pictures via television. Although there are many colors, it is necessary to transmit only the three primary colors to see a full color image. These primary colors are red, blue, and green. With this in mind, color television is really three complete television systems—one for each of the primary colors.

In the color television camera there are actually three pickup tubes. As light enters the camera it is split up according to its color. Some is sent to a green tube, some to the red tube, and some to the blue tube. These three color signals have two important qualities—hue (color) and brightness (intensity). It is necessary to combine all of this picture information on a radio wave just as we once combined black and white colors on a radio wave.

The brightness part of the color signals are modulated onto the radio wave in much the same way as brightness is modulated in black and white television. Thus there are three brightness components combined on the radio wave.

The hue or color information is modulated onto a separate radio wave that is attached to the main radio wave. This separate radio wave is called a subcarrier and acts in a way that is similar to the way FM stations broadcast a stereophonic program. At the receiver, all of this information is disassembled and used to control three color electron beams that scan the face of the picture tube.

Unlike black and white television sets, which have many phosphor dots that become white when hit by the electron beam, the color receiver has many dots that become red, blue, or green when hit by electrons. For every single dot in a black and white set, there are three dots in a color set. One might expect to see three separate colors because of the three dots, but this is not the case. Our minds like things to fit together neatly, and because of the small size of the dots, the brain merges the three dots into a single dot the color of the combined the light which escapes from the three individual dots.

When a black and white picture is being transmitted and a color set is receiving the picture, the same color dots produce a picture that your eye perceives as a black and white image. The design of the present system of color television is compatible with existing black and white television sets and transmitters so that no television sets became obsolete with the advent of color television.

ENGINEERING DECISIONS, ECONOMICS, AND TELEVISION

As mentioned earlier, the FCC allocated thirteen VHF channels for television broadcasting in 1945 hoping that these would satisfy the demand for television channels. The FCC knew that it would be unable to allocate any more VHF frequencies for television broadcasting because it had to accomodate the demands of FM broadcasters, radio amateurs, and many others who wanted part of the

VHF spectrum—the FCC later reduced the original thirteen channels to twelve. In 1945 the FCC believed that if there ever was additional demand for television channels, the channels could be placed in the UHF region of the radio spectrum.[15]

In 1952 the FCC decided that it had not allocated enough channels for television broadcasting and so introduced UHF television by establishing channels 14 and above. These UHF channels were added both to markets that already had VHF television channels and to markets that had no television channels at all. But UHF television has two major disadvantages. First, UHF signals do not travel as far as VHF signals; second, most television sets do not have the capacity to reviece UHF television stations. Consequently, UHF television faced crippling competition from its VHF counterparts. In fact the competition was so great that many UHF television stations were forced out of business. The FCC engineering decision permitted an economic environment that virtually guaranteed a monopoly for VHF television stations.

Not until 1962, when the United States Congress passed a law requiring all television set manufacturers to include tuners that could pick up UHF television stations on all new television sets, did UHF have a chance. Although UHF now makes some profit, the large VHF stations still dominate television broadcasting.

A similar conflict arose when the FCC considered color television. Several companies had plans for color television systems including Columbia Broadcasting System (CBS) and Radio Corporation of America (RCA). During the late 1940s and early 1950s, when the FCC considered color television, the RCA system was more developed than the CBS system. Also, it should be noted that the RCA system was compatible with the existing black and white television system while the CBS system was not. The FCC approved the RCA color system in 1953 and rejected others. At the time, the question was raised whether the CBS system might produce better color pictures than the RCA system. Whatever the case, RCA and the National Television System Committee—an industrial group formed to promote television development—urged the FCC to adopt the RCA system.[16]

When the FCC accepted the RCA color system, it gave RCA a monopoly on color television patents and required CBS and ABC to purchase the rights to use the patents from RCA. This gave RCA a very desirable market position for years. In fact RCA and its network, NBC, were the earliest broadcasters of extensive color television programs.

Many years later, the United States government used the CBS color system to broadcast color pictures from the moon. Presumably, they selected the CBS system because it was superior to the RCA system.

NETWORK RELAY SYSTEMS

Almost from the beginning of radio, broadcasters realized that they needed some way to unite various stations for simultaneous airing of programs. They found that producing their own programs was too expensive for the amount of advertising revenue that individual stations could acquire. They concluded that a central source of programs would benefit a number of stations at once.

Wire Relays

Early broadcasters experimented with connecting stations by wires owned by American Telephone and Telegraph Company (AT&T) since they were readily available. In fact years before broadcasting began, AT&T had connected much of the nation by telephone wires. These wires provided the basis for the first radio interconnections. Also, Western Union provided wires for early radio connections. Although broadcasters found that these wire connections were particularly successful, they felt that sounds were not reproduced with sufficient clarity. AT&T, along with new network companies, began experimenting with different systems of interconnection.

Coaxial Cable

An invention that made possible the transmission of both high fidelity sounds and television pictures was the coaxial cable. As can be seen in Figure 1–19, coaxial is in reality a wire within a wire. The inner wire is suspended by an insulator inside a cylindrical wire shield. Although the coaxial cable requires considerable service, it is used to connect television and radio stations into networks. Coaxial cable is the basis of cable television systems, and network hookups.

Microwave Relays

By using transmitters tuned to radio frequencies well above the television broadcast bands, engineers found that they could relay television pictures for

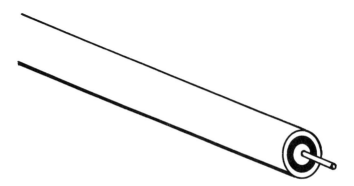

Figure 1–19. Diagram of coaxial cable. The outer surface is an insulating material which protects a cylindrical metal shield just under the insulator. Separating the metal shield and the inner wire is another insulator. Thus, a coaxial cable is really a wire that completely surrounds another wire.

This microwave tower can send pictures, computer data, and telephone calls through the air in a very specific direction. This made possible coast-to-coast network television. (Western Electric.)

distances of at least thirty miles. Microwaves, as these high frequencies are usually called, may be focused in the same way as light from a high power flashlight. This focusing allows for the transmission of radio and television signals from one microwave tower to another across the United States. Like light, microwaves travel in straight lines and cannot bend around the surface of the earth.

AT&T found that by using a combination of microwave transmission and coaxial cable, it could create a link for television that crossed the United States. Their first transcontinental hookup, which had the ability to carry television pictures, was finished in 1951. But microwave connections could not span oceans, nor could they be used effectively in mountainous areas.

This is a more modern version of a microwave tower and antenna capable of transmitting many signals. (Bell Laboratories.)

Scatter Propagation

Although microwaves do not bend around the surface of the earth, they are scattered by the ionosphere and other elements in the atmosphere. This means that, through scattering, a small amount of the microwave energy returns to earth many miles beyond the usual thirty mile limit. In 1955 the Canadians began experimenting with picking up these scattered waves. Their successful experiments led the United States to similar experiments in 1957.[17] Using very sophisticated equipment it was discovered that microwave links could be used over 600 mile distances.

Satellite Links

Most of the earlier links required ground equipment in the forms of coaxial cables, amplifiers, or microwave stations every thirty miles or less. Satellites solved most of these problems by making possible transmissions over great distances without the need for frequent ground stations. In fact one satellite permits coverage of fully one-third of the earth's surface.

The earliest satellites did not have transmitters or receivers, but were merely reflectors that worked as giant mirrors in the sky. These satellites, which were made of metal coatings on large plastic balloons, were of limited value. Later experiments led to satellites which had their own transmitters and receivers. These satellites received a signal from earth and retransmitted the same signal back to earth. Some of the more sophisticated satellites can handle several television pictures in addition to hundreds of telephone conversations.

Satellites hold the greatest promise for inexpensive interconnection for networks. In fact Home Box Office (HBO), which is a company supplying movies to subscribers in return for a fee, already uses satellites to connect some of its systems. As satellite systems develop further, more and more network programs will undoubtedly be sent to stations and cable systems by satellite.

2025134   # DISTRIBUTION SYSTEMS

Cable Television

Cable systems are able to distribute a much greater variety of programs than radio and television stations. Radio and television stations are limited to the number of channels that the FCC has authorized to each of many different services that wish to use the radio spectrum. In the case of cable systems, usually the programs are carried to homes by a wire and do not travel through the air. Consequently, the cable programs do not compete for limited radio frequencies. Cable operators may put as much or as little on the cable system as they desire without competing with any other radio or television use.

Cable was originally envisioned as an auxiliary service to broadcasting, and cable systems were constructed in areas not served by television stations. When people discovered that cable could bring more channels than could broadcasters, cable began extending into markets already served by television stations. Besides offering more programs, cable can bring clearer pictures to

THE ULTIMATE VIDEO FREAK

The choices to the video freak are rapidly becoming endless. Besides a moderate selection of through-the-air television channels, there are a variety of special services. Some cable stations now offer well over twenty channels. Often the same program can be seen on two or more channels.

If the cable system basic service isn't enough, many systems now offer Home Box Office or another pay television channel. These channels provide commercial movies and sports. There are video tape recorders, video disc machines, small televisions, and wall televisions. And you may purchase your own television camera to produce your own video when all else becomes boring.

more homes than can be received out of the air. In New York, for example, skyscrapers obstruct the travel of television waves, but cable systems are not affected by the buildings. Subscribers thus receive much clearer pictures than do those with regular antennas.

Translators

Television stations sometimes use translators to send their signals into areas blocked off by mountains. These translators are low power transmitters that receive a signal from the main transmitter and rebroadcast it into those areas not reached by the main signal. Mountains cast shadows which prevent television pictures from reaching into valley areas. The low power transmitters operate on a frequency other than the frequency used by the main transmitter so that the two transmitters do not interfere with each other. On occasion, translators have been used to carry the signal of a television station beyond the reach of the primary transmitter.

Short Waves

Originally explored as a method for interconnecting radio broadcasting stations, short waves have proven most effective in broadcasting programs across international boundaries. The United States, and almost every other nation of the world, uses short wave broadcasting to send and receive information and propaganda. The use of short wave broadcasting is outside the scope of most commercial broadcasters in this country and, therefore, is of little concern to them.

NOTES

1. Richard Brown, *Media Technology* (New York: Broadcast Institute Of North America, 1974), p. 28.
2. Frederick E. Terman, *Electronic and Radio Engineering* (New York: McGraw-Hill, 1955), p. 8.
3. Walter B. Emery, *Broadcasting and Government: Responsibilities and Regulations* (East Lansing: Michigan State University Press, 1971), p. 30.
4. FCC, "What You Should Know About the FCC" (Washington, D.C.: FCC, 1973), pp. 41, 42.
5. Ibid., p. 22.
6. Terman, op. cit., p. 923.
7. FCC, op. cit., p. 26.
8. Ibid.
9. Ibid., p. 23.
10. Erwin G. Krasnow and Lawrence D. Longley, *The Politics of Broadcast Regulation* (New York: St. Martin's Press, 1973), pp. 86–91.
11. Ibid.
12. FCC, op. cit., p. 29
13. This section is based upon a written but unpublished explanation by Glen Bishop.
14. FCC, op. cit., p. 33.
15. Krasnow and Longley, op. cit., p. 96.
16. FCC, op. cit., p. 34.
17. Keith Henny, ed., *Radio Engineering Handbook*, 5th ed., (New York: McGraw-Hill, 1959), p. 18–1.

History of Broadcasting to 1927

2

The nineteenth century was a period of rapid change. The United States was becoming an industrial power in the midst of a worldwide Industrial Revolution. England with its massive naval and merchant fleets, was still a formidable power. As the world changed a need arose for rapid systems of communications, thus stimulating inventors to look for a new way to send messages.

Inventors sought new devices that might have commercial value in the industrial world. Some, such as Samuel F. B. Morse, strove to fill needs. Morse demonstrated that messages could be transmitted by wire when he invented the telegraph. Of course many other early experimenters were involved in experimenting purely because of scholarly interests. Physicists and engineers both contributed to the growing body of information that led to the invention of radio or wireless. Wireless was the term most commonly used for radio communication prior to about 1919.

Scientists were interested in studying the wireless phenomenon for its scientific value, while other experimenters saw vast commercial and military potential for a wireless system. Long before wireless was a reality, however, experimenters in many parts of the world had to invent the equipment that would make wireless work.

INVENTION AND DEVELOPMENT OF TELEGRAPHY

A trained painter rather than an electrician, Morse had a lifelong interest in electrical gadgets.[1] During much of his early life he supported himself by painting and by teaching painting. It was not until he was forty-one that Morse heard a discussion about the electromagnet and became interested in the telegraph—called writing at a distance. The possibilities so intrigued Morse that he worked out the philosophy of telegraphy—a philosophy that anticipated the entire scope of the telegraph.

Poverty plagued Morse and it was three years before he was able to test his ideas with the aid of a young assistant, Alfred Vail. During the winter of 1835–1836, they successfully strung 1700 feet of wire around their workshop and sent signals from one end to another. But they needed money to develop the device further. With funds from Vail's father the telegraph experiment was demonstrated publicly and a few years later, in 1843, Congress appropriated the funds to construct a telegraph from Washington to Baltimore.[2]

Morse immediately began constructing the new telegraph system, but his project took much longer than he had predicted. He first tried unsuccessfully to bury the telegraph cable in the ground. Morse then hung new wires on poles and the first test of the telegraph came when he was only half finished. The Whig National Convention was held in Baltimore during May 1844, and Morse had the news of the presidential and vice-presidential nominees telegraphed to Washington from Annapolis—the distance the wires had reached at that time. Although onlookers in Washington were initially skeptical of Morse's information, they acclaimed him an instant celebrity when a train arrived an hour later confirming the telegraphed messages.[3] The line was finished only a few weeks later and the famous message "What hath God wrought" was telegraphed from Washington to Baltimore and back to Washington on May 24, 1844.[4]

The telegraph system developed by Morse worked by simply turning electricity on and off to conform to a predetermined code. Each letter of the alphabet and each number had a sequence of on and off pulses which formed a code anyone could learn. Although Morse and his associates made no attempt to send voices through wires, they had demonstrated the important fact that information could be sent through wires with electricity.[5]

At the sending end there was a simple switch to turn the electricity on and off in the predetermined way. This switch became known as a telegraphy key. The device at the receiving end was somewhat complex. It was a pen that rode over a moving roll of paper and moved from left to right in cadence with the keying of electrical signals at the sending end. Sometimes the term "record communication" has been applied to telegraph—a result of the pen recording lines on the moving paper.

For many years Morse's invention served as the basis for all electrical communication, and by 1866 the first successful trans-Atlantic cable was completed under the direction of Cyrus Field.[6] Morse code messages were sent by cable between America and Europe. Rapid international communication had begun.

News Services

The first news service set up for the purpose of providing news to newspapers was the Associated Press of New York (APNY), the forerunner of the modern Associated Press (AP). The organization, begun by newspapers in New York, used fast boats to collect news about Europe from incoming ships. Established in 1848, APNY provided news to all member newspapers.[7]

As the telegraph spread across the nation, APNY began selling its services to inland newspapers. Indeed the reach of AP extended almost as far as the growing network of telegraph lines. For years APNY had a virtual monopoly over the collection and dissemination of news in the United States.

Then when the Atlantic cable was laid APNY began exchanging news with Reuters in Britain, Havas in France, Wolff in Germany, and Stefani in Italy. APNY became the exclusive American distributor for news from the four European news services. AP was reorganized several times in the early 1900s and eventually formed its own international news gathering organization with reporters in many countries besides the United States.

Of course the success of AP led to the formation of other press services across the nation that attempted to compete with AP. Two of the more important of the competitors were United Press Associations, which was formed in 1907, and William Randolph Hearst's International News Service (1909). In 1958 United Press Associations and International News Service merged to become United Press International (UPI).[8a]

THE TELEPHONE

Just as the telegraph had demonstrated the ability of electrical circuits to carry coded messages, the telephone was later to demonstrate that the same electrical charges could carry voices and music. Many people in several parts of the world were interested in the new device. In Germany in 1861 Philip Reis invented the first telephone, but it was so crude that it lacked any practical value.[8]

Across the Atlantic at least two different inventors were trying to discover the secret of the talking wire. In Chicago Elisha Gray, who had been working on a device that might send sounds for Western Union, hoped to develop a talking telephone for commercial purposes. By 1874 Gray had made enough progress that Western Union decided to demonstrate his instrument publicly. It was during that year that the instrument was first called the telephone, but it needed many improvements before it was able to carry the human voice. The improvements came and, two years later, Gray filed an application for a patent with the United States Patent Offices. Ironically, only two hours earlier another patent application had been filed by Alexander Graham Bell for a talking telephone.[9]

Bell, a Scotsman who had been educated at the University of Edinburgh, had come to the United States as a teacher for those with defective hearing. He had long been interest in inventing devices that would make better hearing possible. To this end Bell employed a young mechanic, Thomas A. Watson, for $9.00 per week who constructed the instruments Bell designed.[10] They intended to develop a "harmonic telegraph" that could help the deaf and were not interested in devising a telephone, but their experiments led to a new talking device and a patent application on February 14, 1876.[11]

The two patent applications that were filed for the telephone by Bell and Gray led to a long series of court fights. Eventually Bell won and, with his backers, started a company, Bell Telephone, that was to become one of the most successful industrial enterprises ever launched. Besides beginning a large company engaged in carrying voices by wire, Bell's invention was later to benefit radio. In fact Marconi, the inventor of wireless—wireless was a name for radio in the early years—was to remark in 1902, "I do not know if you are aware that the message received at St. Johns was received through a telephone receiver, and in connection with the telephone the name of Bell is inseparable."[12] The telephone added the dimension of voice, and its invention would later benefit radio experimenters who wished to send voices through the air.

INVENTION AND DEVELOPMENT OF WIRELESS

Much of the ground work for wireless was being laid while other experimenters were working on the telegraph and the telephone. As early as 1843 Professor Joseph Henry, working in the United States, demonstrated that metal objects could be magnetized at a distance.[13] Later, in the 1860s and the 1870s, James Clerk-Maxwell, a Scottish physicist, developed a theory on how wireless waves might work.[14] Maxwell presented a preliminary statement on electricity and magnetism in 1864, but his fully developed theory did not appear until 1873.[15] Maxwell believed that wireless waves traveled through an invisible medium called ether. According to Maxwell's theory, the ether permeates everything and allows wireless waves to travel through all matter. Maxwell even produced a formula that explained how wireless waves worked. He concluded that wireless waves travel at the same speed as light because, as he saw it, light and heat are both vibrations in the ether. Although later scientists have discredited the ether theory, many of the mathematical concepts evolved by Maxwell still survived. While the notion of an ether has died, the ether as a model for discussing how radio waves travel works rather well for simple discussions of radio waves.

While Maxwell produced a theoretical base for wireless waves, Heinrich Hertz, an experimental physicist working in Germany, demonstrated the existence of wireless waves.[16] Hertz was able to show that wireless waves could be reflected, bent, and handled like light waves. He further showed that radio waves do, in fact, have the speed of light. Hertz' experiments were performed with simple spark gap transmitters and receiving equipment. Hertz succeeded in experimentally demonstrating Maxwell's theory, and in 1888 he published "Electromagnetic Waves in Air and Their Reflection" to explain his experiments.[17]

Hertz' interest in wireless waves was that of a physicist and he had no interest in developing a vast commercial system. His experiments effectively demonstrated Maxwell's theory and, as such, would benefit another individual who saw commercial possibilities for the new medium. Although Hertz did not take his work outside the laboratory, his importance was recognized many years later when the name "Hertz" was used for the oscillations of radio waves.

Commercial Wireless Experiments

While Maxwell had created a theoretical base for wireless and Hertz had demonstrated the existence of wireless waves, a twenty-one year old Italian developed wireless into a commercial success. During the summer of 1894 while vacationing in the Italian Alps, Guglielmo Marconi picked up an electrical journal and read about the experiments of Hertz.[18] The work of Hertz so excited Marconi that he returned home to work almost continuously to develop a system of wireless that would be commercially feasible. He brought together the transmitting system used by Hertz, the coherer developed by an English scientist Edouard Branly, the telegraph key used by Morse, and a generator of radio waves called the spark gap. To this he added a new aerial which was vertical, like a telephone pole. This new antenna, combined with the other devices, made radio transmission possible.

After endless weeks of experimenting, Marconi successfully sent cricket-like sounds three-quarters of a mile to a receiving station he had set up.[19] And by turning the transmitter on and off Marconi was able to send letters and words. Just as Morse had sent code over wires, Marconi sent words through the air.[20]

In 1896 Marconi went to England to explore the commercial possibilities of wireless.[21] He hoped to develop wireless for communicating with ships at sea and similar land uses, but Marconi did not anticipate the possibilities of wireless as a medium for broadcasting to large numbers of people.

In England, Marconi applied for a patent, which he received on June 2, 1896, and with the engineer in charge of the British Post Office, Sir William Preece, he began testing wireless on a large scale.[22] So impressed were English businessmen that they formed a company to develop wireless called the Wireless Telegraph and Signal Company, which was incorporated in 1897.[23] The company was later renamed Marconi's Wireless Telegraph Company (British Marconi for short).

This business venture was almost instantly successful. In 1897 an American

MARCONI COMES TO ENGLAND

When Marconi and his mother came to England to show the new wireless instruments to governmental officials, the customs agents were openly skeptical of the box with wires running everywhere. Over Marconi's protests, they smashed the machine fearing that it was a bomb intended to destroy some part of London. Marconi was obligated to create a new instrument before he was able to demonstrate it to the government and business officials who would help develop the new invention.

Source: Lawrence W. Lichty and Malachi C. Topping, *A Source Book on the History of Radio and Television* (New York: Hastings House, 1975), p. 8.

patent was issued for the Marconi wireless system. During 1897 and 1898 Marconi, with the help of British scientist Sir Oliver Lodge, developed a method for tuning wireless. At the same time the Italian Navy began helping Marconi with his experiments.[24]

Later, during 1899, Marconi traveled to New York to transmit bulletins of the American Cup yacht races off the New Jersey coast. While there, Marconi was so certain that his invention would soon span the Atlantic and that the United States would want his wireless services, that he formed an American company to develop wireless. The company, named American Marconi Wireless Telegraph Company and often called American Marconi, began installing wireless stations in America in 1901.[25] The first station, located on Nantucket Island, was soon followed by other stations including one on Glace Bay in Canada.

But Marconi had interests beyond acquiring a contract in America; he hoped to develop a transatlantic wireless system. He achieved his goal on December 12, 1901 when in Newfoundland he and an assistant received the first transmission from England—the letter "s." An ocean had been spanned by wireless![26] In 1902 Marconi equipment transmitted messages between President Roosevelt and King Edward III.[27] Wireless continued to demonstrate its usefulness in times of disaster both when the S. S. *Republic* was wrecked in 1909, and later when the S. S. *Titanic* sank in 1912.

During these years, Marconi very nearly developed an American monopoly in wireless that continued until a United States firm bought American Marconi. In the early 1900s Marconi outfitted both military and merchant ships with wireless by providing both the equipment and an operator on a rental basis. Along with British Marconi and American Marconi, Marconi developed Marconi International Marine Communications in 1900 to help expand the vast international communications business that the companies were developing.

As wireless developed, many companies became interested in it and tried to develop their own wireless system to compete with the Marconi companies. Since Marconi did not sell his equipment or the right to use his inventions, each wireless company had to develop its own patents and equipment. This meant that it was virtually impossible for any single company to have all the patents it needed to construct a sophisticated wireless system. Consequently, Marconi remained the dominant company in the wireless industry despite the fact that other companies in France, Germany, and the United States had entered the field.

During these early years the principal interest in wireless was maritime. It was apparent that wireless could benefit ships in trouble by enabling them to call nearby ships or ground points for assistance. The *Titanic* disaster had been particularly effective in demonstrating this value. Besides the maritime uses of wireless, some companies had shown that wireless could be used to send messages across land.

The potential of wireless was developed by Marconi and his associates and naval uses were quickly found for the new device in both Europe and America. (Culver Pictures.)

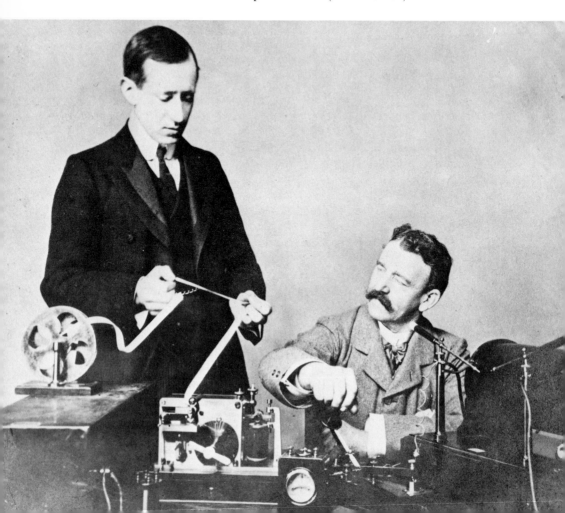

SARNOFF RECEIVES DISTRESS MESSAGES

When the *Titanic* was sinking in 1912, a young wireless operator named David Sarnoff was working for Wanamaker as a radio operator. Sarnoff picked up the first distress messages and sat at the equipment for seventy-two hours picking up every detail of the disaster. He was able to relay safety messages and he kept millions of people posted on what was happening on the *Titanic*. Young Sarnoff was to go on from this experience to become an executive in the as yet unformed Radio Corporation of America.

Four important results came from this event. First, the nation became acutely aware of the importance of wireless in saving lives in a disaster. Second, wireless became well known. Third, wireless proved its worth as an information tool, telling the nation what was happening as it occurred. Fourth, Sarnoff himself had reinforced the power of wireless, and went on to become a leader in the new industry.

Source: Gleason L. Archer, *History of Radio to 1926*, (New York: The American Historical Society, 1938), pp. 110, 111.

WIRELESS INVENTORS AND THEIR COMPANIES

Reginald Fessenden, a Canadian born physicist who spent much of his working life in the United States, conducted early experiments in voice transmission. More than 500 patents were attributed to him. The National Electric Signaling Company was formed in 1902, like other companies before it, to develop the inventions.[28] Fessenden felt that the early developments in wireless had proceeded in the wrong direction and he hoped to rectify this. The Marconi transmitters—called spark gap transmitters—generated their radio waves by causing electricity to jump between two metal points spaced a short distance apart. When in operation, the machine created an incredible noise.

To correct this, Fessenden developed the high frequency alternator—a device that worked much like a conventional generator but created radio waves. The alternator was so successful that Fessenden was able to combine the microphone with his alternator to transmit music and speech. On Christmas Eve 1906 ship operators and amateurs alike must have been astonished to hear sounds of music and the human voice coming through the ether.[29] Fessenden's alternator at Brant Rock, Massachussetts had been successful in transmitting sounds and proved to be an important contribution to the evolution of wireless.

In addition to the alternator, Fessenden developed some of the circuits that are still in use today. In fact Fessenden was credited with developing a detector that was a step between the old coherer and the vacuum tube of modern receivers.[30] Yet with all of his creative force, Fessenden was only one of the inventors who contributed to the evolving system of wireless. Perhaps he could have carried his experiments further had it not been for a long series of legal conflicts over patents.

Unlike other experimenters, Ernest Alexanderson came to explore wireless as an exployee of an established firm—General Electric (GE). When Fessenden wanted an alternator he contacted GE to construct it for him. Alexanderson, who had come to the United States from Sweden, was the engineer to whom the job of developing the new machine was assigned. Working with Fessenden's directions, Alexanderson was able to produce the instrument that was needed for the Brant Rock experiment.

But Alexanderson was dissatisfied with Fessenden's design and set out to build a better alternator. He was successful with his device and, ultimately, a 200 kilowatt alternator was installed at New Brunswick, New Jersey for the Marconi Company. This alternator, which was the most powerful in the world, generated signals that could be heard over much of the Atlantic and by field receivers in France. Alexanderson's interests did not stop at the alternator for he later worked on tuned circuits for wireless and eventually became involved in television.[31]

Unlike the inventions of Marconi, which had been noisy and were consequently limited in their usefulness for transmitting sounds, the devices made by Fessenden and Alexanderson transmitted quiet radio signals. But the alternator was bulky and subject to mechanical failure. Therefore, it was left for someone to devise a system that overcame both of these problems. A substantial step in that direction came when John Fleming, a British physicist, started his experiments.

The Audion

Fleming's exeriments led to the Fleming valve, a glass case surrounding two metal elements and resembling the vacuum tube still used in some modern receivers and many transmitters. Fleming applied for a patent for his invention in 1904, but his tube could only separate sounds waves from radio waves and, therefore, had only limited application.[32] Nevertheless his tube was only the first step in an important development.

Lee de Forest took Fleming's invention farther and created the audion. While Fleming's valve had only two elements, de Forest's audion had three and could amplify sounds in addition to other functions. De Forest, who had been born in Iowa, received a doctorate from Yale in 1896 and had worked for the Western Electric Company, but he decided to experiment independently with radio devices.[33] From his work Abraham White, a business friend, organized the de Forest Wireless Company in 1902 to develop the work and inventions of de Forest. However, the company had many troubles and eventually went bankrupt. De Forest began working independently after the demise of his company. Of course de Forest's 1906 invention, patented in 1907, had defects, but it was a start.[34]

Lee DeForest works on one of his radio devices. It was DeForest who first effectively demonstrated the audion. (Culver Pictures.)

The audion, with refinements, later became known as the triode, referring to the three metal elements in the tube. The third element added by de Forest became know as a grid and could control the flow of electricity between the other two elements. In fact a very small charge of electricity on the grid could control large amounts of electric flow between the other two elements.

Although the audion needed refinement—refinements that came through the work of others—it had the potential to overcome the problems associated with the alternator and the spark gap transmitter. The audion was small, it could amplify sounds, it could create radio waves, and it could add sounds to radio waves—in short the audion provided the basis for all that was to develop in wireless in the future. It created a system that could transmit music and voices to large numbers of people in America and the world.

Early vacuum tubes were large and unsightly, but they made possible electronic transmissions without all of the noise that accompanied spark gap transmitters. Vacuum tubes are still the core of modern radio and television transmitters. (Culver Pictures.)

AUDION'S MAIN PROBLEM

One of the most serious problems with the de Forest audion was that gasses, or air, remained in the tube. De Forest did not think of pumping air out of the tube, but two scientists working independently discovered that removing the gasses improved the tube's performance. Irving Langmuir, a physicist and chemist working for General Electric, turned his attention to the audion in 1912 and developed a vacuum tube that could handle much higher power than the audion. About the same time, Harold Arnold of AT&T achieved similar results. Thus de Forest's audion was improved by others.

Source: Orrin E. Dunlap, Jr. *Radio's 100 Men of Science* (Freeport, N.Y.: Books for Libraries Press, 1944), p. 202.

DeFOREST AND THE PATENT COURT

Lee de Forest always seemed to be in trouble with someone. At one point he was arrested for exploiting an unsuspecting public with stock in a wireless company. He was charged with using the mails to defraud the public. The District Attorney who prosecuted the case argued:

> De Forest has said in many newspapers and over his signature that it would be possible to transmit the human voice across the Atlantic before many years. Based on these absurd and deliberately misleading statements of de Forest, the misguided public, your Honor, has been persuaded to purchase stock in his company, paying as high as ten and twenty dollars a share for the stock. *

The District court demanded that de Forest be sent to the Federal penitentiary in Atlanta. Although de Forest was acquitted, some of the board of directors were found guilty of criminal intent. The judge in the case felt that the jury had not done the job and harshly lectured de Forest, telling him that he should get a common, garden variety sort of job.

*Source: Gleason L. Archer, *History of Radio to 1926* (New York: The American Historical Society, 1938), p. 110.

Unfortunately, others were also to enjoy many of the financial benefits of de Forest's invention because, out of economic necessity, he sold many of the rights to the audion to a representative of American Telephone and Telegraph Company (AT&T) in the summer of 1913 for a mere $50,000.[35] Although he did not relinquish all of the rights to the tube, de Forest lost much of his control over it.

Prior to selling the rights to his tube, de Forest had experimented with transmitting sounds from the Eiffel Tower in 1908.[36] But he did not pursue these experiments, and they did not involve the audion. However, de Forest did return to his audion to experiment with sound transmission when AT&T began experimenting with voice transmissions in 1915.

Early Wireless Laws

Regulation of wireless began in 1910 under the Wireless Ship Act, but this law made no attempt to regulate all four catagories of wireless communication

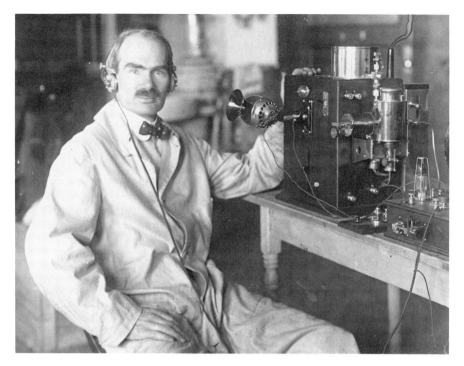

DeForest sits with the device that made his first voice communications possible in 1906. This photograph was taken in 1907. (Culver Pictures.)

noted in "Early Wireless Services." The law required large, sea-going, passenger ships to be outfitted with wireless equipment and operators. Enforcement of that law was left to the Secretary of Commerce and Labor.

Two years later (1912) two events led Congress to pass a second law covering the regulation of wireless. During that year the *Titanic* sank on its maiden voyage across the Atlantic and the success of wireless in saving some of the passengers dramatized the need for more legislation to force operators to keep their wireless equipment on constantly. Also during that year an international radio conference was held in London at which the participating countries agreed to uniform regulations for wireless communication. The United States passed the Radio Act of 1912 to fulfill its obligations under the treaty signed at the London meeting.[37]

The Radio Act of 1912 specified the role of the Secretary of Commerce and Labor in handling wireless, and authorized the secretary to license ship operators. In addition, the law allocated certain frequencies for governmental use, specified the character of radio transmissions, and set up procedures for distress calls. The licensing aspect of the 1912 law permitted the secretary to license both the equipment and the operators.

However, the law had a serious flaw. While it authorized the Secretary of Commerce and Labor to award licenses, it provided no method for him to reject licenses. Thus, the secretary could not portect radio waves from operators who would misuse them. This oversight was not corrected until 1927 when Congress formed the Federal Radio Commission (FRC).

Because wireless was dominated by marine demands, the distribution of radio services was made for the benefit of ships. Since ships could accommodate antennas carrying signals in the 500 kHz range, that frequency was set aside as the international distress frequency. Consequently, when other services wished to use wireless, they were placed on channels around the frequencies devoted to maritime services. Later, when broadcasting came along, it was thought that the frequencies between 300 and 500 kHz would be the best range for broadcasting, but since that would have interfered with the 500 kHz distress frequency broadcasting was placed above the distress frequency.

Military Uses of Wireless

Besides peacetime uses, wireless had distinct wartime advantages, as was demonstrated during the Russo-Japanese War in 1904. Wireless was used by the British Navy for military purposes while journalists from the *London Times* were using wireless to send information back to their newspaper.[38]

During the same years the United States Navy was exploring the use of wireless equipment on its own, but it was not until World War I that military wireless was to be fully demonstrated to the American people. So great was the government's interest in military wireless that the day following the declaration of war in April 1917, President Wilson ordered the Navy to take control of all wireless stations in the United States.[39] Throughout the war, control over wireless remained with the federal government.

The military, particularly the navy, was so delighted with the effectiveness of wireless that it was instrumental in having the Alexander Bill introduced into Congress in 1918. This bill would have given the government monopoly control over wireless had it not failed because of massive lobbying. The National Wireless Association was an important part of the lobby opposing the bill. Because of lobby pressure the bill was tabled in January 1919.[40] Although the Alexander Bill failed, it was not until February 1920 that the government relinquished its control over wireless.[41]

The defeat of the Alexander Bill foreshadowed the future of wireless. Had the bill passed, radio in the United States might have developed in a way much like radio in England. There, the government retains control over much of radio, including broadcasting by radio and television, although in recent years the English government has given up some of this control. But since the Alexander Bill was defeated, it opened the way for private ownership of radio transmitters. Consequently, the first broadcast stations were privately owned by such companies as Westinghouse and AT&T. After the defeat of the Alexander Bill the government was never able to reassert its control over wireless, and broadcasting developed as a privately owned, advertiser supported system. The beginnings of broadcasting were rooted in the massive American company that bought out the American Marconi Company.

AN AMERICAN RADIO CORPORATION IS FORMED

As the United States emerged from World War I, American Marconi was the dominant wireless company in the United States. Over the years American Marconi had constructed some fifty-three coastal stations for communicating with Marconi equipment on board some 370 sea-going ships and 170 coastal vessels.[42] Although Marconi had near monopoly control, it lacked two important elements. First, it did not have the patent for the alternator which was held by GE. Second, American Marconi was not an American owned company and the United States Navy had expressed grave concern over a foreign company controlling wireless, which was so important to any naval effort.

Since Congress had effectively blocked a governmental takeover of wireless, the Navy suggests that an American owned company be established to control wireless manufacture and marketing in the nation. The motivation to create an American owned company became particularly desirable when it was heard that American Macroni had approached GE about buying rights to the Alexanderson Alternator during March 1919.[43]

Under the suggestion of Admiral Bullard, the Naval officer who encouraged the formation of an American Company, Owen D. Young, a young corporate attorney at GE, began the necessary planning and negotiation that led to the creation of a fully American owned company—to be named Radio Corporation of American (RCA). Young's idea was to form a monopoly that would control wireless in the United States by using the patents that GE held, purchasing American Marconi, and by writing cross licensing agreements with other United States companies that had important patents. The cross licensing agreements were commitments on the part of each company to share the use of its patents among all of the RCA partners. Thus each company would have access to enough patents to build the radio equipment authorized to it by the agreement.

The first step was purchasing American Marconi. Members of the Marconi company realized that they were in a weak position when both government and private industry wanted wireless controlled by an American company. Consequently, American Marconi stockholders agreed to sell their stock to GE provided British Marconi would approve the sale. That approval followed, and in 1919 American Marconi changed hands and RCA became the owner of properties and patents held by American Marconi. RCA, of course was largely owned by GE.[44]

But the holdings of RCA were inadequate to create the monopoly envisioned by Young. To make the company complete he negotiated agreements with AT&T, Westinghouse, and their affiliates. Including the affiliates the new consortium consisted not only of GE, Westinghouse, RCA, and AT&T, but of Western Electric, United Fruit Company, Wireless Speciality Apparatus Company, and International Radio Telephone Company as well.[45]

The new group of corporate partners brought together the patents for the alternator, the audion, and patents for several important circuits in addition to

This man, Owen D. Young, created RCA. (Culver Pictures.)

the shore equipment held by the defunct American Marconi. In negotiating the agreement each of the partners was given the right to engage in certain aspects of the newly developing industry. Westinghouse, GE, and RCA (called the radio group) were authorized to manufacture and sell receivers while AT&T and Western Electric, (called the telephone group) retained the right to control telephonic communication by both wire and wireless and to manufacture transmitters. The necessary cross licensing agreements to create this consortium were completed during the years 1919–1921.[46] But the RCA consortium was not without flaw. For example, its monopoly status angered many Americans and the nature of the cross licensing agreements displeased some of the RCA partners. As we shall see later, much was to change.

The Shift from Radiotelegraphy to Radio Telephony

The early years of wireless had been dominated by maritime communications using code transmissions, but with the de Forest voice and music transmissions from the Eiffel Tower in 1908 and the Fessenden Brant Rock experiments in 1906 the advent of regular voice transmissions was foreshadowed. In the Eiffel Tower experiments de Forest had used phonograph records, but only two years later de Forest transmitted a program from the Metropolitan Opera Company in New York City with Enrico Caruso singing. That broadcast may have been heard by only fifty listeners composed of ship operators and amateurs.[47]

The experiments of de Forest and Fessenden had been only that—experiments. Neither man attempted to set up regular broadcasts or cultivate an audience for his station. Fessenden's experiments had been with his alternator and de Forest's had been with a spark gap transmitter that created considerable static.

De Forest continued to contribute to the development of voice wireless with his 1916 experiments, using the audion to generate radio waves. His experiments continued until the beginning of World War I when all nongovernment stations were shut down, but he was successful in transmitting music from phonograph records using the audion.

Another invention, which was to prove invaluable to the development of wireless, was the heterodyne circuit invented by Fessenden in 1905.[48] Although Fessenden lacked some of the components to perfect his device, he was able to construct a circuit that would make a highly sensitive receiver when manufactured with the triode vacuum tube.

Another scientist, Edwin Armstrong, wrote about the heterodyne circuit in 1916 and further paved the way for the modern receiver. His new circuit innovation was called the superheterodyne and was first tested experimentally in 1918.[49] The invention of the superheterodyne circuit along with improvements in the triode led directly to the rapid development of broadcasting. The superheterodyne circuit made radios so sensitive that outside antennas, which had been used up to that time, were no longer needed. Thus the triode and the superheterodyne provided the basis for a sensitive, inexpensive receiver. In addition, the triode was essential to the construction of reliable voice transmitters.

While development of triodes and related devices continued, Alexanderson was at work on the alternator. His alternator, which was like a giant electric motor with a large armature spinning inside some coils and magnets used a wooden armature, but Alexanderson believed that an iron armature would solve some of the problems Fessenden had experienced. The armature was a device that rotated inside the alternator to create the high radio frequencies that resulted from the alternator. Using his method, Alexanderson created a high frequency alternator that was tested in 1907. Alexanderson's alternator was so much better than the Fessenden alternator that Fessenden expressed an interest in it.[50]

In the process of working on the alternator Alexanderson developed a method of coupling a microphone to the alternator which gave GE a strong position in later patent negotiations.[51] Although the alternator provided the basis for voice transmission, the device was so bulky that it was replaced with the triode circuit.

All of these circuits and tubes provided the technical basis for radio broadcasting, but an individual was needed to make wireless broadcasting a reality. That imaginative individual was David Sarnoff—the young man who had received communications from the sinking *Titanic*.

BROADCASTING BECOMES A REALITY

During the early years of wireless, most companies saw radio as a service to assist ships and as a means of communication between businesses on land. Few thought of the new medium as a vast entertainment network serving millions of people throughout the world. The experiments of de Forest anticipated the day when voice broadcasting would become popular, but it was for another person, outside of science, to urge industrial leaders to consider broadcasting.

From receiving distress messages about the sinking Titanic, David Sarnoff went on to become an important part of RCA and its movement towards network broadcasting. (Culver Pictures.)

In 1916 David Sarnoff wrote a note to the general manager of American Marconi in which he proposed a radio music box that would become just as much a household appliance as the record player or the piano. Sarnoff suggested that radio stations with a range of twenty-five to fifty miles could be equipped to play music, which could then be picked up at home by those interested in the new service. Sarnoff's memo suggested that the radio music box would be highly profitable—in fact Sarnoff estimated that the number of sets sold would yield a revenue of about $75 million.[52] Thus the sale of radio sets might support the new venture.

While Sarnoff did not anticipate the possibilities of selling commercials over the air, he did see broadcasting—a term he did not use—as a commercially viable enterprise. The programming would consist of public service including concerts, lectures, and recitals. Sarnoff's memo to Edward J. Nally apparently received no action while the company remained American Marconi—indeed it was several years before the first regular broadcasts were to commence. A world war would intervene between Sarnoff's note and the first broadcast of KDKA.

Some technical improvements helped bring about the development of broadcasting as envisioned by Sarnoff. Besides those mentioned earlier, A. N. Goldsmith developed his "unicontrolled" receiver that made it easier for the inexperienced to operate the radio. Goldsmith's receiver had only one knob for tuning and one for volume compared to the many knobs of earlier sets, making the radio so simple to operate that anyone could enjoy it without special training.[53] Sarnoff could now urge his company to enter the broadcasting field confident that all Americans were potential purchasers of the simplified radio equipment.

KDKA Experiments with Broadcasting

Like other companies interested in radio, Westinghouse had its own engineers and scientists working on the problems of the new medium. Two of these people were Frank Conrad and his friend D. G. Little. Little had been an amateur wireless operator before his association with Westinghouse, and Conrad had become interested in wireless prior to World War I; together they began experimenting with wireless under the license 8XK in April 1920.[54]

Conrad wished to develop a successful voice transmitter and, during 1920, experimented with playing records into the microphone of his test transmitter, located in East Pittsburgh. Amateurs in the area became steady listeners to Conrad's experiments and began requesting favorite music selections.[55] There were so many requests that Conrad began scheduling specific hours each week when he would be on the air.

Then in October 1920, the station was relicensed as KDKA and to inaugurate the new station Conrad and executives of Westinghouse decided to air election returns from the Harding-Cox election on November 2, 1920.[56] This date is often cited as the beginning of scheduled radio broadcasting by a station licensed by the federal government.[57] The election returns carried over

KDKA were heard at great distances from East Pittsburgh because there were no other stations on the same channel to interfere with the station. Consequently, KDKA received listener reports from as far as ships off the coast of Virgina.[58]

Conrad's experiments had led to music broadcasting, but his supply of records was quickly depleted. The Hamilton Music Store in Wilkinsburgh, Pennsylvania, seeing an opportunity to promote itself, offered free records to the station as long as Conrad and his associates would announce that the records could be obtained from the music store—this was undoubtedly the first broadcast tradeout.[59] A tradeout is the exchange of broadcast time for a service or product the station wants.

As an early station, KDKA was the first broadcaster of many events. Some of the firsts of KDKA include the first church service, the first remote broadcast, the first play-by-play baseball and football games, the first boxing match, the first heavyweight championship, and the first world series. KDKA also carried farm services and a barn dance.

Sports formed an important part of KDKA's early broadcasts. The fight between Jack Dempsey and Georges Carpentier for the heavyweight championship was broadcast on July 2, 1921.[60] In August the station carried the Davis Cup Tennis Matches. And on August 5 the station carried play-by-play coverage of a baseball game from Forbes Field. Of course music remained the station's mainstay, but KDKA made many other important contributions to the evolution of broadcasting.

While KDKA may have the honor of being the first radio broadcasting station, it was not long until other companies such as RCA and GE, as well as newspapers, went into the radio broadcasting business. As Figure 2–1 shows in little over one year a number of new stations went on the air. That number continued to grow through the early years of the 1920s until over 570 stations were on the air at the end of 1925.

The growth of on-the-air radio stations created an assortment of problems for the owners, the most difficult problem being interference. Interference results when two stations are broadcasting on the same or nearly the same frequency and are geographically close enough that the two signals are picked up by a listener's receiver. The listener in such a situation may hear the sounds of the two stations jumbled together or may hear squeals resulting from the two signals competing with each other. Interference was eventually to become so major a problem that the federal government would have to intervene and allot

Figure 2-1   Broadcast Stations—1920–1930.

1920	1922	1925	1930
	30	571	618

Source: Lawrence W. Lichty and Malachi C. Topping, *A Source Book on the History of Radio and Television* (New York: Hastings House, 1975), p. 148.

bands of frequencies to stations. In the meantime great changes were occurring for large corporations.

THE COMING OF TOLL BROADCASTING

Sarnoff's 1916 memorandum seemed to suggest that wireless should be supported by those who wished to sell receivers. Although this was not specifically stated, it was a popular philosophy in that stations were owned by manufacturers of wireless receivers and by stores that sold them and other items. In Chicago, Sears Roebuck and Company owned WLS (World's Largest Store) and a newspaper owned WGN (World's Greatest Newspaper). This seemed to be a perfectly plausible method for supporting the new medium, but time was to show that the cost of radio was so high that it needed other forms of support.

One early writer proposed that broadcasting be supported by the government through a tax on receivers, but others were quick to point out what they thought were insurmountable problems.[61] The biggest problem appeared to be the formation of a large governmental agency to collect the tax.[62] While others

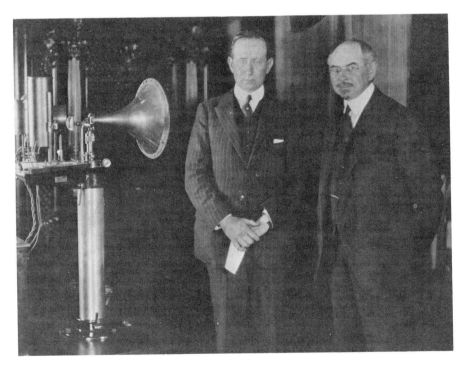

Early broadcasting stations looked much different from their modern counterparts, but they sent out signals that were eagerly sought by the public. Marconi and E. W. Rice, both early pioneers in radio, stand before a G. E. station in 1922. (Culver Pictures.)

were trying to work out a system, one broadcasting company was applying itself to resolving the problem of economics.

AT&T planned to establish two stations in the New York City area so that it could sell advertising on both. Each station was supposed to go on the air with the capability of broadcasting high quality sounds for hire. However, the first station WBAY, which was licensed by the Department of Commerce in 1922, had so many technical problems that it operated only a short while.[63] The second station WEAF, licensed on June 1, 1922, was more successful when it began broadcasting a short time after WBAY went off the air.[64]

By August twenty-eighth WEAF had broadcast its first commercial messages for a land development company in the New York area called the Queensboro Corporation.[65] After the successful airing of messages for Queensboro, others began buying time on WEAF. While other companies had been trying to decide how broadcasting should be supported, WEAF had applied a common method of resolving economic needs—sell what you have to others who might want to buy.

By its choice to start a toll station AT&T unknowingly established the pattern that broadcasting in the United States was to follow. AT&T called their station a toll station because they charged customers a fee for broadcasting commercial messages over the station. Clients were charged a fee or toll based on the number of minutes their commercial message was on the air. What these early business people did not realize was that, because of their *sine qua non* status, advertisers would eventually have great control over radio and television programing. They were establishing a pattern that would lead to frequent interruptions during all forms of programming so that the sponsors could try to influence viewers and listeners to buy their products.

While not everyone agreed with the new method for supporting broadcasting, it was natural that advertising should develop as the economic base of broadcasting. In 1919 Congress had refused to assume control over radio or provide for the support of the medium, and again in 1922 Congress exhibited an unwillingness to get involved in the new medium. Thus government left the problem of devising a method for supporting radio to the private sector.

AT&T, based on its own previous experience, found toll broadcasting the best solution. For many years AT&T had operated telephone companies (the various Bell companies) on a subscription or toll basis and had supported its long distance telephone calls on a per minute rental. It seemed logical to apply the same philosophy to broadcasting. Therefore, AT&T hoped to rent the different time periods to various sponsors on a per minute basis.[66]

AT&T did not intend that WEAF should form the model for all later broadcasting, but with no better plan available and with the public demanding more and more radio programming, sponsored radio seemed the best solution to a growing problem. Two things made the WEAF plan immediately attractive to other broadcasters: (1) when AT&T built WEAF, it used the best possible equipment, making the station the envy of other broadcasters;[67] (2) advertising worked—money, at least some money, was flowing into the station—a claim that other stations were unable to make.[68]

Undoubtedly, advertising did not satisfy everyone and AT&T—along with others who eventually adopted advertising—subjected its advertising to strict standards so as not to offend anyone. For example, early advertisers were not permitted to give prices of products over the air and many personal products could not be promoted. A speech made by President Herbert Hoover in 1924 indicated a real distrust of advertising:

> I believe that the quickest way to kill broadcasting would be to use it for direct advertising. The reader of the newspaper has an option whether he will read an ad or not, but if a speech by the President is to be used as the meat in a sandwich of two patent medicine advertisements there will be no radio left.[69]

The article went on to say that when advertising became the rule only an act of Congress or another Flood could stop it.

NETWORKING BEGINS

Networking, or the connecting of many stations into a chain for simultaneous broadcasting of a program, was the next step in WEAF's development. From AT&T's point of view this seemed a logical step since the potential for renting AT&T programs to WEAF could increase income. Secondly, AT&T had the necessary long distance telephone wires to make the connections between WEAF and affiliated stations. In addition, AT&T was authorized by the RCA agreement to build and operate stations, and AT&T saw networking as merely an extension of this agreement.

On the other hand, networking appealed to stations for several reasons. All stations had large amounts of time and networking provided inexpensive, high quality programming. It was attractive for a station to say it was carrying an important performer live from New York. Also, stations wanted networks because they could carry significant events at the moment they occurred.

AT&T's first network was a two-station hookup between WEAF and WNAC, a Boston station owned by John Shepard III, using telephone lines owned by AT&T. The program consisted of a saxophone solo and a few words.[70] Although this first network broadcast occurred on January 4, 1923, the second network program was not aired until June 7 of the same year.[71] The second program was taken by four stations WEAF, WGY in Schenectady, KDKA in Pittsburgh, and KYW in Chicago.[72]

As networks developed, national advertisers became interested because they were able to advertise on many stations at once for a cost below that of buying time on all of the stations separately. A single call between an advertising agency and a network would confirm many stations quickly.

Because of the network's popularity with stations and advertisers, it is not surprising that a second network was started. The new network was set up by RCA, which bought partial, and then full, control of station WJZ in New York City in 1923 and connected it with WGY, Schenectady, New York.[73] WJZ was originally located in Newark, but it was quickly moved to New York City to be closer to sources of talent.

Both of the early networks were started by partners in the RCA consortium. WEAF and its network were owned by the *telephone group*, while the second network, headed by WJZ, was owned by the *radio group*. But AT&T was not at all happy with this arrangement because the company felt that, according to the cross licensing agreement, only AT&T was authorized to engage in broadcasting, and the other partners were to manufacture radio sets.

Because of its resentment toward RCA, AT&T refused to rent long distance lines to WJZ when it began network broadcasting in 1923. These were special telephone lines that had the capability of carrying radio programs over great distances while preserving the necessary sound quality. Consequently, the hookup between WJZ and WGY in Schenectady—an RCA hookup—was made with Western Union wires which were not equipped to carry high quality sounds. Although the connections were inferior, RCA was in the network business.[74]

WEAF's network developed into a twenty-two station hookup and by October 1924 included stations as far away as KPO in San Francisco, KGW in Portland, and WGN in Chicago.[75] By 1926 the network was deriving $750,000 annually from its sales to advertisers. Thus, AT&T had developed both a vigorous station and a network from its idea of selling advertising to sponsors.

RCA's network did not grow as rapidly as did AT&T's because of the unwillingness of the telephone company to rent telephone lines for the interconnections that were necessary to make the network work. But by late 1925, the WJZ network had fourteen stations in its hookup. The next year, 1926, major changes which would affect broadcasting occurred in the relationship of AT&T and the other partners in the RCA consortium. That year, AT&T withdrew from the RCA organization. There was a great deal of public resentment against the radio monopoly, which was damaging AT&T's image and, of course, could injure its telephone business. The government was considering taking antitrust action against RCA and its partners. Disagreements between AT&T and the radio group strengthened AT&T's desire to withdraw from RCA and from broadcasting. AT&T sold WEAF and its network to an RCA subsidiary for $1 million on November 1, 1926.[76] This new subsidiary, the National Broadcasting Company (NBC), joined the existing network held by RCA with the new network and radio station acquired from AT&T. Thus, the new NBC became the owner of two networks that eventually became known as NBC's Red and Blue networks. NBC was owned 50% by RCA, 30% by GE, and 20% by Westinghouse.[77]

From its beginning, NBC was in a very good position because of the two networks it owned and the many stations affiliated with each. As part of the agreement revising the arrangement between AT&T and the radio group, AT&T agreed not to engage in broadcasting or networking for seven years and

Announcing the

National Broadcasting Company, Inc.

National radio broadcasting with better programs permanently assured by this important action of the *Radio Corporation* of *America* in the interest of the listening public

THE RADIO CORPORATION OF AMERICA is the largest distributor of radio receiving sets in the world. It handles the entire output in this field of the Westinghouse and General Electric factories.

It does not say this boastfully. It does not say it with apology. It says it for the purpose of making clear the fact that it is more largely interested, more selfishly interested, if you please, in the best possible broadcasting in the United States than anyone else.

Radio for 26,000,000 Homes

The market for receiving sets in the future will be determined largely by the quantity and quality of the programs broadcast.

We say quantity because they must be diversified enough so that some of them will appeal to all possible listeners.

We say quality because each program must be the best of its kind. If that ideal were to be reached, no home in the United States could afford to be without a radio receiving set.

Today the best available statistics indicate that 5,000,000 homes are equipped, and 21,000,000 homes remain to be supplied.

Radio receiving sets of the best reproductive quality should be made available for all, and we hope to make them cheap enough so that all may buy.

The day has gone by when the radio receiving set is a plaything. It must now be an instrument of service.

WEAF Purchased for $1,000,000

The Radio Corporation of America, therefore, is interested, just as the public is, in having the most adequate programs broadcast. It is interested, as the public is, in having them comprehensive and free from discrimination.

Any use of radio transmission which causes the public to feel that the quality of the programs is not the highest, that the use of radio is not the broadest and best use in the public interest, that it is used for political advantage or selfish power, will be detrimental to the public interest in radio, and therefore to the Radio Corporation of America.

To insure, therefore, the development of this great service, the Radio Corporation of America has purchased for one million dollars station WEAF from the American Telephone and Telegraph Company, that company having decided to retire from the broadcasting business.

The Radio Corporation of America will assume active control of that station on November 15.

National Broadcasting Company Organized

The Radio Corporation of America has decided to incorporate that station, which has achieved such a deservedly high reputation for the quality and character of its programs, under the name of the National Broadcasting Company, Inc.

The Purpose of the New Company

The purpose of that company will be to provide the best program available for broadcasting in the United States.

The National Broadcasting Company will not only broadcast these programs through station WEAF, but it will make them available to other broadcasting stations throughout the country so far as it may be practicable to do so, and they may desire to take them.

It is hoped that arrangements may be made so that every event of national importance may be broadcast widely throughout the United States.

No Monopoly of the Air

The Radio Corporation of America is not in any sense seeking a monopoly of the air. That would be a liability rather than an asset. It is seeking, however, to provide machinery which will insure a national distribution of national programs, and a wider distribution of programs of the highest quality.

If others will engage in this business the Radio Corporation of America will welcome their action, whether it be cooperative or competitive.

If other radio manufacturing companies, competitors of the Radio Corporation of America, wish to use the facilities of the National Broadcasting Company for the purpose of making known to the public their receiving sets, they may do so on the same terms as accorded to other clients.

The necessity of providing adequate broadcasting is apparent. The problem of finding the best means of doing it is yet experimental. The Radio Corporation of America is making this experiment in the interest of the art and the furtherance of the industry.

A Public Advisory Council

In order that the National Broadcasting Company may be advised as to the best type of program, that discrimination may be avoided, that the public may be assured that the broadcasting is being done in the fairest and best way, always allowing for human frailties and human performance, it has created an Advisory Council, composed of twelve members, to be chosen as representative of various shades of public opinion, which will from time to time give it the benefit of their judgment and suggestion. The members of this Council will be announced as soon as their acceptance shall have been obtained.

M. H. Aylesworth to be President

The President of the new National Broadcasting Company will be M. H. Aylesworth, for many years Managing Director of the National Electric Light Association. He will perform the executive and administrative duties of the corporation.

Mr. Aylesworth, while not hitherto identified with the radio industry or broadcasting, has had public experience as Chairman of the Colorado Public Utilities Commission, and, through his work with the association which represents the electrical industry, has a broad understanding of the technical problems which measure the pace of broadcasting.

One of his major responsibilities will be to see that the operations of the National Broadcasting Company reflect enlightened public opinion, which expresses itself so promptly the morning after any error of taste or judgment or departure from fair play.

We have no hesitation in recommending the National Broadcasting Company to the people of the United States.

It will need the help of all listeners. It will make mistakes. If the public will make known its views to the officials of the company from time to time, we are confident that the new broadcasting company will be an instrument of great public service.

RADIO CORPORATION OF AMERICA

OWEN D. YOUNG, *Chairman of the Board*   JAMES G. HARBORD, *President*

The notice which introduced a new national network, NBC. (Culver Pictures.)

NBC agreed to use AT&T lines to connect its stations where they were available.

About the time NBC was being created, events that would lead to a second national network—Columbia Broadcasting System (CBS)—were in progress. A young man who had once been a violinist but had turned to artist management was concerned about how fair large broadcasters would be in their payments to artists. Young Arthur Judson approached David Sarnoff with a proposal in which Judson would provide talent to NBC once it was operating. In return Judson would collect fees from NBC and distribute payments to the artists. Sarnoff seemed to like the plan; however when NBC was working, Sarnoff failed to contact Judson.

Judson and his new associate, George A. Coats, went to visit Sarnoff to see what he planned to do about Judson's proposal. "Nothing," said Sarnoff. "Then we will organize our own network," declared Judson. Sarnoff reportedly laughed at the proposal. Judson and Coats found others willing to cooperate in their venture. Then they found radio stations willing to affiliate with the new network—a network that promised ten hours of programming and $500 per week to each station that would sign.

United Independent Broadcasters, as the new network was called, had financial difficulties from the very start. It couldn't interest enough sponsors to pay stations their fees or artists their contracts. Then, Columbia Phonograph Record Company brought some of its funds to the new venture on the condition that the network be called Columbia Phonograph Broadcasting System. Finally, the network went on the air September 18, 1927.

From the first broadcast the new network had difficulties. One of the early broadcasts was the Deems Taylor-Edna St. Vincent Millay opera *The King's Henchman*. To give the program status the opera featured Metropolitan Opera artists. But the performance was marred by technical problems. Week after week the network was unable to pay line charges to AT&T or salary to its employees. Columbia Phonograph Records backed out and the network was renamed Columbia Broadcasting System. Other backers invested money, but it seemed that nothing would help.

At the network's darkest moment William S. Paley, the son of a Philadelphia cigar manufacturer, was persuaded to become president of the young network. Paley brought large sums of money and, more importantly, management skills that turned the network into a money-making operation. In September of 1928 Paley became 50.3 percent owner of the new network.

Both NBC and CBS were to develop into national networks with many radio affiliates. Later, when television developed, both organizations added television and offered programs to television stations. ABC was formed in the early 1940s when a Supreme Court decision forced NBC to sell one of its networks. NBC sold the Blue network to Edward Noble, who renamed it American Broadcasting Company. Like its sister networks, ABC added a television service in the 1950s. The fourth radio network, Mutual Broadcasting Company, was formed during the 1930s as a loose cooperative of stations that banded together to sell radio time.

Wireless Regulation is Demanded

Before broadcasting, there was little need to have a systematic law allowing the government to regulate wireless or to take away licenses. There simply were not enough stations on the air to require close governmental regulation. But as broadcasting became popular, more and more people wanted to go on the air as broadcasters or amateurs. With the growing popularity of the new medium, interference between stations became a real problem.

Yet with all of the problems, government had only two laws specifically written to guide it in regulating radio. The Wireless Ship Act of 1910 required that only certain ships carry wireless equipment. The Radio Act of 1912 gave the government very little additional authority. These two laws remained the only wireless laws created by Congress until 1927.

Each of these laws had inadequacies that were exposed by the courts in the Intercity Company Case (1921) in which the Department of Commerce was informed that it could not exceed the very narrow limits of the law.[82] This apparently did not give the Secretary of Commerce the right to deny a license. Thus while the Secretary could award licenses, the department was not free to revoke them. Although the case was appealed, the decision was not reversed.

McPHERSON'S RELIGION

The problems of radio regulation faced by Secretary Hoover were often taxing. One incident involved an extremely popular evangelist of the 1920's, Aimee Semple McPherson, who operated a station from her temple in Los Angeles. She transmitted on any frequency that seemed convenient, often wandering up and down the radio band. An engineer of Hoover's took note of her behavior and Hoover ordered that her station be closed. McPherson immediately sent a telegram to Hoover with the following message:

PLEASE ORDER YOUR MINONS OF SATAN TO LEAVE MY STATION ALONE. YOU CANNOT EXPECT THE ALMIGHTY TO ABIDE BY YOUR WAVELENGTH NONSENSE. WHEN I ORDER MY PRAYERS TO HIM, I MUST FIT INTO HIS WAVE RECEPTION. OPEN THIS STATION AT ONCE.

Hoover persuaded McPherson to employ an engineer before reopening the station.

Source: Erik Barnouw, *A Tower in Babel* (New York: Oxford University Press, 1966), p. 180.

Secretary Hoover's authority was further limited in 1926 when a court in Chicago decided in the Zenith Radio decision that he had no authority to create any regulations regarding wireless.[83] As a result of these two decisions radio was left with no structure for handling stations, which interfered with other stations.

During the years between 1922 and 1926 while the courts were exploring the ramifications of the 1910 and 1912 laws, Congress was considering dozens of bills that might lead to a new law to regulate radio. But each year passed without new legislation. In an attempt to stimulate Congress to action, Secretary Hoover called national radio conferences each year between 1922 and 1925. These conferences were attended by representatives of government, industry, education, as well as interested amateurs.

Since each interest group had its own concerns, the first radio conference was somewhat divisive. It did, however, recommend that Congress regulate the technical aspects of radio. Later conferces produced recommendations for Congress regarding copyright and monopoly in radio.[84] Each year these recommendations were forwarded to Congress for action, making it clear that the industry wanted some governmental regulation.

Not until the historic Zenith decision of 1926 did Congress decide to act. Although interference had been a problem before 1926, after the Zenith decision bedlam reigned and Congress was forced to act. Working from suggestions gleaned from the radio conferences and from previous bills, Congress came up with a new law that was approved by the House of Representatives on January 27, 1927 and the Senate on February 18, 1927. President Calvin Coolidge signed the bill into law on February 23, 1927.[85]

The newly created Federal Radio Commission (FRC) came into being on the basis of an important concept. To provide a reason for creating a new agency, Congress reasoned that the public owned the radio waves. This arises from the notion that all people in the United States (according to the Constitution) have a right to enjoy their share of the nation's resources. Thus, everyone has the right to drive down roads, travel on waterways, and use oil. But when a resource is limited—as is the case with radio—then this public ownership authorizes Congress to step in and regulate in the interest of all citizens. Radio was (and still is) a limited resource because it is impossible for everyone to have their own radio station without creating chaos. So Congress passed a law authorizing a commission (FRC) to regulate radio in the "public interest, convenience, and necessity."

By passing the Radio Act of 1927, Congress was giving the government ownership of the radio waves so that it could parcel out the different channels to private citizens. These private citizens, it was expected, would broadcast programs.

The FRC had many of the recommendations from the four radio conferences incorporated into its legislation. The FRC was authorized to regulate the technical aspects of radio including setting the power a station may use, the number of hours that station may be on the air, and the location of the station. In addition the new agency had the right to write its own regulations, it

RCA BROADCASTS SPORTS

Early broadcasters often had problems. RCA and its new General Manager David Sarnoff—the young man who had received signals from the sinking *Titanic*—saw his company moving into broadcasting quickly. He proposed setting up a station in New Jersey to broadcast the Jack Dempsey-Georges Carpentier fight scheduled for July 2, 1921 in Jersey City. Others in the company agreed, but RCA lacked a transmitter. Scouting around, Sarnoff found that GE had a new transmitter that was not yet delivered to a customer. Sarnoff convinced GE to loan him the transmitter just long enough to air the fight, and moved it into an experimental yard owned by the Lackawanna Railroad. Railroad technicians strung antenna wires around the yard for Sarnoff, and provided a metal shack for the manager to use during the fights, but failed to tell Sarnoff that the shack was used by porters of the railroad. At that time all of the porters were black and no white person had ever entered the shack. The porters threatened the transmitter with violence and Sarnoff found himself guarding the equipment day and night with firearms.

By the day of the fight the transmitter had been tested and was operating properly. Some of Sarnoff's associates stayed at the transmitter while others went to see the fight that was to be held outside. That August day rain and clouds kept would-be broadcasters at the sports arena wet and uncomfortable while, in the transmitter shack, the technician was being blinded by the bright glow of the vacuum tubes. In spite of the weather a blow by blow account reached the transmitter, but all was not well. The transmitter had not been intended for continuous operation and as the fight got hotter so did the transmitter. About three-quarters through the fight one tube exploded and the operator grabbed the broken base with his bare hands replacing it with a new one. The new tube got the transmitter through the fight, but sent the operator to the hospital with burned hands. The troubles were not yet over. Almost immediately after the fight the transmitter seemed to disintegrate into a molten mass of glass and wire. RCA was now in the broadcasting business with one borrowed, demolished transmitter, one operator with a burned hand and slightly blinded eyes, and a wet sportscaster. Undaunted, RCA set up new facilities in Roselle Park, New Jersey.

Source: Gleason L. Archer, *History of Radio of 1926*, (New York: The American Historical Society, 1938), pp. 212–215.

could take stations off the air, and it could modify licenses. To make sure Congress did not overlook anything important the FRC was provided with authority to regulate in other areas such as the public interest, convenience, or necessity might require.

When the FRC was initially formed, Congress gave it total control over radio for only one year. At the end of the year the administrative power of the FRC was to revert to the Secretary of Commerce, however the FRC was to receive applications for licenses and for renewals or modifications of licenses. Apparently, Congress felt that the need for a strong FRC would vanish when the chaos on the radio waves was cleared up.

As a new commission, the FRC immediately set out to remove the interference resulting from stations operating on the same or adjacent frequencies and audiences quickly noticed a change for the better. It became possible to hear stations quite clearly and broadcasters and listeners alike were pleased with the success the FRC was having in handling technical matters.

In forming the FRC, the government accepted the idea that it had the right to hold radio frequencies for the public. There was no attempt on the part of the government to decide if some other method for regulating radio might be devised, however. One possibility might be for the government to sell radio channels to the highest bidders and to regulate them in much the same way that other property is now regulated. With this approach, private citizens, not thM government, would own radio vernment might step in only to protect citizens from excesses.

Of course, there is the other extreme—government might have taken upon itself the task of operating all of the radio stations and only let people come in to broadcast their views. Between these two extremes, one might devise dozens of alternatives. But in the United States, the people, through their government, own the radio waves, and the government loans the use of these frequencies to individuals.

NOTES

1. Orrin E. Dunlap, Jr., *Radio's 100 Men of Science* (Freeport, N.Y.: Books for Libraries Press, 1944), p. 35.
2. Ibid., p. 39.
3. Gleason L. Archer, *History of Radio to 1926* (New York: The American Historical Society, 1938), p. 28.
4. Ibid., pp. 28, 29.
5. Ibid., p. 28.
6. Ibid., p. 42.
7. Edwin Emery, *The Press and America* (Englewood Cliffs, N. J.: Prentice-Hall, 1972), p. 330.
8. Dunlap, op. cit., p. 64.
9. Archer, op. cit., pp. 47–49.

10. Ibid., p. 47.

11. Ibid., p. 49; Dunlap, op. cit., p. 85. There is some disagreement on the exact date of the invention of the telephone in that Archer argues for February 14 or 29, 1876 while Dunlap places the date at March 10, 1876. Both authors take note of the February date.

12. Speech at a dinner of the American Institute of Electrical Engineers, January 13, 1902 quoted in Dunlap, op. cit., p. 86.

13. Ibid., p. 50.

14. Ibid., p. 66.

15. Ibid.

16. Archer, op. cit., p. 54.

17. Elliot N. Sivowitch, "A Technological Survey of Broadcasting's Prehistory, 1876–1920," *Journal of Broadcasting*, Vol. XV, No. 1 (Winter 1970–71), pp. 1–20.*

18. Dunlap, op. cit., p. 172.

19. Ibid.

20. Ibid.

21. "Wireless Signals Across the Ocean," *New York Times* (December 15, 1901), pp. 1, 2.*

22. Dunlap, op. cit., p. 172.

23. Archer, op. cit., p. 57.

24. "Wireless Signals Across the Ocean," op. cit., pp. 1, 2.

25. Thorn Mayes, "History of the American Marconi Company," *The Old Timer's Bulletin*, Vol. 13, No. 1 (June 1972), p. 11.*

26. "Wireless Signals Across the Ocean," op. cit., p. 1.

27. Dunlap, op. cit., p. 174.

28. Ibid, p. 138.

29. Sivowitch, op. cit.

30. Ibid.

31. Dunlap, op. cit., p. 190.

32. Ibid., p. 93.

33. Sivowitch, op. cit.

34. Dunlap, op. cit., p. 166.

35. Ibid., p. 202.

36. Ibid., p. 98.

37. Federal Communications Commission, "Information Bulletin 14-G" (November 1975), p. 1, 2.

38. Archer, op. cit., pp. 74–75.

39. Ibid., p. 137.

40. Ibid., pp. 157, 158.

41. Ibid., p. 158.

42. Mayes, op. cit., p. 11.

43. Erik Barnouw, *A Tower in Babel* (New York: Oxford University Press, 1966), p. 49.

44. Archer, op. cit., pp. 178–180.

45. Ibid., pp. 178–189, 194, 195.

46. Ibid.

47. Ibid., pp. 97, 98.

48. Ibid., p. 89.

49. Edwin H. Armstrong, "The Story of the Super-heterodyne," *Radio Broadcast*, (July 1924), p. 198.*

50. Archer, op. cit., p. 116.

51. Dunlap, op. cit., pp. 190–192.

52. Archer, op. cit., pp. 112, 113; Sivowitch, op. cit., pp. 19, 20 places the date of the memo as Sept. 30, 1918.

53. Dunlap, op. cit., pp. 224–226.

54. "History of Broadcasting and KDKA Radio," Westinghouse Broadcasting Company, undated news release, p. 1.*

55. Ibid.

56. Ibid., p. 2.

57. It should be noted that other stations claim the same honor. WWJ owned by the Detroit News claims to have broadcasted as early as August 31, 1920 with the call letters 8 MK and WBL (see Archer pp. 207, 208). Other stations that claim early broadcasts include KQW in San Jose, California in 1909; 2 ZK in New Rochelle, New York in 1916; and WHA in Madison, Wisconsin. In any event KDKA is, according to Department of Commerce records, the oldest station with appropriate federal license to engage in airing programs for the general public on a regularly scheduled basis.

58. "History of Broadcasting and KDKA Radio," op. cit., pp. 2–5.

59. Ibid.

60. Ibid.

61. H. D. Kellogg, Jr. "Who Is to Pay for Broadcasting—and How?" *Radio Broadcast* (March 1925), pp. 863–866.*

62. Ibid., p. 866.

63. Archer, op. cit., p. 264,

64. FCC, "Early History of Network Broadcasting (1923–1926) and the National Broadcasting Company," *Report on Chain Broadcasting* (Commission Order No. 37, Docket 5060, May 1941), pp. 5–20.*

65. Lawrence W. Lichty and Malachi C. Topping, *American Broadcasting: A Source Book on the History of Radio and Television* (New York: Hastings House, 1975), pp. 195–196.

66. Ibid., pp. 196, 197.

67. Archer, op. cit., pp. 265, 266.

68. Lichty, op. cit.

69. Ibid., p. 203.

70. Ibid., pp. 187, 286.

71. FCC, "Early History of Network Broadcasting (1923–1926) and the National Broadcasting Company," op. cit.

72. Ibid., pp. 5, 6.

73. Ibid.

74. Ibid.

75. Archer, op. cit., p. 346.

76. FCC, "*Early History*," op. cit., pp. 5–10.

77. Ibid.

78. FCC, "The Columbia Broadcasting System," *Report on Chain Broadcasting* (Commission Order No. 37, Docket 5060, May 1941), pp. 21, 22.*.

79. Ibid.

80.   Ibid.

81.   John Wallace, "What We Thought of the First Columbia Broadcasting Program," *Radio Broadcast*, (December 1927), pp. 140, 141.

82.   Marvin R. Bensman, "Regulation of Broadcasting by the Department of Commerce, 1921–1927," p. 549.*In the *Intercity Company* case, the Department of Commerce refused a commercial radio license to a company on the grounds that unacceptable interference would occur. However, the courts directed Hoover to award the license, saying that Hoover should use only the authority granted the department in the statute. The courts were saying that Hoover and the Department of Commerce could not exceed the specific language of the two radio laws that had been enacted in 1910 and 1912.

83.   Ibid., p. 554. In the Zenith Radio Corporation case, the court told the Department of Commerce that it could not establish any regulations. This in effect prevented Hoover from even assigning a channel or power to a station. Thus while Hoover had been assigning power and frequency to stations after the *Intercity* case, now all he could do was grant a license. What the licensee did with that license after it got the authorization was up to the license holder.

84.   Edward F. Sarno, Jr., "The National Radio Conferences," *Journal of Broadcasting*, Vol. XIII, No. 2 (Spring 1969), pp. 189–202.

85.   Bensman, op. cit., p. 547.

*Citations are printed in Lawrence W. Lichty and Malachi C. Topping, *American Broadcasting: A Source Book on the History of Radio and Television* (New York: Hastings House, 1975).

History of Broadcasting After 1927

3

RADIO ENTERS ITS "GOLDEN AGE"

The Radio Act of 1927 brought order to the radio waves so that listeners could pick intelligible programs out of the ether. But the Radio Act had its shortcomings: the FRC had jurisdiction only over radios and not wire communication, the FRC had been created as a temporary agency, and the first commissioners on the FRC served without pay. In time Congress made the FRC a permanent body subject to annual review and gave the commissioners some pay, but the FRC was still considered a second class agency.

Whatever the frailities of the FRC, it gave radio broadcasting a secure foundation upon which to work and, with the passage of the Radio Act, a twenty year period spanning the Great Depression and World War II began called the "golden age of radio." This period saw the building of vast business empires by commercial broadcasters. Radio's popularity was to grow immensely during a depression that forced people to conserve their income and a war that limited the production of consumer products.

The very growth of radio pointed out some of the weaknesses of the FRC as an agency responsible for regulating radio. For one thing the FRC had no authority to regulate telephone companies, or for that matter any of the other companies engaged in using wires to communicate. Yet the newly developing radio networks had to use telephone company wires to interconnect all of the stations in the network. Telephone companies in different states charged different rates and the quality of service was apt to vary. Networks needed consistent telephone service.

Indeed, Felix Frankfurter, a Harvard professor of law who became a United States Supreme Court justice, noted that state commissions were simply unable to adequately regulate these telephone companies. Frankfurter's comment in 1930 was followed by a study done by W. W. Splawn, a special council for the House Committee on Interstate and Foreign Commerce, which led to the suggestion that a new federal commission be set up to study all aspects of telephone companies.[1]

Public concern led President Franklin D. Roosevelt to direct the Secretary of Commerce to study the problem of regulating wire and wireless communication. This study resulted in the recommendation that all electrical communication be regulated by one federal agency. The FRC regulated radio while the President, the Postmaster General, and the Interstate Commerce Commission (ICC) had been variously responsible for some aspects of wire communication.[2]

Even David Sarnoff, the president of RCA, testified before the House of Representatives Committee in 1934 urging the formation of the central agency.[3] That same year, Congress formed a new commission—the Federal Communications Commission (FCC)—by passing the Communications Act of 1934. The new FCC had control over both radio and wire communication. This meant that the FCC could regulate telephone companies when their wires crossed state lines as well as regulate radio as the FRC had done. Thus Congress, at Roosevelt's suggestion, brought together under one agency the

TABLE 3-1   Radio Set Sales and Saturation, 1922–1972

	RADIO RECEIVER SET SALES		
Number Sold		Percent of Sets With FM Radios	Homes With Radio
1922	100,000		0.2%
1925	2,000,000		10
1930	3,827,000		46
1935	6,026,800		67
1940	11,800,000		81
1945	500,000		89
1950	9,218,000		95
1955	7,327,000	4%	96
1960	18,031,000	11	96
1965	31,689,000	23	97
1970	34,048,000	59	99
1972	42,149,000	57	99

Source: Lawrence W. Lichty and Malachi C. Topping, *A Source Book on the History of Radio and Television* (New York: Hastings House, 1975), p. 521.

powers that had once been held by the Postmaster, the President, and the ICC. With its new power the FCC could grant, deny, or revoke broadcast licenses. It could, and did, regulate technical and nontechnical matters related to broadcasting—but the FCC could not censor any broadcast and it could not intervene in the business of a station.

Yet some problems still existed. The FCC did not have specific control over networks. The networks—CBS and NBC—were still young when Congress created the FCC and it did not anticipate how important networks were to become in the development of radio. This failure would eventually cause the FCC some difficulties. And, of course, the Communications Act could not possibly have anticipated some of the revolutionary developments that were to occur twenty to thirty years after its formation—such as cable television.

Perhaps one of the most difficult problems of the FCC concerned the poorly defined "public interest, convenience, or necessity" phrase that Congress included in the Communications Act. This phrase was tested in courts—if for no other reason than that it was imprecise. Despite its vague nature, the FCC could and has used the phrase as the basis of much of its regulatory decisions.

RADIO DURING THE DEPRESSION 1928–1937

Some feared that the depression, which occurred just as radio was developing, would destroy it. But this concern turned out to be unfounded since, if anything, the depression helped the growth of radio. As jobs vanished and as people's economic situation became more strained, the popularity of radio seemed to grow. People who had a radio did not have to spend money on movies, plays, or any other entertainment—radio brought entertainment to them. Those who could not afford dinner out could sit before their radios and enjoy music, drama, and comedy. Radio was so popular that almost four million sets where sold in 1930 and by 1935 over six million were being sold each year. This meant that fully 67 percent of all homes were equipped with radios by 1935.[4]

Network Programming During the Depression Years

In the 1927–1928 season networks and syndication companies provided only a few programs to radio stations such as variety shows, like one sponsored by the Eveready Battery Company, and a few news, religious, and music shows. Most of the programs has been on the air for only a year or less.[5] In only one season—1928–1929—networks doubled the number of musical shows, and they offered five variety shows, two dramas, and at least one public affairs program each week. Within the two years following the formation of the FRC, business had shown a considerable interest in the developing medium.[6]

By the 1929–1930 season—the first full year of the depression—industry began cutting back and unemployment was widespread, yet broadcast

DR. J. R. BRINKLEY

J. R. Brinkley operated a radio station and a hospital in Milford, Kansas where he dispensed cures for all kinds of ills to patients he never saw. Brinkley used his radio station to encourage people to write for medical advice and suggestions for medicines which might help solve their problems. Then, over the radio, he would prescribe the cure. His broadcasts went something like this:

> Here's one from Tillie. She says she had an operation, had some trouble 10 years ago. I think the operation was unnecessary, and it isn't very good sense to have an ovary removed with the expectation of motherhood resulting therefrom. My advice to you is to use Women's Tonic Numbers 50, 67, and 61. This combination will do for you what you desire if any combination will, after three months' use.*

Not only did Brinkley use the air to prescribe cures, he performed operations in his hospital, and he dispensed drugs through the Brinkley Pharmaceutical Association. When Brinkley applied for a license renewal in 1930 for station KFKB, the FRC denied the renewal on the grounds that he broadcast to individuals rather than to the public by answering individual medical questions over the air. The FRC, in addition, argued that Brinkley used the station solely for his own personal use.

Brinkley appealed to a court, but it agreed with the FRC and Brinkley was forced to take his station off the air. It should be pointed out that Brinkley's claim to his medical degree came because he paid $100—not because he completed medical school.** The American Medical Association declared that his operations were a fraud. Although the FRC took no action on the AMA claim, it did find that Brinkley had misused his license.

*KFKB Broadcasting Association, Inc. v. Federal Radio Commission 47 F.2d 670 (D.C. Cir.) (1931).
**Erik Barnouw, A Tower in Babel (New York: Oxford University Press, 1966), pp. 168–173.

programming continued to increase. "Adventures of Helen and Mary" was introduced as a daytime light drama or "soap opera," so called because soap products were advertised during breaks. A radio minister, Billy Sunday, had the "Back Home Hour" and concert music, light music, and thrillers were being aired. Broadcasters had an extensive choice of programming as the years of the depression passed, and radio seemed to be offering the American public more and more of what it wanted. By 1931 "Death Valley Days" and "Sherlock Holmes" were on the air.[7]

As others were trying to entertain, churches were finding broadcasting to be an effective way to communicate their message. The Catholics had an hour, CBS offered time to churches on a rotational basis, and the Jews had the "Message of Israel." While advertising and entertainment were trying to solve the economic problems, ministers tried to serve spiritual needs.

Many of the famous broadcast entertainers were on the air for most of the depression. Bob Hope sang through the last five years; Burns and Allen were broadcasting through all but the first season and were still going strong; and Kate Smith had been on the air for nine seasons by 1940. There were other long timers, still remembered by many, such as Gene Autry, Bing Crosby, and Fibber McGee and Molly. Indeed the depression was the proving ground and the growth period for radio programming. Most program types began in radio during these lean years and grew into successful series. People turned to radio in great numbers and listened with intense interest to their favorite series.[8]

One of the popular programs—"The Lone Ranger"—featured a masked man and an Indian companion who traveled the West trying to restore order. The program was so popular that when a free pop gun was offered some 24,905 requests for it were received in only three days.

And then there was Jack Benny, a comic who was the target of most of his own jokes. His comedy centered around such situations as the selling of an old, 1918 Maxwell car that was so broken-down that no one would buy it. One of his most famous standing jokes was that he was a brilliant violinist. However, every time he would attempt to play, the instrument would squeak horribly.

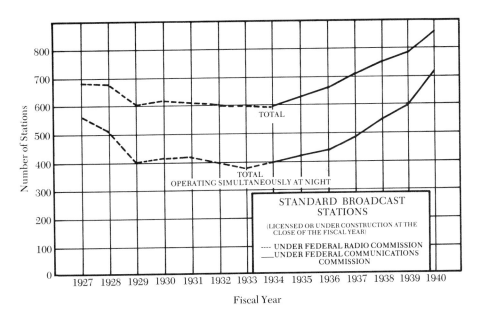

Figure 3–1. Graph of broadcast licenses 1927–1940. Source: FCC Sixth Annual Report (Washington, D.C.: Government Printing Office, 1940), p. 121.

FATHER COUGHLIN

Charles Edward Couglin was a Roman Catholic priest who originated controversial broadcasts from his Shrine of the Little Flower
in Royal Oak, Michigan during the depression years. He began
broadcasting in 1926 over WJR in Detroit, but later he used CBS for
his religious and political speeches.

For sometime he led listeners to believe that he had close ties
with President Roosevelt and had advised the President. During
these years Coughlin urged listeners to support the President. Then
Roosevelt fell from the list of Coughlin's friends and Coughlin called
the President a "great liar and betrayer." Thereafter Coughlin
aligned with Huey Long of Louisiana.

Coughlin's political fervor extended to chosing a presidential
candidate, William Lemke of North Dakota. Coughlin guaranteed
that he would cease broadcasting if Lemke was not elected in 1936.
Lemke received fewer than one million votes and Coughlin continued broadcasting. Coughlin undoubtedly saw himself as a great
reformer and leader in the nation. But CBS saw him as one misusing
the air waves and removed him from the air. Coughlin was a racist
who had great admiration for Hitler and as the nation turned against
Hitler and all he stood for, they rejected the narrow views of
Coughlin. by 1940, Coughlin had largely lost his audiences.

Source: Frank Buxton and Bill Owen, *The Big Broadcaster* (New York: The
Viking Press, 1972), p. 82.

Franklin D. Roosevelt—A Consoling Voice

Entertainment was not the only fare that kept listeners coming back to their
radio sets. Often, during the worst years of the depression, the consoling voice
of the President of the United States, Franklin Roosevelt, could be heard on
the air, assuring the nation that the government was doing all it could to solve
the problems that confronted everyone. Then Roosevelt would tell listeners
about the programs that had been initiated to cope with the depression. Many
of his programs ended with a reminder that the depression would soon be over
and that people should sustain their courage. But Roosevelt's skill went beyond
just saying the right words—he showed the American people that he was a man
they could identify with.

One hot Washington day as Roosevelt was talking to the nation, he com-
mented on the heat. Then he asked his radio audience to wait a moment while
he took a drink of water. He paused, then resumed his chat. After going off the
air, Roosevelt was told by his staff that the pause was the perfect action.

Whatever his effect on the audience, Roosevelt undoubtedly had great persuasive powers. The "Fireside Chats" were the first extensive political use made of radio. The success of these chats encouraged other politicians to use radio and, later, television as persuasive tools. The fireside chats established personality as an essential ingredient for the effective use of radio as a political tool.[10]

THE EVOLUTION OF THE DISC JOCKEY

Drama, comedy, and talks were complemented by a liberal amount of music. Without a doubt, the largest segment of a radio station's day was filled with music. During the early days of radio those music programs were live, but as the depression came along and as advertising revenues available to local stations became more scarce, radio stations began to look for more inexpensive programming. One solution was recorded music. To play a record the station needed only an announcer, a record player, and a supply of records. This form of programming became popular with both networks and stations as we shall later see and it has since become the mainstay of the radio industry.

Recorded music took its place along with live music shows, variety programs, newscasts, live drama, and comedy programs. The notion of using recorded music was later to create some complex economic problems that would have to be confronted in a somewhat protracted flight between the producers of music and the broadcasters of music.

By 1938 fully 52 percent of all radio programming was music—most of it recorded.[11] Using recorded music led to the rise of the disc jockey format. Probably the first disc jockey show was evolved by Al Jarvis in the early 1930s and was called "Make Believe Ballroom." Jarvis did not have a monopoly on record playing for long. Martin Block took the idea—along with the title—and began his own disc jockey show in Southern California. Later he moved to New York to begin "Make Believe Ballroom" on WNEW.[12] Both Block and the station were to reap large financial rewards from this type of programming.[13]

The disc jockey program format was later to develop into more elaborate formats—the form was to replace radio network programming when the networks turned their attention to programming for television. In fact the next step in the development of record playing stations was specialized music. That step was taken in 1953 when a station owned by George McLendon in Texas began programming specialized music and news plus, as it was called, "razzle-dazzle promotions."[14] This led to the Top-40, middle of the road (MOR), and other specialized stations. Top-40 stations specialize in rock and current music and try to reach the young. MOR stations are more interested in middle-aged people and, therefore, program more old favorites.

As network executives turned their attention away from radio to television and listeners became viewers, radio networks began to stop sending dramas and other live programs to their affiliates. Little by little music and reruns began to creep in. In fact Martin Block and others began spinning records on networks in the late 1940s. By the early 1950s Mutual Broadcasting System (MBS) was feeding fifty minutes of music and ten minutes of news an hour to its affiliates.

Copyright

Playing records, or for that matter bringing live performers into the studio to perform musical selections, required broadcasters to pay fees on copyrighted material to the American Society of Composers, Authors, and Publishers (ASCAP). This practice had begun in 1922 when the creators of music believed that broadcasters should pay a fee for using records.[15] The authority to collect copyright fees was a result of a copyright law passed by Congress in 1909. Although it predates commercial radio by several years, it gave the creators of music the right to collect fees from all users. Many young stations were in such weak financial shape when ASCAP began charging copyright fees that they simply had to close. Others decided to use music without permission, but a few large stations began paying the fees.

In order to fight ASCAP a group of broadcasters organized the National Association of Broadcasters (NAB), but ASCAP continued charging fees to broadcasters—fees that increased as broadcast revenue climbed.[16] By 1935 ASCAP demands had become so high that the NAB decided to take some action. It found its opportunity in 1937 when ASCAP announced a new rise in royalties. That same year ASCAP was under investigation by the Department of Justice for possible violations of the antitrust laws and so was in a particularly vulnerable position.

In 1937 the broadcast industry formed its own Broadcast Music, Incorporated (BMI) to compete with ASCAP in licensing and collecting fees for the use of copyrighted music. Broadcasters hoped that BMI, by competing with ASCAP, would keep music fees low. Furthermore, broadcasters planned for BMI to license new artists who would be willing to sell rights to their music for lower prices. Stations would then play only the music licensed by BMI and propel the new composers to fame, benefiting both the station and the composer. As it happened ASCAP came in line with the demands of broadcasters so the need for BMI was reduced, although not eliminated.[17]

Radio Threatens Newspapers

As the depression advanced, radio broadcasters were collecting larger and larger revenues while newspaper advertising was decreasing. Needless to say this angered newspapers, especially when they saw broadcasters airing the very news they would be carrying only a few hours later. Indeed newspapers found that they were being scooped by radio stations at every turn. The "extra" issue of a newspaper to cover an important event could not compete with the speed of radio. While editors and printers in a newspaper office were writing, editing, and setting type, a newscaster in a radio station might be reading the news that would be on the street five or six hours later. Most newspapers felt threatened by the turn of events.

An inactive radio committee of the American Newspaper Publishers Association in 1933 persuaded Associated Press (AP), United Press (UP), and International News Service (INS) to stop sending news to radio stations and networks.[18] CBS decided to retaliate and started organizing its own news gathering bureau, but newspapers in the areas where CBS had affiliates immediately stopped printing station listings. CBS lost its nerve and gave up on the news bureau. This incident convinced CBS and most other stations and networks that they would have to make peace with the newspapers.

In 1933 representatives of both networks, the ANPA, AP, UP, and INS met at the Hotel Baltimore in New York and signed an agreement in which the networks agreed never again to engage in news gathering. In return, the news organizations agreed to provide two five minute news summaries each day. Also the news organizations would provide occasional bulletins of great importance.

The newspaper boycott was never very successful because some stations refused to abide by the agreement and because the controls set up by the press were not very effective. One of these controls was the Press Radio Bureau, which went into operation on March 1, 1934. It was intended to be the police arm of the ANPA.

Another serious problem that arose was the formation of Trans-Radio Press— an independent news gathering organization that provided broadcasters with news. It was so successful that by 1935 the ANPA amended its agreement with broadcasters to permit UP and INS to sell news to broadcasters as well. Although the newspaper boycott remained officially in operation until 1940, its intent had been largely compromised by 1935.[19]

RADIO DURING THE SECOND WORLD WAR 1938–1945

Radio had survived the depression in good form. Networks had grown and stations—at least most of them—had been able to pay their bills. But with the coming of a war, radio was confronted with a new problem. The Government stopped the production of consumer goods so that military needs could receive industry's maximum attention. Gasoline was rationed, metal was in short supply, and the best foods were being shipped to the soldiers. There was no apparent need to advertise since there was little to sell, but many advertisers were willing to use some funds in promoting business or products via radio.

A major reason for this advertiser spending arose from a federal ruling that permitted advertisers to treat money spent on advertising as a cost of operation. Thus they could take advertising dollars as a tax deduction. Consequently, during the war, money spent on advertising continued to grow. In 1935 advertisers spent 113 million dollars on radio. By 1940 that amount had risen to $216

TABLE 3–2   Advertising Dollars Spent on Radio

	1935	1940	1945
DOLLARS (Add 000,000)			
Radio	$112.6	$215.6	$423.9

Source: Lawrence W. Lichty and Malachi C. Topping A *Source Book on the History of Radio and Television* (New York: Hastings House, 1975), p. 256

million and during the war years advertiser support of radio continued to increase until it reached $424 million in 1945 when the war ended.[20]

Radio was riding high with sponsors like Jergens Lotion, Johnson and Johnson, and Lever Brothers. Consumer products were advertised to assure a market when the war ended and to encourage fair distribution of the limited supply of products then available.

Just as important was the right advertisers had to take advertising dollars as a tax deduction. Since many companies were making large profits supplying products to the military, they needed business expenses which would reduce profit and thereby taxes.

Networks, Advertising, and Programming

NBC, which was formed by RCA and the other partners in the RCA consortium, was the first radio network and is still in existence. The first broadcast on the new NBC was carried during 1926 (see p. 62). The announcement publicizing the creation of NBC stated that the network had been formed to bring the highest quality programs to the people of the United States. It also indicated that the new network would provide, when possible, a national hookup for covering important national events that people could not otherwise hear.[21]

Providing high quality programs to its affiliates was not the only purpose in forming radio networks. A network organization was in a unique position to sell advertising time over affiliate stations to national sponsors. Thus, affiliates could derive both programs and money for their station by affiliating with a national network. On the other hand, the network could derive income from selling time in the programs. The network would take a portion of the money derived from selling advertising to pay for producing programs, for renting the telephone lines used to connect stations, and to generate profit. The remainder went to the affiliates for their time and was usually a fraction of the amount the station charged to local sponsors.

THE INFLUENCE OF NETWORKS ON RADIO PROGRAMMING

One of the principle functions of a radio network is to provide programs to its affiliates and, in this respect, the four networks—ABC, CBS, MBS, NBC—were highly successful during the war.

The networks offered a wide variety of public affairs and entertainment programming designed for many listener tastes and intended to convince all advertisers to buy radio time. The spectrum was sprinkled with names that became household words, such as H. V. Kaltenborn, Lowell Thomas, and Drew Pearson. Some of these had been commentators through the Press-Radio War. As World War II approached, America turned to broadcasting for news of what was happening in Europe and Asia, and radio networks responded with eighteen news series each week.[22] Some of the series offered one program a week, others three programs, and still others five programs.

Sarnoff and Marconi on a visit to "Radio Central," 1933. (Culver Pictures.)

The nation was also hearing about the war first hand with reporters like Edward R. Murrow in Europe. The listener tuning into one of the Murrow broadcasts might well hear sounds of war in the background—guns firing, mortars exploding, engines roaring. A sense of immediacy was there that listeners had never experienced before.

In addition to the traditional programming there was a group of programs intended to instill patriotism in the minds of listeners—these programs, like others on the networks, had sponsors. Wrigley Gum for example, sponsored "America in the Air," "First Line of Defense," and "Service to the Front." While the nation was being informed and entertained, famous actors and actresses were urging the public to buy war bonds to support the military.

WAR OF THE WORLDS

There were serious programs on the networks like the Mercury "Theatre of the Air" that carried a different play each week. Perhaps the most important, or at least the most remembered, play this program presented was Orson Welles' "The War of the Worlds" in which Martians were attacking the world. The program, done like a newscast with interruptions in a music program, related news of the fire and destruction the Martians were bringing to the world. Wells told of destruction in New Jersey, armies being destroyed, and people hiding underground. The fear caused by the program caused many people across the nation to actually flee their homes.

It all happened on October 30, 1938, when writer Orson Welles gave his Halloween gift to the nation over CBS radio. The program featured many fictitious interviews and on-the-scene reports of happenings as the invaders were supposedly crossing the world. Announcers described moments of chaos and destruction. The consequences of the program were vastly different from what was expected. Although the producers of the program intended that it be merely dramatic entertainment, the program was filled with such realistic events that it caused actual fear and panic.

Before the program ended, people were praying, crying, and fleeing to escape the "death" the Martians brought. People even began to stock their basements with provisions for the inevitable. People tried to warn their friends of danger. People said things like, "I knew it was dangerous as soon as I heard all those military men were there and the Secretary of State."

The intense public reaction to "War of the Worlds" demonstrated dramatically the power and credibility of radio.

Source: Hadley Cantril, *The Invasion From Mars* (Princeton: Princeton University Press, 1940), pp. 1–7.

OFFICE OF WAR INFORMATION

The United States government set up the Office of War Information (OWI) to broadcasters during World War II to be used for their use in preparing programs for airing. This office produced and distributed a series of pamphlets entitled "Radio Background Material," which were distributed to writers three times a month. Although stations were not required to use the material, most writers felt that it provided valuable backgrounds for their stories.

Besides providing background material, OWI engaged in preparing programs for international broadcast over high power stations operated by the United States, and it served as a consultant to the producers of many different shows. An example was "Front Page Farrell" in which the writer derived much of the material for the program directly from OWI. In fact, OWI checked all of the scripts for accuracy before they were aired.

Source: George A. Willey, "The Soap Operas and the War," *Journal of Broadcasting*, Vol VII, No. 4 (Fall 1963), pp. 339–352.

Not only did the listening public want to be informed about what was happening in the war zone, but they needed to relax. Entertainment programming remained on the air through the war and undoubtedly helped some to forget for brief periods the horrors of war. There were thrillers such as "Death Valley Days," which had been on the air twelve seasons, and there were new programs like the "Green Hornet" and "Mr. District Attorney;" there was comedy, with the long running "Amos 'n' Andy" and newer shows like "Blondie."[23]

The war, like the depression, brought new shows such as quiz programs like "Doctor I Q" and "Double or Nothing." The 1944–1945 season, the last full season during the war, was a very successful year for radio by most standards—there were over 340 network programs of which all but a few were sponsored.[24] Networks were thoroughly involved in the business of entertaining and informing America by radio.

Radio did a great deal to aid the nation in successfully coping with the war. Sponsors and radio stations alike readily supported patriotic programs. Entertainers and broadcasters led in the drive to support the war through the purchase of war bonds while newspeople created programs glorifying the fighting soldier. It is safe to assume that this support aided in creating the national spirit of cooperation that existed.

The public seemed to be approving of the work of radio, whatever its role. Reasearchers who examined the impact of radio on the American household during 1946 discovered some interesting facts. When people were asked to rate several institutions on how good a job they were doing, they rated radio over

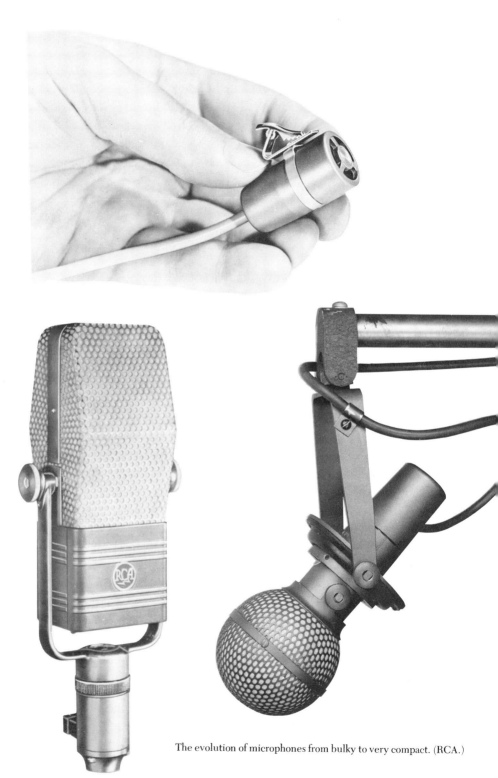

The evolution of microphones from bulky to very compact. (RCA.)

churches, newspapers, schools, and local government.[25] Indeed there were few things for listeners to criticize about radio. Furthermore, the study found that more people got their news from radio than from any other medium. It appeared that radio was the dominant medium in the nation and that people had an allegiance to it.

THE BUSINESS OF NETWORKS

Both CBS and NBC were set up as profit-making corporations intended to serve the affiliates with programming—the two companies had their own corporate structure and were not owned by member stations. On the other hand a new network—Mutual Broadcasting System (MBS) formed in 1934 by four stations—came into being as a group of stations banded together for the purpose of selling time on all of the stations.[26] In addition, the new network would negotiate with AT&T for the use of telephone lines to connect the stations.

One of the stations involved in starting the new network—WXYZ in Detroit—had left CBS because it was dissatisfied with CBS affiliate policies. To start a new network that would have policies more compatible with its view, WXYZ entered into agreements, with WOR in Newark, New Jersey; WLW in Cincinnati, Ohio, and WGN in Chicago, Illinois. After each of the stations was assigned duties to help the new network operate, other stations were persuaded to join MBS.

Each of the three networks that existed in 1934 had organizational elements that made it strong in some way. NBC owned two networks and could offer programs to at least two stations in each market. CBS had a network-affiliate contract that was particularly attractive to the network and its stations. The CBS contract gave the network the right to sell time on an affiliate's station without securing permission from the affiliate to do so. This meant that CBS could sell time the day before a broadcast and know that the commercials would be carried on all stations chosen by the advertiser. In return for giving this control to CBS the stations were given 24 hours of programs. During unsponsored periods, stations could find their own sponsors. MBS, on the other hand, was attractive to stations that wanted to have strong input in how the network was run. It should be noted, however, that MBS had great difficulty in acquiring affiliates for several years because NBC and CBS had the most desirable stations affiliated with them.

The strength of national networks becomes apparent when one realizes that only 6 percent of all radio stations were affiliated with a national network in 1927, but by 1940 fully 50 percent of all radio stations had an affiliation with a national network.[27] Interestingly by 1945 94 percent of all radio stations had network affiliations, but the figure had dropped to 55 percent in 1950 and has remained at a low figure. During those years CBS and NBC dominated the network picture.

The economic health of networks seemed to be very good. In 1935 national networks were charging sponsors almost 40 million dollars, and that amount rose to 74 million in 1940 and over 133 million in 1945. During those years about half of all of radio's revenues came through the networks.

MBS Complains   The young MBS, which had been formed in 1934, attempted to make inroads into the number of affiliates connected with the other two networks. The success of this project was apparent by 1940 when MBS had some 160 stations in its network line up. This amounted to more stations than were affiliated with CBS and almost as many as were involved in the various NBC arrangements.[28] Yet these gains were more on paper than actual since

---

JAMES L. FLY

James L. Fly, who chaired the FCC during the early years of the 1940s, directed the investigation that led to the court case dissolving NBC's second network. His antitrust actions caused bitter resentment in the broadcast industry, which demanded that Congress impeach Fly. One of the Congressmen concerned with removing Fly was Representative Eugene Cox of Georgia. One of Fly's colleagues, Commissioner Durr, angered by Cox's investigation, attempted to prevent Cox from completing his study.

FCC investigators had found a cancelled check in the possession of an Albany, Georgia radio station that had been given to Cox in return for influencing federal agencies—a clear violation of the law.* The FCC had once shown the check to several members of Congress, hoping to get Cox removed from the Fly investigation. Neither House Speaker Sam Rayburn nor the Department of Justice had shown any interest in the check. Durr, seeing no aid coming from government, went to the *Washington Post* with copies of the cancelled check and other information about Representative Cox—the next day the *Washington Post* printed "A Public Letter to Speaker Rayburn.**

Durr also gave one hundred copies of the check to the public information office at the FCC.† As a result, Cox resigned the next day as chairman of his probe of the FCC. In commenting on the event Rayburn insisted, "Confidence in his [Cox] honor is unshaken.‡

*Erik Barnouw, *The Golden Web* (New York: Oxford University Press, 1968), p. 175.

**Washington Post*, September 27, 1943.

†Barnouw, op. cit., p. 178.

‡*Washington Post*, October 1, 1943.

James L. Fly tried to reform relations between networks and stations by getting the FCC to promulgate regulations which specified how station-network contracts should be handled. The industry was so angered that he finally resigned. (Culver Pictures.)

NBC and CBS had all but two of the thirty-fifty kilowatt stations and over half of the regional stations during the 1930s.[29] As a result MBS complained to the FCC that the other two network organizations had a virtual monopoly over radio and urged the agency to do something about the problems that they felt existed.

The FCC began investigating the problems of network control in 1938. This action was urged not only by MBS, but by President Roosevelt. The investigation led to a report from the FCC in 1941 urging that NBC be forced to sell one of its two networks and CBS be required to rewrite its network-affiliate contract in such a way that the network would have to consult the stations before selling their time to advertisers. In this way the FCC wanted stations to regain control over their broadcast time. The FCC's report led to a series of new FCC regulations, called the chain broadcast regulations, which were designed to limit CBS and NBC.[30]

CBS and NBC objected to the FCC's new regulations and went to court to fight them, but the Supreme Court agreed with the FCC in a 1943 decision. The result of this opinion was that NBC sold its Blue network to Edward J. Noble, a candy manufacturer and owner of WMCA in New York, who named the new network American Broadcasting Company (ABC).[31] There was a secondary result in that MBS became more successful in acquiring affiliates—many of the affiliates were connected to one of the other networks. It was easier for MBS to acquire affiliates after the 1943 decision because the Supreme Court required networks to permit stations to affiliates with more than one network. By 1946 MBS had 384 radio affiliates.[32]

The Supreme Court decision forcing NBC to divide its two networks

---

DUMONT TELEVISION NETWORK

An energetic engineer who once worked for Westinghouse tried his luck at building a television network in the 1940s. Allan B. DuMont secured an experimental television license in 1940 that was relicensed as commercial in 1944. Using this station, WABD, DuMont began network experiments with W3XWT (later WTTG) in Washington. While his experiments paralleled those of the three larger networks, DuMont failed to develop a profitable organization.

Although Paramount owned half of his company, the movie firm showed little interest in developing network programming and was not willing to carry DuMont programs on the one Paramount-owned television station. Without the backing of the larger company, DuMont had to produce inexpensive programming to compete with the higher cost shows offered by ABC, NBC, and CBS. As a result, many of the television stations which had become affiliated with DuMont refused to carry its shows.

By 1954 DuMont was losing so much money that the network and laboratories were separated and the DuMont network served out its contractual requirements. The remnants of the network were sold to Metropolitan Broadcasting Company (Metromedia), ending a valiant attempt to create a new national network.

Source: Lawrence W. Lichty and Malachi C. Topping, *American Broadcasting: A Source Book on the History of Radio and Television* (New York: Hastings House, 1975), pp. 190–192.

resulted in the formation of the last national network to be instituted in this country on a commercial basis, ABC joining MBS, NBC, and CBS.

THE EMERGENCE OF FM BROADCASTING

Radio broadcasting during the 1920s and 1930s was characterized by static, and during electrical storms the interference was almost intolerable. Some, like Sarnoff at RCA, dreamed of a static free system of broadcasting–he even speculated with his friend Edwin H. Armstrong on the possibility of a receiver that would eliminate static. Since this was the same Armstrong who had worked on the superhetrodyne receiver and who had developed an antenna that would fit into the case of a radio, he was a good choice to develop a new system of radio. For several years Armstrong worked on his invention and, after acquiring several patents, demonstrated frequency modulation (FM) radio to Sarnoff and some RCA engineers.

RCA was so impressed with FM that Armstrong was invited to test his instrument in the Empire State Building in 1934.[33] Engineers conducted tests, wrote reports, and examined the invention, then there was silence while Armstrong waited for a verdict.

In 1935 he was asked to remove his equipment from the Empire State Building so that RCA could use the space to expand its television experiments. Sarnoff apparently saw greater commercial possibilities for the visual medium than for FM. RCA then publicly announced that it was allocating $1 million for television tests. Armstrong had not publicized his FM system during the years he had worked on it, but with RCA's change of mind he decided that it was time to publicly demonstrate FM.[34] In fact the turn of events at RCA had so thoroughly angered Armstrong that he decided he owed nothing to the company.

In November 1935 Armstrong read a paper before a meeting of the Institute of Radio Engineers explaining FM.[35] There had been no hint of a public demonstration, but at the appropriate time Armstrong suggested that they have a little demonstration. The sound quality was so astounding that Armstrong followed the demonstration with an application to the FCC for FM channel space. Armstrong's petition placed him in opposition to RCA, which also petitioning the FCC for channel space for television.

The legal battles aside, Armstrong acquired permission to operate an FM station in Alpine, New Jersey as Station W2XMN.[36] The channels used by Armstrong were experimental channels authorized by the FCC for studying FM and were not intended for full broadcasting to the public. Not until May of 1940 did the FCC authorize commercial FM broadcasting. Later, by 1942, when the FCC stopped authorizing station licenses because of war shortages, there were thirty stations licensed.[37]

During the same years manufacturers, led by Philco, had built some 40,000 FM sets and it appeared that once the wartime freeze on licenses was lifted FM

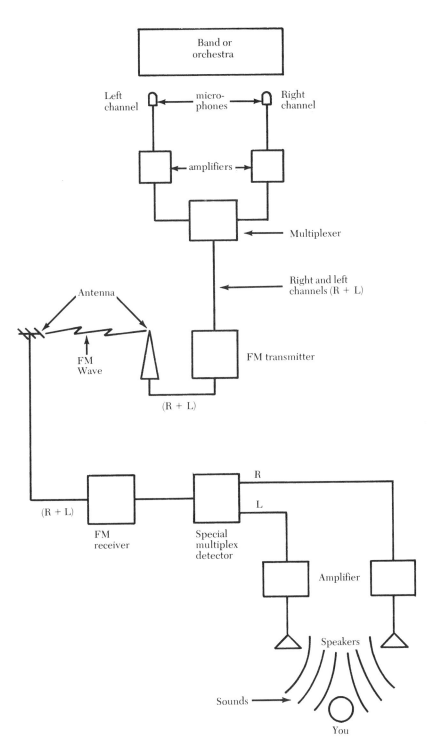

Figure 3–2. Stereo FM.

would have a good future. The band of frequencies allocated to FM in 1940 was between 42 and 50 mHz, but when the war was over the FCC conducted a series of hearings regarding FM and ultimately decided to change the FM broadcast band to 88–108 mHz.[38] This, of course, made all of the existing transmitters and receivers obsolete and set FM back in its development. A second event also slowed the development of FM—the rise of television.

The number of FM stations authorized by the FCC has followed a bizarre course because of the problem it had. In 1945 there were some forty-six stations authorized. By 1950 the number had risen to 691, but FM stations were having such a difficult time surviving that the number of FM stations having FCC licenses and permits dwindled to 540 in 1955. Most of these FM stations were owned by AM stations that hoped someday to make a profit from their FM holdings. The number of FM stations on the air began to increase again and by 1960 there were 1,343 FM stations. In 1970 the number had risen to over two thousand and in 1976 there were over 3600 FM stations on the air.[39]

The course of FM began changing during the late 1950s largely because of three factors: more people were purchasing FM sets that were better than ever before; broadcasters were beginning to take FM seriously by programming their stations carefully; and interest in high fidelity music was developing rapidly.[40]

Then in the early 1960s stations began experimenting with FM stereophonic or two channel broadcasting. Stereophonic sound differs from usual radio signals in that sounds coming from the left side of an orchestra or band are carried on a left channel while sounds from the right side are carried on a right channel. In more traditional broadcasting all sounds are transmitted on a single channel. To reproduce stereo programming two speakers placed a small distance apart are needed. By using this two channel reproduction the performing group sounds as if it is spread out in front of the listener rather than coming from a single point, as is the case with ordinary broadcasting. This form of broadcasting required a special "multiplex" converter to modulate both the left and right sound channels to the FM carrier. In the same way the receiver needed a special converter to separate the two channels of music—of course, a conventional FM radio could pick up the FM station broadcast as a single channel program. WTMJ-FM in Milwaukee, for example, began experimenting with stereophonic broadcasts over its FM station in 1961 and by 1965 its music was fully stereo.[41] Most FM stations currently program their music in stereophonic sound and it has benefited FM in acquiring new listeners.

THE END OF RADIO'S GOLDEN AGE 1948–1956

In October of 1945 the FCC lifted its wartime ban on licensing broadcast stations and the number of AM applications that deluged the FCC foreshadowed a tremendous growth in stations broadcasting in the United States. In 1945 there were 931 stations on the air, but that number jumped to 961 in 1946, to 1,693 in

1948, and to 2,118 in 1950. By the end of the television freeze there were 2,333 AM stations operating in the United States.[42] In many areas local service was available for the first time.

As the number of radio stations was increasing the quantity of sponsored network programs supplied to affiliates was decreasing because networks were turning to television. With the decline in sponsored programming available to affiliates, network revenue began to vanish. Network radio revenue decreased from over 131 million dollars in 1950 to less than 65 million dollars in 1955.[43] During these years a great change in radio programming occurred.

The national networks—CBS and NBC particularly—were uncertain about the future of radio and took steps to acquire television outlets. This was followed by a change in programming as the networks began putting their best programming on television.

Change in Radio Programming

By 1952, the number of network programs offered to affiliates was still high, but the number of sponsored programs had already begun declining and only slightly over half the programs were regularly sponsored as compared to a high of 80 to 90 % sponsorship in the best years of radio.[44] Three related reasons accounted for the movement of sponsors to television. (1) Television was very expensive and networks, which were interested in developing the new medium, placed their best programs on television to attract sponsors; (2) networks took some of the radio profits to promote television. To increase these profits the networks were using reruns on radio. This lowered the cost of programming, but it made radio programs less attractive to sponsors; (3) for many advertisers using both television and radio was too expensive, so they began shifting to television, where they could show products. Nothwithstanding the change, most of the traditionally successful programs were still on radio.

Bob Hope had been on radio sixteen seasons, Jack Benny had been on the air through 20 seasons, and "Amos 'n' Andy" had completed 23 years. Over the next three year period, networks continued to offer many programs, but sponsors were turning to television in greater numbers. Popular, long running shows lost their sponsors. By 1956 "Charlie McCarthy-Edgar Bergen" had lost sponsorship; Arthur Godfrey was only offering taped repeats; the longest-running show, "The New York Philharmonic Orchestra," had lost its sponsor after running twenty-eight seasons on radio.

But a new type of programming was coming to the air. NBC, beginning with the 1955–1956 season, was offering a short variety program called "Monitor"—some called it a magazine type program since it was a combination of many elements—interviews, music, and news. "Monitor" symbolized the change in radio's status perhaps more than any other program in that it was inexpensive, using neither costly actors nor elaborate production techniques.[45]

Serial radio had gone to television and the advertisers had gone too. Radio appeared to be dead. Local stations could depend upon networks for only occasional newscasts, magazine-type programs, and recorded music as provided by

MBS. But the new form of network programming began to supplement the disc jockey format that was growing up in stations all across the nation. Stations could run 50 or 55 minutes of disc jockey programming and then switch to the network for five or ten minutes of news each hour. Using the alternating music and news formula radio has been able to develop into a highly profitable medium.

Of course, not all stations had the benefit of network news and those that lacked a network developed a new form of news reporting sometimes called the "rip-and read" newscast. Local stations acquired an AP or other news service wire to provide printed news to the station. Then a disc jockey who needed news would simply tear off the latest news from the teletype machine and read it over the air.

Radio, then, after 1955 became a music and news service—largely unchanged into the 1970s. When all stations were appealing to the same audience with the same music, advertisers had little or no reason to pick one station over the other. Consequently, as mentioned earlier in this chapter, the specialized music format arose. In the early 1960s stations were experimenting with the Top-40, classical, Middle of the Road (MOR), progressive, and "good music" formats. Each was intended to satisfy a particular taste. The advertiser could pick the desired audience by selecting a station with a particular format. To further specialize, a few stations gave up music altogether and became all-talk or all-news stations.

THE DEVELOPMENT OF TELEVISION

Early Experiments

The theory of television goes back to the late 1800s when experimenters were thinking of the possibility of sending pictures through telephone wires.[46] But it was impossible to transmit a whole picture at once because of the limited capacity of wire and radio channels; therefore it was necessary to break pictures up into small segments or dots (see Chapter one, page 20). The problem of sorting out light from a picture so that it could make images that could be carried by wire was evolved by Paul Nipkow, a German experimenter, in 1883 and patented by him in 1884.

Nipkow's theory required a three part system in which a lens focused the light from a scene, a rotating disk with holes punched in it divided up the light from the lens into rows of light, and a light sensitive photo cell converted the light into electrical impulses. The round disk was punched with small holes in a spiraling pattern with each hole slightly closer to the center of the disk than the last opening.

As the disk rotated each hole in its turn allowed light from part of the scene to fall upon the photo cell. Thus, as the first hole rotated behind the lens, it permitted light from the top of the scene to fall upon the photo cell. As the disk revolved further the second hole passed behind the lens and permitted a second slightly lower row of light to fall on the photo cell. This process continued until the entire scene was "scanned" by the rotating disk. But Nipkow lacked some of the necessary electrical components to fully develop his television system; therefore, it was several years before the system was demonstrated.

Early mechanical television was very crude and produced low-quality pictures. This picture of Felix the Cat in the late 1920s was a poor indication of what was to come. (RCA Corporation.)

By 1887 the French physician M. Senlecq transmitted pictures projected on a screen by tracing them with a special light-sensitive instrument.[48] His invention required that the picture image be both projected and still while it was being traced. Senlecq's problem of relying on a still image was overcome as Nipkow's disk was made technically possbile. But both of these systems relied heavily upon mechanical devices—a spinning disk or a tracing tool. A fully electronic system of television was needed before television could be sold to the public.

In 1908 A. A. Campbell-Swinton wrote, in the British publication *Nature*, about a theory of electronic television that was very similar to that developed later by Alexander Zworykin.[49] A similar theory was advanced by Rosing in Russia during the same year, but both men lacked the machinery to develop their ideas.

Zworykin, who had come to the United States from Russia, used his doctoral research to develop the theory of an iconoscope, as he called it, or television camera pickup tube that helped to make televiion fully electronic.[50] His first patent had been filed in 1923, but faced several years of litigation over who first invented the iconoscope before he was able to develop the tube further. Zworykin received other patents related to television in 1928 and 1938 as he expanded the scope of the pickup tube and attempted to produce color television.[51] Zworykin worked for Westinghouse until 1930 when RCA opened an experimental television station and borrowed Zworykin to direct the project.[52]

Working independently, Philo Farnsworth a young scientist, developed a system of electronic television that grew out of his childhood interest in electronics. Farnsworth went to work for Leslie Gorrell and George Everson of San Francisco who had agreed to finance his experiments.[53] The first practical results of Farnsworth's experiments were evident in 1927 when a picture of a dollar sign was transmitted over a short distance by a crude form of television. Both Zworykin and Farnsworth had developed their television systems to the point at which they were transmitting television pictures with 240 scanning lines in 1933, but both required mechanical scanning using the Nipkow disk at the receiving end.[54]

Experimental telecasting was taking place during the years that Zworykin and others were experimenting with the equipment. In 1927 Bell Laboratories sent a television picture by wire between New York and Washington, and RCA demonstrated a television set at a New York theater in 1930.[55] By 1937 seventeen experimental television stations were in operation and the networks were trying to show the public that television was on its way. In 1938 CBS built its first television studio at Grand Central Station in New York. Many companies were beginning to experiment with the new medium of television, including Zenith, General Electric, Westinghouse, and Paramount.[56]

NBC demonstrated television publicly during the 1939 World's Fair in New York, showing an episode of "Amos 'n' Andy." Subsequent broadcasts included a speech by Franklin D. Roosevelt, the first President to appear on television. As the year wore on, others came to New York to perform on television shows which included opera, comedy, music, puppet shows, and kitchen demonstrations.[57]

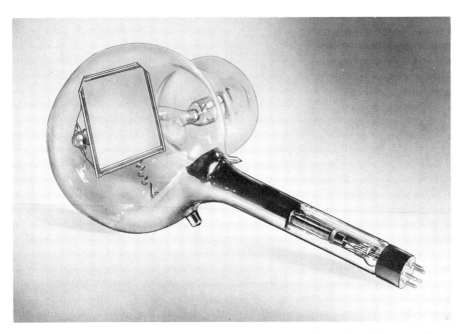

The iconoscope made television without mechanical scanning possible. Although this early device was very crude, it was the basis for modern television. (Culver Pictures.)

During the same year NBC began its first regularly scheduled broadcasts for the public during a two hour period each week. These programs were carried under an experimental authorization from the FCC using the Zworykin television system that by this time had 441 scanning lines.[58]

The First Television Licenses

So far television was only an experimental gadget. Then in 1940 the FCC, hoping to resolve any technical disputes, began hearings to determine how to license television. The FCC found that there were a variety of television standards, such as the one adopted by the Zworykin system, which used 441 scanning lines in the picture. The FCC had to resolve these many standards before it could grant any permanent television broadcast licenses.[59]

In order to solve the standards problem, the National Television System Committee (NTSC) was formed to negotiate areas of conflict in television transmissions and to advise the FCC. This committee settled upon the standards still in use today; that is, 525 scanning lines and thirty complete scannings of the picture each second (thirty frames per second). (These standards are discussed more fully in Chapter 1). In the same hearings the FCC decided that the television picture would be modulated by AM and the sound would be modulated by FM. These standards were adopted on April 30, 1941. The first station application under the new standards was filed by the Journal Company of Milwaukee, whose station became known as WTMJ-TV.

This opened the way for the first commercial television stations to be authorized, which began commercial operation on July 1, 1941.[60] Although ten stations received licenses to begin operation in 1941, only six of them remained on the air throughout World War II. The FCC freeze on broadcast licenses during the war (1942 to 1945) included television as well as AM and FM, and no new stations were authorized until 1945 when the FCC began licensing stations again on a regular basis. The six stations that remained on the air necessarily had to limit their broadcasts since there were very few people to either sponsor or view programs. Indeed by the time the war came there were about 10,000 television sets in existence. But when the war was over more and more people began applying for station licenses and the television boom began. Those six prewar television stations were to jump to 108 by 1948.

POSTWAR EXPANSION OF TELEVISION

When peacetime returned in 1945, 158 requests for television station licenses awaited the FCC's attention. Although many of the pending applications were eventually withdrawn, there were many others who wanted licenses.[61] Almost immediately after the war the FCC began authorizing new television stations in the VHF channels of one through thirteen (in 1948 the FCC deleted channel one). In 1946 there were forty-six FCC approved stations and that number rose to sixty-six in 1947 and 109 in 1948.[62]

The increase in television coverage in the years immediately after the second world war is particularly impressive when one realized that by 1950, 106 of the 109 authorized stations which were on the air were bringing television coverage to some sixty-four cities and metropolitan areas. According to the FCC's estimate this meant that some 87 million people could view at least one television station and these people were distributed among forty-three states.[63] Of course the freeze on television station licenses between 1948 and 1952, to be discussed shortly, slowed the development of television somewhat, but the nation was strongly interested in the new medium.

Since television stations needed people who had receivers to pick up the signal, manufacturers were building more and more sets. For example, in 1950

TABLE 3-3   Growth of Broadcast Stations
The figures in this table represent stations on the air and authorized on the last day of the fiscal year indicated and were derived from appropriate FCC and FRC records.

Type of Service	1930	1934	1938	1942	1946
Commercial AM	618	593	747	925	1215
Commercial FM	—	—	—	—	456
Commercial TV	—	—	—	10	30
Educational FM	—	—	—	—	24
Educational TV	—	—	—	—	—

*Data for this year as for mid-year.

over seven million sets were sold and nine percent of all homes had at least one television set, however, fully sixty-five percent of all homes were equipped with at least one television set in 1955.[64] The tremendous rise in television set ownership, of course, stimulated broadcasters interest in acquiring more television stations.

Equipment Development

The early iconoscope that had been developed by Zworykin had two major problems. First, it required so much light the actors were subjected to intensely hot working conditions; second, the picture quality of the iconoscope was so poor that viewers had difficulty recognizing the picture. An invention in 1945 at CBS solved both of these problems—the image orthicon pickup tube.[65] Like the iconoscope, the image orthicon tube picks up the image of a scene and converts it into electrical impulses that can be transmitted. But the added quality of the image orthicon vastly improved television signals. As a result, the image orthicon has become the heart of the modern television camera and is still used by networks and major television stations.

Another technical development that advanced television—specifically network television—was the expansion of a cable and microwave system connecting the East and the Midwest. This new cable and microwave system made it possible for television networks to connect stations in cities such as Chicago, Detroit, Cleveland, and New York. In fact the new hookup connected fourteen metropolitan areas in 1948 and made it possible for about one-third of the nation's population to view the same television program at the same time. This development was especially important when one remembers that all television during the late 1940s and early 1950s was live and a cable hookup was the only way to supply the same program to many television stations.[66] By 1951 coast-to-coast network television had been achieved.

Of course film existed during these early days of television, but neither stations nor film producers considered using film in television applications. The other medium for recording and preserving programs, video tape, was not yet available. Television was mostly a live medium, and network interconnection of stations was quite important. One form of recorded television, Kinescope recording, was available to networks and stations. Film cameras were used to record television programs from a special television screen. Although picture

1950	1954	1958	1962	1966	1970	1974	1977*
2303	2697	3353	3886	4153	4370	4477	4543
732	569	634	1191	1744	2260	2796	3075
109	573	665	654	735	823	751	770
82	123	157	209	302	462	821	976
—	30	53	79	144	212	253	103

These three photographs show how television sets changed during the 1940s and early 1950s. (Culver Pictures.)

quality was not great, kinescoping delivered network programs to the West Coast before the completion of a coast-to-coast network hookup. Of course, kinescoping had many other uses in news, educational, and network programming.

THE LICENSING FREEZE OF 1948–1952

When the war ended and the military no longer needed all of the materials that the nation could produce, industry turned to manufacturing consumer goods again. The abrupt change put several strains not only on the manufacturers but also on broadcasters and government. There were unresolved questions involving just what to do with television; how to handle educational uses of television; and the use of the ultra high frequency television channels (UHF). Broadcasters were unsure whether to keep programs on radio or transfer them to television and advertisers did not know which medium would be the most effective in selling products.

If broadcasters and networks were unsure of television's future, the FCC was even less certain about its role in regulating the new medium. The FCC believed that the medium needed to be regulated, but the form that regulation should take was an open question. This uncertainty led the FCC, on September 30, 1948, to impose a freeze on all new licensing of television transmitters while it considered the problems of television.[67]

During the freeze the FCC conducted a number of hearings inviting those from the broadcast industry and education, as well as other interested people, to testify. The hearings covered a considerable period of time and a large number of topics. There was, of course, a good deal of lobbying by all interested parties. The hearings led to the FCC's Sixth Report and Order.

The television freeze was lifted in 1952, after a period of three and one-half years, when the FCC issued the Sixth Report. The new order explained the FCC's view on how television should be regulated with a series of new standards. First, the FCC decided there should be twelve VHF television channels and seventy UHF television channels. (The VHF channels had already been in existence and the FCC added the UHF channels because it believed there would be a need for more television channels).

To designate the localities in which television channels might be used the FCC came up with a table of allocations which was a list of communities in the United States and the television channel or channels alloted to each community. In its new allocation scheme the FCC decided that both VHF and UHF stations should exist in a number of communities.

In addition to commercial television stations the Report established an educational class of television stations. The FCC created 242 channels for educational use.[68] Eighty of the channels were VHF and 162 were in the UHF band. The move for these allocations was led by Frieda B. Hennock, the first

Frieda Hennock, the first women commissioner of the FCC, was a friend to educators and helped them get television channels. (Culver Pictures.)

female commissioner on the FCC. Commissioner Hennock, who was appointed in 1948, soon learned that educators had not received a fair deal when AM channels were given out in the late 1920s, and she was determined that the same would not occur with television.

One of Hennock's discoveries was that commercial broadcasters had promised the FRC that they would carry educational programs, eliminating the need for alloting radio channels to education. In this way commercial broadcasters received almost all AM radio channels; but in the years that followed, the commercial owners had failed to fulfill their promise. During the television freeze broadcasters were again promising to carry educational programs, but now Hennock and others were naturally suspicious of the promises.

The broadcast industry vigorously opposed Hennock's position but a number of educators, especially in the midwest, supported her. Similarly, a large portion of the FCC staff believed that there was a need for educational television channels.

Finally, the Sixth Report specified the distance between television stations that shared the same channel. It concluded that two VHF stations on a common channel should be 190 miles apart and two UHF stations should be 175 miles apart. Thus station A, which is on channel two, must be at least 190 miles from station B, which is on the same channel two.[69]

After the report had been issued the FCC began processing applications again and the number of television stations authorized by the FCC increased rapidly. In fact the original 109 stations that had FCC licenses and permits during the freeze rose to 458 by 1955; and along with the rise in the number of stations, viewer interest in television rose.[70] By 1955 fully 65 percent of all homes had television sets.

THE DEVELOPMENT OF COLOR TELEVISION

One of the problems the FCC considered during the television freeze was color. The difficulties of color required more than just the freeze years to resolve because of the complexity of the issue. But first, let us examine the development of color television.

Color television is a primitive form was first demonstrated by John L. Baird, a British television engineer, in 1928. He used color filters to break light up into red, blue, and green components and used a spinning disk in the receiver to bring the colors back together. The next year Herbert Ives, at the Bell Laboratories, demonstrated a mechanical television system using photo cells as had been used in some of the early black and white sets. But the work of these two people received a boost when RCA entered the picture.[71]

In February 1940 RCA demonstrated an electronic color system to the FCC, but it was so bad that the company did not engage in a public demonstration and returned to its Princeton laboratories to refine its system. While RCA was developing its system, Peter Goldmark was working on a color system at CBS. Both Goldmark's and RCA's system lacked good quality—although the CBS system may have been a bit better.

The FCC in 1941 declared that color was an innovation for the future and refused to take any action on the matter.[72] During the Second World War little happened to color development because of the material shortages. However, both CBS and RCA continued their experimentation hoping to someday demonstrate a viable system.

When the war was over, color television continued its development. RCA demonstrated a color system that divided the color into three primary colors and transmitted quite good stable color, but when someone moved on the screen colors tended to run together. Although RCA announced that its color system was superior to all other's CBS created some competition when it asked the FCC permission to use its color system commercially.[73] CBS supported its request with a demonstration that showed that its color television could produce very pure and faithful colors that were stable and did not smear.

In 1947 the FCC denied CBS's request on the grounds that it had not done enough testing and on the vague possibility that there might be other better color systems. Then, after the freeze began, the FCC chose to approve the CBS color television equipment in 1950 while refusing to approve other systems.[74] RCA and several other companies contested the FCC's decision in court, but were overruled in favor of the FCC. Untimately, circumstances were to go

Microwave communications towers like this one are used (with cable) to connect television networks with their stations. In addition, these microwave transmitters and receivers can carry hundreds of telephone conversations. (AT&T Co.)

against CBS and the company was not able to enjoy the FCC's approval since all color production was stopped on October 19, 1951 because of the Korean War.[75]

In that same year the National Television System Committee (NTSC) became interested in the potential of color and, by 1953, chose to endorse the NBC color system, which had been developed considerably since 1950. In December 1953 the FCC, bowing to industry views and the new evidence, reversed its decision and approved the NBC system. To be sure NBC color had some advantages, for example, black and white sets could pick up the color picture in black and white and the system was fully electronic. But the NBC color also had some disadvantages: the cost of an NBC equipped color station was

TABLE 3–4   TV Set Sales and Saturation

Figures show the number of monochrome and color sets manufactured, the % manufactured outside the U.S. and the % with UHF, the average cost (manufacturer's value) of monochrome and color sets, and the % of U.S. homes with television, color, two or more sets and UHF.

	NUMBER OF SETS SOLD PERCENT					HOMES WITH		
	Monochrome	Color	Imported	UHF	TV	Color	Multi	UHF
1946	6,000	—	—	—	.02%	—	—	NA
1950	7,355,000	—	—	—	9	—	1%	NA
1955	7,738,000	20,000	—	15%	65	.2%	3	11%
1960	5,709,000	120,000	—	8	87	.7	13	8
1965	8,753,000	2,694,000	3%	100	93	5	22	16
1970	7,647,000	7,274,000	25*	100	95	39	33	63
1972	5,600,000	7,908,000	21	100	97	64†	44	86
1975/76	4,968,000	6,485,000	36	100	97	79	46	90

*Imported does not include sets with a "domestic label" (U.S. name) but manufactured outside the U.S. local imports were actually about 35% of the market in 1970.
†1976

Source: *Broadcasting Yearbook, Television Factbook.*

much higher than the cost of CBS equipment; the price of a color television set was very high, about $1,000 per set; and very bright lights were required to produce a program in color. On the other hand, the CBS system had the advantage of being less expensive and black and white sets could be adapted to their color system inexpensively.

With the approval of the NBC color system, which used three separate pickup tubes to produce a color signal, both CBS and NBC went into limited color television production, however, new color sets had yet to be constructed and the market for color television grew slowly. Part of the problem was that people were unwilling or unable to spend large sums for new sets. Although CBS began colorcasting "The Red Skelton Show," "Shower of Starts," and "Climax," the cost was so high that CBS was forced to abandon all regular color by 1958. Consequently, between 1958 and 1964, only NBC had an extensive regular schedule of color shows. By the 1966–1967, however, season all three television networks were broadcasting all of their prime time shows in color.[76] Color television broadcasting has been the regular practice ever since.

With the growth of color broadcasting, the number of homes with color sets has steadily increased. In 1960 less than one percent of all homes had color sets, but that figure had risen to five percent in 1965 and 39 percent in 1970. By 1974 about 65 percent of all homes had color sets.[77]

THE UNSTEADY GROWTH OF UHF

Although the FCC's 1952 table of assignments created a large number of UHF stations intended to compete with VHF, the FCC's action hardly assured the success of the new channels. (See Chapter 1 page 31 for a discussion of UHF channels.) In fact the FCC's action created as many problems as it was supposed to solve. By authorizing more television channels the FCC apparently provided enough space for all the television stations the nation would need. That seemed quite a worthy goal.

However, the problems of the new assignment seemed to eclipse any benefits to be realized from the seventy UHF channels. The primary problem was that television sets manufactured during the early 1950s could not tune in UHF stations and the FCC took no action to correct this problem. The result was that most televisions could not receive UHF stations and most viewers had no idea that there were more than the channels between two and thirteen. In fact if one wished to pick up the UHF stations, it was necessary to order either a special television set at a higher cost or a separate adaptor.

UHF stations had at least two other problems. The high frequencies at which UHF stations operated meant that their signals simply would not go as far as those of VHF stations. Thus VHF stations not only reached more sets because of the limitations of the set, they also reached out farther into the fringes and acquired additional viewers that were out of the reach of UHF. Finally, VHF stations tended to be older than UHF stations and they had first pick at network affiliation. Of course networks preferred to have VHF stations as affiliates since they had greater coverage. Consequently, many UHF stations were obliged to survive on old films and reruns without network affiliation.

Even the FCC in 1955 admitted that the plan for UHF stations had been a failure. The FCC noted that out of the 325 UHF licenses it had granted, only about one-third were on the air.[78] Later in 1960 the UHF situation was no better, with only seventy-seven UHF television stations in operation.[79] Because of these problems, the FCC began considering a number of proposals to resolve the UHF situation.

One of the proposals the FCC considered for resolving the UHF dilemma was the elimination of all VHF channels and the transfer of all television to the UHF band of frequencies. The proposal was rejected primarily because there were a number of stations established in the VHF band by the late 1950s. A solution that seemed more appropriate was the FCC's request that Congress amend the Communications Act of 1934 permitting the FCC to require television set manufacturers to incorporate UHF tuners in all new television sets. Congress complied with the FCC's request in 1962 and the FCC directed that all new sets manufactured after April 30, 1964 be equipped with UHF tuners.[80]

But the UHF tuners did not click from channel to channel like the VHF tuner, and the difference made it difficult for many people to tune in UHF stations. So while progress was made in resolving the UHF problem, it still existed and in 1970 the FCC adopted additional regulations requiring that UHF dials be compatible with VHF dials. Whether this change will improve the status of UHF television is as yet unknown.[81]

In addition to regulatory activities, the FCC in 1961-1962 conducted a study in New York City to determine the distance a UHF television signal could reach. Using a transmitter in the Empire State Building, the FCC found

TABLE 3–5 Number of Television Stations Reporting Profit or Loss by Amount of Profit or Loss, 1971*

	TOTAL		NETWORK AFFILIATED		INDEPENDENT	
	VHF	UHF	VHF	UHF	VHF	UHF
Number of stations reporting	453	149	422	101	31	48
Stations reporting profits	366	47	352	41	14	6
Profitable stations as percent of total	80.8	31.5	83.4	40.6	45.2	12.5
Stations reporting profits of						
15,000,000 or over	14	—	14	—	—	—
3,000,000–5,000,000	22	—	22	—	—	—
1,500,000–3,000,000	36	—	32	—	4	—
1,000,000–1,500,000	41	—	38	—	3	—
600,000–1,000,000	33	1	31	—	2	1
400,000– 600,000	40	3	57	3	3	—
200,000– 400,000	64	8	63	7	1	1
100,000– 200,000	46	11	45	9	1	2
50,000– 100,000	36	9	36	8	—	1
25,000– 50,000	15	5	15	5	—	—
Less than 25,000	19	10	19	9	—	1
Stations reporting losses	87	102	70	60	17	42
Unprofitable stations as percent of total	19.2	68.5	16.6	60.0	53.1	85.7
Stations reporting losses of:						
Less than $10,000	5	4	4	3	1	1
18,000– 25,000	9	8	9	8	—	—
25,000– 50,000	15	8	14	7	1	1
50,000–100,000	16	16	15	11	1	5
100,000–200,000	19	19	16	15	3	4
200,000–400,000	14	20	10	13	4	7
400,000 and over	9	27	2	3	7	24

*Excludes part-year stations and satellite stations. Profits are before Federal income tax.

Source: FCC 1972 Annual Report Washington, D.C.: (Washington Government Printing Office), p.18)

that by broadcasting on channel thirty-one it could produce UHF pictures up to forty miles from the transmitter that were as good as VHF television signals coming from the same building—all seven of New York's VHF stations have their antennas on the Empire State Building. So enthusiastic was the city of New York that it purchased the station from the FCC and began broadcasting on Channel thirty-one.[82]

The least successful of the FCC's attempts to promote UHF television was the move to "deintermix" UHF and VHF stations in the same market. By deintermixing the FCC intended to convert those markets that had both VHF and UHF television stations into markets that had only VHF or UHF stations, but not both. In its 1952 table of allocations the FCC had placed both UHF and VHF channels in some communities. The move to deintermix these markets would have created a table of television assignments that had only VHF or UHF stations in any given market. The move failed largely because VHF stations were unwilling to give up their prime channels to move to a UHF assignment and there were not enough VHF channels to deintermix UHF stations into VHF channels.

By 1971 the FCC found that UHF television was still not on a firm footing because, out of 149 UHF television stations, 102 reported that they were loosing money. Thus only forty-seven reported a profit and twenty-four indicated that they made less than $100,000 gross profit.[83] This compares very poorly with VHF television, which reported that 366 out of 453 stations were making a profit.

THE ESTABLISHMENT OF NATIONAL TELEVISION NETWORKS

The early television experimenters included national radio networks who had a vigorous interest in anything that might affect their networks. In fact both CBS and NBC possessed experimental stations prior to 1941 when the FCC authorized commercial television operation. NBC operated W2XBS, which became WNBT (later WNBC), and CBS operated WCBW (later WCBS), which retained its call letters as a commercial station.[84]

After World War II both network organizations became interested in developing television networks and by 1948 NBC had nine affiliates while CBS had three. Although ABC did not come into being until after the 1943 Supreme Court decision to break up NBC's two networks, it was able to acquire six television affiliates by 1948.[85]

While each network had affiliates, NBC was especially successful in adding stations during the early years of network television. By 1950 NBC had more than twice as many affiliates as CBS and more than four times the number of affiliates connected with ABC. The gap between CBS and NBC closed somewhat in the years after 1950, with NBC having 218 stations in its line up compared to CBS's 212 in 1974.

ABC, on the other hand, had a long, difficult time in acquiring affiliates because it lacked the necessary funds to produce strong competitive programming. Unlike the other two networks, ABC did not have large radio revenues to help support the new medium. Then in 1953 ABC merged with the Paramount theater chain after a court decision forced Paramount Pictures to separate the theaters from the studios.[86] The merger strengthened ABC's position since it made additional funds available, but ABC was never able to acquire as many affiliates as the two competing networks. However, by 1974 ABC had 181 affiliates which made it more competitive with the other networks.

CBS gained an advantage when ABC and Paramount merged because both Paramount and ABC owned television stations in Chicago. Since FCC rules prohibit one organization from operating two stations in the same market, Paramount sold its station to CBS. CBS gained an important new element for its network and was able for the first time to secure more viewers than its competitor, NBC.

ABC used the new economic leverage gained from its merger to embark upon a new philosophy in programming its network. While the other networks were using programs produced live by the networks, ABC began programming Hollywood productions. Its first step in the new direction was made when ABC and Walt Disney signed an agreement to carry a series called "Disneyland." The Disney deal was followed by an agreement between ABC and Warner Brothers in which Warner would produce a series of one hour programs for television entitled "Warner Brothers Presents." ABC added other filmed programs rapidly after these two 1954 agreements. The Warner series reached television during the 1955–1956 season.[87]

TELEVISION PROGRAMMING

When speaking of television programming, reference is made mostly to network programs because networks provide the largest portion of a station's programming. Of course not all stations are affiliated with a national network, but these stations often use programs that were once run on a national network. As a result, our discussion of television programming will be largely limited to network programs.

Television in the early 1950s was live and when entertainers "goofed" they were seen by millions of viewers across the nation—there was no opportunity to edit the mistake. Television became a national participation sport; viewers wondered who would err next and performers feared that they would. A wide variety of shows existed even in the early days of television. There were comedies like "I Love Lucy" with Lucille Ball; variety shows like Ed Sullivan's "Toast of the Town;" Arthur Godfrey's "Talent Scouts," and Sid Ceasar and Imogene Coca's "Your Show of Shows."[88] Variety and comedy were not the only fare. There were also dramas like "Lights Out," "Suspense," and "Cisco Kid." Many shows moved from radio to television, such as "Amos 'n' Andy," "The Goldbergs," and "The Aldrich Family." And NBC developed at least one unique program, "Today," which was started in 1951 and consisted of talk, news, and interviews.[89]

Television carried events of national importance such as President Truman's message to Congress in 1950—the first time such an event had been televised. National political conventions were carried on networks in 1952 and, of course, eight years later two presidential candidates, Richard M. Nixon and John F. Kennedy, debated each other on national television.

So successful was television in attracting viewers that at least one group, the major motion picture producers, feared that television would consume theater.

TABLE 3-6   Network Affiliates

Figures show the number of stations for the national radio and television networks and the Keystone syndicate.

	1927	1930	1935	1940	1945	1950	1955	1960	1965	1970	1974	1976
NBC Red/NBC	22	22	27	53	150	172	208	202	209	223	232	
NBC Alternates		32	41	69								
NBC Blue	6	17	20	60								
ABC					195	282	357	310	355			
ABC Information										334	407	
ABC Entertainment										241	347	
ABC Contemporary										213	317	
ABC FM										182	216	
CBS	16	60	97	112	145	173	207	198	237	246	248	
Mutual			3	160	384	543	563	443	501	576	635	
Mutual Black											90	
Keystone System*				50	202	395	852	1100	1140	1154	1060	
Television												
NBC-TV					9**	56	189	214	198	215	218	195
CBS-TV					3**	27	139	195	190	193	212	216
ABC-TV					6**	13	46	87	128	162	181	223
Dumont						52	158					
% of total affiliated with national net												
AM	6%	16%	21%	50%	94%	55%	49%	33%	32%	43%	52%	
TV						92	82	86	88	82	87	

*Keystone not interconnected; but syndicated.

**1948.

Source: Compiled by Lichty with C. H. Sterling from *Broadcasting Yearbook*, FCC and the networks. Figures are usually for January 1.

As audiences turned away from the theaters to their television sets, film producers decided to fight back by refusing to let television use motion pictures. In addition, filmmakers adopted all kinds of technical refinements such as Cinemascope, Cinerama, three-dimensional, and Todd A-O in an attempt to lure people back to the theater.

Without motion pictures, the early to mid 1950s produced a new kind of television—unique in that it had not appeared in radio years—anthology drama. These series did not have fixed actors or situations from week to week since each play was original, complete and written specifically for one television showing. The anthology was a kind of "Broadway for television," and shows appeared under such numerous titles as "Goodyear Television Playhouse," "Kraft Television Theater," "Studio One," and "Motorola Playhouse." This new art form resulted in a new breed of writers, such as Rod Serling and Paddy Chayefsky, and gave them the opportunity to do serious dramatic work on television.

FEAR OF COMMUNISM THREATENS BROADCASTING

Broadcasting and its programming was seriously affected in the late 1940s and early 1950s by the fear of communism, a fear that plagued the entire nation. Many felt that the United States, through its timid international policies, had allowed the Soviet Union to gain control of such large portions of Eastern Europe that the Soviet Union might try to use its power to expand into other parts of the world. Government leaders in Washington became just as concerned as the rest of the nation. President Truman instituted a loyalty oath that government employees were required to take. In Congress, Senator Joe McCarthy ran vigorous investigations into the lives of alleged communists. The nation seemed bent on purging any influence of communism.[90]

Outside government there werepeople like Eleanor Johnson Buchanan, daughter of a Syracuse, New York supermarket owner, who was among those determined to stamp out communism. Publications like "Red Channels: The Report of Communist Influence in Radio and Television" and "Counterattack" were published to expose communism in broadcast circles, among others.[91]

Like other organizations, radio and television networks were affected by the fear of communism and CBS began blacklisting performers with alleged ties to communism. The advertising agency BBD&O followed suit. In addition, broadcasters found that many of their entertainers were blacklisted by outside groups for the most trivial reasons. Eleanor Buchanan began telephone campaigns to networks demanding that many performers be taken off the air, others called advertising agencies, and still others called advertisers directly. Broadcasters had to confront some serious questions concerning how they were going to deal with the issue of intimidation.

The broadcasters' problems were two pronged. On the one hand, if broadcasters were to refuse to fire the alleged communists, advertisers were threatening to remove their support from the networks. Broadcasters would thereby loose their only menas of income. But if they failed to expose the unreasonable fear of communism for what it was, broadcasters would be violating what they had long held to be one of the basic reasons for their existence—the exposure of wrong in public agencies. Many broadcast journalists and executives believed that because so many people received all or most of their news from radio and television, they had a great responsibility to uphold reason and expose corruption.

Networks found their journalistic function in conflict with their economic health. People like Fred Friendly, a vice president of CBS, found themselves in serious conflict with others at the networks. For a time the need for economic security triumphed as networks failed to expose people like Senator Joe McCarthy while terminating contracts of many innocent people accused of being communists.

In time network journalists persuaded management to expose the unwarranted fear of communism. Networks carried live coverage of the McCarthy hearings which permitted the nation to see that McCarthy was an antagonistic, glory hungry person. Edward R. Murrow, a news anchorman at CBS, went on the air with a documentary exposing McCarthy's damaging techniques, and news programs covered trials of innocent people damaged by those fearful of communism.[92] Although Murrow's program served a desirable purpose—that of reducing McCarthy's influence—some of Murrow's tactics were unethical. Ed Murrow edited bits and pieces of McCarthy's filmed speeches and comments to achieve the desired effect. Some of these filmed comments were taken out of context and may have been outright misrepresentations. Indeed, Murrow used some of the very tactics that he was engaged in condemning. Tactics aside, television played an important role in both promoting and destroying the harmful influences that arose during this period of the so-called Red Scares.

THE INVENTION OF VIDEO TAPE

The move away from live television began with ABC's use of films and RCA's invention of the first video tape recording system in 1953.[93] RCA's machine required that tapes be run at high speeds, 360 inches per second, which consequently, meant that a great deal of tape was needed to record a thirty-minute program. Despite high tape costs, networks and other large broadcasters found the convenience of recorded programs to be worth the price.[94]

Ampex, in 1956, developed a refined video tape recorder that ran the tape at a much slower speed and cost about $75,000. After Ampex's machine was introduced, many different companies entered the video tape machine market and today it is possible to purchase large high cost broadcast recorders or small home video tape machines that cost only $1,000 or less.

Video tape has several advantages that make it attractive to broadcasters and others. Most important is the immediate replay capability of tape. Processing is unnecessary, therefore, one need not wait for laboratory work. Secondly, picture quality of video tape is just about as good as the original images picked up by a television camera. Thirdly, like film, video tape can be readily edited.

Some of the first uses of video tape included recording segments of otherwise live shows that required actors to change costumes or that required such large sets that not all of the sets used in a program could be constructed in one studio. When actors had to change clothes, the portion of the program when they were wearing one costume was video taped. Then the remaining part of the show—with the actors wearing a second costume—was done live and the video taped portions was simply played at the appropriate time.

Some shows used sets so large that one set filled an entire studio which of course, made the construction of other sets in the studio at the same time impossible. In these cases the large sets were erected and the scenes played in them were recorded, then this set was removed and new sets were brought into the studio for the live part of the program while the recorded portions were inserted at the appropriate time. In this way a program could be contained in one studio, and other studios that the network might own could be used for other productions.

Currently video tape is used in recording news shows produced by the three national television networks. Every network produces three newscasts each evening—one at 6:00, 6:30, and 7:00. Each newscast carries essentially the same stories and, thus, affiliates have a choice of three times when they may carry a news program. The 6:00 newscast is recorded on video tape and replayed at 6:30 and 7:00 if there is no new late-breaking news or no major flaws in the 6:00 program. If everything goes perfectly, the news staff may leave at 6:30 and the first tape will simply be replayed twice for the two later newscasts. But when important events are breaking after 6:00 or when someone makes a mistake, then the news staff will have to produce a second and perhaps a third newscast. Thus, video tape is used by network news departments to reduce the amount of work that must be done each evening.

More recently—in fact during the early 1970s—Norman Lear began using video tape to record his comedy programs as they were performed before live audiences. Lear uses video tape to gain the advantages of both live and recorded television. Every program is performed without interruption before a live audience so that the spontaneity of live theater may be captured. Each program is performed twice before audiences. Since programs are recorded on video tape, Lear may edit the best of each program into the final version that is shown on television. With this technique, Lear hopes to gain the excitement of live television, without showing the nation the mistakes of his performers.

Of course, videotape finds many other uses in sports, documentaries, and public affairs. Yet with all of its advantages, video tape has yet to entirely re-place motion picture film. Most of the evening dramas on television are produced on film because of the advantages film has over video tape. Film cameras are smaller and lighter than television cameras and, consequently, they are much easier to handle on location. Just as important, television cameras require elaborate back up equipment, such as video tape machines and switching equipment, to handle more than one camera. Therefore, the com-pactness of film recording remains more desirable for location shooting than video tape and since most evening television is shot on location, film remains the choice.

There are three other advantages in using film over tape for shooting loca-tion dramas: (1) Film may be used on all television systems while video tape must be converted to new line systems when the tape is sent to other nations using a television system different from our own. (See Chapter 1, page 20 for a discussion of line systems). (2) Film tends to be more permanent than video tape and much of the profit for evening programs is derived from reruns and syndication, therefore, permanence is important. (3) Finally, television equip-ment requires more adjustments and is more sensitive to vibration than film equipment and is, therefore, less desirable in location work.

Quiz Program Scandals

One of the favorite forms of television during the 1950s, which had been popular on radio and had made the transition to television, was quiz programs. These programs pitted the intellectual skills of two contestants against each other. The contestants were playing for large sums of money—some won up to $100,000 and there was no indication of dishonesty or fraud. The popularity of this type of program is evidenced by the fact that some quiz programs such as "The $64,000 Question," "The Big Surprise," and "Twenty-One," reached the top spots on the ratings. In 1958 Edward Hilgemeir, a stand-by contestant, discovered a notebook that one of the contestants had dropped. Upon examining it, he found that it contained the questions and answers that the contestant was answering.[95]

Although the producer attempted to buy Hilgemeir's silence, Hilgemeir contacted the FCC. Others like Herbert Stemple also told their stories and, eventually, the networks were forced to remove all big money quiz shows from the air. Herbert Stemple was an interesting key to breaking the quiz show rigging in that he had been a brilliant and honest contestant on "Twenty-One." "Twenty-One" producers thought that Stemple lacked the kind of personality that would help the program's ratings and wanted him off the air, but they were unable to find anyone bright enough to beat him. He finally lost to a contestant who had been primed with answers. When he discovered what had happened, Stemple willingly exposed the quiz show rigging.

As a result of the revelations about quiz show rigging, the FCC urged Congress to enact new laws making rigged quiz programs illegal. Congress followed the FCC's suggestion and, as a result of a series of hearings conducted during 1959–1960, amended the Communications Act of 1934 (§509) to include a section forbidding quiz programs that attempted to deceive the public.

Filmed Television and the Violent Years

Both video tape and motion picture film contributed to converting television from a medium specializing in live programming to one that specialized in carrying recorded programs. Even more importantly, film helped to change the content of television programs. The change began in the mid-1950s when Disney Studios and Warner Brothers agreed to pruduce some films for ABC.

By using motion pictures many of the limitations on television programming vanished. There was no need to produce the program at the exact time it was aired; it was easy to take the camera outside for location filming; and editors of film had great freedom to select shots that best contributed to the development of a program. The new freedom led to many outdoor series filled with physical violence such as cowboy series, detective programs, and spy shows and with them came a violence that was unknown during the live television. Producers quickly learned that the new programs captured larger audiences than had been possible with other types of television and it was not long before most live television programs gave way to filmed episodes.

One of the new programs, "Cheyenne," was so successful that it became a long-running series that lasted for seven years. Its success led to imitators like "Sugarfoot," and "Colt 45." Film producers found that they could produce television films at very low costs by using old footage to cover things like cattle stampedes and Indian battles.[96] Cowboy series during the early years of television film were among the most popular programs and they remained at the top of the rating charts for a long time. The series "Gunsmoke" attests to this as it holds the record for being on television more seasons than any other show.

By 1960 another type of programming was becoming popular beginning with the "The Untouchables." The program, an ABC entry which reached and held the top position in the Arbitron ratings for sometime, depicted conflicts between the law and gangsters and was the most violent program yet to reach television. "The Untouchables" was so successful that specialized in dramas of physical violence like "Hawaiian Eye" and "77 Sunset Strip."[97]

The violent programming that viewers saw on their television sets in the early 1960s expanded during much of the decade and remained on television into the 1970 with shows like "The Man From U.N.C.L.E." and "Mission Impossible." These two spy shows featured master spies who used illegal tricks to solve problems for their governments.

The violence in television programming concerned many Americans and, during the 1969 Congressional season, Senator Pastore and is committee directed the Surgeon General of the United States to conduct a study of the effects of televised violence on the public to determine if any restrictive legislation was needed. The study cost the government about one million dollars and indicated that there was some relationship between viewing television violence and violent behavior. However, the conclusiions were somewhat tentative.[98] (The findings of this study are more fully discussed in the chapter on research in broadcasting. See page 220.)

Although no new laws resulted from the Surgeon General's report or from the Congressional hearings, which were conducted after the report was released, the NAB, the national television networks, and National Association of Independent Television Broadcasters decided to create the "family viewing hour." The family hour came into being because broadcasters feared new laws if they failed to take some action. The period from 7:00 to 9:00 (Eastern time) each evening was declared the family hour and networks and stations agreed not to program shows containing excessive sex or violence during this period.[99] (See Chapter 11, page 281 for a discussion of the details of the family hour.)

Of course, there were many programs during the 1960s that did not feature acts of physical violence, but this type of program was certainly in the minority. Prominent among the nonviolent programs was hillbilly comedy which included "The Beverly Hillbillies," "Green Acres," and "Petticoat Junction." Then there were urban comedies like "Dick Van Dyke," which featured a typical family in which the husband was a television writer.

Violence in the News

The dramatic program was not the only source of acts of physical violence on television during the 1960s and early 1970s. In 1963 John F. Kennedy was assassinated in Dallas. While network television did not show the actual event as it occurred, the nation was able to see Jack Ruby killing Lee Harvey Oswald, Kennedy's alleged assassin, in the basement of the Dallas Jail two days later. Networks suspended all prgramming for several days to cover the the slain President's funeral in Washington.

In 1968 Martin Luther King, the leader of the black movement, was assassinated by a sniper's bullet and, during the same year, Robert Kennedy was assassinated while campaigning for the Democratic nomination to the presidency. When the Democrats went to Chicago to nominate a presidential candidate to run in November, the convention hall was surrounded by protesters demanding that Democrats cease aggressive acts of war in Vietnam. Television covered the protesters as a news event. Consequently, viewers of nightly news programs saw a Chicago that looked like a war zone.

Television newscasts have a special ability to cover visual events with much action. As a result they have long specialized in visual material by going to college campuses when students were rioting for better social conditions; by going to the streets of America's cities when the ethnic poor had protested their living and working conditions; and by giving live coverage of the war in Vietnam.

As radio had once covered World War II, television covered the Vietnam war, but the perspective, the consequences, and the medium were different. Many newscasters opposed the Vietnam war, particularly in the later years, while most newsmen had urged support for World War II. Thus, through film editing, word choice, and the amount of time devoted to military events, thelevision newsmen showed America the worst of the war. Of course, the medium itself contributed to this distaste for war. When viewers nightly saw the blood, death, and fear war causes, many must have turned away in anger.

One newscast included film of a soldier being shot while a reporter discussed the atrocities of the war. The unpleasant scene probably was selected because a reporter wished to use the medium to influence the audience.

TELEVISION PROGRAMMING IN THE 1970s

Broadcasters feared dealing with controversial materials on television and radio because they thought they would lose viewers andsponsors. To support their fears broadcasters pointed to the low ratings that documentaries and issue-oriented drama received. Then, during 1971 Norman Lear in association with CBS presented a new program entitled "All in the Family."[100] The program, which treated controversial subjects traditionally considered taboo for television such as black-white relations, abortion, and racial bigotry, became, to the astonishment of network executives, the most popular program on television. Other Lear programs in the same vein followed. Following Lear's example, other producers also began treating controversial topics with success.

Another production company, named after the actress Mary Tyler Moore (MTM), decided to treat urban topics from a less controversial but still modern point of view than Lear's and found that its programs fared very well in the popularity race. One of its programs, "The Mary Tyler Moore Show," is the story of a successful businesswoman who lives alone in a large city. Moore is portrayed in the series as a person who is not dependent upon a man for security or happiness. Although the character's lifestyle undoubtedly bothered some, the program reached and remained in the top ratings.

Violence in programming did not vanish from network schedules during the 1970s with the advent of the new controversial comedy of Lear and MTM. One of the most popular styles of programming was police drama, which included "S.W.A.T.," "Kojak," and "The Streets of San Francisco." There was also the on-location police show from Hawaii called "Hawaii Five-O." Other action shows included private detective features such as "Canon," and "Mannix."

A remarkable shift in the relationship of networks and in their programming appeared in the 1976–77 season. Since the dawn of network television, CBS had received the highest ratings, followed by NBC, with ABC trailing behind them both. In the mid-1970s, ABC began improving its ratings, and in the 1976–77 season, ABC finished well ahead of the other two networks. Indeed, by season's end ABC was able to say that it had seven of the top ten programs and eleven of the top twenty programs. Not only was ABC the most-watched network during the 1976–77 season, it set the record for the most watched network for any season—ever.

ABC offered popular comedy ("Laverne and Shirley" and "Happy Days"), detective, and super-people shows ("Bionic Woman" and "Six Million Dollar Man"). Even the mini-series like "Rich Man-Poor Man" gave ABC a strong rating edge.

But perhaps most spectacular of all was the success of "Roots," an eight-night series tracing the history of a black family from its home in Africa to slavery and ultimate freedom in the United States. "Roots," which was based on the book by Alex Haley, has the distinction of being the most-watched television program in history. About 52% of the nation watched one episode. "Roots" had serious educational elements and attracted millions of viewers. Indeed, the program laid to rest the myth that television viewers will not watch serious programming.

As the network moved towards the 1977–78 season, ABC decided to make a concession to citizen groups opposed to violence on television and eliminated all but two of its most violent programs. Whether ABC's action signals a trend towards less violent television is yet to be seen, but the potential for change is clearly there.

NOTES

1. Walter B. Emery, *Broadcasting and Government* (East Lansing, MIchigan State University Press, 1971), p. 32.
2. Ibid. p. 33.

3.   Ibid.

4.   Lawrence W. Lichty and Malachi C. Topping, *A Source Book on the History of Radio and Television* (New York: Hastings House, 1975), p. 521.

5.   Harrison B. Summers, ed., *A Thirty-Year History of Programs Carried on National Radio Networks in the United States: 1926–1956*, reprint (New York: Arno Press, 1971), pp. 9, 10.

6   Information on programming in this section is compiled from Summers and represents the author's evaluation of Summers' work.

7.   Ibid., p. 27.

8.   Ibid., pp. 83–93.

9.   Lichty, op. cit., p. 300.

10.   Erik Barnouw, *The Golden Web* (New York: Oxford University Press, 1968), p. 9.

11.   LIchty, op. cit., p. 307.

12.   Ibid., p. 309.

13.   David T. MacFarland, "Up From Middle America: The Development of Top 40," in Lichty, op. cit.*

14.   Lichty, op. cit.

15.   Llewellyn White, *The American Radio* (Chicago: The University of Chicago Press, 1947), p. 28.

16.   Ibid.

17.   Ibid., pp. 48, 49.

18.   Ibid., pp. 44, 45.

19.   Ibid.

20.   Lichty, op. cit., p. 256.

21.   Barnouw, op. cit., pp. 185–188.

22.   Summers, op. cit., pp. 83–94.

23.   Some writers have indicated that "Amos 'n' Andy" went off the air briefly during the war because its sponsor, Campbell's Soup, could not acquire metal for soup cans. Almost immediately after Campbell's terminated sponsorship, Lever Brothers started sponsoring the program. Campbell's had sponsored the program as five weekly episodes of fifteen minutes; Lever Brothers changed the format to a weekly thirty minute program. If the program was off the air, it was for less than a season.

24.   Summers, op. cit., pp. 123–130.

25.   Harry Field and Paul F. Lazarsfeld, *The People Look at Radio*, (Chapel Hill: University of North Carolina Press, 1946), p. 6.

26.   FCC, "The Mutual Broadcasting System," *Report on Chain Broadcasting (Commission Order 37, Docket 5060, May 1941).* *

27.   Lichty, op. cit., p. 193.

28.   Ibid.

29.   White, op. cit., p. 40.

30.   *National Broadcasting Company et al.* v. *United States et al.*, 319 US 190 (1940).

31.   White, op. cit., pp. 40, 41.

32.   Ibid., p. 35.

33.   Barnouw, op. cit., p. 40.

34.   Ibid.

35.   Ibid., p. 41.

36.   Ibid., p. 42.

37.   White, op. cit., p. 22.

38. Erwin G. Krasnow and Lawrence D. Longley, *The Politics of Broadcast Regulation* (New York: St. Martins Press, 1973), p. 90.

39. Lichty, op. cit., p. 148; and *Broadcasting* (May 31, 1976), p. 68.

40. Christopher H. Sterling, "WTMJ-FM: A Case Study in the Development of FM Broadcasting," *Journal of Broadcasting*, Vol. XII, No. 4 (Fall 1968), pp. 341–352.*

41. Ibid.

42. Lichty, op. cit., p. 148.

43. Ibid., p. 148.

44. Summers, op. cit., pp. 192–202.

45. Ibid.

46. David T. MacFarland, "Television: The Whirling Beginning," in Lichty, op. cit.*

47. Ibid.

48. Ibid.

49. Ibid.

50. Orrin E. Dunlap, Jr., *Radio's 100 Men of Science* (Freeport, N.Y.: Books for Libraries Press, 1944), p. 242.

51. Ibid.

52. White, op. cit., p. 23.

53. Dunlap, op. cit., p. 281.

54. White, op. cit., p. 24.

55. FCC, "Broadcast Services" (Washington, D.C.: FCC Information Bulletin #3, 1976), p. 32.

56. White, op. cit., p. 24.

57. Barnouw, op. cit., pp. 125, 126.

58. Ibid.

59. FCC, op. cit., p. 33.

60. Ibid.

61. FCC, *Twelfth Annual Report (1946)* (Washington, D.C.: Government Printing Office, 1947), p. 17.

62. FCC, *Sixteenth Annual Report (1950)* (Washington, D.C.: Government Printing Office, 1951), p. 102.

63. Ibid., p. 103.

64. Lichty, op. cit., p. 522.

65. Donald G. Fink and David M. Lutyens, *The Physics of Television* (Garden City, N.Y.: Anchor Books, 1960), pp. 94–96.

66. FCC, *Fifteenth Annual Report (1949)* (Washington, D.C.: Government Printing Office, 1950), p. 42.

67. FCC, "Broadcast Services," op. cit., p. 34.

68. Barnouw, op. cit., pp. 293, 294.

69. The FCC has divided the United States into three zones for purposes of licensing television stations in the VHF channels. In Zone I, which contains part of the northeast and part of the midwest, the minimum separation between licensees on the same channel is 170 miles for VHF and 155 miles for UHF. The mileage separation given in the text is for Zone II, which includes the remaining portions of the northeast, the midwest and the west. Zone III separations are 220 miles for VHF and 205 miles for UHF and include Florida, parts of Georgia, Alabama, Louisiana, Mississippi, and Texas. Source: FCC, "Broadcast Services," op. cit., p. 36.

70. Lichty, op. cit., p. 148.

71. Lynn A. Yeazel, "Color it Confusing: A History of Color Television," p. 73, Lichty, op. cit.*

72. Ibid.

73. Ibid.

74. Ibid., p. 76.

75. Ibid., p. 77.

76. Ibid., p. 79.

77. Lichty, op. cit., p. 522.

78. FCC, *Twenty-first Annual Report (1955)* (Washington, D.C.: Government Printing Office, 1956), p. 95.

79. Emery, op. cit., p. 151.

80. *Broadcasting Yearbook 1975* (Washington, D.C.: Broadcasting Publications, 1975), p. A-6.

81. Ibid.

82. Emery, op. cit., p. 153.

83. FCC, *Thirty-eighth Annual Report (1972)* (Washington, D.C.: Government Printing Office, 1973), p. 183.

84. Poyntz Tyler, ed., *Television and Radio* (New York: H. W. Wilson, 1961), p. 40.

85. Lichty, op. cit., p. 193.

86. Barnouw, op. cit., pp. 290–292.

87. Erik Barnouw, *The Image Empire* (New York: Oxford University Press, 1970), p. 62.

88. Ibid., pp. 21–40.

89. Barnouw, *The Golden Web*, op. cit., p. 297.

90. Merle Miller, *The Judge and the Judged.* (Garden City, N.Y.: Doubleday, 1952), pp. 61–95.

91. John Cogley, *Report on Blacklisting*, reprint (New York: Arno Press, 1971), pp. 1–9.

92. Barnouw, op. cit., pp. 45–56.

93. R. E. B. Hickman, "The Development of Magnetic Recording" *Magnetic Recording Handbook: Theory, Practice and Servicing of Domestic and Professional Tape and Wire Recorders* (London: George Newness Limited, 1956), pp. 1–7.*

94. Ibid.

95. Barnouw, *The Image Empire*, op. cit., pp. 122–124.

96. Ibid., p. 63.

97. Ibid., p. 148–152.

98. Surgeon General's Scientific Advisory Committee on Television and Social Behavior, *Television and Growing Up: The Impact of Televised Violence* (Washington, D.C.: Government Printing Office, 1972), pp. 183–186.

99. Statement of Richard E. Wiley, Chairman before the Subcommittee on Communications of the HOurse Committee on Interstate and Foreign Commerce, March 11, 1975, pp. 30–32.

100. "The Winning Ways of William S. Paley," interview, *Broadcasting* (May 31, 1976), pp. 25–44.

*Citation is reprinted in Lawrence W. Lichty and Malachi C. Topping, *American Broadcasting: A Source Book on the History of Radio and Television.*

Financial Organization and Programming Practices 4

In many ways, broadcasting is like most other businesses in the United States. Broadcast owners range from conglomerates with several broadcast properties to small town businesspeople who own a single AM station. Regardless of the type of broadcast property they have, all broadcast owners are in the business to make a profit.

Broadcasting differs from other businesses in that broadcasters do not make their money from selling a product directly to the listener or the viewer. Instead, they get their money from the advertiser, who pays them to carry the advertising message to the broadcast audience—all potential consumers of the advertiser's product. If the broadcaster presents programming that attracts a large audience, the broadcaster becomes more attractive to the advertisers and hence is able to make a greater amount of money. Thus, success in the business of broadcasting is determined primarily by popular programs, large audiences, and advertising dollars.

Broadcasting also differs from other businesses in the degree of government regulation it is subject to. The government limits the number of stations that can be owned by an individual or company, sets forth regulations for the operation of these stations, and has the power to grant and renew station licenses.

As can be seen in Figure 4–1, the networks, individual stations, advertisers, program producers, syndicators, and the government are all part of the structure of the broadcast industry. Although it is an industry noted for its glamour and social influence, broadcasting is first a business and, as such, cannot be understood without understanding its economic structure. In the discussion that follows, we will concentrate on this business structure and how it influences decision making in the broadcast industry.

BROADCAST OWNERSHIP

One of the basic principles behind broadcast regulation is that, in order to protect freedom of speech and the public's right to a range of freely expressed ideas, no single individual or corporation should be allowed to gain too much control over the broadcast system. In order to insure that this did not happen, the government, through rules and regulations, put limits on broadcast ownership. The rules and regulations prescribe that an individual or corporation can own no more than seven AM, seven FM, and seven television stations (often called the seven-seven-seven rule). In the case of television, the rules specify that no more than five VHF stations can be owned by the same party. The rules and regulations also limit owners to one station of each type (AM, FM, VHF, or UHF) in a single geographical area. For example, you cannot own two AM stations in a single city, but you can own one AM, one FM, and one TV station.

The regulations limiting station ownership were intended to give many different persons and organizations access to the broadcast spectrum. These rules, however, did not take into account that station location might be even more important than the number of stations that any one person owned. As broadcasting grew, it was apparent that a station in a large population area was more powerful and valuable than a station in a small population area. Therefore, owners who had stations in cities such as New York and Los Angeles could exercise greater influence and attract a much larger share of advertising dollars than stations in areas such as Grand Rapids or Omaha.

In order to understand the American broadcasting system it is necessary to look at two aspects of ownership: market areas and ownership patterns.

MARKET AREAS

As the broadcast industry began to grow, the system of market areas evolved. The term *market area* refers to the geographical area that is reached by a radio or television signal, and to the population living within that area. For example, New York is the number one market area because it has the greatest number of people in a geographical area reached by a broadcast signal. New York has over six million households with at least one television set; Los Angeles (the number

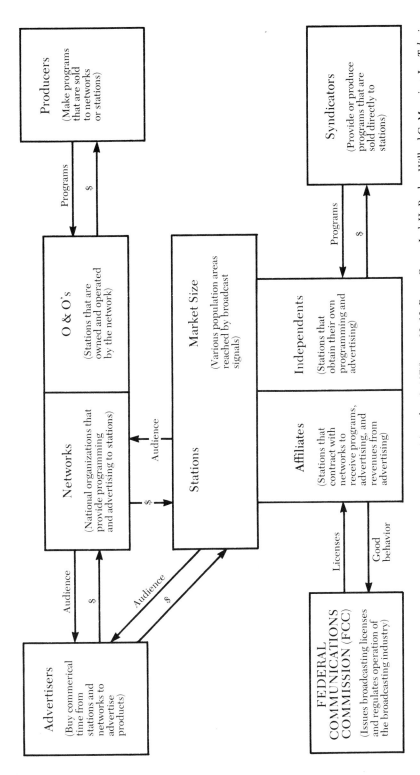

Figure 4–1. The economic structure of television. Sources: *Access 20* (October 6, 1975), pp. 10–12; Bruce Owen, Jack H. Beebe, Willard G. Manning, Jr., *Television Economics*, Lexington Books, 1974, p. 7.

123

two market) follows, with three and a half million; and Chicago (number three) is next, with almost three million.

A broadcast property in a major market (the top fifty markets are considered major) is more valuable than property in minor markets because the larger the population, the greater the audience for advertising messages and, hence, for potential sales. When broadcast stations were still widely available, those who were aware of the importance of market areas were quick to obtain licenses in major markets. For example, all three national networks—ABC, CBS, and NBC—acquired licenses for stations in New York, Los Angeles, and Chicago, as well as in several other major market areas. Today these network owned-and-operated stations are among the most powerful and profitable in the United States. Not only do they reach a substantial portion of the nation's population, but they also provide almost one-third of the networks' profits.[1]

BROADCAST OWNERSHIP PATTERNS

Multiple and Single Ownership

The network owned-and-operated stations, known as O & Os, are an example of *multiple ownership*. Multiple ownership exists when an individual or a company owns two or more stations in different communities. The networks are typical examples of multiple owners. Over 50 percent of all of the television stations in the United States are owned by multiple owners. More importantly, such stations reach 74 percent of the total potential audience in the United States. The most important multiple owners own stations in the largest markets. Some of the giants of American broadcasting are listed in Table 4–1.

TABLE 4–1   The Ten Largest Television Multiple Ownership Groups Ranked by Average Daily Audience, 1972

		Number of Stations Owned			Average Daily Audience		
Rank	Group	VHF	UHF	Total	Households (in thousands)	As % of all stations	As % of 50 largest groups
1	CBS	5	0	5	1,406	6.0	9.4
2	NBC	5	0	5	1,253	5.3	8.4
3	ABC	5	0	5	1,213	5.2	8.1
4	Group W—Westinghouse	5	0	5	749	3.2	5.0
5	Metromedia	5	1	6	666	2.8	4.4
6	Storer Broadcasting	5	1	6	604	2.6	4.0
7	Capital Cities	5	1	6	543	2.3	3.6
8	Tribune Community Stations	4	0	4	492	2.1	3.3
9	RKO General	4	0	4	434	1.9	2.9
10	Taft Broadcasting	5	2	7	403	1.7	2.7

Source: Walter S. Baer et al., *Concentration of Mass Media Ownership: Assessing the State of Current Knowledge* (Santa Monica, Calif.: The Rand Corporation, 1974), p. 49.

Although there are still those who own a single station or several kinds of stations in only one market area, the trend has been toward multiple ownership. In the 1950s television stations were more likely to be owned by single owners than by multiple owners. By the 1970s, however, the situation had reversed; a substantial majority of television stations were owned by multiple owners. The trend toward multiple ownership affects both radio and television stations. For example, with the exception of two stations, WBLS-FM and WMCA-AM, all other commercial radio stations in New York City are either owned by multiple owners or owners with other media interests.

The potential influence of large multiple owners is illustrated by the following statistics: the stations owned by the fifty largest multiple owners reach about two-thirds of all television homes in the nation; the twenty-five largest multiple owners reach one-half of all television homes; and the ten largest multiple owners reach one-third of all television homes.[2]

Cross-Media Ownership

Cross-media ownership occurs when an individual or group owns media property in two or more different media in the same market area. The most common type of cross-media ownership is owning broadcast property along with newspapers, magazines, or both. When radio first began to develop, newspaper publishers were among the first to establish radio stations; later they moved into both FM and television. Presently, many newspapers own AM-FM-TV combinations. In major markets, for example, the New York Times Company owns WQXR-AM and FM in New York. The *Washington Post* owns WTOP AM-TV; the *St. Louis Post-Dispatch*, KDS television and radio; the *St. Louis Globe-Democrat*, KTVI television; and the *Milwaukee Journal*, WTMJ AM-FM-TV. In several minor markets, single owners own all of the newspaper and broadcasting facilities. This system of single ownership in minor markets means that most media information comes from one source.

Although the FCC has often expressed concern that newspaper and broadcast combinations could reduce the public's access to differing opinions and decrease competition for local advertising, it has not prohibited cross-media ownership.[3] In 1977, however, the United States Court of Appeals ruled that the same company could not own a newspaper and a television or radio station in the same city unless the company could clearly demonstrate that cross-ownership was in the public interest. Although the effect of this ruling is not yet clear, it is likely that for the next several years newspapers will argue that their ownership of broadcast property is in the public interest and will therefore be able to avoid or delay selling their broadcast property.

Conglomerate Ownership

Many of the country's corporations also own broadcast stations. Some of the giant corporations such as CBS, have broadcasting as their primary interest, but other stations are subsidiaries of corporations which are not primarily en-

HEARST CORPORATION

The Hearst Corporation is an example of a multi-media giant. Hearst owns one newspaper in Maryland, two in New York, two in Massachusetts, one in the state of Washington, two in California, and one in Texas. Some of these papers are in major cities such as Albany, Baltimore, Boston, Los Angeles, San Francisco, and Seattle. Hearst also owns a comic weekly that is a newspaper supplement.

In addition, Hearst owns the following magazines: *Cosmopolitan, Good Housekeeping, Harper's Bazaar, Town and Country, House Beautiful, Motor Boating and Sailing, Sports Afield, Popular Mechanics, Science Digest,* and *American Druggist.* Hearst also owns Avon Books.

Hearst properties in broadcast stations include an AM, FM, and TV station in each of the following cities: Pittsburgh (market number 10), Baltimore (19), and Milwaukee (22). The corporation also owns an AM station in Puerto Rico.

Source: *Broadcasting Yearbook 1976* Broadcasting Publications Inc., (Washington, D.C., 1976), p. A-47.

gaged in broadcasting or other media. An example of such an organization is Wometco Enterprizes Inc. Wometco, chiefly known as a soft drink bottler and vending machine operator, also owns the Miami Seaquarium, ninety-seven movie theaters, cable television systems in seven states, and three wax museums. Wometco's station holdings are relatively small, one FM and three TV stations. Nevertheless these broadcast properties account for 55 percent of Wometco's profits.[4] Other examples of corporate owners of broadcast properties include: General Tire and Rubber Company, Dun and Bradstreet, General Electric, Schering-Plough Company, Kansas City Southern Industries, Kaiser Industries, Pacific Southwest Airlines, Rust Craft Greeting Cards, and many others.

One of the main sources of information about the business of broadcasting could come from the financial records of the corporations. When large corporations are involved in broadcast ownership, however, the actual ownership of the property and its financial status can often be obscured in a maze of complicated ownership structures. For example, Corinthian Broadcasting Corporation, the licensee for five television stations, is a wholly owned subsidiary of the wall street investment firm of Dun and Bradstreet. But eight different banks own 34.1 percent of the shares of Dun and Bradstreet, so it is difficult to determine who actually owns the stations.[5]

Corporations that are privately owned are not required by law to disclose any financial information unless they buy or sell broadcast property. An example of a private corporation that owns a broadcast property is the *Chicago Tribune*, which owns WGN-TV. Publicly owned corporations are required to disclose their earnings, but financial information concerning their broadcast can easily be buried in the overall holdings financial report. Westinghouse, a major owner of broadcast stations, lists its broadcast earnings under the category of "Broadcasting, Learning, and Leisure Time." Since this category includes earnings from other Westinghouse activities such as soft drink bottling, watch manufacturing, and the Westinghouse Learning Corporation, it is impossible to obtain very much information about the financial workings of the Westinghouse stations.[6]

COLUMBIA BROADCASTING SYSTEM

CBS is a conglomerate whose primary interest is still in broadcasting. The broadcasting part of CBS is also the most profitable—network O & O stations provide 46 percent of CBS revenues, 74 percent of net profits. Columbia Records, a division of CBS, is also very profitable.

In 1964 CBS began to diversify and buy companies that were not part of the broadcasting business. CBS now owns the following:

Musical instruments: Fender Guitar, Rhodes, Electro Music, V. C. Squier, Rogers Drums, Steinway, Gulbransen.

Publishers: Holt, Rinehart & Winston, W. B. Saunders, Anthony Blond (British), Popular Library, Nueva Editoriale Interamericana SA, Movie Book Club, Praeger Publications, Fawcett Publications.

Records: Discount Records.

Magazines: *Field and Stream, Road and Track, Cycle World, PV4, World Tennis, Sea Magazine, Women's Day.*

Educational films: Bailey Films, Film Associates.

Audio: Soundcraft, Pacific Stereo.

Music publisher: Tunafish Music.

Posters: April House.

Toys and hobbies: Creative Playthings, National Handcraft Inst., X-Acto, Needle Arts Society.

CATV: Two systems in the United States and several in Canada.

Source: *Forbes*, May 1, 1975, p. 23.

THE FAILURE OF DIVERSIFICATION OF BROADCAST OWNERSHIP

Although the Communications Act of 1934 had the intent of creating a system in which many people would have access to broadcasting licenses and in which broadcasters would be part of the local community where the stations were located, it is now clear that the effort to ensure diversification has failed. Much of broadcasting is in the hands of large corporations, and most broadcasters live far away from the communities where their stations are located. Broadcast licenses—at least in desirable market areas—are all taken, and there is likely to be little change in the pattern of broadcast licensing.

Since diversification was a concept originally created in order to promote public exposure to a wide range of ideas, the failure of diversification forces us to consider whether the result has been a limiting of ideas and free speech. Those who favor concentrated ownership argue that this type of ownership is more stable economically, that the owners are able to make greater programming efforts, and that they are more likely to attempt innovations in technology. Those who argue against concentrated ownership claim that it presents greater potential for abuse in advertising rates, for information control, and for conflicts with other business interests. They also argue that if concentrated interests were broken up, there would be more of an opportunity

---

THE BROADCAST BUSINESS

Number of Stations

Total Radio	8,240
Commercial AM	4,497
Commercial FM	2,873
Noncommercial FM	870
Total Television	984
Commercial VHF	517
Commercial UHF	211
Noncommercial UHF	155
Noncommercial VHF	101

Set Saturation

71.5 million homes with TV sets (97 percent of all homes)
54 million color sets
425 million radio sets (estimated)

Source: *Broadcasting Yearbook 1977* (Broadcasting Publications, Inc.: Washington, D.C., 1977) p. A-2.

for minorities and other under-represented or unrepresented groups to own stations.

In 1974, a project group of the Rand Corporation gathered and assessed all of the past research that has been done on media concentration and broadcast performance. After analyzing all of this research, they concluded that there was no convincing evidence to either prove or disprove the theory that media concentration affects program content.[7] But David Halberstam, in his 1975 study of CBS, argued that as CBS grew into a giant corporation it became much less likely to engage in controversy and controversial commentary in its news and public affairs programming.[8] Thus, it is clear that issues concerning the impact of media concentration are by no means resolved.

The fact remains, however, that broadcasting is big business and the decisions that are made about programming, sales, and personnel are all fundamentally business decisions. In order to understand how this business works, we will look more closely at the structure of the networks and the stations.

THE EXTERNAL STRUCTURE OF NETWORKS AND STATIONS

Networks

There are three full-time commercial radio and television networks in the United States: the American Broadcasting Company (ABC), the Columbia Broadcasting System (CBS),* and the National Broadcasting Company (NBC). There is also one sizable national radio network—the Mutual Broadcasting System (MBS), as well as several regional or special interest radio and television networks.

Networks provide three basic services for their member stations, which are known as *affiliates:* 1) they purchase or produce programming for distribution to their affiliates; 2) they sell commercial time to national advertisers and give a certain percentage of the revenue from such sales to their affiliates; and 3) they arrange for technical interconnection so that affiliates can receive network programs.

Contrary to popular belief, the stations are not in the business of producing programs—they are in the business of providing audiences. Although most stations produce a small amount of local programming, it would be too expensive for individual stations to produce their entire program schedules; therefore, the stations depend on networks for most of their programming.

By offering "desirable" programming to their affiliates who are located throughout the country, the network is able to attract a nationwide audience. The network then offers this audience to national advertisers. The network that

*The Columbia Broadcasting System changed its name to CBS Incorporated in 1974.

offers the most desirable programming attracts the largest audience and, consequently, the largest share of the advertising dollar.

The money that the network gets from advertising accounts for the greater share of its revenues and profits. The advertising revenues from a program (and its reruns) pay the cost of purchasing or producing a program and distributing it to the affiliates. Networks also make a substantial profit from their owned-and-operated stations.

Networks are highly profitable business organizations. In 1976, CBS network had a pretax profit of $129 million while NBC and ABC each had a pretax profit of $83 million. These figures represent an increase, from 1975, of 22 percent for CBS and 13 percent for ABC. Due to ABC's new programming strategy, which made it the top rated network, ABC had a startling 186 percent increase in profits from 1975![9]

Owned-and Operated Stations

Each of the three networks owns and operates five commercial VHF television stations. These stations, called O&O's, are the aristocrats of television stations. Not only are they all located in major markets, but they also provide almost one-third of each network's yearly profit and they are training grounds for entertainment talent, news personnel, and management before they reach the big time of the networks. As well as being owned and operated by a network, each O&O is also an affiliate of the network that owns it.

The three networks combined also own 17 AM and 17 FM stations. Many of these stations are located in cities where the network owns TV stations (See Table 4–2).

Network Affiliates

Although many radio stations affiliate with networks, this affiliation is not very crucial to the operation of a radio station: a radio station will usually depend on a network only for news and public affairs programming. In addition, the greatest percentage of commercial time in radio is sold locally, and so, although the radio station might earn revenue from national advertisers, such earnings are only a small percentage of its total revenues.

Eighty-five percent of all television stations affiliate with networks. NBC has 213 affiliates; CBS has 197; and ABC has 183, with an additional 67 *secondary affiliates*.[10] Secondary affiliation means that the stations might also have an affiliation with another network.

For television, network affiliation is the most practical and profitable way of running a station. The affiliate takes programming from the network for two basic reasons: the money the affiliate makes from the network is more than the affiliate could make if it developed its own programming; and the network offers certain programming that stations must provide in order to meet FCC requirements.

A portion of the money that the networks get from national advertisers goes directly to the network affiliates as payment to them for airing the commercials. The network-affiliate contract calls for a complex exchange of funds. Basically, the network pays the station for each commercial the station carries from the network. The amount of payment is determined by the size of the station's audience—the larger the audience, the greater the payment. The networks also offer another source of revenue to their affiliates by leaving a certain amount of time open around the network prime time programming that the affiliate is free to sell to local, regional, or national advertisers. In return for providing programming and commercials, the network charges the affiliate for the interconnection between the affiliate station and the network, but the affiliate gets more money from the network for carrying commercials than it pays to the network for the interconnection.

When the affiliate station is not receiving network programming, it is free to sell commercials for all the programs it purchases or produces. Stations most commonly sell commercial time for locally produced programs, feature films, and programs they buy from syndication companies.

The FCC regulates contracts between networks and their affiliates. The Commission has ruled that no network can have an exclusive agreement with a

TABLE 4-2   Network Owned-and-Operated Radio and Television Stations

	AM	FM	TV	Market Number*	Location
ABC	WABC	WPLJ	WABC	1	New York
	KABC	KLOS	KABC	2	Los Angeles
	WLS	WDAI	WLS	3	Chicago
	KGO	KSFX	KGO	5	San Francisco
	WXYZ	WRIF	WXYZ	7	Detroit
	KXYZ	KAUM		12	Houston
CBS	WCBS	WCBS	WCBS	1	New York
	KNX	KNX	KNXT	2	Los Angeles
	WBBM	WBBM	WBBM	3	Chicago
	WCAU	WCAU	WCAU	4	Philadelphia
	KCBS	KCBS		5	San Francisco
	WEEI	WEEI		6	Boston
	KMOX	KMOX	KMOX	15	St. Louis
NBC	WNBC	WNWS	WNBC	1	New York
			KNBC	2	Los Angeles
	WMAQ	WNIS	WMAQ	3	Chicago
	KNBR	KNAI		5	San Francisco
	WRC	WKYS	WRC	8	Washington, D.C.
			WKYC	9	Cleveland

*Figures compiled by the American Research Bureau

Source: *Broadcast Yearbook 1977* (Washington, D.C.: Broadcasting Publications, Inc., 1977) pp. A34, A35, A41, B80, B81.

station that would prevent the station from using another network's programming. In fact, in some cities with only one or two television stations, stations use programs from two different networks. Other regulations state that network-affiliate contracts are limited to two years, that stations may refuse any unsuitable programming, and the network cannot require the station to clear time whenever the network wants. Networks are also prohibited from influencing advertising rates for nonnetwork programs.

Although these rules are designed to protect the stations, and sometimes the network, they do not prevent the station from complying voluntarily with network wishes. Generally the most profitable stations are those that are affiliated with networks, and a station that earns the network's favor is able to negotiate for better rates on its next contract. Therefore, stations usually strive to comply with network requests.

Independent Stations

Some television stations—the independents—are neither affiliated with or owned by a network. They account for 10 to 15 percent of the total commercial television stations and are usually found only in large and medium markets. Generally, independent stations do not enjoy as much financial success as network affiliates because they do not have as much money available for talent and programming. Not only do they have to produce or purchase all their programming, they also must sell all their own advertising time. In 1972, 67 percent of the VHF independents showed a profit, while only 21 percent of the UHF independents were profitable. In comparison, among the network affiliates 86 percent of the VHF stations and 44 percent of the UHF stations were profitable.[11]

There are also independent radio stations. However, the question of independent status versus affiliation is not nearly so important in radio as in television, since radio stations are not so dependent on networks for programming and advertising revenue.

A Fourth Network?

When Norman Lear created "Mary Hartman, Mary Hartman," he offered the program to the networks. After the networks refused it, he sold the program to many independent stations throughout the country. The program was so successful in generating advertising revenues that the independents began to think about creating a limited network of their own. By 1977, the independents, acting collectively, began to commission some of their own programs. Rather than following the established network practice of selling most of the commercial time on a national basis with revenues returning to the networks, the independents decided to sell the majority of commercial spots in their own market areas. This strategy has been so successful in creating substantial profits for the independents that, although an independent network is still in an experimental stage, the independents are confident that they will soon be able to compete with the networks for advertising dollars and audiences during the prime time period.

THE INTERNAL STRUCTURE OF NETWORKS AND STATIONS

As with all businesses, networks and stations are divided into various operating departments that have specific jobs to do. The divisions are basically the same for both the stations and the networks, although in the case of smaller stations some of the jobs may overlap. Generally, there are seven divisions; management, programming, production, sales, traffic, engineering, and broadcast standards.

Management

Management is responsible for the overall operation of the networks and stations. Management personnel set the direction, philosophy, and programming format of each station or network, and all of the various divisions operate within management guidelines. In a network operation there may be as many as fifty people in top management positions, whereas a smaller station's operations may be managed mostly by the station owner.

Programming

At the network level there are hundreds of people who operate in the programming departments. They range from those who make decisions about what programs to purchase or produce to those who actually produce, write, and appear in programs. Those who work in news departments are separate from the rest of the programming staff. News department personnel range from executive producers to correspondents and writers. The most successful programming executives are those who purchase and produce programming that appeals to the widest possible audience.

At the local level, if the station is a network affiliate, the majority of programming will come from the network. Local station programmers must fill up the remainder of the broadcast schedule with local programming, feature fiims, and programs from syndication companies. In a radio operation, where music is the most common format, those involved in programming must choose the records that will best fit the station's format.

Production

In the networks, production personnel are separate from the programmers. Network production staffs include directors and camera and sound equipment operators. At the local level, programming and production functions often overlap—one person may both write and direct a program or, in radio, one person may write, announce, and run the audio control board.

Sales

Since the primary economic support of broadcasting is advertising, the sales department is the heart of any broadcast organization. The sales department sells advertising time. If the organization is a network, commercials are most often sold on a national level. For an individual station, the sales staff will concentrate on local or regional sales. Sales are so important to the success of network and station operations that most top management positions are held by those who have moved up from the ranks of sales.

Traffic

The traffic department is responsible for organizing the flow of programming material and commercials. This department sees that commercials are aired at the right time, that films and other programs are available to be shown, that production work is done on time, and that each department is aware of programming and production deadlines. Traffic departments work closely with sales departments; they provide the salespersons with frequent updates of the commercial time that is available so that the sales staff can advise their clients of present availabilities.

Engineering

Engineers see that the station is operating in accordance with FCC technical standards. This includes keeping the broadcast tower lights on, maintaining transmitter power and frequency, checking heating and cooling systems, and ordering and repairing equipment.

Broadcast Standards

The networks all have departments that monitor programming and commercial acceptability. These departments serve a censorship function, and if they find any material unacceptable, they help producers and writers restructure the material so it will be suitable for the network. At individual stations, decisions about acceptability of broadcast material are usually made at the management level.

BROADCAST PROGRAMMING

The key to the success of any broadcast operation is its programming. The records, the news, the soap operas are all designed to attract the listener and the viewer to the broadcast media so that networks and stations can sell the audience to advertisers. Programming functions to bring the advertiser's message and the audience together. When a program attracts a large audience, advertising revenue increases; with a small audience, it decreases.

Prime time television programming is very expensive, so programs must attract huge audiences to justify the advertiser's investments. An audience of only a million people would be considered a catastrophe at the networks—a weekly program series aired during prime time needs approximately 30 million viewers to be considered a success. However, the networks are not interested in just any thirty million households. The ideal audience for network prime time programming is considered to be between the ages of 18 and 49 and preferably female—these are the persons who do most of the buying of consumer goods in the American economy.

Market size is particularly important to network programming. If programming appeals to the top fifty markets, the broadcaster has a potential audience of most of the U.S. population. Since large markets contain the majority of the population, they are all in urban areas. Therefore, the urban population is more important to the programmers than the rural population. Also, advertising rates are much higher in the major markets. For example, the cost of a 30-second television commercial in a popular prime time program would be about $9000 at WCBS-TV in New York City; about $140 at KGGM-TV in Albuquerque; and approximately $80 at WWNY-TV in Watertown, New York.[12] Thus, it becomes more efficient and more profitable for network broadcasters to direct programming to major markets than to minor ones.

Although major market radio stations are generally more profitable than minor market stations, market size is not nearly as crucial to radio as it is to television. Radio stations program for a local rather than a national audience, and they generally depend on national advertisers for only a small share of their revenue. Radio stations sell most of their time to local advertisers, and the main concern of the advertiser is that the local audience will be persuaded to buy the advertiser's products. As with television, radio stations with the largest audiences are the most profitable.

Regardless of whether their audience and advertisers are national or local, all networks and stations have one thing in common; they constantly strive to develop programming that will attract the "right" audience for their advertisers. Even though some programming is considered enlightening, fascinating, and of tremendous social value by media critics, in the business of broadcasting it is a failure if it does not attract enough of the right kind of people.

Although no one has ever discovered a magic formula for successful programming, the broadcast industry makes certain program decisions—

generally based on successful past experiences. In the section that follows we will discuss radio and television programs with regard to program sources, the selection process, and the program options that are available.

RADIO PROGRAMMING

When television became popular with the American public, it took away the large nationwide audience that had listened to radio. Television also absorbed much of radio's programming. Entertainers and comedians involved in program series soon realized that if they were going to survive, their future was with television, not with radio. Therefore, radio station management and program personnel realized they would have to develop new programming formats. Music was the obvious choice since it appealed to the ear rather than to the eye, and by the late 1950s most radio stations had changed to an all-music format.

At the same time radio was making programming changes, it also had to change its way of making money. Since most national advertising had gone to television, the only way for radio stations to survive economically was to develop their local advertising sources. Radio time salespersons did precisely that, and although national advertising revenues to radio have remained constant, local advertising revenues rise every year.[13]

Radio formats largely depend on market size. Large market areas can support several stations with different formats, while a minor market may only be able to support one or two stations and, consequently, programming choice is limited. In a small market with a single radio station, the station will usually offer a combination of programs. In the morning, for example, a station might use a middle-of-the-road (MOR) format, which mainly consists of easy-listening music. In the afternoon and late evening, the station is likely to program contemporary/Top-40 music which will appeal to a young audience.

In larger market areas, stations program a single format. A medium market area is likely to have stations that use only Top-40 or MOR programming. In the largest markets, stations can offer even more choices. A typical Top-ten market may have stations that specialize in classical music, jazz, soul, or country music. As FM radio began to develop, there also came to be a number of "beautiful music" or "good music" stations—a term the broadcast industry uses to describe stations that play standard musical favorites. Although stations provide a variety of formats, listeners prefer contemporary/Top 40 followed by MOR—as can be seen in Table 4-3.

Programming specialization opened the door for advertising specialization. MOR stations, for instance, often advertise banks and family-type restaurants, while Top-40 stations are more likely to advertise record stores and quick-food places. The more specialized the audience, the more specialized the advertiser becomes in trying to reach that audience.

TABLE 4-3   Trends in Radio Listening Preferences in the Top 25 Markets (1972–1976)

	1972	1973	1974	1975	1976	% change from '72
Good Music	15.1	15.3	15.1	15.7	15.5	+ 2.6
Country Music	4.4	4.7	6.1	6.9	6.7	+52.3
News	3.2	3.5	4.3	4.8	5.2	+62.5
MOR	19.7	18.8	18.2	17.0	17.4	−11.7
Cont./Top 40	19.2	19.0	19.5	19.3	19.5	+ 1.5
Progressive	4.8	5.4	5.8	7.2	7.7	+60.4
Black	4.8	5.0	5.2	5.6	5.0	+ 4.2
Talk	5.6	4.7	4.2	3.5	3.3	−41.1
Classical	1.8	1.5	1.5	1.6	1.4	−22.2
Oldies	1.4	1.5	1.3	1.1	1.2	−14.3
Other	20.0	20.6	18.8	17.3	17.1	

Source: *Broadcasting*, May 2, 1977, p. 51.

Today, most of the program formats for radio depend on music with occasional breaks for news. Many stations still receive news from the networks; other stations use the wire services and supplement this news with local reporting. Although some stations have all-news or all-talk formats, the mainstay of radio programming is music.

Stations that program MOR and "beautiful music" formats have uncomplicated program choices, since there is an identifiable list of music that appeals to their audiences. Even specialized music stations have little difficulty; there are only so many choices available in classical music, beautiful music, and jazz. These stations have predictable formats, steady personnel, and consistent profits; all in all, they are the bread-and-butter stations of the radio industry.

The Top-40 stations are quite a different matter. They are the flashiest of the radio stations—their programming changes weekly, they have a great turnover of personnel, and they can make huge profits—both for themselves and for the record industry. Since they are unique, we would like to concentrate our discussion on Top-40 radio. Although some aspects of the business, such as playlists and trade magazines, are common to most radio stations, they take on a special importance for Top-40 radio.

Playlists.   The most important programming element for an all-music radio station is the station's *playlist*, the lists of records the station plays each week. These records are carefully selected by the program director, usually in consultation with his or her staff, and these are the only records that will be used during the life of the particular playlist. At a Top-40 station the total playlist contains an average of thirty-seven to thirty-eight records but only twelve to fourteen of these records get concentrated play. Although the list changes every week, it does not change very much. In a top-market station, the program director may replace only one or two records with recent releases.

Since there are well over a hundred new releases every week, it becomes very difficult for a new record to get air time—especially a record by a new performer or group.

Program directors do not pick playlists haphazardly. They know that a successful playlist means higher ratings for the station. Therefore, in addition to consulting with the members of the station's staff, the director will usually seek outside information. The most important record information comes from the trade magazines, the tipsheets, and the record promotion people.

Trade Magazines.   There are three trade magazines for the record industry: *Billboard, Cashbox,* and *Record World.* Most people in the business consider *Billboard* to be the most influential and the best of the three. All of these magazines publish charts listing the top 100 records. They also indicate which records are moving up on the charts. Generally the trade magazines base these charts on record sales and information about playlists of stations throughout the country. These charts may be the single most important information source in the entire record industry. As one record executive puts it: "Every week the trades get hundreds of calls from artists, managers, and promotion people saying how *tragically* they erred in this week's list."[14]

Tip Sheets.   Most program directors also subscribe to newsletters about singles records. These newsletters are called *tip sheets,* and the editors of these publications have correspondents at radio stations throughout the country who report on which records are rising and falling, and which records are being added to playlists in the correspondents communities. The best-known tipsheets are *The Gavin Report, Friday Morning Quarterback,* the *Tip Sheet,* and the *Hamilton Report.*

Record Sales.   Some radio stations periodically check with the major record stores to see which records are selling in their area. Record stores can be a useful source of information—especially about performers who have local and regional, rather than national, appeal.

All-Music Stations and the Record Industry.   All-music programming turned out to be a boon for the record industry. All-music formats created a demand for a constant supply of new records, new performers, and new sounds. Usually only radio can create a hit single record, and every record company hopes that its record will be the one. Although at least 25,000 copies of a record must be sold before it can break even, record companies make a five-cent profit on every copy after that. Often a hit single inspires people to buy the performer's album—an even more profitable sale for the record company. Because of the potential value of radio exposure, record manufacturers provide free albums and singles to commercial radio stations. Stations located in larger markets often receive tapes of new songs even before the records have been pressed. The tapes are duplicated from the master recording and distributed with the hope that advance exposure will improve sales of the new release. Because of the interest record companies have in promoting their records on the radio, stations receive albums and singles from the record companies every week.

Although stations pay nothing to the record companies, they pay annual fees to ASCAP (American Society of Composers, Authors, and Publishers) and BMI (Broadcast Music, Inc.), for music performance licensing. The fee that is paid to the two licensing organizations is usually in the form of a percentage of the station's gross billings for the year. It is, however, possible to pay on a per-use basis for the use of records, but most stations have found the accounting problems of per-use charges so great that they simply settle for the amount based on gross billings.

Because of the value of radio coverage, record companies have devised many methods to encourage stations to play their records. One tactic has been the use of promotion people. Promotion people go directly to radio stations to promote their records. Although they try to get the major market stations to play new releases, they are generally unsuccessful because these stations do not want to take a chance with an unknown record. Therefore promotion people try for the secondary markets. If a record is played first in a number of secondary markets, promotion people may then be able to persuade stations in the major markets to play it. A good part of successful promotion is going from station to station and telling program directors who is playing what.

Payola

Some record manufacturers were less than satisfied with the results attained by legal methods of persuading disc jockeys to play their records. Consequently, they began to offer, and disc jockeys accepted, enormous fees to act as consultants to record companies. Favors such as free records, stereo systems, and money were given in return for playing the manufacturer's record releases. During the late 1950s and the early 1960s, a Senate investigating committee discovered the practice of paying for the playing of records. As a result of the investigation, the Communications Act was amended to make the practice illegal.

The playlist system was instituted as a result of these scandals. When a station had a rigid playlist the air personalities had few opportunities to make record choices and hence they were not so vulnerable to temptations offered by the record companies.

Because the record companies depend on radio stations to create hit singles, station personnel are still not totally immune to bribes from record companies. During the 1970s, several payola scandals erupted again. At least one record company was accused of offering cocaine to station personnel, and several stations were offered bribes by concert promoters. Since it is so difficult to get a single on a playlist, small-scale payola scandals will probably continue to occur from time to time. Many performers and promotion people believe that if most records were only played, they would be successful. This belief makes it very tempting to offer bribes.

TELEVISION PROGRAMMING

Program Sources and Costs

The program sources that are available to television are both more complex and more varied than those sources available to radio stations. Stations that affiliate with a network have most of their programming problems solved; they get approximately 65 percent of their programs from the networks, 25 to 30 percent from program distributors called syndication companies, and they produce the remaining 5 to 10 percent themselves. Independent television stations have greater programming problems. They generally choose their programming from various program series that once ran on network television, as well as from motion pictures, free films, regional networks, and their own locally produced programming.

In this section we will discuss the three major sources—two local and one national—of program material, and some of the costs that are involved in producing programs for television. The local sources are local production and syndication, and the national source is networks.

Local Productions

The most common type of locally produced programming consists of news and public affairs programs. Since the FCC requires that stations meet the needs of their local communities, most television stations have decided to do this predominately through their news and public affairs programming. Local television stations are likely to have at least two or three local newscasts a day as well as one or two half-hour weekly programs about subjects that are of particular interest to their communities. Many stations also have a weekday morning program that is intended to attract a largely female audience. Stations vary greatly in local programming, but most of them stay away from programs that are purely entertainment, since the networks and independent production companies can do a much better job of providing that kind of program.

Syndication Companies

Syndication companies provide programs for stations to use when the stations are not receiving network programming. If the station is an independent, it gets most of its programming from syndicators. Syndicated programs are not carried on network lines; they are sent through the mail or by air or rail express to the individual stations.

Stations that obtain programs from syndicators have exclusive rights to show the programs in their markets. The price of the programs depend on the market size. Generally, stations buy several episodes of the program series and their contract with the syndication company specifies the number of times they can show the program.

Syndication companies provide both new and old programming. New programs are those which are produced specifically for syndication purposes. Examples are "Hollywood Squares," the "Merv Griffin Show," "Let's Make a Deal," and the "Lawrence Welk Show."

Old programming consists of feature films and off-network programs; that is, program series that have already been aired by the network. In order for an off-network program to go into syndication, it usually must have 120 episodes. Off-network programming is a very profitable business. "Happy Days" was sold for $35,000 per episode to individual stations in major markets. Each station has the right to run each episode six times, beginning in the fall of 1979 when enough episodes are available for syndication.[15]

Network Programming

Although networks supply about 65 percent of their affiliate's programming, they produce very few of the programs that they carry on their schedules. Actual network production is limited to news, documentary, and sports programs, and talk shows such as the "Tonight" show.

The networks obtain the majority of their programming from independent production companies or the television divisions of Hollywood movie studios. Although we associate prime time programming with the networks, almost all prime time programs are actually produced by these companies. Every independent production company or movie studio that works for television has the hope of selling a program series to one of the three networks. If the program is bought and attracts a large and faithful audience, both the independent production company and the networks make substantial profits.

The networks also buy the rights to show feature films that have already been shown in movie theaters. The more successful the film has been in the theater, the higher the price the network is willing to pay for the right to show it on television.

In the early days of television, advertisers provided many television programs. This practice meant that the advertiser also paid for all of the commercial time within the program. Since today's prices for commercials are so high, this practice of providing and sponsoring the entire program is not so common. Most advertisers prefer to spread their advertising dollars over a wide variety of programs in the hope of attracting as wide an audience as possible. An example of an advertiser that still owns and supplies television programs is Proctor and Gamble, which owns several soap operas.

Program Costs

One of the problems networks have had to face in recent years is the rapidly rising cost of the shows they buy from independent producers. In 1949 a typical one-hour drama could be produced for about $11,000; in 1961 a one-hour drama cost networks about $87,000, and by 1976 the cost was over $300,000.[16]

The costs of other types of programming have also risen rapidly. Because of these rising costs of production, networks have had to increase the cost of commercial time.

A consequence of high production costs has been a reduction in the number of new programs produced each year. Networks once purchased as many as thirty-six original episodes for each season a series was on the air, but rising costs caused networks to reduce the number of original episodes to as few as thirteen. Recently, networks have begun purchasing an average of twenty-four original episodes for a series. Thus, reruns start after only five months—in about February—and, with only twenty-four episodes produced per year, each one is shown on an average of about two and one-half times on the network in a year's time. Although many critics have protested the number of reruns, there is little reason to believe that shows will return to thirty-six episodes per season schedule. By showing each episode two or more times instead of creating new ones, networks are able to make a profit—something they often cannot do by only running the original episode.

The Selection Process

The process that networks use to reach a final decision on what programs they will buy from independent producers is a slow and risky one. A program idea is usually developed a good eighteen months prior to the time it actually appears on the air. At least 300 program ideas are considered by all the networks each year, but only a small percentage go into production and an even smaller percentage are actually successful once they are broadcast.

When a network believes that a program idea is promising, it commissions the production company to produce a pilot or demonstration program. Because of the high cost of pilots—each network spends about $20 million a year—networks resist paying for too many.[17] Once the pilot is produced, it undergoes extensive testing by the network. The network will air it in the season before it is to become a regular series in order to gauge public reaction; it will test show it in theatres and on cable systems, and it will be subjected to considerable scrutiny and modification by top network management.

If a pilot is judged acceptable after it has been tested and analyzed, it is considered for the following fall lineup. Network management must then decide where to put it in the broadcast schedule. Although management hopes that the pilot program will receive a good rating based on its own merits, it must also consider the programs that precede and follow it in order to get the highest possible rating for an entire evening's programming. A single program series is considered as only part of the entire schedule, and if the program cannot fit into the schedule, it may be dropped.

Once the schedule is put together for the following fall, the networks get all of their affiliates together to view the new season's offerings. At such meetings, network executives promise gigantic improvements in the ratings, stars are brought in to mingle with station managers, and food and drink flow profusely.

Although affiliate station managers have the right to protest the networks' choices, which they often do, their complaints seldom bring about immediate change.

Once the affiliates know what will happen in the fall, the networks release stories about the forthcoming shows to *TV Guide* and other television-related magazines, hoping to build audience interest in the new season. In addition, during the summer "doldrum" months when sales are low, networks engage in elaborate self-promotion with unsold network commercial time.

Once the schedule is put together, the three networks combined will program about sixty-three hours of prime time programs a week and 135 hours in nonprime time periods during the week days. NBC programs more hours than the other two networks, since it programs talk shows into the early hours of the morning.

Types of Programming

Dramatic and Comedy Shows.   The mainstay of prime time television is comedy and drama. This programming is also the most expensive to produce. In the 1976–77 season "All in the Family" cost $170,000 and "Kojak" cost $340,000 for each episode (including the right to one re-run).[18]

Situation comedies have always been the leaders in ratings. Comedy in rural settings ("The Beverly Hillbillies") was big in the 1960s, but in the 1970s the trend has been more toward urban comedy, with programs such as "The Jeffersons" and "Good Times." Program preferences change in dramatic programs. At one time the broadcast schedule was filled with Westerns, but the latest trend has been toward situation comedies. The most common strategy in providing prime time programming for a new season is to imitate what has been the most popular program in a previous season, a process called "spin-offs" in the industry.

Mini Series.   The 1976–77 season saw a new development in programming called the mini series, which is a series that presents a serialized novel in several episodes. The most successful of these series, "Roots," had the largest prime-time audience of the entire season. Mini series differ from regular series in that they have a limited number of episodes and are developed from best-selling novels. Because of their success in the 1976–77 season, they are likely to become an established form of television programming in the years to come.

Feature Films.   There are three types of feature films: old feature films that are generally shown in nonprime time; recent feature films that are shown in prime time; and made-for-television films. Made-for-television films are a fairly recent phenomenon. Although there has always been an audience for feature films, the television industry quickly used up all of the older films that had been shown in theaters. Their solution was to make films for television. Regardless of the type of film, networks pay an average of $900,000 to fill up a two-hour time slot with a film.

Specials.   Specials are programs that are not part of a program series. They are intended to be shown only one time and they are known in the industry as O.T.O.s, or "one-time-only's." They are, however, subject to being rerun, as is any prime time program. Specials appear in many different forms. Generally they bring us programming that would be too expensive or too specialized to produce in a regular program series. They may be dramatic (such as the Hallmark specials), they may be documentary (such as the network news specials), or they may take on a cartoon format, as do some of the children's programming shown around the holiday seasons.

Variety Shows.   Although variety shows were very popular in the early days of television they have generally decreased in recent program schedules. The present variety show is usually organized around well known performers such as Carol Burnett. An episode of a variety show is often not re-run which makes its cost even higher because the network has to pay for a replacement. In 1976–77 an average episode of the "Carol Burnett Show" cost $265,000.[19]

News.   Each network news operation employs hundreds of people and has a yearly budget of millions of dollars. Most of the budget and personnel go toward producing the evening news program, although a certain percentage will also go toward the documentaries that are aired on the networks.

Local stations also have news staffs that cover the local community. Although a major market station might have a news staff that numbers as many as twenty or thirty people, stations in small or medium markets might have only four or five people, and they are often also involved in other programming at their station.

Both stations and networks depend on the wire services for news. The two national wire services are Associated Press and United Press International. Both of these services have reporters throughout the United States and the world to provide written news, commentary, headlines, weather reports, and even photographs. In order to obtain the special equipment necessary to receive these services, the stations and networks pay a subscription fee to the news services.

Sports.   Since sports often attract large audiences they are very profitable to the networks. Networks occasionally carry regularly scheduled sports but they are more likely to offer special sports events as they occur. An important game brings great financial reward to the network. For example, in 1976 an estimated 73 million people watched the Super Bowl. A one minute commercial for the program cost $230,000![20]

Game and Quiz Shows.   Although quiz shows were very popular in prime time programming in the 1950s they were withdrawn from the air when Congress discovered that producers were rigging the questions so that certain contestants would win. The quiz shows were replaced by game shows in which people were asked to perform stunts rather than answer questions. In the 1970s quiz shows reappeared in nonprime time with much smaller prizes.

Game and quiz shows are commonly found in both daytime and early evening programming. Compared to prime time program costs, they are very cheap to produce—about $25,000 for half an hour.[21]

Soap Operas.   Soap operas, more respectfully known as daytime drama, are often owned and produced by the advertisers. Although the ratings are low compared to prime time, the audience is very faithful. Soap operas are also one of the cheapest forms of programming. For example, it costs NBC $170,000 to produce an entire week of "Days of Our Lives," while the daily advertising revenues are $120,000.[22]

Children's Programs.   Children's programming is most commonly found on Saturday mornings, but since National Association of Broadcasters, under pressure from the FCC, recently created the family viewing hour (from 7:00–9:00 PM) programs that are free of excessive sex and violence can be seen nightly. The Saturday morning programming always makes a profit for the networks.

Religious Programming.   Most religious programming comes from the networks or from church-related organizations that have programs in syndication. Stations often charge these groups to carry syndicated programming. Religious programming is most often carried on Sunday morning—a time which is of little interest to the advertisers.

CONCLUSION: CHANGE AND THE FUTURE

As we have seen from the preceding discussion, the ownership patterns and the programming practices in the broadcast industry are organized in a way to make the broadcasting business as profitable as possible. Since the present system is profitable, the broadcast industry works to preserve the status quo. However, the system does change from time to time.

Changes in programming are most likely to come about because the industry discovers that some new form of programming is more profitable than the old. The best examples of this type of change are situation comedies that have social themes. When Lucille Ball's real life pregnancy also provided a story-line for "I Love Lucy" in 1953, the industry proceeded with great caution and hired script consultants from several religious organizations to make certain that her pregnancy was not presented in an offensive manner. By the 1970s, however, similar situation comedies were dealing with social problems that ranged from impotency to alcoholism. "All in the Family" was the first program to try any of these subjects, but when it became clear that this program attracted huge audiences several other programs quickly followed with controversial subject matter of their own. Similarly, persons who appeared on the television screen became more varied—especially during the 1970s. For instance, several major market stations hired both black people and women to take anchor positions on local news programs. When it became clear that the presence of these individuals did not hurt the ratings—indeed they often improved ratings—other stations were quick to follow. Obviously, this sort of change cannot take place unless a station or a network is willing to take the first risk. But broadcasters must take a certain number of risks, since it is clear that the same type of programming will not continue to attract audiences indefinitely.

Ownership patterns are not likely to change as quickly as programming patterns. Station ownership is most likely to change hands only when a station is losing money—a situation that is more likely to occur in a minor market than a major one. During the 1970s, however, both the Justice Department and citizens' groups have been working to break up current ownership patterns. Their efforts seem to indicate that if change is to occur in ownership, it is more likely to come from external forces than from forces within the broadcast industry.

Since the broadcast industry is organized according to a profit-maximizing model that is common to almost all other businesses in the United States, dramatic change is not likely to occur. Since this sort of change is not imminent, it remains practical and realistic to analyze the broadcast industry as a business enterprise with economic motivations; in short, broadcasting is a business.

NOTES

1. A Primer on the Economic Structure of Television," *Access*, 20 (October 6, 1975), pp. 11–12.

2. Walter S. Baer, et al., *Concentration of Mass Media Ownership: Assessing the State of Current Knowledge* (Santa Monica, Calif.: The Rand Corporation, 1974), p. 47.

3. *Ibid.*, pp. 2–3.

4. *Broadcasting Yearbook 1976* (Washington, D. C.: Broadcasting Publications Inc., 1976) p. A-43; and Richard Bunce, *Television in the Corporate Interest* (New York: Praeger, 1976), p. 103.

5. *Media Report to Women* (Washington, D. C.: Media Report to Women, 1975), 2:3, pp. 6–7.

6. *Access, 20*, op. cit., p. 9.

7. Baer, op. cit., p. 143.

8. David Halberstam, "CBS: The Power and the Profits," *Atlantic* (January 1976), pp. 33–71.

9. *New York Times* (May 9, 1977), p. 57M.

10. *Broadcasting Yearbook 1976*, pp. D17-D28.

11. FCC, *Thirty-ninth Annual Report*, p. 234.

12. *Access, 20*, op. cit., p. 10.

13. John Blair and Company, *1975 Statistical Trends in Broadcasting*, 11th Edition, (New York: Blair Television Blair Radio, 1975), p. 41.

14. Clive Davis, *Clive: Inside the Record Business* (New York: William Morrow, 1975), p. 200.

15. *Broadcasting* (January 10, 1977), pp. 34–36.

16. *Broadcasting*, April 26, 1976, pp. 28–29.

17. Bob Shanks, *The Cool Fire: How to Make it in Television*, (New York: W.W. Norton, 1976), p. 104.

18. *Broadcasting*, (April 26, 1976), pp. 28–29.

19. *Ibid.*

20. *Broadcasting Yearbook 1976*, p. A-2.

21. Stephanie Harrington, "To Tell the Truth, the Price is Right," *New York Times Magazine* (August 3, 1975), p. 17.

22. "Sex and Suffering in the Afternoon," *Time*, (January 12), 1976, p. 47.

Broadcast Advertising

5

Not long ago, a Japanese electronics firm decided to introduce a tape recorder it had developed into the American market. Since successful marketing of this recorder would depend on a large advertising campaign, the company hired a New York advertising agency to plan and develop the campaign.

The agency quickly decided on the focus of its advertising strategy. The tape recorder had a unique selling point—it could play for many hours without being reloaded. The advertising agency decided to base the entire campaign on this point and looked for a theme that would best illustrate the recorder's uniqueness. After considering many ideas, the agency decided to use the theme of a dance marathon—a form of entertainment that was popular in the United States in the 1930s. Since the dance marathon lasted for many hours it seemed uniquely suited to illustrate the ability of the tape recorder.

Once the agency set out to produce the commercial, it had to find a proper location. After settling on an old hotel in Atlantic City that had an appropriate ballroom, the agency next had to research and plan, thirties costumes, hair-styles and makeup.

In addition to solving the special problems of producing a period commercial, the agency had to handle the routine planning that is necessary for all commercials. A script was written, actors, actresses, and a production crew were hired and a shooting schedule was arranged.

The planning for the commercial took several months, the shooting took a few days, and several additional days were spent on the editing. Finally the commercial was finished: it had cost $100,000 and it was 30 seconds long. The only thing left to do was to buy television time to air the commercial. Our story, however, takes a surprising turn. After the commercial was finished, the Japanese company decided that they did not want to market the tape recorder in the United States after all, and so, obviously, there was no use for the commercial. Although the company had to pay the agency, the commercial has never been shown and is now gathering dust in some library.

This true story is a good illustration of advertising in America. Admittedly most commercials that are filmed are actually shown, but this commercial is a good example of the time, human resources, detail, and money that go into the making of a television commercial.

Advertising is a subject that repels some and fascinates others. Regardless of one's position, it is a system we can hardly ignore. Not only is advertising crucial to the support of mass media in America, it is also crucial to the entire American economy. Thus, we would like to look at the system of advertising in greater detail.

THE ROLE OF ADVERTISING IN THE U.S. ECONOMY

Advertising is not a new idea. Immigrants were lured to America by the idea that the streets were paved with gold—an early example of both advertising and propaganda. Slaves were advertised before the Civil War and advertising brought lonely men on the western frontier and mail-order brides together. Eighteenth and nineteenth century newspapers were filled with advertisements, and late in the nineteenth century, catalogs devoted exclusively to advertising were issued by Montgomery Ward and Sears Roebuck. It was not until the twentieth century, with the advent of broadcasting, that advertising became so widespread and pervasive.

Advertising went hand in hand with the mass production of goods. The mass production and distribution of goods depends on mass consumption, and the best way to encourage mass consumption is by advertising through the mass media, magazines, newspapers, and broadcasting, which can reach hundreds of thousands of people with a single advertising message.

Advertising provides a way to dramatize the marginal difference between products. There is not much difference among the various laundry detergents that are on the market, for example, so the advertiser's job is to create the mythology that one is really better by persuading us that the detergent being advertised will get clothes whiter, works in cold water, and so on. In many cases numerous new goods that we have neither heard of nor knew we needed are advertised. Marshmallows and pop tarts, for example, are hardly necessary to our existence, but advertising makes us believe that they will enhance our lives.

Since advertising helps to distribute mass produced goods and creates a demand for products it is no surprise that it is a major industry. In 1976, an estimated $33 billion was spent on advertising in all media. This was an increase of 18 percent over 1975.[1] Assuming that the country's population is about 215 million, this means that approximately $153 was spent on advertising for every woman, man, and child in America!

Because newspapers run so much local advertising, more dollars are spent on newspaper advertising than on any other kind. Newspapers are followed by television (which has the greatest amount of national advertising), direct mail, radio, and magazines. Table 5-1 shows how the ten largest advertisers spend their money.

Yearly broadcast advertising trends beginning in 1960 show that television has steadily increased the volume of local and national advertising it broadcasts each year. During election years, television shows an unusually sharp advertising increase. Radio advertising trends since 1960 show a sharp increase in local advertising and a moderate increase in spot advertising; network advertising has remained about the same from one year to another.[2] These increases indicate that as long as broadcast expenses do not increase disproportionately, broadcasting is in a very healthy economic state.

ADVERTISING AND THE MASS MEDIA

Advertising plays an important role in mass media industries. Not only does it support most media, it also influences media content. Advertising provides 50 percent of magazine income, 75 percent of newspaper, and almost 100 percent of radio and television.[3]

If any mass medium is going to be successful it must be able to attract an audience that will be attractive to advertisers. This means that mass media must appeal to mass audiences and that if media content gets too specialized it will lose the audience and hence the advertiser.

The ideal media program for an advertiser is one that attracts a large audience, and does not offend potential consumers of the advertiser's product. These unwritten rules mean that when media industries plan their content they must seriously consider the advertisers. A television network can run an occasional documentary critical of American business, but if it does it too often it is out of business in America. A magazine that centers on food must be careful not to be too critical of the food industries because it depends on these very industries for most of its advertising.

When media depend on advertising, there is often a very thin line between media content and media advertising. If a newspaper features a page of recipes and every recipe contains olives, you can be pretty sure that the recipes have come from an olive manufacturer rather than a local food editor who has invented all of these recipes. As any television game show viewer knows, it is im-

TABLE 5-1   Use of Media by Top Ten Advertisers, 1976[1]
(In millions of dollars spent)

Advertiser	Total	Spot TV	Net TV	Spot TV	Net TV	Maga-zines	News-papers	Farm Pub	Out-door	Unmea-sured	Other
1. Proctor & Gamble	445.0	145.75	193.0	.25	—	16.0	7.0	—	—	83.0	—
2. General Motors	287.0	68.7	72.0	20.4	1.7	37.0	38.9	1.9	7.7	23.7	15.0
3. General Foods	274.0	66.3	128.9	.85	.32	20.5	8.1	—	.03	50.0	—
4. Sears Roebuck	245.0	23.3	57.1	3.2	—	18.4	—	—	—	143.0	—
5. Warner Lambert	199.0	26.0	53.79	1.81	5.1	1.5	.45	—	.25	110.0	—
6. Bristol Myers	189.0	17.8	102.7	5.0	—	25.7	1.4	—	—	36.4	—
7. Ford Motor	162.0	28.2	50.0	11.3	2.0	21.3	15.0	2.2	2.0	30.0	—
8. American Home Products	158.0	33.5	97.4	3.6	1.5	6.4	2.2	.40	—	13.0	—
9. Philip Morris	149.0	6.3	24.4	1.8	—	38.9	44.6	—	18.3	14.7	—
10. Mobil Corp.	146.5	26.2	7.6	.40	—	2.6	5.7	1.0	—	103.0	—

1. Local advertising is not included in this chart.

2. Unmeasured includes point of purchase, direct mail, premiums, and various other forms of advertising and sales promotion.

Source: Figures adapted from *Advertising Age*, August 29, 1977.

possible to distinguish media content and advertising. Authors who appear on talk shows to promote their books are providing program content but they are also involved in a good deal of self-advertising.

Although publishers and broadcasters are not advertisers, they interact and interrelate with advertisers in many ways. There are some media industries, such as public broadcasting and movies, that do not depend on advertisers for their support. These industries, however, are exceptions to the media industry structure. In our present system, advertising support is a fact of life for most media.

ADVERTISING AND THE BROADCASTER

The most important difference between the print and the broadcast advertiser is that print sales people sell space and broadcast sales people sell time. Unsold time is worse than unsold space. A magazine or newspaper publisher has the option of increasing or decreasing pages depending on the amount of space sold. In broadcasting, however, there is no way to regain unsold time; time that is not sold is gone forever.

Time is also more interruptive than space to media audiences since print advertisements are more easily ignored than are broadcast commercials. Thus, broadcasters must take great care to integrate advertising with broadcast programming.

The integration of commercials with programming is a very complicated process. Commercial broadcasting is precise in its timing, and programs are timed so exactly that they are not a single second long or short. Most broadcast programs start exactly on the hour or half hour, which enables broadcasters to know how much of the remaining time can be used for commercials.

If all commercials were shown at the beginning or end of programs the job of scheduling would be much easier. But since commercials appear at intervals throughout the program, they must be integrated within it. This calls for cooperation between the programming and advertising departments. Typically, program script writers write material that can be interrupted at points at which viewer interest is high. This suits the needs of the advertisers, who obviously do not want viewers switching channels during the commercials. If the program is good enough the viewer will not take the risk of missing anything and will stay with the program through the commercials.

The practice of integrating advertising and programming results in scripts written in a formula style. If you watch a one hour police drama, you will discover that the main criminal is never captured until the last ten or fifteen minutes of the program. There will be close calls throughout the program to keep you interested but the arrest will not take place until the end.

Another aspect of timing in broadcast programming is the placement of commercials within the broadcast schedule. Commercials are run during programs that have an audience likely to be receptive to the product being advertised. Detergent commercials are often placed with daytime serials because their audiences consist largely of women, the potential buyers of the detergent. Products with a wide consumer appeal are placed in evening programming, which attracts a large general audience.

All networks and stations run material other than commercials with their programs. Virtually all broadcast operations periodically broadcast public service announcements (psa's) which promote nonprofit charitable, community, or government organizations. Stations and networks commonly run promotional advertisements (promos) to advertise their programming. Stations are also required by the FCC to identify their call letters and locations at least hourly.

The style and timing of commercials is controlled by the Federal Trade Commission (FTC), the Federal Communications Commission (FCC), and the National Association of Broadcasters (NAB). The FTC's concern is that commercials are not deceptive or misleading. The FCC requires the advertiser to be identified and requests that broadcasters control the loudness of commercials and distinguish between commercials and program content. The NAB, which has no enforcement power, requests that advertising not exploit children, unfairly attack competitors, or advertise hard liquor, fortune telling, or astrology. They also have guidelines prohibiting the use of medical personnel and the use of children's programming hosts or cartoon characters to advertise products. The most important NAB guidelines involve the length and frequency of commercials and commercial interruptions during broadcast programming.[4] These guidelines are shown in Table 5-2.

The FCC has set no limits on commercials since it approves of the NAB guidelines. Since the NAB has no enforcement power, however, its recommendations depend on the good faith of broadcasters. Although there are many

TABLE 5-2   NAB Guidelines for Commercials

	NO. OF MINUTES PERMITTED/ CLOCK HOUR		INTERRUPTIONS PERMITTED/ CLOCK HOUR	
	Prime Time	*Non-Prime Time*	*Prime Time*	*Non-Prime Time*
Independents	12	16	4*	8*
Network Affiliates	9:30	16	4	8
Children's Programs	12	12	4	8
Children's Weekend Programs	9:30	12	4	8
Radio	18	18		

*Five interruptions per hour are permitted on variety programs broadcast in prime time.

Source: NAB, *The Television Code*, 17th ed. (Washington, D.C.: January, 1974), pp. 14–17; NAB, *The Radio Code*, 18th ed. (Washington, D.C.: January, 1974), p. 15.

broadcasters who conscientiously follow the guidelines on length and frequency of commercials, there are many who do not.

Even though broadcasters follow NAB guidelines for the amount of advertising time and the number of program interruptions, there is an increase in commercials every year. This increase occurs because commercials are getting shorter. Commercials are now generally thirty seconds long rather than the sixty seconds they were during the 1950s and the early 1960s. For example, if a station is permitted to have nine and a half minutes of commercials in a one hour time period, it is possible for the station to run eighteen different thirty-second commercials with the remaining thirty seconds devoted to a station identification and a shorter commercial. Although it is unusual to see eighteen commercials, it is not unusual to see fifteen during a popular prime time program.

The number of commercials run is even greater on independent stations. For example, it is not unusual for WNEW-TV, a New York independent station, to run twelve thirty-second commercials in a program scheduled from 11:00–11:30 P.M.

The commercial chaos is not only the concern of the hapless viewer, it is also a concern to advertisers. They question how any viewer will remember a commercial that is sandwiched in with twelve or fifteen others. Yet there does not seem to be much chance of change. Since the trend is toward shorter commercials, many broadcast and advertising personnel believe that the fifteen-second commercial may become the standard length in the near future.

BUYING AND SELLING ADVERTISING TIME

Any advertiser buying broadcast time must make three basic decisions: the best medium for the product, the best type of advertising arrangement, and the best choice of stations or networks.

The Medium.   One of the most important pieces of information for the advertiser is CPM, or cost per thousand. CPM refers to how much it would cost to reach a thousand people with an advertising message. For example, if it cost you $1000 to produce and to buy time for your message and your message reached 1000 people , your CPM would be $1. Media vary in their CPM. In broadcasting, prime-time network television has the highest CPM while local radio generally has the lowest. The advertiser must also decide which medium is best suited to the product. In broadcasting the choices are television, AM radio, and FM radio.

Advertisers who are interested in reaching a national audience for their product would probably conduct a national television campaign. Virtually every American home has a television set and a commercial on the highest rated program could reach as many as 80 million people. National television is commonly the choice of advertisers who sell products that all Americans use. Year after year, the largest amount of money for national television advertising is for food and food products, toiletries and toilet goods, medicines, automobiles and soaps, cleansers, and polishes.[5]

Radios are found in 99 percent of all American homes. Although national advertisers buy time on network radio, radio time is much more likely to be sold to advertisers who have more specialized products. One of radio's greatest advertising advantages is that it can reach selective audiences. Advertisers reach young listeners on rock stations, older on easy listening stations, people with higher educations on classical music stations, and other listeners on minority and ethnic stations. AM radio also reaches most drivers—in fact the most expensive advertising time on AM radio is when listeners are going to and from work.

When advertisers buy radio and television time they can also choose between national time and local time. The majority of advertising time for television is spot and network, while the majority of time sold for radio is for local advertising.

The second choice the advertiser must make concerns the best type of advertising arrangement. When advertising time is sold on a program, the program is considered to be *sponsored*. If no advertising time is sold the program is called *sustaining*. Some companies will buy all of the available commercial time on a single program. This is called *sole sponsorship* and it is the least common way of buying commercial time since it is so expensive. Generally when it is done, it is done for occasional specials such as the Bell Telephone Hour and the Hallmark Hall of Fame. Rather than engaging in the costly and restrictive practice of sole sponsorship, most advertisers prefer *alternating* or *participating sponsorship*. In alternating sponsorship advertisers agree to buy so many commercials at specific intervals such as every other week. Participating sponsorship, also known as scatter plan buying, occurs when several sponsors buy time in one or more specific programs. The advertiser also has the choice of appearing in the program on a regular or irregular schedule and of buying one commercial or several. Participating sponsorship is the most common way of buying broadcast time.

Rather than buying from the networks, many advertisers prefer to buy *spot time* from individual radio and television stations. This time can be bought in ten, twenty, thirty, and sixty second lengths, but the thirty-second spots are the most common. The main advantage of spot time is that the advertisers can buy into the markets that will do them the most good. Although this option is also available when buying network time, it is even more flexible in spot television. An example of buying spot would be an advertising campaign for grits. Since grits are not widely eaten outside the South, a grits company would probably do best with an advertising spot campaign designed to reach Southern markets. Advertisers are also able to buy the highest rated stations in a market when they buy spot time and if they have a limited budget they only buy into as many markets as they can afford. Thus, spot time is useful to advertisers who have specific needs, who want only the highest rated stations, and who want to reach specialized markets.

The last choice the advertiser makes is the best network or station on which to advertise. To aid in this choice both networks and stations publish *rate cards* that list how much radio and television time costs throughout the broadcast day. Station rate cards also list their coverage area, power, frequency, ownership, and network affiliation. *Standard Rate and Data Service*, a monthly publication, summarizes rate cards for all stations throughout the country.

AM Radio.   The broadcast day in radio is generally sold by time periods. The time that attracts the greatest number of listeners is the most expensive; this is called *drive time*—the hours when people are commuting to and from work. On most stations, drive time is from 6–10 A.M. and afternoon from 4–7 P.M. A commercial bought for a drive time period will appear at any time during that period. The next most expensive time is *daytime*, between 10 A.M. and 4 P.M., followed by *evening time*, from 7 P.M. to midnight, and *nighttime*, from midnight to 6 A.M. All of these time periods are for weekdays; weekend rates are classified separately. Radio usually refers to its time in classes of A, B, C, D, or AAA, AA, or A. Depending on the classification the station uses, A time or AAA time is the most expensive. Radio stations also sell Run-of-Station (ROS) time, which means that the station can run the commercial whenever it pleases. ROS time is always cheapest on a rate card.

FM Radio.   The most expensive time for FM advertising will vary from station to station. Unlike AM, FM stations usually do not consider the category of drive time since many cars still do not have FM radios. Prime time for FM radio varies depending on the type of station and its audience. An FM station in a college town might have its largest number of listeners in the evening, while a beautiful music FM station might have a large daytime audience of homemakers. When a station owner owns an AM/FM combination, time is often sold in an AM/FM package with commercials appearing on both stations. This package is often cheaper than an AM package alone.

Television.   The most expensive television time is *prime time*, which runs from 6 P.M. to 10 P.M. or 7 P.M. to 11 P.M. depending on the part of the country in which you live. Prime time is followed by *fringe time*—the hour or so that occurs before and after prime time. Some stations' rates are based on only two classifications: prime time and nonprime time. Other stations have five or six different rate classifications, all based on the size of the viewing audience at different times.

Networks and stations offer advertisers a variety of discount plans. Some offer *frequency* and *quantity* discounts—the more spots an advertiser buys and the more often they are run, the cheaper they are. Stations also have weekly package plans for a flat rate. These plans offer a number of spots spread over different time periods during the week. In radio, for example, an advertiser might buy a weekly package consisting of one-third drive, one-third daytime, and one-third weekend. In television, the package might consist of a combination of prime time, fringe time, and weekend time. Additionally, a television advertiser often has the choice of buying time that will occur in a fixed place in the broadcast schedule or cheaper time that is *preemptible*. Preemptible time can be changed to a different place in the broadcast schedule based on the need of the station. There are also two different rate classifications for preemptible time. The most expensive can be preempted with two weeks notice; the cheapest can be preempted until broadcast time. As well as permitting advertisers to buy cheaper time, preemptible time allows the station greater flexibility. Time not sold by broadcasters can never be regained. Preemptible time gives broadcasters a greater chance of selling their time, and it also offers them a chance of reselling it if a higher bidder comes along.

These are the most common ways of selling time to radio and television. Additionally, however, some radio and television stations engage in practices known as *tradeouts* and *bartering*. Tradeouts is a practice whereby a station gives a company advertising time in exchange for goods and services. For example, a station airs commercials for a local office supply store and the store in turn gives the station office furniture. This practice, which began in the late 1920s, is still used by some stations. Bartering usually occurs at the national level. In some barter arrangements, advertisers provide shows that are already produced and filled with their own commercials with the exception of some spots that are left empty for the local station to sell. In other barter arrangements, the barter house provides prizes or premiums to the station in return for the right to sell a certain amount of the station's time to barter house customers. Neither tradeouts nor bartering are common to all broadcasters—the practices are more likely to be used by stations that have the lowest ratings in their particular markets.

In some situations, products are advertised by promotional announcements rather than by commercials. This practice is very common in shows that offer prizes. This type of advertising is not free. If the product is cat food, worcestershire sauce, or a similar low price item, the manufacturer donates the produce and pays a $250 promotion fee. Merchandise that costs between $350 and $1500 is traded for time, while the network pays the wholesale price for more costly items. If the network wants to give away a car, for example, it has to pay the dealer's cost. For every ten seconds the car is shown, the car's price is reduced by $300 for a daytime show and by $1400 for an evening show.[6]

ORGANIZATIONS CONCERNED WITH ADVERTISING

Advertising Agencies

There are presently almost 6,000 advertising agencies in the United States. Of this number, 200 are major agencies that together do 70 percent of the total volume of business.[7] The major advertising agencies are located largely in New York City, although they may have numerous branches throughout the United States and the world. They are likely to plan national advertising campaigns, while the smaller agencies are more likely to work on regional and local accounts. Table 5-3 shows the top twenty advertising agencies that advertise on radio or television.

TABLE 5-3 The Top 20 Advertising Agencies and Their Radio–TV Billings, 1976

	Combined broadcast billings	Total TV	TV network	TV spot	Total radio	Radio network	Radio spot	Broadcast share of agency's total billings	Broadcast billings change from 1975	Agency's rank in 1975
1. J. Walter Thompson	$341.1	$321.1	$214.0	$107.1	$26.0	$9.1	$16.9	70.0%	+77.7	1
2. Leo Burnett	302.0	288.0	202.8	85.2	14.0	2.4	11.6	60.0	+60.5	2
3. Young & Rubicam	278.5	248.2	165.0	83.2	30.3	6.0	24.3	60	+67.0	3
4. BBDO	247.0	227.0	144.0	83.0	20.0	3.5	16.5	64	+39.5	4
5. Grey Advertising	199.3	190.8	131.2	59.6	8.5	2.5	6.0	62.9	+59.3	10
6. Ogilvy & Mather	193.0	180.0	120.0	60.0	13.0	5.0	8.0	60	+52.5	9
7. Ted Bates & Co.	187.2	174.3	117.2	57.1	12.9	8.1	4.8	65.8	+32.6	5
8. Benton & Bowles	185.5	178.6	117.8	60.8	6.9	1.0	5.9	78	+51.9	11
9. McCann-Erickson	168.0	145.0	95.0	50.0	23.0	3.0	20.0	65	+24.8	7
10. Dancer-Fitzgerald-Sample	166.0	156.3	86.4	69.9	9.7	1.7	8.0	68.6	+15.5	6
11. Foote, Cone & Belding	143.8	129.5	99.4	30.1	14.3	5.0	9.3	52.4	+2.3	8
12. D'Arcy-MacManus & Masius	138.0	116.0	75.4	40.6	22.0	5.5	16.5	57	+34.7	13
13. Doyle Dane Bernbach	122.0	110.0	70.0	40.0	12.0	2.0	10.0	51.7	+47.0	19
14. Wm. Esty	114.0	102.0	69.0	33.0	12.0	6.0	6.0	65	+7.0	12
15. SSC&B	101.0	93.5	71.2	22.3	7.5	1.0	6.5	69	+5.8	15
16. Wells, Rich, Greene	99.1	85.4	62.7	22.7	13.7	1.7	12.0	51.9	−0.4	14
17. Needham, Harper & Steers	98.6	92.5	69.1	23.4	6.1	1.6	4.5	57.4	+8.3	16
18. Compton	89.0	87.2	64.1	23.1	1.8	0.0	1.8	76.7	+8.3	17
19. Kenyon & Eckhardt	87.9	80.3	44.5	35.8	7.6	2.7	4.9	73.3	+13.2	20
20. Cunningham & Walsh	85.2	81.0	56.7	24.3	4.2	0.4	3.8	68.9	+8.6	18

Source: *Broadcasting*, December 6, 1976, p. 44.

Any large corporation that wishes to advertise is likely to plan its campaign through an advertising agency. Since many of these companies have their own advertising, public relations, and marketing departments, these departments will work hand-in-hand with the agency. If the company has several products, it is likely to work with several agencies, each handling a different product line. These companies pay the advertising agency based on the amount of work done. The negotiated fee is determined by the amount of media time or space that is bought and the cost of producing the print ad or the broadcast commercial.

Large agencies that handle mass media accounts usually break down their staff into the following areas of responsibility: *Management* is responsible for running the agency. Management hires and fires key personnel, develops the agency style, and finds new accounts. *Plans group* consists of department heads who help to set the strategy and direction for various accounts. *Account management* acts as a liaison between the client and the agency and oversees the planning and execution of the advertising campaign. *Creative* consists of the art directors and copywriters who plan the content of the commercials.

Generally the work of producing the final product is done by outside specialists. *Media specialists* plan, select, and buy media time. *Research* tests commercials for their effectiveness. Often the agency hires special research companies for this testing rather than doing it within the agency. *Accounting* handles billing of clients and all other day-to-day financial needs of the agency.[8]

Media Buyers

Media buyers have always been a division of advertising agencies. In the 1960s, however, some of these specialists broke away from the agencies and formed their own companies. Media buyers buy time for the advertiser or the agency and are not involved in the creation of the commercial. They will plan which stations to use, buy the time, and check to see that the commercial is properly run. Media buyers also offer the advantage of buying large blocks of radio-television time at wholesale rates to resell to their clients at a price below the card rates of the individual stations. These services are paid for in two ways—either by a fee based on the total billings of the media buyer's client or on a percentage of the money saved for the client.

Station Representatives

Independent and affiliate stations do not have access to every advertiser who is planning a national spot advertising campaign. Since these advertisers may be anywhere in the country, no station has the time or financial resources to pursue them. To get some of this advertising money, the station signs on with a station representative. These "reps" have offices in major advertising centers

---

DOUBLE YOUR PLEASURE

The music most often heard in the United States is the humble jingle. Although the jingle may be no more than half a minute long the business of getting it recorded and on the air requires many people and months of work.

The advertising agency writes or provides the idea for the lyrics. The lyrics are then sent to a number of musicians who compose the music and make demonstration tapes called "demos." The agency then chooses the best music and pays the musician. Payment for a local or regional commercial generally ranges from $1000 to $2500. A jingle for a national campaign, however, can bring the successful musician anywhere from $20,000 to $40,000. The jingle musicians lose their right to the music once it is sold to the agency. They have the satisfaction of knowing, however, that they have a bigger audience than Brahms, Beethoven or Bach ever did!

Source: James C. Condon, "Those Who Stand (Unnoticed) Behind the Music," *New York Times*, October 31, 1976, F3.

---

and act as sales agents for many different stations. Station representatives provide national advertisers with information about an individual station's coverage, ratings, advertising prices, and availability and give the station they represent advice on advertising rates and programming trends. Station reps are paid by a commission of 5 to 15 percent of the sales they make for the station.

THE PROBLEMS OF ADVERTISING

The role that advertising should play in broadcasting was debated as early as the 1920s. The arguments that were heard then are very similar to those heard today. Critics complain that advertising puts too much emphasis on consumption, that it has an adverse and even dangerous effect on children and adults, and that it uses huge amounts of money that could be better spent for the public good. The general public, however, has a generally favorable attitude toward broadcast advertising. When polled by the Roper Organization, 74 percent of those queried believed that commercials were a fair price to pay to watch television.[9]

At least one group of people, however, is saying that some programming should have no commercials at all. In 1970, Action for Children's Television (ACT) filed a petition with the FCC requesting the commission to ban commercials from children's programming. Although the FCC received 100,000 letters in support of the ACT petition, it decided that a total ban might affect the amount and quality of children's programming and so it decided not to ban commercials.

The complaint most often received about commercials by the Federal Communications Commission in 1973 was that advertising was offensive, in bad taste, or both. The commission also received many complaints about the amount of advertising and false or misleading advertising.[10] These and other issues are often as great a problem to the broadcaster and advertiser as they are to the viewer and listener.

Offensive Commercials

Television writers and members of the broadcast industry are fond of the concept that radio and television are guests in your living room. Broadcasters say that, as guests, they should be on their best behavior—specifically, they should not offend anyone. The main problem is deciding just what is offensive. When broadcasters first advertised a product that offered relief for hemorrhoids, the entire industry was in an uproar. Yet in the early 1970s, when the broadcasters and advertisers decided to advertise sanitary napkins on television, there was very little controversy.

During the late 1960s and 1970s, many of the advertising complaints have come from members of identifiable protest and pressure groups. Many women have been upset by the sexual stereotyping in commercials: to them, portraying women only as housewives or beauty queens is highly offensive. Mexican-Americans, Italians, and blacks have also complained about the stereotyping in advertising and programming. In fact, in the mid-70s many women's groups organized and demonstrated at annual meetings of major advertisers to protest the stereotyping of women in the company's commercials.

Excessive Commercials

Since commercials provide the main support of the broadcast industry they cannot be eliminated completely. The question, then, is how many commercials are needed to support the commercial broadcast system. The answer lies in how well one thinks the industry should be supported and how much profit broadcasters should be permitted to make. If the broadcasters increase their commercials they usually increase their profits.

How many commercials and commercial interruptions should be in a program is somewhat controlled by the guidelines set by the NAB in its radio and television codes. Additionally, the FCC has stated that program-length commercials are not in the public interest. These are programs in which the program content and commercials are so interwoven that the program itself becomes a commercial. For example, a station broadcast a program on Colorado real estate eighteen times over an eight-month period. The station was notified that it was in violation of FCC rules.

False and Misleading Advertising

In the past, many commercials were filled with exaggerated claims. When the consumer movement began to grow, consumer groups pressured the government to put some restraints on advertising. Acting on these complaints against specific advertising, the Federal Trade Commission (FTC) began to use its already existing power to investigate and stop advertising that gave false information or misled the public. FTC powers will be more fully discussed in Chapter 10. Basically, the FTC can order advertisers to provide research that backs up the claims they made in advertising. If a company says, for example, that its insect spray kills roaches, it had better be able to prove it. Additionally, the FTC can force advertisers to go on the air and correct previously misleading commercials in a process known as corrective advertising. This has been done in the past, for example, by advertisers for Profile bread and Ocean Spray cranberry juice.

The main problem with FTC action is that it is so slow that the commercial may be broadcast for several months before the FTC bureaucracy can bring about a change. Also, the FTC can only deal with facts and evidence—proving that a certain toothpaste will not lead to greater popularity is almost impossible.

ADVERTISING AND PROGRAM CONTENT

Perhaps the greatest concern about broadcast advertising is the extent to which it influences the content of television programming. Sometimes advertisers have a direct influence. During the 1976–77 season, several advertisers, including General Motors and Sears, Roebuck, stated that they would no longer advertise on programs with excessive violence.[11] The effects of this decision were apparent in the program schedule for the 1977–78 season: there were no new police/adventure series and several of the existing ones were dropped.

In most cases, however, advertisers have had a more indirect influence on program content. With few exceptions, programs that cannot attract advertisers are never broadcast. Therefore, when networks, stations, and independent producers develop programs and program ideas, they develop those ideas and programs that they hope will attract advertisers. For example, they know that advertisers, particularly in prime time, are interested in audience members between the ages of eighteen and forty-nine because these viewers have the greatest buying power. Producers would never create a program for older people for this time period because it would never sell. Producers also know that advertisers are wary of too much controversy; a "successful" documentary producer, for example, has a better chance of getting a program aired about railroads and rivers than programs about abortion and the Equal Rights Amendment.

Since program producers are well aware of the industry's structure and of the necessity for advertising revenue, they work to fulfill the needs and expectations of the advertisers. In this way advertising influences most of what we see on television.

Advertising Research

No one knows why some commercials work and others do not. Even favorites of the public and prize winners in advertising competitions are sometimes unsuccessful in motivating people to buy the product.

Whether a commercial will work is a subject of great interest to advertisers—especially when they have a quarter of a million dollars invested to make and run the commercial. Specialists in advertising research use a wide variety of techniques to predict the success of a commercial. Some show commercials in theaters to an audience whose members can turn a dial indicating interest or disinterest at any given moment. Other research organizations simply ask their audiences to judge commercials; some make telephone calls to discover which commercials people remember. Still other researchers use sophisticated technology to measure contractions in the pupil of the eye or reactions from muscles and nerves in the fingers.

Although a number of research techniques have been developed, no single one can claim unqualified success. Only two things are known for certain: that although people like the commercial they may never buy the product; and that no amount of advertising can sell a poor product—at least not more than once.

It has often been said that television exists to deliver audiences to national advertisers. By the same token radio could be said to exist for local advertisers. Certainly all roads in the broadcast industry lead back to the advertiser. Stations are valued according to their ability to reach the largest possible audience with the advertiser's message. Programs are geared to those groups that include the most active consumers who are most likely to pay attention to radio and television commercials. Even a good part of the government regulation of broadcasting is concerned with advertising.

No program in radio or television is immune from the need to attract advertisers. Creativity, innovation, and originality are all valued in programming *if* they can attract advertising dollars. Walter Cronkite will be permitted to read the evening news for CBS for as long as advertisers are attracted to his program. As long as commercials on his show sell for top dollar, producer Norman Lear can continue to turn out programs on social themes. The broadcast industry is open to virtually any ideas as long as it is legal and it makes money.

People work in the commercial broadcast industry because it is a very good way of making money. Broadcasting is a major business in the United States and even though it deals with the products of information and entertainment its primary function, as with any other business, is to make money. Virtually all of this money is made from advertising, and without advertising we would not have a broadcast system as we know it today.

NOTES

1. John Blair & Company, *Statistical Trends in Broadcasting*, 13th ed. (New York: Blair Television Blair Radio, 1977), p. 1.

2. Ibid., pp. 12, 25, 40

3. Peter M. Sandman, David M. Rubin, and David B. Sachsman, *Media: An Introductory Analysis of American Mass Communications*, 2nd ed. (Englewood Cliffs, N.J.: Prentice-Hall, 1976), p. 127.

4. NAB, *The Radio Code*, 18th ed. (Washington, D.C.: NAB, January 1974); NAB, *The Television Code*, 17th ed. (Washington, D.C.: NAB, January 1974).

5. *Advertising Age*, February 14, 1977, p. 34.

6. Stephanie Harrington, "To Tell the Truth, The Price is Right," *New York Times Magazine* (August 3, 1975).

7. Otto Kleppner, *Advertising Precedures*, 6th ed. (Englewood Cliffs, N.J.: Prentice-Hall, 1973), p. 571.

8. Elizabeth J. Heighton and Don R. Cunningham, *Advertising in the Broadcast Media* (Belmont, Calif.: Wadsworth, 1976), pp. 43–44.

9. *Broadcasting*, April 4, 1977, p. 42.

10. FCC, *39th Annual Report*, p. 220.

11. Ibid., p. 82.

12. *Advertising Age*, February 14, 1977, p. 1.

Public Broadcasting

6

In the early days of broadcasting, no distinction was made between educational and commercial stations, in fact, in 1925, 171 educational institutions and organizations were operating AM broadcast stations. As interest in broadcasting grew, however, the commercial broadcasters began to take over the educational broadcaster's licenses. Since many educational stations could not afford to run broadcast stations, especially during the depression, they put up little resistance and by 1937 the educators only held licenses for thirty-eight stations.[1]

In deciding on early radio regulation, Congress was uncertain about the role of educational broadcasting. When it debated the revision of the Federal Radio Act of 1927, one of the main considerations was whether a certain percentage of channels should be reserved for educational use. Since no educators insisted on reserved educational channels and since such a reservation would have meant a delay in passing the Communications Act of 1934, Congress passed the Act without reserving educational channels. In 1935 the newly instituted Federal Communications Commission (FCC) stated that the commercial stations would provide enough chances for educational programming and, thus, there was no need for separate educational channels.

The belief that commercial stations would fulfill educational needs proved to be overly idealistic Although stations and networks began by offering educational programming, it soon became a negligible part of their programming schedules. The idea of educational programming remained mainly rhetorical— many commercial broadcasters thought it was a fine idea but few did anything about it.

In 1940 the FCC realized that if educational programming was to exist it would have to create separate educational channels, therefore, the commission created five FM channels for noncommercial educational broadcasting.[2] These five channels were increased to twenty in 1945 when the FCC decided to change FM allocations to a higher band. This was the beginning of a steady growth in educational FM radio as can be seen in Table 6-1. In 1948 the FCC gave even more broadcast power to educational institutions when it authorized low-power ten watt stations for noncommercial use, thereby creating many of the stations that are used by schools, colleges, and universities today.

Although FM broadcasting is now well established, in 1945 the allocation of FM channels to educators was no great advantage to the recipients since few people had FM receivers. Thus, many stations existed for years with very few listeners. When FM began to grow, however, these channels became more valuable. Also, the principle had been established that government should set aside channels for non-commercial broadcasting—a principle that became even more important when it came time to allocate television channels.

TABLE 6-1   Growth of Noncommercial Radio Stations: 1919–1973 (at the End of Calendar Year)

Year		Number of Stations	Major Developments
1919	AM	1	First noncommercial radio station
1925	stations	171	In 1934 Communications Act enacted & FCC established
1937	only	38	
1938		1	First FM broadcasting (experimental)
1939		2	
1940		4	
1941		7	FM broadcasting authorized by FCC
1942		8	
1943		8	
1944		8	
1945		9	FCC reserved 20 FM channels exclusively for noncommercial educational channels
1946		10	
1947		15	
1948		27	FCC authorized low power (10 watt) educational FM broadcasting
1949		48	
1950		73	
1951	FM	85	
1952	stations	98	
1953	on	112	
1954	reserved	122	
1955	channels	123	
1956	only	125	
1957	counted*	141	
1958		151	

When the reserved FM channels became available to the educational broadcasters, it was clear that educational radio might have a future. The National Association of Educational Broadcasters (NAEB) received foundation grants which enabled it to set up a radio tape mail "network" and to make grants for program series. The tape network was particularly useful since it enabled radio stations throughout the country to exchange programs.

Early in the 1950s it was clear that if the educational broadcasters wanted to get into television they were going to have to make some systematic and organized demands. Accordingly, in 1950, the NAEB and the U.S. Office of Education formed the Joint Committee on Educational Television (JCET)—a committee made up of a variety of collegiate and educational associations. The main function of JCET was to represent the interests of the educational broadcasters before the FCC. Although the FCC had already allocated some television channels in 1948, the commission froze further television allocations while it determined the best system of allocations for the entire country (see Chapter 3). The freeze gave educators the opportunity to propose that some of the television channels be reserved for educational use.

Although there was little opposition to reserved educational channels, members of JCET felt that their case would be even stronger if they could show that commercial broadcasters were not providing well-rounded programming. They gathered their evidence by monitoring commercial television offerings in several cities. The New York City viewers alone found that there were 2,970

Year	Number of Stations		Major Developments
1959	162		
1960	175		
1961	194		FCC authorized FM "stereo" broadcasting
1962	209		
1963	237		
1964	255		
1965	268		
1966	296		
1967	326		Public Broadcasting Act enacted and CPB established
1968	362		HEW's Educational Broadcasting Facilities Program applied to public radio
1969	AM & FM stations on both reserved & nonre- served channels	438	(73)**	73 stations qualified, but Community Service Grants were not given until 1970
1970		497	(96)**	
1971		536	(109)**	NPR begins network operations
1972		598	(132)**	
1973		677	(147)**	APRS established

*From 1938 to 1968, the number of stations includes those stations broadcasting on reserved FM channels for educational broadcasting only. Source: Federal Communications, "Educational Television," *Information Bulletin*, April, 1971, p. 5 and CPB.

**Number in parentheses indicates the number of stations qualified for CPB's

Source: S. Young Lee and Ronald J. Pedone, *Status Report on Public Broadcasting*, (Washington, D.C.: U.S. Govt. Printing Office, 1975), p. 8.

acts or threats of television violence in a single week—many of them occurring when children were likely to be watching. Many people were shocked by these results and felt that they clearly indicated the need for an alternate system.[3]

When the freeze ended in 1952, it was clear that JCET had been successful; the FCC set aside 242 channels (80 VHF and 152 UHF) channels for educational use. By 1974 the FCC had revised the Table of Allocations and the number of noncommercial channels was increased to 672 (132 VHF and 540 UHF).[4]

Although the educators had their channels it was again apparent that the FCC had not been overly generous. As in the case of radio, the educational broadcasters were second to the commercial broadcasters. They did not receive channels in several major markets (New York, Philadelphia, Washington) and most of the channels they did receive were UHF—at a time when few persons had UHF receivers. Again, the situation was somewhat improved in later years; some of the educational interests were able to obtain outlets in major markets by buying existing commercial stations, and the receiver situation improved when Congress ruled that after April 30, 1964 all new television receivers must be equipped to receive both VHF and UHF.

Although the allocation of reserved channels had been a major hurdle for educational broadcasting, there were many more problems to be solved. The major issue was money to finance the new broadcast operations. Many educational institutions helped to support their own broadcast systems, but the principle source of funding was the Ford Foundation.

The Ford Foundation played a key role in educational broadcasting in broadcasting's earliest days by providing funding both for stations and programs. The Foundation also provided a $1 million grant to establish the first television mail network. The "network," the Educational Television and Radio Center (ETRC) located in Ann Arbor, Michigan, duplicated and distributed programs to stations across the nation. In 1959 ETRC moved to New York, and in 1963 changed its name to National Educational Television (NET). At this point NET also changed its direction; it dropped its distribution function and began to produce programs of its own with additional funding from the Ford Foundation.[5] NET programming did much to advance the prestige and influence of educational television.

Although the Ford Foundation funding was invaluable to the development of educational television it was clear that the Ford Foundation—even when its resources were combined with other public and private sources—could not continue to support educational broadcasting indefinitely.

In 1962 the federal government began to take on some of the responsibility for funding with the Educational Television Facilities Act. This Act authorized the Department of Health, Education, and Welfare to provide federal funding to applicants to construct and expand broadcast facilities. During this period the number of noncommercial television stations either going on the air or under construction increased from 76 to 239. In the five years that radio stations were eligible for grants, they received forty grants to construct new stations and sixty-four grants to expand existing ones.[6] The Educational Facilities

Act was a tremendous incentive to the development of noncommercial broadcasting. In a sense, however, the Act created stations that were "all dressed up with no place to go." Stations had new buildings, new studios, and new equipment but the Act provided little money for programming. Another problem was that there was still no interconnection between NET stations.

In 1967, a solution to the continuing problem of funding for educational broadcasting was tackled by the Carnegie Foundation. The Foundation set up a committee known as the Carnegie Commission on Educational Television. The Commission, made up of representatives of government, business, the broadcast industry, and education, was given the responsibility of making a comprehensive study of the future of educational television, and of making recommendations to President Lyndon B. Johnson.

After studying the problem the Commission recommended, in 1967, that federal, state, and local government should provide facilities and adequate support for educational television and that Congress should establish a nonprofit, nongovernmental corporation to oversee the operation.

In February of 1967, President Johnson requested specific legislation based on the Commission's recommendations. During the same year, Congress passed the Public Broadcasting Act of 1967, the Act then becoming part of the Communications Act of 1934.

As well as extending the Educational Facilities legislation for another three years, the Public Broadcasting Act authorized the establishment of the Corporation for Public Broadcasting (CPB). CPB was set up as a nonprofit, nonpolitical corporation with a Board of Directors consisting of fifteen members appointed by the President of the United States. The act stipulated that no more than eight members could be from one political party and that the term of office would be six years. Congress also prohibited CPB, and indeed all noncommercial stations, from editorializing or supporting or opposing any political candidate.[7]

The Act states that CPB responsibilities are to help develop programs, obtain grants from private and governmental agencies, to distribute these grants to stations for program production and services, and to set up the interconnection between stations.

Once CPB was established and funded, one of its most important jobs was to set up the interconnection, or network. To this end CPB established and funded the Public Broadcasting Service (PBS) to provide an interconnection for television, and a few years later it created National Public Radio (NPR), an interconnection for radio. Once PBS was established, there was no longer a reason to operate the NET mail network. Consequently, NET merged with the public television channel, WNDT in New York City, and it took WNET as its new call letters.

Both the Public Broadcasting Act of 1967 and the Educational Facilities Act of 1962 were responsible for many new stations going on the air. As can be seen by Table 6-2, 1967 began a major growth period for public television, although it was not long before the public broadcasting system encountered some major problems. The first big crisis came in 1972 for the Corporation for Public

Broadcasting. Despite overwhelming Congressional support for CPB appropriations, Richard M. Nixon, then president, vetoed the bill. Basically Nixon had two objections to CPB: he felt that it was supporting news and public affairs programs that were biased, and that it was becoming too powerful and centralized. Nixon believed that CPB was creating a fourth network whose power was centered in the Eastern cities—particularly New York and Washington. Instead he favored grassroots participation; a system in which all local stations would participate in the programming and decision-making process.

Some who were involved in public broadcasting believed that Nixon's attack, especially in reference to CPB centralization, was justified. The public broadcasters had already been divided over whether public broadcasting should be centralized or based more on local and regional needs.

There was also a power struggle between CPB and PBS. Although PBS had originally been established to provide the interconnection, it was also making important decisions about scheduling and programming that, in the opinion of CPB, overstepped PBS responsibilities. Finally a compromise was worked out

TABLE 6-2   Growth of Public Television Licensees and Stations: 1953–1973 (at the End of Calendar Year)

Year	Number of Licensees	NUMBER OF STATIONS			Major Developments
		Total	VHF	UHF	
1953	1	1	1	0	The first noncommercial television
1954	10	10	8	2	station
1955	16	17	13	4	
1956	19	21	17	4	
1957	25	27	22	5	
1958	33	35	28	7	
1959	41	44	34	10	
1960	48	51	37	14	
1961	57	62	44	18	
1962	68	75	50	25	HEW's Educational Broadcasting
1963	73	84	53	31	Facilities Program established
1964	85	101	61	40	All television channel receiver
1965	93	114	65	49	legislation in effect
1966	99	126	71	55	
1967	111	152	75	77	Public Broadcasting Act enacted
1968	117	180	79	101	CPB established
1969	124*	189	82	107	CPB in operation
1970	130*	200	87	113	PBS begins operation
1971	138*	216	92	124	
1972	147*	233	94	139	
1973	152*	242	93	149	New PBS emerged

*Includes stations operated independently from the parent licensees' operations: one such station for 1969 through 1972 and four for 1973.

Source: S. Young Lee and Ronald J. Pedone, *Status Report on Public Broadcasting*, (Washington, D.C.: U.S. Government Printing Office, 1975), p. 13.

in 1973: PBS and CPB reached an agreement that provided PBS with the right to choose and schedule programs and CPB with the right to oversee and object to PBS choices.

Although there was never a very specific decision made as to whether public broadcasting would be national or local, a compromise was reached giving local stations a greater role in providing and choosing programs than they had previously had. The issue of bias in news and public affairs programming was not so easily solved. The first president of CPB, John W. Macy, had resigned in protest because of the Nixon administration's interference with programming. Thus, it became clear that public broadcasting was vulnerable to political pressure and, consequently, the public broadcasters reduced the number and intensity of controversial news and public affairs programs.

Although many stations, which had been previously considered educational, became public broadcasting stations, the education designation did not entirely disappear. However, the term "educational" is more useful to the FCC than it is to the general public.

The numerous noncommercial radio stations that are not part of public broadcasting bear very little resemblance to each other. They range in power from low power FM stations to stations with power equivalent to commercial FM stations. Programming formats range from Top 40 to classical music. Economic support for educational radio ranges from colleges, which pay the entire bill, to municipal, state, or local sources. There are also noncommercial stations that are supported by listeners and foundations. The Pacifica Foundation is an example of a group that runs radio stations of this nature.

The only noncommercial educational stations that share common programming and economic characteristics are part of the public broadcasting system. We will limit our discussion to the public television stations that are affiliated with PBS, and the public radio stations that are affiliated with NPR, and the operations and policies of these networks and stations.

THE ECONOMICS OF PUBLIC BROADCASTING

When radio and television frequencies were reserved for educational use the FCC stipulated that stations that used these frequencies must be run as noncommercial operations. This meant that noncommercial stations had to find an alternative source of money to keep the system in operation.

Although the Public Broadcasting Act of 1967 provided federal funding, the support was always inadequate for all the needs of public broadcasting. In the beginning, the federal government paid almost half of the funding for organizations such as CPB, PBS, and NPR, while it paid less than 10 percent of the cost of running individual radio and television stations.[8] Obviously then, public broadcasting funding depends on several agencies and institutions in addition

TABLE 6-3   Percentage of Cash Income of
Public Television Licensees by Source, 1974

Intra-Industry (incl. CPB)	12%
Federal	6
Local Boards of Education	10
Local Government	2
State Boards of Education	14
State Government	17
Universities	8
Foundations	7
Business & Industry	5
Subscriptions	11
Auctions	4
Other	4

Source: CPB Report, December 15, 1975

to the federal government. In Table 6-3 we can see the sources of cash income for public television licensees for 1974. In the following section we will examine these funding categories in greater detail.

Federal Funding

The Corporation for Public Broadcasting (CPB).   When Congress makes its yearly appropriation to public broadcasting the money goes to CPB. CPB then channels this funding to the various institutions and organizations involved in public broadcasting. A portion goes to the television network, PBS, to be used for the interconnection between stations and to assist in program scheduling. The radio network, NPR, receives funding for interconnection, programming, and promotion.

CPB also distributes a substantial portion of the money to individual radio and television stations in the form of Community Service Grants. Stations are free to use these grants as they please and commonly use them to produce or purchase programming.

Another portion of the CPB money goes for program development. CPB will fund pilot programs and program series intended for national distribution for a two year period. If producers want to continue their program beyond this point they must find other funding sources. The remainder of CPB money is used to support a research office and to maintain its own offices and staff.

Federal Grants.   As well as the annual congressional appropriations which are made to CPB, the federal government has made program funding available through various government agencies. Agencies such as the National Endowment for the Humanities and the National Endowment for the Arts have supported a good deal of cultural public television programming. The Children's Television Workshop, which produces "Sesame Street" and "The Electric

Company," has received a portion of their funding from the U.S. Office of Education.

State and Local Government Funding

The single greatest source of money for public broadcasting comes from state government. States have a variety of ways of supporting public broadcasting. Some states fund a state educational network or individual stations with money appropriated directly by the state legislature. Other states channel money to public broadcasting through the state board of education. States also support colleges and universities—many of which run public broadcasting stations.

Many local schools and local governments also contribute to the support of public broadcasting. Local schools are most likely to give financial support to stations when the station's programming is used in the classroom for instructional purposes.

PROFILE OF A LOCAL PUBLIC TELEVISION STATION

Although there is no typical public television station, WITF-TV is a station that represents some of the triumphs and problems of public broadcasting. WITF is owned and operated by the South Central Educational Broadcasting Council. Its signal reaches a 10-county area of South Central Pennsylvania and it is a member of the Pennsylvania Public Television Network, which serves the entire state.

WITF began operations in 1964 with a budget of a quarter of a million dollars. By 1975 their yearly budget exceeded $1 million. Twenty-eight percent of their budget for the 1975–76 season came from the state network, which is funded by the state legislature. Twenty-one percent came from grants and foundations, 18 percent from fund raising efforts, 15 percent from the school district, 11 percent from CPB, and 7 percent from the Pennsylvania Department of Education.

WITF has been successful in producing programs that have been carried on the PBS interconnection. Although this is expected from larger stations in cities such as New York and San Francisco, it is not very common for small and medium-market stations. Since its beginning WITF has received program grants from the National Endowments for the Arts and Humanities, the Ford Foundation, and CPB, just to name a few.

The annual budget of WITF would not begin to pay for a single evening of commercial network prime time programming. Yet it is stations such as WITF that are able to provide both innovative and creative programming—even on a very limited budget.

Foundations

Several private foundations have supported both educational and public broadcasting throughout the years. Their money has been used for programming, equipment and facilities, and research. Substantial contributions have come from the Rockefeller, Carnegie, and Markle Foundations. The greatest contributor of all has been the Ford Foundation—contributing over $268 million to educational broadcasting between 1951 and 1973.[9]

Foundation funding, however, may be less of a factor in the future support of public broadcasting. Between 1973 and 1974 foundation grants to public television decreased by 14.5 percent. This was the only funding category to decrease during this time period.[10]

Corporate Underwriting

Several private corporations have taken on the responsibility of underwriting public television programs. Notable programs made possible by partial or total corporate underwriting are "Upstairs, Downstairs" and "The Adams Chronicles."

Programming that is underwritten by corporations is inexpensive for the local station since the station only has to pay a portion of the cost of acquiring the program from the network. Consequently, practically all PBS stations carry these programs. Although underwriting corporations get only a brief line of credit, they generally gain a great deal in terms of public relations.

Although there has been little abuse of corporate underwriting there is concern that corporate influence may interfere with program content. PBS has developed guidelines for private underwriters that are designed to limit their control over programming.

WHO WATCHES PUBLIC TELEVISION?

According to a 1975 Roper study, when the public television audience is compared to the population at large, the PTV viewer is:
—more likely to have a college education and income over $15,000
—more likely to live in the Northeast, Midwest, or West
—slightly more liberal in politics
—more likely to be female (55 percent)
—likely to be between 22 and 44 (53 percent)
—overwhelmingly likely to be white (93 percent).

Source: *CPB Report*, February 2, 1976

Individual Station Fund Raising

As any public broadcast viewer or listener knows, stations engage in a good deal of individual fundraising. Most stations have at least one full time person and many volunteers whose sole responsibility is to promote the station and raise money. This effort pays off for the station—a good fund raiser may raise anywhere from fifteen to thirty percent of the station's total budget.

The major fund raising effort usually comes from membership drives during which the station tries to secure commitments from members of the viewing or listening audience for annual pledges of money. In return for a pledge, members have a sense of direct participation in station affairs and, in most cases, they also receive a monthly program guide. Many stations also run a successful yearly auction. Local merchants donate merchandise throughout the year and the stations take a few days of prime time programming to auction the merchandise to its viewers and listeners.

Most stations also take on the responsibility of raising programming money by applying for grants to produce programming. These grant proposals are sent to a variety of organization including CPB, private foundations, and business and industry.

PROGRAM SOURCES AND FUNDING

As we have seen, public broadcasting depends on a variety of sources for funding. Table 6-4 shows how public television stations use their money. Programming, combined with the interrelated technical and production categories, uses almost two-thirds of the total budget. Therefore, most of the focus of fund raising is for programming.

Program funding comes from federal, state, and local government; business and industry; private foundations; and public broadcasting audiences. Sometimes a single source will fund an entire program series. However, it is much

TABLE 6-4 Operating Costs of Public Television Licensees, by Percentage, 1974

Technical	23%
Programming	11
Production	29
Instructional & School Services	6
Development and Fund Raising	6
Promotion	3
Training & Personnel	1
General and Administrative	16
Other	5

Source: CPB Report, December 15, 1975

TABLE 6-5 Program Sources for Public
Television, 1974 by Percentages

PBS Interconnection	46%
Local	17
Other Interconnection	10
Other sources	27

Source: CPB Report, December 15, 1975

more characteristic for program funding for a series to depend on several sources. In the discussion that follows we will describe some of the principle types of arrangements that public broadcasting uses to produce and acquire programs. A breakdown of the sources of programming to individual stations can be seen in Table 6-5.

Programs Carried on the PBS Interconnection

The Station Program Cooperative (SPC).   Unlike the commercial affiliates who depend on the networks to make programming choices, public television stations have a voice in network decision making about programming. This station involvement began in 1974 when CPB and the Ford Foundation provided funding to PBS to set up and administer the Station Program Cooperative (SPC).

The Cooperative offers all public television stations the opportunity to buy and submit television programs. Any station that is interested in producing a program or program series submits a proposal to the Cooperative. PBS puts these proposals into a catalog that is circulated to all member stations. Stations then indicate the programs in which they are interested. The programs in which stations have no interest are eliminated and then stations make their purchases from the remaining programs.

The money that a station uses to acquire a program series must come out of its own budget. Some stations depend almost entirely on their CPB Community Service Grants to buy programming. Other stations with aggressive fund raising departments will be able to use some of this income to buy programs. A smaller station with limited funds might only be able to afford the cheaper series.

At the time of this writing, the Cooperative is partially subsidized by CPB and the Ford Foundation. This means that these two organizations pay a portion of the production costs and the stations that desire the program series divide the remaining costs of production among themselves. However, both Ford and CPB plan to eventually phase themselves out of the Cooperative, which means that programming offerings will cost more to the individual television stations. CPB plans to offset this increased cost to stations by offering stations larger community service grants.

Programs do not have to be chosen by all stations (or even a majority) to be scheduled by PBS. The more stations that choose a program the lower the price since the production costs are then divided among a larger number of stations. If only a few stations choose an expensive program the corresponding price might be so high that stations would eventually decide that the program would not fit into their budgets. The stations would decide not to carry the program and it would, therefore, be dropped by the Cooperative.

The Cooperative is not without critics. Supporters believe that this system enables local stations to better serve community needs and that the system encourages local decision making. Critics believe that cheap programming will drive out expensive programming. For example, it is cheaper to produce exercise and cooking shows than it is to produce documentaries and operas. Another criticism is that controversial public affairs programming will not fare well when put into the marketplace and left to individual station determination. Others maintain that stations are more willing to puchase programs produced by bigger, well-known stations in urban centers, whereas they are afraid to risk programs from smaller, lesser-known stations. Regardless of one's position, the Cooperative has been a way to decentralize programming and it will probably continue to be the system by which most of the programming is chosen to be carried.

Individual Station Productions.   Not all stations depend on the Cooperative to get their programs on the network. Stations will seek funding for a program or program series that they want to produce. A station will make a direct approach to a funding group and will ask that group to underwrite the cost of producing the program. Generally, only the larger stations have the resources to develop this type of funding since it requires a good deal of time in making personal contacts and writing program proposal grants.

A program that exemplifies this kind of funding was "The Adams Chronicles," a series that was first run in the 1976 season. The program was produced by WNET in New York. Since the series was so expensive, $2 million dollars for 13 programs, the funding came from a variety of sources: the National Endowment for the Humanities (federal government), the Andrew W. Mellon Foundation (private foundation), and the Atlantic-Richfield Company (business-industry). Since the production cost was funded by these sources, individual stations only had to pay the cost of having the program distributed to their station.

Outside Program Sources.   Some programs are produced by organizations other than public broadcasting stations. The Children's Television Workshop (CTW), a nonprofit corporation, produced "Sesame Street" and "The Electric Company." Part of the program's costs are paid by CPB and the U.S. Office of Education. CTW also gets money by selling its programs abroad and by offering its name and characters to businesses that sell articles based on the programs.

John Adams (George Grizzard) is sworn in as the second President of the United States in the sixth chapter of "The Adams Chronicles," shown in 1976 over the Public Broadcasting Service. The series of thirteen weekly one-hour programs tracing 150 years and four generations in the lives of the Adams family was produced by WNET/13-New York. (Photo by Carl Samrock.)

The remainder of the production cost is picked up by individual stations, which pay for the program through the Station Program Cooperative. Since the program is partially subsidized by the government and by income generated by CTW, the cost to the individual station is lower than if it had to pay the total production cost.

PBS also has an underwriting office, the purpose of which is to persuade corporations and foundations to underwrite the cost of programs. Sometimes PBS is underwriting for already existing series that have been aired elsewhere. An example of this is "Upstairs, Downstairs," which came from the British Broadcasting Corporation. In the case of this program, Mobil Oil was the underwriter.

Locally Produced Programs

Every public television station produces programs that are intended for local audiences and are not carried on the PBS interconnection. Many stations do a great deal of programming in the area of public affairs. These programs typically deal with problems of their local communities. Most stations also devote programming time to local cultural activities such as dance, art, and music. Depending on the station's money and resources, the programs range from talk shows, in which participants sit and discuss community problems and activities, to documentaries or the actual filming of local events.

Stations that are run or supported by educational organizations and institutions often produce instructional programming designed for classroom use. When school is in session, public television stations devote an average of 30 percent of their total broadcast hours to classrom programming.[11] Some of this programming is locally produced, while some of it comes from regional or national sources.

Regional Networks

There are several regional educational networks in the United States. The Eastern states, for example, are covered by a network called the Eastern Educational Television Network. Stations that are in the states covered by these networks acquire programs collectively, with each station paying a portion of the cost. Individual stations within the network range also produce programs that are shown on the regional network.

Some states also have networks and, as with the regional networks, the stations in the state will produce or purchase programs intended for use within the state.

Other Program Sources

There are hundreds of organizations that produce programs that public broadcasting stations can rent or show for free. Many of the programs that are available for commercial stations are also available to public television stations—the difference being that public television stations cannot insert commercials. In addition to the commercial sources, public television stations also use organizations that produce educational programming. There are many program choices, ranging from the types of films that are shown in classrooms to programs that are produced specifically for instructional television use.

National Public Radio

Unlike the public television network, National Public Radio produces a good deal of its own programming. In 1974 it supplied about forty hours of live programming a week to its member stations. As with the television network, member stations supply programming to public radio. Additionally, NPR gets programming from freelance producers.

Most of the funding for public radio comes from CPB and from sources generated by individual stations. There is also a certain amount of underwriting for programming but it is not as common as it is for public television. Some program underwriters, for radio have included Xerox, the Foreign Policy Association, and *Psychology Today*.

THE PUBLIC RADIO STATIONS

In 1975 there were 177 public radio stations that covered about 60 percent of the United States. The audience for public radio is smaller than the audience for public television since there are no public radio stations in 34 of the 100 largest population areas.

In 1974 the average public radio station broadcast 121.7 hours weekly. Almost 65 percent of this was locally produced, 11 percent came from the interconnection, and the remainder came from other sources. Most of the local stations had music as their dominant programming. Of the total broadcast music hours programmed, classical music accounted for 61 percent. The next highest music category was jazz with 9.9 percent followed by several other conventional music formats.

The number of NPR stations is limited since stations must meet qualifications in staff, facilities, programming, power, and hours of operation before they become eligible for affiliation.

Source: CPB Report, December 21, 1975; CPB Report, February 16, 1976

THE DIVERSITY OF PUBLIC BROADCAST PROGRAMMING

Throughout its short history, public broadcasting has offered great diversity and richness in programming. Programs such as "Sesame Street," "Upstairs, Downstairs," and "The Adams Chronicles" are examples of programs that have both delighted and stimulated viewers.

Public television has also made it possible for viewers outside of major cities to see some of the great performers from cultural institutions such as the American Ballet Theatre and the Metropolitan Opera. Film lovers have been able to watch films by the major international film directors—an opportunity that is available in few American cities.

As well as offering a great variety of classical music programming, public radio has also been active in generating news and public affairs programming. While most radio stations depend on the wire services for their news, NPR has often ventured into the area of investigative reporting and has often been the first news organization to discover important stories.

Although public broadcasting has been plagued by internal squabbles, inadequate funding, and governmental pressures, it has been able to present some of the most innovative programming in American broadcasting. For many people, public broadcasting often achieves broadcasting's great potential.

PROBLEMS FACING PUBLIC BROADCASTING

The single greatest problem that public broadcasters face is finding enough money to operate. Although public broadcasting does not have the commercial problem of attracting huge audiences for advertisers, the public broadcaster's preoccupation with money is just as intense as it is in the world of commercial broadcasting.

When public broadcasting first started it appeared that federal funding would solve a good many of its financial problems. In reality, however, the federal government pays only a small proportion of the total operating cost of public broadcasting.

The Public Broadcasting Financing Act of 1975 authorized funding for public broadcasting for the next five years. The Act provides a maximum of $88 million in 1976, which will increase to a maximum of $160 million in 1980. However, the Act does not guarantee that the maximum will be appropriated—the actual amount is ultimately determined by the House and Senate Appropriations Committee and it could be much lower than the maximum authorized funding. Further, the Act only provides funding on a matching basis; that is, public broadcasting must raise $2.50 from nonfederal sources in order to get $1.00 of federal funding. In other words, public broadcasting does not get any federal money unless it can produce nonfederal dollars at a 2.5:1 ration.[12]

This type of funding places a good deal of responsibility both on PBS and on the individual station. PBS must search for program underwriters while local stations must continue to cultivate underwriters, state and local government, and audience support. Unless the public broadcasting system concentrates on funding by aggressively seeking funding sources it will be in serious trouble.

As well as facing economic problems, public broadcasting is also vulnerable to political pressures. Politics and economics are closely related, for those who pay the bills are likely to call for specific programming politics. During the Nixon administration there was strong feeling against the federal government's support of public affairs programming—particularly when it was unfavorable to the Administration. In order for public broadcasting to get its annual appropriation it had to "reform" by presenting fewer hours of both controversial and non-controversial public affairs programming. Congress has also influenced programming by granting funding on an annual basis. Public broadcasters have believed that if they presented programming that was "acceptable" to Congress, Congress would reward them with increased yearly appropriations. State governments have also used their influence. Any number of governors and state legislators have made strong recommendations about what their stations should program.

Public broadcasters have long argued for long-range federal funding—a system by which public broadcasting would be funded for several years rather than on a year-to-year basis. The broadcasters argue that long-range funding would enable them to engage in long-term planning and that long-range funding would make the system less vulnerable to yearly political pressures. The

Public Broadcasting Financing Act of 1975 provided such funding for the first time. The Act authorized the system to be funded for the 1976, 1977, and 1978 seasons. Although it is still too early to tell what the impact of this funding might be, it is possible that programming might be less vulnerable to federal government pressure because of this Act.

The public broadcast system does not have to remain poor; numerous people and organizations have come up with creative ideas for means of support. The Carnegie Commission recommended that the system be supported by an excise tax. Under this system everyone would pay a yearly excise tax on their radio and television sets (much in the same way that one pays for the license plate on a car) and this money would be used to support the public broadcast system. Others have suggested that since business and industry already underwrite program costs it is hypocritical to call the system noncommercial. These people recommend that public broadcasting carry commercials, but only at the end of programs and with the stipulation that advertisers could not sponsor specific programs—they could only buy time.

Both of these systems of support have been used successfully to support European systems of broadcasting. Why, then, have they never been seriously considered as a form of support for American public broadcasting? Although the answer to this question is not clear cut, we can offer some speculative answers. Basically we believe that it is in the interest of both Congress and commercial broadcasters to keep the public broadcasting system poor. As we have already pointed out, if the system is dependent on Congress for a portion of its funding, the system is likely to come up with programming that will be acceptable to Congress. If the system were largely self-sufficient, it would be free to program as it wished.

As far as the commercial broadcasters are concerned, they do not want a fourth network that would compete either for audience or for advertising dollars. As long as public broadcasting offers programming that only reaches a few million people it does not provide any real competition for commercial broadcasters. Therefore, it is in the interest of commercial broadcasters to oppose additional funding. If it appears that public broadcasting might become too powerful, we suspect that commercial broadcasters would be the first to protest.

Although the public broadcasting system has only existed since 1967, it is already locked into a system that resists reform or change. Public broadcasting is not likely to disappear—it is too firmly established. Its future economic health, however, will depend on how well it can appease various political and economic sources that supply its funding.

NOTES

1.   S. Young Lee and Ronald J. Pedone, *Status Report on Public Broadcasting* (Washington: U.S. Government Printing Office, 1975) p. 7.

2. Edwin G. Krasnow and Lawrence D. Longley, *The Politics of Broadcast Regulation* (New York: St. Martin's Press, 1973), p. 86.

3. Erik Barnouw, *The Golden Web* (New York: Oxford University Press, 1968), p. 294.

4. Lee and Pedone, p. 11.

5. Lee and Pedone, pp. 14, 16.

6. Lee and Pedone, p. 17.

7. Communications Act of 1934, Section 399.

8. Lee and Pedone, pp. 22, 26.

9. Lee and Pedone, p. 15.

10. *CPB Report*, December 15, 1975.

11. *CPB Report*, December 15, 1975.

12. *CPB Report*, February 16, 1976.

Ratings

7

In preparation for a recent television season, CBS contracted for one of the most lavish and expensive television series of all time, "Beacon Hill." The new series, unabashedly modeled after the popular BBC series "Upstairs, Downstairs," was the fictional story of the Lassiter's, a wealthy family living in Boston during the 1920s. CBS spared no expense in producing the series: extensive research was conducted to guide the re-creation of the 1920s settings, some of Broadway's best actors and actresses were hired to play the roles, and the program was shot in a variety of exterior and interior settings. As one network executive put it, "Beacon Hill" was "the Tiffany of TV series."[1]

Even though CBS lavished money and attention on the series, it also risked a great deal by producing the program, for "Beacon Hill" was decidedly uncharacteristic of the typical television programming of police adventure and situation comedy. CBS could, however, afford to take this risk because for the past nineteen television seasons it had been the number one network in national ratings—meaning that it attracted more viewers than any other network. Even though CBS was number one, it was still concerned about "Beacon Hill's" ability to attract a large enough audience to keep the series going. The network developed several strategies: more money was used to promote the series than for any other program, the series was premiered a week earlier than its competitors, and the premiere was scheduled opposite the low-rated NBC baseball night.

After the premiere it looked as though the strategy had been successful, for according to the Nielsen ratings, the premiere program attracted a sizeable audience. By the second week the series' ratings were down, and in the third week the program was in third place—far behind ABC and NBC programs. During the fourth week the program increased its ratings a little and the producers and network executives were a little more hopeful. By the fifth week, however, catastrophe struck: not only was "Beacon Hill" in third place— so was CBS! When CBS again appeared in third place for the sixth week, it was clear that there was no time left for sentiment. CBS had to drop all of the poorly rated programs, and clearly "Beacon Hill" was one of those that had to go.

After the demise of "Beacon Hill" there was speculation about what went wrong. NBC claimed it had always known that the series would never attract audiences. The producer and the writer of "Beacon Hill" blamed each other and some industry personnel and television critics blamed the American viewer for not having enough taste to appreciate the program.[2]

The failure of "Beacon Hill" illustrates the nature of the American commercial television business. The series disappeared, as have countless other series, because it could not attract a large enough audience. Audience size is measured by the rating services, and since programs succeed or fail on the basis of their ratings, understanding the rating system is an essential element in understanding American broadcasting.

THE REASONS FOR RATINGS

When advertisers decide to commit thousands of dollars to buying broadcast time for the commercials, the first question they are likely to ask is "who is watching or listening to the show or the station?" Answers to this question are provided by the rating services—companies that are set up to measure audience size and composition. Advertisers, stations, and networks subscribe to the rating services and make advertising and programming choices based on the data they receive.

Since broadcasters depend on advertising revenues for their support, ratings are essential to their economic survival. If the number of potential consumers for a particular program is not satisfactory, the advertiser will switch support to another network or station.

Ratings also work in favor of a station or network. Since advertisers prefer to have their commercials appear on the highest-rated programs, the stations with the best ratings will usually get the best prices for the sale of broadcast time. Thus, broadcasters use ratings to "sell" their stations and networks to advertising clients.

The ratings not only offer information about audience size, but they also provide information about audience composition—called *demographics*, or "demos." This demographic data, which typically gives information about the age and sex of the viewers, is crucial to the advertisers so that they can identify the target audiences for their products. For example, demographics (and common sense) tell the advertiser that the audience for Saturday morning cartoons is predominantly children. Since children are a logical target audience for products such as toys or chewing gum, manufacturers of these products buy Saturday morning time to advertise.

Thus, we can see that as well as providing information about audience size and composition, the ratings services tell the stations and networks how well their programs are doing in attracting the right kinds of audiences. Since this information is only available through the rating services, these services are vital to the economic well-being of the commercial broadcast industry.

CONDUCTING RATINGS RESEARCH

Market Areas

If all broadcast advertising and programming was intended for a national audience, the rating services' problems of measuring audience size and composition would be greatly reduced. Because much advertising is spot or local, however, and since no station has a signal that reaches the entire country, the

TABLE 7-1   The Top 50 Television Markets, as Ranked by the American Research Bureau

Ranking	Market
1	New York, NY
2	Los Angeles, CA
3	Chicago, IL
4	Philadelphia, PA
5	San Francisco, CA
6	Boston, MA
7	Detroit, MI
8	Washington, DC
9	Cleveland, OH
10	Dallas-Fort Worth, TX
11	Pittsburgh, PA
12	Houston, TX
13	Minneapolis-St. Paul, MN
14	Miami, FL
15	St. Louis, MO
16	Atlanta, GA
17	Tampa-St. Petersburg, FL
18	Seattle-Tacoma, WA
19	Indianapolis, IN
20	Baltimore, MD
21	Milwaukee, WI
22	Hartford-New Haven, CT
23	Denver, CO
24	Sacramento-Stockton, CA
25	Portland, OR
26	Kansas City, MO

rating services must also provide audience information about specific areas of the country.

In order to provide information about local, regional, and national audiences, the rating services have divided the entire country into market areas, that is, areas that are reached by radio and television signals. They have done this by taking all of the 3,141 counties in the United States and grouping them into 209 market areas. Where the population is dense, such as in the New York area, there will be only a few counties in the market area; where the population is sparse, the market area will contain many counties. Each county, however, is assigned to only one market area.

Two rating services, Arbitron and Nielsen, originated this system of defining market areas according to counties. Arbitron's market areas, the most widely used by the industry, are called "areas of dominant influence" (ADI). Nielsen's are called "designated market areas" (DMA).

Both Nielsen and Arbitron assign rankings to the designated market areas. The markets that are ranked highest are those which have the greatest number of households with working television sets. In Table 7-1, Arbitron identifies the

Ranking	Market
27	Cincinnati, OH
28	Buffalo, NY
29	San Diego, CA
30	Providence, RI
31	Nashville, TN
32	Phoenix, AZ
33	Charlotte, NC
34	Columbus, OH
35	Memphis, TN
36	Greenville-Spartanburg-Ashville, SC/NC
37	Oklahoma City, OK
38	New Orleans, LA
39	Louisville, KY
40	Orlando-Daytona Beach, FL
41	Grand Rapids-Kalamazoo, MI
42	Albany-Schenectady-Troy, NY
43	San Antonio, TX
44	Charleston-Huntington, WV
45	Harrisburg-York-Lancaster-Lebanon, PA
46	Dayton, OH
47	Raleigh-Durham, NC
48	Norfolk-Portsmouth- Newport News, VA
49	Wilkes Barre-Scranton, PA
50	Birmingham, AL

Source: *Broadcasting Yearbook 1977*, (Washington, D.C.: Broadcasting Publications Inc., 1977), pp. B80–81.

top five markets as being New York, Los Angeles, Chicago, Philadelphia, and San Francisco.

The market area information provided by the rating services is important because the larger the market aera, the greater the potential audience for the advertising message. Thus the number-one market, New York City, has far greater audience potential than the Albany-Schenectady-Troy market, which is ranked number forty-two. An advertiser who reaches the top ten markets will reach a substantial portion of the United States population. Therefore, advertising time is more expensive in major markets than it is in medium or small markets.

Coverage and Circulation

Advertisers not only need information about the potential audience in market areas, but also information about how much of the market area a given station can reach. For example, a low-powered station in a market area that contains many counties might only reach a small percentage of that market area's

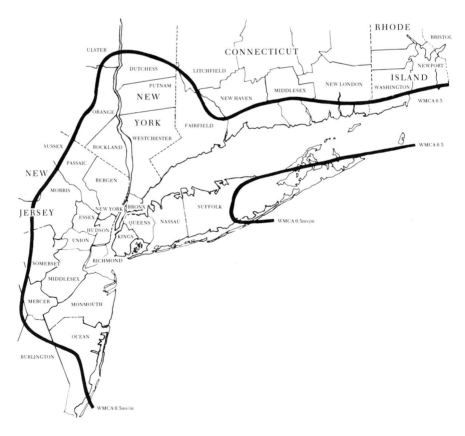

Figure 7-1. Radio coverage map of New York. (WMCA).

viewers or listeners. Therefore, when advertisers decide to buy broadcast time they must consider stations in terms of their *coverage* and *circulation*. *Coverage* refers to the station's signal and how much geographical area it can reach. This is generally determined by the strength of the signal and the contours of the land. Figure 7-1 shows the coverage area of radio station WMCA in New York. *Circulation* is the term used to refer to the station's potential audience for programming; if at least 5 percent of an audience within a particular county tunes into the station at least once a week, that county is considered to be part of the station's circulation area.

Networks need to know the coverage and circulation of their affiliates, and such information is also essential to individual radio and television stations. Before advertisers buy broadcast time, they want to know the geographical boundaries of a station's audience. However, both coverage and circulation are only indicators of a station's potential audience. Even if a station can reach an audience, there is no assurance that the audience will want to listen to or watch the station. The question of how many people are actually in the audience can best be answered by the rating services.

The Measurement of Audiences

The United States has approximately 68.5 million homes with television sets. To discover what every household is watching on television would obviously be an overwhelming task; by the time the job was completed the information would be history. In order to facilitate the rating process then, the rating services take a *sample*, or small segment, of the population, monitor its viewing choices and then generalize about the viewing habits of the entire population on the basis of what was learned from the sample.

Sampling is a well tested and well accepted research technique among natural and social scientists. If you are going to have your blood tested, for example, you know that it is not necessary to drain your whole body—a sample will suffice, for what is true of that sample is very likely true of all the blood in your body.

The rating services, then, apply this sampling principle. They do not test the entire population, but instead test a sample of the population. It should be emphasized, however, that this sample is not chosen haphazardly. The samples the rating services use are designed to accurately represent the entire United States population, and every member of this population has an equal chance to be chosen as part of the sample. Further, the sample is broken down into segments. For example, if 10 percent of the entire United States population earns over $15,000 a year, then 10 percent of the sample should earn over $15,000 a year. This technique of matching the sample to the population is called *stratification*. Different rating services may stratify their samples in different ways, but usually the sample reflects differences in income, age, race, sex, and geographical area.

Because the rating services use stratification in choosing their samples, they automatically have the demographic information that is so important to advertisers. This demographic information in turn provides information about CPM (see page 154). For example, if the rating services discover that the audience for an afternoon soap opera is predominantly adult women, advertisers who wish to reach such an audience will be guided by that information when they make decisions about which time slots to buy for their messages. Thus sample stratification provides demographic information about audience composition, which in turn enables advertisers to figure CPM for the variety of audiences that are reached by the broadcasters.

Data Gathering Techniques

After the rating services have selected their sample households, they use a variety of techniques to discover what these households listen to or watch on radio and television. The techniques most commonly used are as follows:

Electronic Monitoring.   The most influential television ratings are provided by the A. C. Nielsen Company, which gathers its information by electronically monitoring all the television sets in its sample homes. A device known as the Storage Instantaneous Audimeter, or SIA (commonly referred to simply as the Audimeter), is installed by Nielsen representatives in approximately 1,160 households across the United States. The Audimeter is wired directly to the household's television sets and is able to record when each set is turned on and what channel it is tuned to (see Figure 7-2). The Audimeter monitors the sets continuously, at 30-second intervals, which means that it can keep very accurate track of channel switchings. Each Audimeter is linked, by means of a separate telephone line, to Nielsen's main computer center in Dunedin, Florida. At least twice a day a "collecting" computer dials each home unit and gathers the information stored by the Audimeter. The collected information is then transferred to a "processing" computer, which organizes the data and generates the many reports that Nielsen issues.

Nielsen offers a wide variety of ratings reports to its subscribers, who choose from the range of reports according to their individual needs for information. The subscriber services offered by Nielsen fall into two basic categories: reports that provide information on a national basis, and reports that provide information on a local basis. Nielsen calls its national service the Nielsen Television Index (NTI) and its local service the Nielsen Station Index (NSI). Table 7-2 describes briefly the main ratings report services available from Neilsen.

The main strength of the Audimeter system is that it allows Nielsen to report data faster than any other rating service. Before Nielsen engineers developed the latest model Audimeter, it took one to two months to compile the ratings data. Now Nielsen can report data within a time period that ranges from overnight to one or two weeks.

On the other hand, the Audimeter system also has weaknesses. One

WMCA RATE CARD # 45

Effective November 15, 1976

GRIDS/FREQUENCY		AA—5AM–10AM 3PM–8PM Mon.–Fri.		A—10AM–3PM Mon.–Fri. 5AM–8PM		B—8PM–10PM Mon.–Sat. All Day Sun.	
		60 sec.	30 sec.	60 sec.	30 sec.	60 sec.	30 sec.
I.	6x	$170	$136	$140	$112	$90	$72
	12x	150	120	120	96	80	64
	18x	130	104	100	80	70	56
II.	6x	$140	$112	$110	$ 88	$80	$64
	12x	120	96	90	72	70	56
	18x	100	80	70	56	50	40
III.	6x	$120	$ 96	$ 90	$ 72	$70	$56
	12x	100	80	80	64	60	48
	18x	80	64	70	56	50	40
IV.	6x	$100	$ 80	$ 80	$ 64	$60	$48
	12x	90	72	70	56	50	40
	18x	80	64	60	48	40	32
	24x	70	56	50	40	30	24

CHECK STATION FOR GRID NUMBER IN EFFECT–HIGHER GRID PRE-EMPTS LOWER.

10-second spots 50% of minute rate.

SPECIAL PROGRAMS:

BARRY GRAY	1x		7x		14x	
10PM–12 Midnight	60's	30's	60's	30's	60's	30's
Mon.–Fri./Sunday	$100	$80	$70	$56	$60	$48

LONG JOHN NEBEL			
CANDY JONES	1x	7x	14x
12 Midnight–5:00AM	2 minutes	2 minutes	2 minutes
Mon.–Sunday	$100	$70	$60

55 MINUTE SPONSORSHIP
7:00 PM–10:00 PM $2000
MONDAY–SUNDAY

Figure 7–2. Sample rate card. (WMCA.)

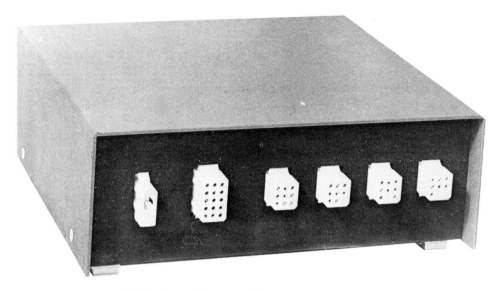

1971 Audimeter. (Courtesy of the A.C. Nielson Company.)

problem stressed by critics of the system—and acknowledged by Nielsen itself—is that although the Audimeter records the times when the set is in use
and the channels it is tuned to, the instrument has no way of determining
whether anyone is actually watching the set. Television sets are often turned on
to provide background noise while members of the household are busy with

TABLE 7-2   Nielsen Ratings Services

Local Services

Overnights. Available only in the three largest markets (New York City, Los Angeles,
and Chicago), these reports are issued by 10:00 AM each morning, with ratings data on
the previous day's programming in those markets. Even though the overnights only
cover three markets, many network executives look at them as an indication of national program preferences.

Multi-Network Area Reports (MNAs) These reports, available one week after a viewing date, provide information about the total audience, the number of stations carrying a program, and the percentage of coverage of the nation. The MNA ratings apply
to the seventy largest population centers in the United States.

National Services

SIAs, or Dailies. SIA reports are issued 36 hours after a viewing day and contain information on program ratings and share of audience.

National Television Index Reports (NTIs). NTIs are comprehensive reports issued at
two-week intervals and covering two weeks of programming. They contain information about average audience, number of households using television (HUT), share of
audience, as well as demographic information about audience composition.

activities other than viewing. When the television set is left on, the Audimeter reports the set in use, even if the household cat is the only viewer.

Critics of Nielsen's system also complain that not enough care is taken to maintain the demographic mix of the sample. They claim that when the members of a sample household move away, Nielsen is sometimes reluctant to remove its Audimeter promptly. This means that the sample gets distorted if the new occupants of the house do not have the same demographic characteristics as the original occupants. For example, if the sample household was originally made up of a young married couple with two children and they are replaced by a middle-aged couple with no children, the demographic characteristics of that household are significantly changed. If Nielsen sticks with the second couple instead of finding another family similar to the one that moved away, the sample becomes less representative of the United States population.

Diaries.   Two of the rating services, Arbitron and Nielsen, use diaries to obtain viewer and listener information. Respondents are asked to make entries in the diary listing the times they spent viewing, the channel numbers they were

---

SWEEP WEEKS AND BLACK WEEKS

Since a good rating is so essential to a station's economic well-being, stations are tempted to try to increase their ratings by a process called "hypoing." Although the blatent forms of hypoing such as contests, give-aways, and promotion stunts during rating weeks are discouraged by the FTC, the FCC, BRC, and the rating services, the more subtle forms are harder to control.

One example of hypoing occurs during sweep weeks—the three weeks out of the year that Arbitron and Nielsen "sweep" the country to measure the audiences of the network affiliates. During these weeks the networks provide special programs on nights that have been doing poorly in the program schedule. This special programming offers popular performers, recent hit movies, and so on. If this special programming is successful, the affiliates will be able to gather bigger audiences and thus charge a higher price for advertising time.

Although the sweep weeks may glitter, the networks offset them with black weeks. Black weeks are the four weeks a year when Nielsen doesn't do ratings—therefore a low rating during those weeks won't hurt anyone. If you see a number of cultural and documentary programs all within a single week, you can be pretty certain that it's a black week.

Source: Les Brown, "TV Notes: How 'Sweep Weeks' Hype the Ratings," *New York Times*, December 7, 1975, p. D 37.

1942 Audimeter. (Courtesy of the A.C. Nielson Company).

1971 Audimeter. (Courtesy of the A. C. Nelson Company.)

Audimeter. (Courtesy of the A.C. Nielson Company.)

1950 Audimeter. (Courtesy of the A.C. Nielson Company.)

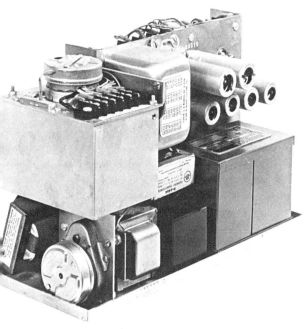

1958 Audimeter. (Courtesy of the A.C. Nielson Company.)

tuned to, the stations' call letters, the names of the programs they watched, and the age and sex of the viewers. After completing the diary, the sample household mails it back to the rating service, which analyzes and reports the data to its subscribers. Figure 7-3 shows a page from an Arbitron diary.

Arbitron uses counties as sample units and chooses its respondents from within the county by using a computer to randomly select telephone numbers of county residents to be contacted for participation in the survey. The size of the sample will range from 300 to 2,400 households, depending on the size of the market where the research is being conducted.

Nielsen uses the diary system to supplement its Audimeter system. In addition to the approximately 1,160 households that it monitors by means of the Audimeter, Nielsen also has roughly 2,300 households that keep diaries. Nielsen calls its diaries *Audilogs*. Households that participate in Nielsen's Audilog system fill out their diaries for the third week of every month from September to February, as well as for other selected periods during the year. Generally, a Nielsen household will keep a diary for a total of eleven or twelve weeks each year. Nielsen also uses diaries for Sweep weeks.

The Nielsen Audilog diary system also employs an electronic device known as a *Recordimeter*, which is attached to the television set to record the amount of time the set is in use. An additional function of the *Recordimeter* is to emit an audible signal every thirty minutes that the set is in use to remind viewers to make entries in their Audilog diaries. Nielsen compares the record of set use provided by the Recordimeter to the Audilog entries as a check of the diary keeper's accuracy.

The main advantage of diary sampling is that it can measure actual viewing and can provide valuable information about the composition of the audience. The main disadvantage of diaries is that they are subject to human error. Respondents often misunderstand the instructions, fill their diaries in improperly, mail them in too late to be counted, or forget to mail them at all.

Telephone Interviews.   Rating services generally use two types of telephone interviews, *coincidental* and *recall*. In a *coincidental interview*, the interviewer asks the respondent what she or he is watching or listening to at the time of the interview. In a *recall interview*, the interviewer asks the respondent about use of broadcast media for the past day or so. Sometimes telephone interviewers use *aided recall* techniques where they read off a list of what was on radio or television or the call letters for the stations in the area. Aided recall helps respondents to remember details about their recent viewing or listening that they may have forgotten. Telephone interviewers will often ask the sex and age of the respondent, as well as information about those who were present when the viewing or listening took place.

Telephone interviews are widely used by rating services and individual stations to gather rating information. Telephone interviewing systems have the advantages of measuring behavior as it is taking place, and of being inexpensive and easy. The disadvantage of using the telephone is that some people do not have telephones or their telephone is not listed. An even greater problem is

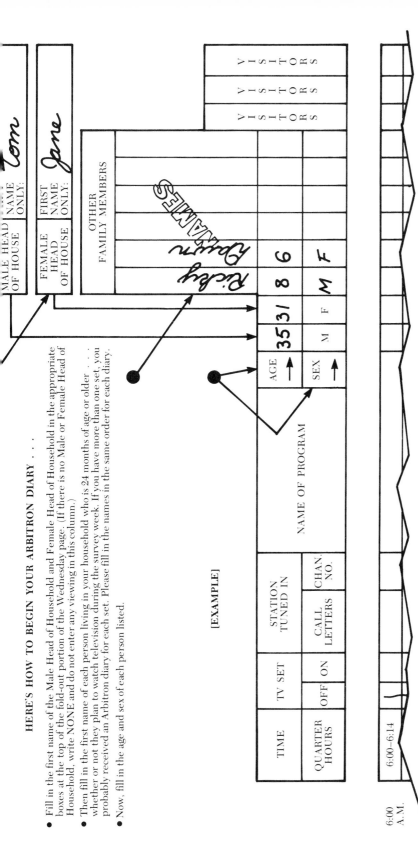

HERE'S HOW TO BEGIN YOUR ARBITRON DIARY . . .

MALE HEAD OF HOUSE | NAME ONLY: *Tom*

FIRST NAME ONLY: *Jane*
FEMALE HEAD OF HOUSE

OTHER FAMILY MEMBERS

- Fill in the first name of the Male Head of Household and Female Head of Household in the appropriate boxes at the top of the fold-out portion of the Wednesday page. (If there is no Male or Female Head of Household, write NONE and do not enter any viewing in this column.)

- Then fill in the first name of each person living in your household who is 24 months of age or older . . . whether or not they plan to watch television during the survey week. If you have more than one set, you probably received an Arbitron diary for each set. Please fill in the names in the same order for each diary.

- Now, fill in the age and sex of each person listed.

[EXAMPLE]

	TV SET		STATION TUNED IN		NAME OF PROGRAM	Ricky Bryan JAMES 35 31 8 6 M F M F
TIME	OFF	ON	CALL LETTERS	CHAN. NO.		AGE → SEX →
QUARTER HOURS						V I S I T O R S V I S I T O R S V I S I T O R S

6:00 A.M. | 6:00–6:14

Figure 7–3. Source: Arbitron Television, American Research Bureau, 1350 Avenue of the Americas, New York, New York 10019.

197

TABLE 7-3   What Happened to the Original Sample in a Telephone Survey

	No.	%
Total predesignated sample	5000	100
Disconnects or nonworking telephone numbers	483	9.7
Total usable household sample	4517	100
Lines busy	69	1.5
No answer/Selected respondent not available	676	15.0
Refused/Partial interview/ Language barrier	1461	32.3
Tabulated interviews	2311	51.2
Total households contacted	3906	100
After call-backs		
Refused/Partial interview/ Language barrier	1461	37.4
Not available	134	3.4
Tabulated interviews	2311	59.2

Source: Trendex: *Research by Telephone* (Westport, Conn.: Trendex, Undated)

that it is difficult to reach all of the people designated as part of the sample. Table 7-3, based on a Trendex survey in a metropolitan area, illustrates the types of problems telephone interviewers must face. The interviewers who conducted that survey were able to complete just 59.2 percent of the interviews—even after call-backs.

Personal Interviews.   One of the best ways to conduct rating research is through personal interviews. Pulse, which measures radio listening, uses this method. Pulse chooses its sample from telephone directories or census reports and then goes directly to the homes of its respondents. Depending on the population size of the area surveyed, Pulse will interview anywhere from 500 to 2500 respondents.

Pulse personal interviewers use aided recall techniques. Since radio does not have clearly defined shows, Pulse asks questions about time periods. Repondents identify which stations they listened to the previous day, from the time they woke up until the time they went to bed. Respondents are also asked to tell which stations they listened to during the previous week. In all cases, Pulse asks for specific listening information rather than for general listening preferences. Pulse reports station listenership data by age, sex, and the time of day repondents listen.

Personal interviews are the best way to get a good response from the persons in the sample. The disadvantage of personal interviewing is that it is expensive; the rating service must hire and train interviewers, and the interviewing itself takes a good deal of time—especially in areas that are sparsely populated or in areas where people are often away from home.

Reporting Results

Once the rating service has selected a sample and has found a method of testing the sample, its next problem is to organize and report its results in a meaningful way. Although there are a variety of rating services, most of them make use of a common language in reporting their results.

The two measurements most commonly used are a *program rating* and a *share of audience rating*. A *program rating* represents the percentage of *all* the sample television households that are watching a specific program.

The most important ratings measurement, however, and the figure that most influences programming decisions, is called a *share of audience rating* or "share." To calculate a share of audience rating, it is necessary to first add up all the program ratings for all stations and networks for a given time period. The sum of all the program ratings for the time period is a figure that is referred to as a *HUT* ("households using television") *rating*, and it represents an estimate of the percentage of the total potential audience that was actually tuned in to the programs that were shown during that time period. Once the HUT rating for the time period is known, the share of audience rating for any program that was aired during the time period can be derived by calculating what percentage of the total viewing audience was tuned to that particular program. The share of audience rating thus provides an indication of how popular a program was in relation to the other programs that were aired at the same time. If a program gets a share of audience rating of 14, that means that 14 percent of the actual viewing audience watched the program, while 86 percent of the audience watched other programs in the same time slot. For a network prime time program to survive, it must usually get at least a 30 percent share. If it has a 40 percent share, it's a solid hit.

It is possible to have a seemingly high numerical rating and a mediocre share of audience and vice versa. During prime time, for example, a program may reach 15 million television households. This may represent a high rating, but if the program's competitors are reaching three-quarters of the audience with their sets tuned, the program's share of audience is not very good. Conversely, during late-night programming a show might only reach two million people, which would represent a low rating. But if those two million people represent two-thirds of the actual viewing audience for that time period, the program has won a sizable share of the audience. From the national advertisers point of view, the ideal situation would be one in which every set in the entire United States was tuned to the program that they were sponsoring. This would mean a 100 rating and a 100 percent share. Since this never happens, advertisers must be content with sponsoring programs with large audiences or, more importantly, programs with the largest share of viewers or listeners.

Both ratings and shares are computed on a national and local basis. The networks and national advertisers are interested in national figures, whereas local stations are often more concerned with ratings in their particular coverage areas.

Program ratings are also refined by measuring them under three different circumstances: instantaneous, average, and cumulative ratings. An *instantaneous* rating is taken during a particular time period during a program. For example, an instantaneous rating could tell you the percentage of your sample that is watching "All in the Family" at 9:07 P.M. An *average* rating gives the average percentage of the audience watching over a time period. In the case of "All in the Family" an average could be calculated over a fifteen minute period or over the entire thirty minutes that the program is on the air. A *cumulative* rating (often called a *cume*) gives the percentage of the audience that was watching over two or more time periods; we might want to know, for example, the cume for "All in the Family" for a four or five week period. The rating one finds most useful will depend on the program being broadcast. The audience for a documentary that is broadcast only once would have its rating figured on an instantaneous or average basis; a cumulative rating would be more useful for a continuing series.

NETWORK AND STATION REPONSE TO RATINGS

Television Scheduling Strategies

As we have seen, good ratings are essential if networks and radio and television stations are going to survive. Since the dollar stakes are the highest at the network level, the networks have evolved a variety of scheduling strategies intended to improve their ratings.

A common strategy is *counter programming*, whereby a network puts its most popular program opposite a popular program on another network in the hope of taking the competitor's audience away. Another counter programming strategy is to put a different type of program in competition with opposition programming. For example, NBC might program a variety show opposite ABC and CBS situation comedies in the hope that the variety show would attract an audience that did not like comedies. Also, networks often put low-rated programs such documentaries opposite each other. The philosophy behind this move is that it is better to do poorly together—in that way no one is the loser.

Networks often run similar programs back to back during a particular time period in order to keep the same audience. This strategy, called *block programming*, is designed to produce a good audience "flow" from one program to another. Typical examples of block programming are an afternoon of soap operas or an evening of police adventure programs. A similar programming technique is *strip programming*, whereby a network or station runs the same programs at the same time every day. Soap operas and evening newscasts are examples of strip programming. This strategy appeals to viewers' loyalties and habits; if you watched it on Tuesday you will probably watch it on Wednesday too.

A network never looks at a program as an isolated entity; an individual program is always considered part of the overall schedule and must be placed on the schedule in a way that will enhance both itself and the surrounding programming. One network strategy is to move a strong program to a time period in which the program schedule is weak, in the hope that the strong program will strengthen the schedule. "All in the Family" has moved five times in six years—always taking the audience with it and thus improving the schedule on the night on which the program appears. This strategy does not always work, however. "M*A*S*H," a very strong program, almost failed when CBS moved it from Tuesday to Friday night in the 1975–76 season. Once CBS moved it back to Tuesday, it regained its rating strength. A new program's rating potential is often enhanced when it is scheduled between two highly rated programs—a practice known in the industry as "hammocking."

Every viewer at one time or another is the victim of timing strategies. For instance, a network may begin an hour-long program at 8:30, hoping to get you so involved that you will not think of switching to the other networks for their 9:00 programs. The winner at this game is the network that can keep the same audience for the entire evening.

Programming

Besides influencing the scheduling of the networks, ratings also have a strong influence on the kinds of programming the networks offer. Since ratings indicate which shows are popular and which are unpopular, the network programmers try to use ratings to make predictions about the kinds of programming that are likely to be successful. They know, for example, that public affairs and cultural programming attracts small audiences and few advertisers and so they provide very little programming of that kind.

Determining the ingredients of successful programming is more difficult. Since no one is very certain what kind of rating an innovative program will attract, the programmers try to limit their risks by providing new programs that resemble past successes. If a police adventure show works well in one season, there will be similar shows in the future. If a series has several strong characters, the programmers may take some of the characters away from the original series and create a new series around them—shows created according to this strategy are known as *spin-offs*.

Figure 7-4 gives a summary of prime-time programming diversity from 1953 to 1974. As the figure shows, although there was a good deal of diversity in 1953, diversity began to decline steadily from that point on, reaching its lowest point in 1974. At that time, 81 percent of all prime time programming fell into one of three program categories: action/adventure, movies, and general drama.[3] Although this study ends in 1974, there is no reason to believe that programming is becoming any more diverse.

Programming may also change because the rating demographics are wrong for the advertisers. "Gunsmoke" was cancelled after twenty years, even though at the time of cancellation it was still one of the top twenty-five programs, with

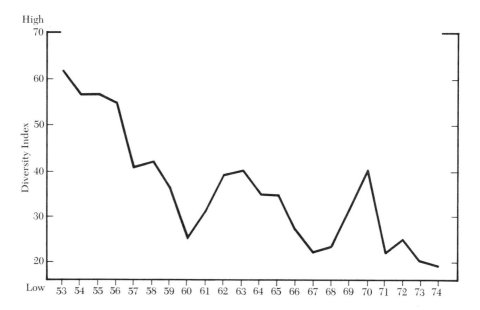

Figure 7–4. Diversity in network prime-time schedules, 1953–74. Source: Joseph R. Dominick and Millard C. Pearce, "Trends in Network Prime-Time Programming, 1953–1974," *Journal of Communication*, Vol. 26, No. 1 (Winter 1976), p. 77.

an audience of about 36 million. A CBS vice-president explained that it was cancelled because "the show tended to appeal to rural audiences and older people. Unfortunately, they're not primarily the ones you sell to."[4] "Gunsmoke" is not the only show to have suffered this fate. All three networks have dropped a number of shows because they were not appealing to the right kind of audience.

Programming has also been influenced by the new rating service technology. The 1974–75 television season was the first season to make full use of Nielsen's improved Audimeter, the Storage Instantaneous Audimeter. Prior to that season, Nielsen used Audimeter instruments that recorded viewing data on film. Since the film had to be mailed back to Nielsen, it was a much slower procedure than the present one. The new system has meant that networks and advertisers are able to make much quicker decisions about programming choices. Although network executives buy 13 weeks of a program at a time, they have shown no reluctance to drop a program that earns a poor rating, sometimes after only one or two shows have been aired.

Radio Ratings

Ratings are as important to radio as they are to television. In a medium market, stations compete to be the number-one rated station. In a major market, ratings also distinguish between stations with similar formats. For example, in a market with two or three Top-40 stations, ratings will tell which of these stations has the largest audience. There have also been cases where stations with consistently low ratings will change their formats in the hope that their ratings will improve.

The most important rating time for most AM stations is drive time. Most stations will make an effort to make the programming in this time period as appealing as possible.

MONITORING THE RATING SERVICES

Although audience measurement has existed since the early days of broadcasting the question of audience size became critical when stations began to increase in numbers and advertising time became more and more expensive. Advertisers were not interested in "hit-or-miss" advertising. They wanted assurance that their messages were reaching enough of the right kind of people.

Only rating services were equipped to provide this audience information. Although many of them had existed for years, their role in the broadcast industry gradually became essential rather than peripheral. However, it became clear that some rating services were not doing a very good job when in 1962 the Federal Trade Commission (FTC) ordered three of them to stop misrepresenting the accuracy and reliability of their figures. The FTC order was followed by a Congressional investigation of the rating services in 1963. The investigation revealed that the rating services sometimes doctored data, were careless, and engaged in outright deception.[5]

THE MOST VALUABLE PLAYER IN BROADCASTING

Network executives who work out successful programming strategies are well rewarded for their efforts. In 1975, Fred Silverman, who was responsible for the CBS 1974–75 program schedule, left CBS to go to ABC. Industry sources said that ABC gave him a three-year contract at $250,000 a year, $1 million-worth stock, $750,000 in life insurance, and apartments in both Los Angeles and New York City. Within a week of the announcement of his move to ABC, ABC stock increased in value by a total of $85 million. For ABC, the hiring of Silverman paid off, in the 1976–77 season, ABC held the first place in ratings for the first time in its history.

Source: Jeff Greenfield, "The Fight for $60,000 a Half Minute," *New York Times Magazine*, September 7, 1975, p. 75.

The Broadcast Rating Council

Probably in response to the fear of government regulation, the industry decided to set its own house in order. In 1964, the National Association of Broadcasters established the Broadcast Rating Council (BRC) and made it responsible for setting standards for the rating services and accrediting and auditing them. In order to get BRC accreditation, a rating service must disclose its methodology and procedures to the council. The BRC also conducts a periodic audit of the accredited services to make certain that they are following the methodologies they have described. Arbitron, Nielsen, and Pulse, as well as two smaller services, are currently accredited by the BRC.

The Committee on Nationwide Television Audience Measurements

The second response of the industry to the government's investigation of rating services was to set up its own research committee to investigate the methods used by the rating services. Formed by the NAB and the three television networks, this group was known as the Committee on Nationwide Television Audience Measurements (CONTAM).

CONTAM's job was to answer some of the questions that were raised by the Congressional committee. The first question was whether measurements based on a small random sample of the national television audience could accurately reflect the viewing behavior of the audience as a whole. By drawing and measuring its own sample, and by comparing it to the rating service sample, CONTAM discovered that the sampling method used by the rating services was basically accurate. The second question CONTAM investigated was whether people who cooperated with rating services had different viewing habits than those who did not cooperate. CONTAM found that cooperators watched more television than noncooperators, and thus rating service results were biased toward cooperator viewing habits. CONTAM therefore recommended that the rating services use better strategies to persuade people to cooperate. Finally, CONTAM compared the different rating services and found that, even when rating services used greatly different methods in measuring audiences, their results were very similar.

Basically the CONTAM study gave assurance that when rating services used methodologies that were well established in statistical theory they would get results that would give reasonable estimates of television's audiences.[6]

The All Radio Methodology Study

The National Association of Broadcasters and the Radio Advertising Bureau also organized a study of radio methodology. The study, called the All Radio Methodology Study (ARMS), was initiated in 1963. The main objective of the study was to examine and compare the various methods of measuring radio audience, and the main conclusion of the research was that the coincidental telephone interviewing method was the most reliable.[7]

As a result of the congressional hearing, the subsequent research studies, and the establishment of the Broadcast Rating Council, many of the methodological problems of the rating services have been solved. There are still problems, however, with those who subscribe to and use rating service data.

Since all of the rating services follow complex methods of gathering rating data, not all subscribers to the services understand the exact meaning of that data. It is important to keep in mind that ratings are *estimates* that are based on statistical theory. There is a built-in error of approximately three rating points on either side of the point estimate. This means that a program rating might be three points higher or three points lower than the rating that is actually reported. Because of this margin of error, one cannot necessarily assume that a program with a rating of 30 has more viewers or listeners than a program with a 28 rating, although managers of small stations have actually fired programming personnel on the basis of such a fallacious assumption. As well as being subject to statistical error, ratings are also subject to human error. These errors can range anywhere from a mistake in filling out a diary to erroneous data being entered into a computer.

Although rating services take the responsibility for their methods, they are quick to point out that they are not responsible for how their data is used—they insist that they are merely collectors of information. One might say that blaming the rating services for dropping a program is like blaming the mirror because you do not like your face—both the rating services and the mirror only reflect reality; they don't create it.

Most commercial broadcasters will agree that program quality, artistry, and creativity are all desirable but that the rating game is the only game in town. Every fall season the network executives, program producers, and program talent anxiously await the latest ratings report. Those who are involved in the top fifteen shows can plan a cruise or buy a new house, while those in the bottom fifteen prepare for a long and hard winter. The poor folks in the middle range have the most anxious time of all, since their shows could go either way.

And we, the viewers, turn our dials and hope that something new and interesting will catch our attention. If it does, we hope it will survive or that the show we like will appeal to forty million Americans all between the ages of eighteen and forty-nine who will all go out and buy the sponsors' products. With these ideal conditions, our favorite show could go on forever.

NOTES

1. *Broadcasting* (November 3, 1975), p. 40.
2. *Broadcasting* (September, October, November 1975).
3. Joseph R. Dominick and Millard C. Pearce, "Trends in Network Prime-Time Programming, 1953–1974," *Journal of Communication*, Vol. 26, No. 1 (Winter 1976), p. 77.

4. Jeff Greenfield, "The Fight for $60,000 for a Half Minute," *New York Times Magazine* (September 7, 1975), p. 62.

5. House of Representatives, Committee on Interstate and Foreign Commerce, *Broadcast Ratings*, 1966.

6. Martin Mayer, *How Good are Television Ratings?* (New York: Television Information Office, 1966).

7. *ARMS: What it Shows, How it has Changed Radio Measurement* (Washington, D.C.: National Association of Broadcasters, 1966).

Broadcasting Research

8

When the first radio stations went on the air, radio was regarded as a fad—a novelty that would soon fade away. But after radio became a part of American life, many people went to another extreme; they believed it to be capable of miracles. Some saw radio broadcasting as a powerful tool for propaganda—others saw it as an educational tool that could reach the nation's students. Still others believed that radio was responsible for breaking up the family—that families would listen to the radio rather than communicate with each other.

In 1939, an estimated one million Americans panicked as a result of a radio play which portrayed the United States being invaded by Martians. When psychologist Hadley Cantril investigated this phenomenon he discovered that people who were afraid had a poorer education, were more religious, and were more suggestible than those who realized that it was only a drama.[1] Other researchers studying daytime radio serials discovered that many people identified with soap opera heros and heroines and listened to them for personal advice and guidance.[2] Although "Amos 'n Andy," the well-known comedy serial, was never studied for its effect on its audience, it certainly had an impact. The show was so popular that many factories and businesses closed early on the nights it was on so that their employees could hear it. Even President Coolidge was said to have given orders that he was not to be disturbed when the program was on.

An outstanding case of mass persuasion by radio took place in 1943 when the popular singer Kate Smith went on the air for an eighteen-hour marathon to sell war bonds. She succeeded in raising $39 million in war bond pledges. Robert K. Merton, a sociologist who conducted research on a sample of those who bought the bonds, found that half of the sample already intended to buy bonds—they just needed to be prodded. About a third of the sample was predisposed toward buying bonds, and although they had not intended to do so at that time, they were persuaded by Miss Smith. The remainder of the sample bought bonds because they wanted to be associated with a celebrity or because they became fascinated with the drama and structure of the marathon.[3] This marathon provided a model for the wide variety of television charity appeals that we see each year.

After two decades of radio broadcasting, it became clear that although radio was not bringing about any miracles, it was definitely affecting American audiences—often in a very significant way.

In 1948, Merton teamed up with another sociologist, Paul F. Lazarsfeld, to develop a comprehensive theory about how media affected Americans. Their theory stated: 1) that media confer status—that any person or event that the media cover becomes important because of the media coverage; 2) that media enforce social norms by showing what is and what is not acceptable; and 3) that media have a numbing effect on their audiences—that audiences receive so much information that they become well-informed but unable to act.[4]

The Lazarsfeld and Merton study came at an excellent time: the transitional period between radio and the advent of television. With the rapid growth of television broadcasting, it soon became apparent that what Lazarsfeld and Merton said about the other mass media could also be said about the newest medium, and, in fact, most media researchers abandoned radio and began to study television instead. Many of the questions that were raised about radio were also raised about television: Would it destroy the family? Could it replace the teacher? What would be its effect on children? Could programming bring about changes in behavior? All of these questions and many more were being asked. In the section that follows we will discuss the methods that have been used for conducting broadcasting research, as well as the four major concerns of such research: the communicators—those who create programs and make policy decisions; the audience—those who watch and listen to the programs; the message—the programs themselves; and the effects—the impact the programs have on their audiences.

RESEARCH METHODS

Researchers in broadcasting use a wide range of methods or research techniques to study the communicators, the audience, the message, and the effects of programming on the audience.

One of the most widely used methods is *survey research*—research that is most commonly used to study audiences. In survey research the researcher takes a regional or national sample of the population he or she wishes to survey and then studies each member of the sample in an identical manner. Survey research is the technique used by most of the rating services—such as Nielsen, Arbitron, or Pulse—and by polling agencies, such as Gallup and Roper. As well as studying audience size and composition, survey researchers study viewer-listener attitudes toward radio and television and audience preferences—what the audience wants to see or hear.

Some survey researchers have also concentrated on how radio and television influence day-to-day behavior. For example, how do members of the audience fit television into their daily routine, how does it affect their relationships with family and friends, or how much attention do audiences give to what they see and hear?

The most common research method used to study messages is called *content analysis*. As the name implies, this research is used to analyze the actual content of the message—the programs we see and hear. At its simplest level, content analysis involves counting the number of times that certain people, issues, or ideas appear in programming. At its more complicated level, it is used to analyze attitudes or editorial bias. Most researchers who conduct content analysis look at some aspect of the program they are studying. For example, in a content analysis of a police adventure program researchers might focus on violence. They might count the number of violent acts, they might classify violent acts into those leading to death and those leading to injury, they might try to identify the types of persons who commit violent acts, and so on.

Many researchers have used content analysis to study news and editorial bias. For example, a researcher studying network news coverage of a political campaign might count the number of minutes devoted to the Democrats and to the Republicans or the researcher might study when the candidate appears in the newscast on the theory that stories that appear at the beginning of the newscast are more important than stories that appear at the end.

Another commonly used research technique in broadcasting is *experimental research*—research that is mainly concerned with the effects of radio and television on its audience. Experimental research in broadcasting uses many techniques that were developed in the social sciences; in fact a good deal of experimental research in broadcasting is being conducted by sociologists and psychologists.

In experimental studies, the researchers set up and manipulate the research circumstances rather than observing behavior or attitudes in a natural setting. For example, a researcher might show one group of children a film containing violence and then observe this group playing with other children to see if their play is consequently more aggressive.

Survey research, content analysis, and experimental studies account for the great majority of studies that are conducted in broadcasting. However, they are not the only studies that have yielded important results. Some researchers have had success with *panel studies*—studies in which the same persons are measured on two or more occasions. This type of study has been particularly useful in measuring children's behavior and attitudes regarding violence as the children grow older. Other researchers have been successful with *participant-observer studies*. In these studies the researcher observes what happens in the actual media operation. For example, he or she might study a newsroom to see who makes decisions about what news will or will not be broadcast. These studies are particularly useful in identifying policy makers in stations and networks.

When compared to research in the natural and physical sciences, broadcasting research—and indeed social science research in general—is still in its infancy. Broadcast researchers can neither place their subjects in a controlled laboratory setting nor can they count on their subjects to always act consistently. Although the entire area of mass communications raises serious questions, there are still very few answers about the effects of media exposure on people.

In fact, in many cases, we don't even know how to go about finding answers to these questions. Thus, researchers constantly look for new methods of analyzing the media. The existing research is important, but it is only a beginning.

THE COMMUNICATORS

In recent years there has been a trend toward policy research—research that often leads to recommendations for future legislation. The best known study of this type is the report of the Carnegie Commission on Educational Television; a report that led the government to set up a public broadcasting system.

In the 1970s there have been several studies concerned with the area of broadcasting and economics. Noll, Peck, and McGowan have done an economic analysis of television and the interaction of the industry with the Federal Communications Commission. Owen, Beebe, and Manning have researched television economics and have made recommendations regarding future use of the broadcast spectrum. The Rand Corporation has studied the effect of cross-media ownership on programming and competition, and Bunch has studied the influence of corporations in broadcasting. Although Halberstam's study on CBS was written for a popular rather than an academic audience, it has provided valuable insight into the connection between profit-making and program choices.[5]

There have been a handful of studies about communicators—the media managers who make choices about program content and what should be broadcast. Many of these studies about communicators have been in the area of news. Kurt Lang and Gladys Engle Lang conducted a study, which is now a media classic, of the McArthur Day Parade that took place in 1951. The researchers observed the media coverage of the event and the actual parade itself, as well as the media and nonmedia audiences. The Langs discovered that the television coverage of the event was much more exciting and dramatic than the actual event. Additionally, they found that, while the television event matched its viewers' expectations, for the actual onlookers, the parade did not meet their expectations. The researchers concluded that television structures events in order to please the viewers.[6]

Another study related to news broadcasting is Edward Jay Epstein's research concerning network television news. Epstein discovered that there were forces other than network officials that helped to determine news policy—namely, network affiliates and the FCC. He observed that network newscasts must be acceptable to the affiliates or they can refuse to take them. Although this is not likely to happen, the networks are still put into the position of trying to please the affiliates. The FCC influences the news by such policies and guidelines as the Fairness Doctrine and the expectation that stations will all broadcast a reasonable amount of news—news that is partially provided by networks.

Epstein also found that news coverage is influenced strongly by economic factors. The newscast is expected to attract a large audience that will, in turn, attract advertisers. The pressure to attract an audience compels a producer to look for interesting stories, star newscasters, and so on. The make-up of a newscast is also influenced by internal economic factors. Since network news departments have to stay within their budgets, they are more likely to cover stories in New York, Washington, Los Angeles, and Chicago—where they already have film crews as part of the staffs of their owned-and-operated stations (see page 130).

Finally, Epstein noted that the structure of the newscasts is determined by the demands of the organization; that is, the network itself. The networks have certain values and thus recruit producers and newscasters who also display these values. In reference to hiring reporters at NBC, one senior executive said, "It is simply not in our enlightened self-interest to employ reporters with too firmly fixed ideas on how the world ought to be."[7]

Although there have been many studies about the effects of media on children, there have been few studies about the communicators who plan and structure children's programming. One of the most interesting studies is Cantor's research on the role of producers and writers in choosing content for these programs. Cantor interviewed almost all the producers and writers of children's programs for one television season. He found that none of them had any academic training specifically directed toward producing children's entertainment. He found that all of them had training in film techniques or in business rather than in any aspect of children's behavior such as education or psychology. Half of them had been film animators, with the rest coming from advertising, promotion, publicity, and writing. Most of them regarded themselves as businesspersons and were indifferent to the possible harmful effects of the programming they produced.[8]

A study similar to Cantor's was conducted by Baldwin and Lewis, except that they interviewed those persons responsible for producing and writing prime time programs that contained substantial violence. When questioned about the high incidence of violent acts in these programs, their respondents defended violence. They said that conflict was essential to a plot and that violence was synonymous with conflict. They also pointed out that shows with conflict and violence attracted the largest audiences, and that if their shows did not have it, their competitors' would. Baldwin and Lewis also found that no one actually took the responsibility for introducing violent acts into television programs. Since television scripts are usually the result of a team effort, no single individual could claim the work as his or her own.[9]

THE AUDIENCE

Almost 98 percent of all American homes have television sets, and the sets in each of these homes are in use an average of six to seven hours a day with the average person viewing about three hours of television a day.

Americans spend 28 percent of all of their leisure time watching television as a primary activity, which means giving their total attention to the television set. Not surprisingly, those who watch the most television are those who are home the most. Women watch more television than men, but men are more likely to watch it as a primary activity than are homemakers or employed women.[10]

Even before they enter the first grade, children are regular television viewers with favorite programs. In a week's time, one study found, first graders watched about twenty-four hours of television, sixth graders watched a little more than thirty hours, and tenth graders viewed about twenty-eight hours. In program preference, first graders liked cartoons and situation comedies, sixth graders preferred adventure shows, and tenth graders watched adventure and musical and variety shows. All of the children reported considerable conflict with other household members about program selections. Ninety percent of the sixth graders and tenth graders objected to commercials, and the majority of these children mistrusted commercials.[11]

Teenagers are one group who do not watch as much television as the rest of the population. In 1960 they were the heaviest viewers, but by 1970 they watched television less than any other age group.[12] The decrease in teenage viewing is probably due to the increased availability of media that was geared to their specific interests such as film, radio, and records. Teenagers' loyalty to other media is only a temporary condition. When they reach their twenties, their viewing is similar to that of the rest of the population.

Black audiences for the broadcast media exhibit somewhat different viewing patterns than those of white audiences. During prime time, black audiences watch slightly less television. However, during nonprime time, blacks watch substantially more television: black women watch 41 percent more daytime and fringe time television than white women. Black and white women listen to the same amount of radio. Black men, however, listen to radio 16 percent more than white men.[13]

Among the urban poor, radio and television ownership is about 10 percent below the national average.[14] One researcher found that, in comparing the

ARE DIARIES ACCURATE?

The results of one research study would seem to indicate that people do not record their television viewing very accurately. When the researchers made film records of families viewing television in their own homes, they found that the families recorded four hours of viewing, while the cameras only recorded three actual viewing hours. This research would indicate that rating services that rely on diaries for viewing information could be off by as much as 25 percent.

Source: R. B., Bechtel, C. Archelpohl, and R., Akers, "Correlates Between Observed Behavior and Questionnaire Responses on Television Viewing," in E. A. Rubinstein, G. A. Comstock, and J. P. Murray (eds.), *Television and Social Behavior*, v. 4. *Television in Day-to-Day Life: Patterns of Use*, Washington, D.C.: Government Printing Office, 1972, pp. 274–344.

urban poor to the rest of the American population, children and adolescents from that segment of the population watch television more and have a greater belief that television accurately portrays reality. The urban poor audience watches television more than the general population but has less access to other media, particularly newspapers.[15]

In one study of older adults (those between 55 and 80) the researcher found that they preferred news and public affairs programming. Their program favorites also differed from the population at large: of the top 15 programs, as rated by Nielsen, they only considered four as their own favorites. Generally, older adults thought that television was satisfactory and provided good companionship. Seventy-eight percent, however, denied that television advertising influenced their buying choices.[16] Other researchers who have studied older adults have found that when social isolation increases, they become more dependent on television.[17]

A few studies have concentrated on more specialized television viewing. A researcher studying the audience for television soap operas discovered that the most typical audience member was a Southern or Midwestern woman from a large household with a low income and education.[18] Another researcher discovered that people with a high anxiety level were more likely to prefer fantasy programming.[19] As far as educated audiences are concerned, although they express dissatisfaction with television, they watch the same programs as anyone else—and do not limit their viewing to informational and educational programs.[20]

Although there are variations in viewing patterns and program preferences among the various demographic groups, research would indicate that there are more similarities than differences in responses to television and television

SOAP OPERAS AND THE MENTALLY ILL

Soap operas may help a mentally ill patient to recover faster. Several researchers and psychologists have observed that patients often identify with the soap opera characters they see on television. Although patients may not be able to talk about themselves in group or therapeutic sessions because they find those situations threatening, they are often able to talk about conflicts and highly charged emotional events by identifying with soap opera characters. Research on this subject is still in its beginning stages, but soap opera therapy may become a future method of treating mental illness.

Source: H. R. Lazarus, and D. K. Bienlein, "Soap Opera Therapy," *International Journal of Group Psychotherapy*, 17 (1967), pp. 252–256.

programming. Regardless of age, income, political beliefs, and education, almost every one owns a television set. Nielsen and Arbitron also show, with great regularity, that viewers like some programs and avoid others.

Media Preference

Research about media preference is frequently contradictory. For many years the Roper organization has conducted a yearly poll on American attitudes toward various media and every year they have found that those surveyed increasingly cited television as their major source of news. In 1977, when people were asked where they got most of their news about the world 64 percent answered television. The closest runner-up was newspapers (49 percent), with radio, magazines, and people trailing far behind.[21]

When Roper asked people about which medium would they believe if they were to get conflicting news stories, the majority (51 percent) again said television. Newspapers, the next preferred medium, only got 22 percent. When questions were asked about elections, most people said they got their news about local elections from newspapers. Those surveyed also said that newspapers gave them the clearest understanding of local issues. In state and national elections, however, television was the leader.[22]

Other studies contradict Roper's results. Robinson found that on an average weekday 78 percent of the adult population read a newspaper while the total audience for any one of the three television national newscasts was only about one-quarter of the population. He also found that half of the adult population did not watch a single television newscast in a two-week period.[23] Clark and Ruggels also found that newspapers were preferred over television. Their research indicated that the broadcast media are used as a source of news by those who have an average or below average interest in and knowledge of public affairs. They also found that those who preferred newspapers were better educated.[24] A study by Lemert confirms the Roper study that television is preferred for national news, while newspapers are the choice for local news.[25]

The above studies are a good example of some of the contradictions found in broadcast research. The contradictions can only be explained by differences in methodology, such as sample selection, how the questions were asked, and so on. Whenever contradictions occur, however, it is clear that the research question is by no means answered.

A question related to media preference is where do people see or hear news that is of great importance and interest? One study seems to suggest that media play an important role.[26] When Lyndon B. Johnson announced that he would not run for President for 1968, 77 percent of the adult population heard the news from the original telecast. Seventeen percent heard it later from reports on the mass media, and 5 percent heard it from other people. This study suggests that mass media, particularly radio and television, are the most important means of communicating news of national importance.

Media Satisfaction

As well as examining where people get information, researchers have asked questions about satisfaction with the media. Roper discovered that people were generally happy with both programming and commercials. The majority of viewers liked the existing balance between entertainment and news and public affairs. The majority of those surveyed also believed that it was acceptable to have commercials on children's programs.[27]

Television was named as the most desirable medium, followed by newspapers, radio, and magazines.[28] But despite the preference for television, people still valued other household items over the television set. In a poll conducted by Bower in 1970, when people were told they could only keep one item, they choose the refrigerator, the automobile, and the telephone—before the television set.[29]

THE MESSAGE

Much of the research about the message of broadcasting has concentrated on news and news bias. Lang and Lang claim that the media do not simply report on news as it occurs but instead give us a constructed image of events.[30] In television news, for example, film is edited and the editor typically omits the dull portions, the poor camera shots and so on. The stories are also structured by the reporters, the writers back in the newsroom, the producer, and the director. Thus, the news story that we see and hear becomes a new reality; one which may be considerably different than the actual event. This kind of procedure is obviously necessary; the viewer does not have time to listen to the entire politician's speech or to listen to all of the details from a murder trial. However, this kind of restructuring leaves broadcasters open to accusations of distortion and news bias—especially by those who have been the subject of news stories. Thus, many researchers have done analyses of news programs and have attempted to determine whether claims of bias or distortion were true. Since such studies deal with persons and issues within certain time periods, they quickly become dated and so we will not discuss them here. But we would like to point out that studies concerned with news bias are especially prevelant around election periods and are available in the professional journals about the communications industry.

Some of the most interesting message research has documented how the broadcasters cover race relations and portray black people. A study of network news between 1968 and 1970 concluded that NBC gave more coverage to race issues than did ABC and CBS. NBC also portrayed officials and authorities more sympathetically than did CBS.[31] In another study of blacks appearing in television commercials, the researchers discovered that between 1967 and 1970 there was a marked increase of black people in commercials. However, even as late as 1970, black people "typically did not speak or hold the product.[32] In the same study, researchers discovered that in prime time programming half the program had black actors or actresses and that a typical black male worked in law enforcement. In daytime television, blacks were only represented in one quarter of the programs and were most likely to have roles associated with medicine. An interesting finding of this study was that prime time blacks gave and took more orders than daytime blacks.[33]

Sexual stereotyping has been a popular subject for recent broadcasting research. A study of sex roles in cartoons, for instance, revealed that there were three times as many male characters as female characters. Males were shown in a wide variety of occupations, while females were typically portrayed as pretty teenage girls or housewives.[34] Another study of nonprime time programming found that women most often played comic roles or were wives and mothers. Female roles were dependent, subservient, and less rational than male roles. Personal appearance, family, and home were the main concerns of television women.[35] A 1971 study of commercials revealed that men had more important roles than women. They were more often portrayed as experts about products—even when the products were mainly used by women. When men and women used the product, men were often rewarded by career and social advancement, while women were rewarded by approval from others.[36]

There has also been research about particular types of programming. Characters on soap operas are mostly adults. Male professionals are given a great deal of attention, as are their wives, female assistants, lovers, and secretaries. Ninety percent of soap opera conversations are about family, romance, and health problems.[37] In a study of crime and law enforcement shows, researchers found that 64 percent of all prime time shows in the 1972 season had at least one crime, while 42 percent had more than one. Not only does television crime stress murder and the more dramatic forms of crime, but it also portrays crime as being almost always unsuccessful.[38] DeFleur also found that television's portrayal of occupational roles was very different from real life and that high-status occupations were over-represented on television.[39]

Although content analysis centers on the message of a program, some researchers believe that their findings also reveal information about the society to which the message is addressed. George Gerbner and Larry Gross, television researchers, stress that television violence, rather than being meaningless action, actually tells us a good deal about our society by communicating a variety of messages, "most of them dealing with who gets away with what, how, when, why, and against whom."[40] In their study of violence, Gerbner and Gross have analyzed the victims and the violents (those who commit violence) who appear in dramatic television programs to better understand what kinds of characters are portrayed as powerful. They have discovered that there were more victims than violents in terms of getting hurt but in terms of getting killed, there were more killers than killed. The violents were most likely to be young, lower-class, foreign, and nonwhite men. Young men were also likely to get away with killing—for every one killed there were four killers. The victims were most likely to be women—especially lower class, nonwhite, and old women. Of all groups, single women were the most likely to be killed. If a woman was married or foreign, she was not so likely to be a victim.[41]

Another part of the Gerbner-Gross research examines trends in violent programming. Since 1967 they have been conducting a detailed yearly analysis called the Violence Profile, of one week of prime time programming on all three commercial networks.[42]

They have discovered that there has been little decrease in violent programming from the 1967 season to the 1975 season. During the 1975 season eight out of ten prime-time programs still contained violence as did nine out of ten weekend children's hour programming. Of the leading characters, beetweeen six and seven (eight and nine for children) were still involved in some violence. The family hour did not reduce the overall pattern of violence. Although violence was reduced *during* the family hour, it increased during later program hours thereby keeping the overall averages about the same.[43]

THE EFFECTS

The area of broadcast research that has received the most attention and that has been the most controversial is that which deals with the effects that radio and television have on their audiences. Generally, research about effects tries to answer the question of whether broadcasting can bring about changes in people's attitudes and behavior.

Many people fear that broadcasting has the power to manipulate people; that it is so powerful that it can exert some control over people's lives. In recent history a number of Presidents have tried to surpress the media, especially the broadcast media, because they believed and feared that broadcasters were capable of molding public opinion against them.

Generally, however, researchers have discovered that the media are more likely to reinforce our existing attitudes than to change them in any way. For example, in a study of a television antismoking campaign, the researcher discovered that nonsmokers were more likely to find the antismoking commercials effective than were smokers. The antismoking commercials were influential with those who wanted to stop smoking, but, even so, only half of them were able to cut back in their smoking habits.[44]

When "All in the Family" first appeared on the air many people regarded it as a satire on bigotry. The researchers discovered, however, that those who were themselves prejudiced were likely to admire Archie and to perceive him as victorious over his more tolerant son-in-law, Mike. The researchers have suggested that the program is more likely to reinforce racism and prejudice than to combat it.[45]

Other studies on the effects of broadcasting suggest that the audience is not a passive recipient of the broadcast message. Bauer labels the audience for mass media as "obstinate" and points out that the audience will pay no attention to the communication unless there is something in the communication that the audience needs and wants.[46] Researchers have also found that broadcasting usually does not affect any viewer or listener individually, for audience members do not try to understand what they hear and see in isolation. Instead they see, hear, and discuss messages with a wide variety of other people, such as family members, friends, and people they work with. Messages are then interpreted and restructured in reference to these groups. To understand just how this process works, some researchers have studied the leaders of opinion—defined as those persons we turn to for advice. They have discovered that opinion leaders listen to and watch more media than do their followers. They also use the media for the advice and information that they pass along to their followers. Media messages then become more important to opinion leaders than they are to the general mass audience.[47]

In reference to media influence, many people fear that children are much more vulnerable to programs than are adults. In a study of advertising and children, the researchers found that the younger the children, the more likely they were to be confused or misled by television advertising. As children grew older, their attention to and trust in commercials declined.[48] Researchers have also investigated the role of television in educating children. Research on the effects of "Sesame Street" had indicated that children who are encouraged to view the program have greater gains in skills than children who do not have this encouragement.[49] There are also several studies that indicate that children learn social skills from television. For example, when children were shown 30-second commercial spots that stressed sharing, they were later more likely to play games cooperatively rather than competetively.[50]

The most controversial question in discussion of the effects of television on the audience has been that of whether watching violent programs on television increases aggressive behavior on the part of viewers. Although there have been some studies conducted on this subject with adults, the main concern has been the effect of violence on children. Attention to this question increased in 1975

TELEVISION EPILEPSY

The medical profession has recognized a new disease known as "television epilepsy." Patients with no previous history of epilepsy have been known to have epileptic seizures while watching their television set. Television epilepsy is most likely to occur if the patient is a child, if the room is dimly lighted, or if the television set is faulty and flickering. Television epilepsy is most likely to occur in Europe where the scanning and line systems are different.

Source: F. R., Ames, and M., Pietersen, "A Case of Television-Induced Epilepsy with Repetetive Head Movements during the Seizure," *South African Medical Journal*, 46, (1972), pp. 542–44.

with the widely quoted figure that from age five to age fifteen the average young person sees 13,500 people come to a violent end on the television screen.

The relationship between television or film violence and aggressive behavior by children has been studied more intensively than any other broadcast research question. Generally, these studies are experimental and very complex, but, the simplest level, the researcher typically assigns the children into one of two groups—those who see the violent program and those who do not. After the children see the program, they play with each other and the researcher observes which children play aggressively. In virtually all the studies of this nature, a significant percentage of children who have watched the violent programs act aggressively in their play. Although most researchers agree that children who observe aggressive models become more aggressive, there is not enough evidence to indicate that viewing violent programming contributes to crime and juvenile delinquency.[51]

Not only is violence research prevalent but it is also very controversial. Even though most researchers agree that violent programming increases aggression, members of the broadcast industry argue that violent programming only reflects an already violent society. Any research is open to criticism, and research on violence is no exception. Besides broadcast industry criticism of violence research, there is also a good deal of criticism among the researchers themselves over matters such as the methodology of the experiments and the language used to describe the results.

In 1969, in an attempt to resolve some of this controversial research, Senator John Pastore requested that the Surgeon General appoint a committee to determine whether television programs had any harmful effects on children. Specifically, Pastore hoped that such a study "would help to resolve the question of whether there is a causal connection between television crime and violence and anti-social behavior by individuals, especially children."[52]

Pastore's request led to the appointment of a twelve-person committee. Three years later, in 1972, the committee issued their findings in a five-volume research report called *Television and Growing Up: The Impact of Television Violence.* The report contained the results of twenty-three research projects that involved 7,500 young people ranging in ages from three to nineteen and from all geographic areas and socioeconomic groups throughout the United States. The report also contained analysis and criticism of past and ongoing research on the subject of television and aggression.

What did the report actually say? To the dismay of everyone looking for a conclusive answer, the report was largely equivocal. Couched in careful language, the committee unanimously stated that it found "preliminary" and "tentative" indications that there is a connection between programs containing violence and aggressive behavior on the part of viewers. The committee, however, was "unable to conclude how many children were likely to be affected or what should be done about it."[53]

As well as being controversial, the report was almost incomprehensible to the layperson because most of it was written in social science jargon. To compound the problem, the report's results were widely misrepresented in the press. Some newspapers stated that the report linked television programs and violence, while other papers reported that the report had found no link at all. Still others labeled the entire report a "whitewash."[54]

Because of the controversy that followed the release of the report, Senator Pastore feared that its integrity might be compromised. Therefore, he called for two Senate hearings in the hope of bringing order to the controversy. The first hearing, held in 1972, concluded that the networks should remove "gratuitous violence" from programs that children watch. At the second hearing, held in 1974, network executives assured Senator Pastore that they were reducing violence in their programming.[55]

Violence and Adults

Not all research on violence has been limited to its effects on children. Gerbner and Gross, who were mentioned earlier for their work on the Violence Profile, have also done some preliminary work on the effects of television violence on adult viewers. Although their work is still in its preliminary stage, their results show that heavy viewers of television (those who watch four or more hours daily) are much more likely to overestimate the possibility of danger to themselves in everyday life. In other words, they accept the television version of reality.[56]

FUTURE RESEARCH

Although there is a considerable amount of research being conducted concerning all aspects of broadcasting, there are still many subjects that need attention. One area of growing concern to all academic disciplines is that of policy research. In commercial broadcasting it is often very difficult to identify policy makers. Who, for example, determines overall programming policy? Is it the network, the advertiser, or the independent program producer? What role, if any, does the station affiliate play? Program policy is equally unclear at radio stations. Who decides what records should be played on a Top-40 station? Is it station management, the program director, or the disc jockey? Is this decision made solely by the station or is it influenced by record promotion people, trade publications, record sales, and underground music magazines?

One disadvantage of broadcast research is that it is often short-term—it investigates a single phenomenon over a short period of time. For example, if Gerbner and Gross had only conducted a Violence Profile for 1967, the first year of their study, it would be of little value today. But now, whenever this profile is compared to subsequent profiles, it becomes a valuable indication of broadcast trends in programming over the years. Many of the present broadcast research studies would be enhanced if they were designed to examine their subjects over a longer period of time.

Another area that needs research is that of future technology. As Alvin Toffler points out in *Future Shock*, we are inclined to introduce new technology in the name of progress without looking at its possible consequences to society. He argues that we should assess the impact of possible new technology and then decide whether we want to introduce it. Researchers must not only be content to research what is—they must also be concerned about what might be.[57]

Media research also needs more generalists: people who are able to look at all the media and to formulate broad hypotheses about how media affect human beings. We need media ecologists: persons who try to put media into perspective with regard to the total environment. This is not to say, however, that there is no longer any need for specialized research that enables us to fit pieces into the puzzle of the entire system.

There are two areas of specialized research that have been almost entirely neglected; one has been forgotten, and the other has hardly been covered. The forgotten area is radio, which has lost out to its more glamorous colleague, television. Although there have been studies of radio in recent years, they are few and far between. There are several million teenagers who consider their car radios, portable transistor radios, and home radios crucial to their lives. Radio is essential to the multimillion dollar record industry and to the rise and fall of singers and musicians. Radio may also be responsible for forming many of the values held by teenage audiences. It may be that radio is neglected by researchers because it is primarily a medium for teenagers and researchers are usually well past their teenage years.

One area of research that has been almost completely neglected is the study of listeners and viewers as consumers of advertising messages. For every hour of radio, listeners are likely to hear eighteen minutes of commercials; for every hour of television, twelve to fifteen minutes. There is no society in the world, past or present, that is exposed to such a barrage of advertising messages. What is the meaning of all these commercial messages? Do they teach us our roles in society? Do they make us more content? Less content? Do they make us different from other human beings in our values and aspirations?

Research on the impact of broadcasting is still in its infancy. There are thousands of questions that remain unanswered—questions to be answered by the curious. There is also a sense of urgency about these questions for there is no other single institution in American life that consumes as much time and attention as broadcasting.

NOTES

1. Hadley Cantril. "The Invasion from Mars," *The Process and Effects of Mass Communication*, rev. ed., Wilbur Schramm and Donald F. Roberts, eds. (Urbana: University of Illinois Press, 1971), pp. 579–595.*

2. Herta Hertzog, "What Do We Really Know About Daytime Serial Listeners?", *Radio Research, 1942–43*, P. F. Lazarsfeld and F. N. Stanton, eds. (New York: Duell, Sloan and Pearce, 1944) pp. 3–33.

3. R. K. Merton, *Mass Persuasion*, (New York: Harper & Row, 1946).*

4. P. F. Lazarsfeld and R. K. Merton, "Mass Communication, Popular Taste, and Organized Social Action," Schramm and Roberts, op. cit., pp. 554–578.*

5. Roger G. Noll, Merton J. Peck, and Jack J. McGowan, *Economic Aspects of Television Regulation* (Washington, D.C.: Brookings Institution, 1973); Bruce Owen, Jack H. Beebe, Willard G. Manning, Jr. *Television Economics* (Lexington, Mass: Lexington Books, 1974); Walter S. Baer, et al., *Concentration of Mass Media Ownership: Assessing the State of Current Knowledge* (Santa Monica, Calif.: The Rand Corporation, 1974); Richard Bunce, *Television in the Corporate Interest* (New York: Praeger, 1976); David Halberstam, "CBS: The Power and the Profits," *Atlantic* (January and February 1976).

6. K. Lang and G. E. Lang, "The Unique Perspective of Television and its Effect: A Pilot Study," *American Sociological Review*, 18 (1953), pp. 3–12.

7. Edward Jay Epstein, *News From Nowhere* (New York: Random House, 1973).

8. M. G. Cantor, *The Hollywood TV Producer* (New York: Basic Books, 1971).*

9. T. F. Baldwin and C. Lewis, "Violence in Television: The Industry Looks at Itself," *Television and Social Behavior, Vol. 1, Media Content and Control*, G. A. Comstock and E. A. Rubinstein, eds. (Washington, D.C.: Government Printing Office, 1972), pp. 290–373.*

10. J. P. Robinson, "Television and Leisure Time: Yesterday, Today and (Maybe) Tomorrow," *Public Opinion Quarterly* (1969), pp. 210–223.*

11. J. Lyle and H. R. Hoffman, "Children's Use of Television and Other Media," *Television and Social Behavior, V. 4. Television in Day-to-Day Life: Patterns of Use*, E. A. Rubinstein, G. A. Comstock, and J. P. Murray, eds. (Washington, D.C.: Government Printing Office, 1972), pp. 129–256.*

12. Robert T. Bower, *Television and the Public* (New York: Holt, Rinehart and Winston, 1973).*

13. L. Bogart, "Negro and White Media Exposure: New Evidence," *Journalism Quarterly*, 49 (1972), pp. 15–21.*

14. C. E. Block, "Communicating with the Urban Poor: An Exploratory Inquiry," *Journalism Quarterly*, 47 (1970), pp. 3–11.*

15. B. S. Greenberg and B. Dervin, "Mass Communication Among the Urban Poor," *Advances in Communication Research*, C. D. Mortensen and K. K. Sereno, eds. (New York: Harper & Row, 1973), pp. 388–397.*

Also B. S. Greenberg and B. Dervin, *Use of Mass Media by the Urban Poor* (New York: Praeger, 1970).*

16. R. H. Davis, "Television and the Older Adult," *Journal of Broadcasting*, 15 (1971), pp. 153–159.*

17. P. W. Gregg, "Television Viewing as a Parasocial Interaction for Persons Aged 60 or Older," Master's Thesis, University of Oregon, 1971.*; T. F. Schalinske, "The Role of Television in the Life of the Aged Person," Doctoral Dissertation, Ohio State University, 1968.*

18. N. I. Katzman, "Television Soap Operas: What's Been Going On Anyway?," *Public Opinion Quarterly*, 36 (1972), pp. 200–212.*

19. W. R. Hazard, "Anxiety and Preference for Television Fantasy," *Journalism Quarterly*, 44 (1967), pp. 461–469.*

20. Bower, op cit. p. 179.

21. The Roper Organization, *Trends in Public Attitudes Toward Television and Other Mass Media, 1959–1974* (New York: Television Information Office, 1975), p.3.

22. Roper, op. cit., pp. 4, 8–9.

23. J. P. Robinson, "The Audience for National TV News Programs," *Public Opinion Quarterly*, 35 (1971), pp. 403–5.*

24. P. Clarke and L. Ruggels, "Preference Among News Media Coverage of Public Affairs," *Journalism Quarterly*, 47 (1970), pp. 464–471.*

25. J. B. Lemert, "News Media Competition Under Conditions Favorable to Newspapers," *Journalism Quarterly* (1970), pp. 272–280.*

26. I. L. Allen and J. D. Colfax, "The Diffusion of News of LBJ's March 31 Decision," *Journalism Quarterly*, 45 (1968), pp. 321–324.*

27. Roper, op. cit. pp. 19–23.

28. Ibid. p. 5.

29. Bower, op. cit. p. 13

30. K. Lang and G. E. Lang, *Politics and Television* (Chicago: Quadrangle Books, 1968).*

31. R. A. Pride and D. H. Clarke, "Race Relations in Television News: A Content Analysis of the Networks," *Journalism Quarterly*, 50 (1973), pp. 319–328.*

32. J. R. Dominick and B. S. Greenberg, "Three Seasons of Blacks on Television," *Journal of Advertising Research*, 10 (1970), pp. 21–27.*

33. Ibid.

34. R. M. Levinson, "From Olive Oyl to Sweet Polly Purebread: Sex Role Stereotypes and Televised Cartoons," Paper presented at the meeting of the Georgia Sociological Society, Atlanta, November 1973.*

35. M. L. Long and R. J. Simon, "The Roles and Statuses of Women on Children and Family TV Programs," *Journalism Quarterly*, 51 (1974), pp. 107–110.*

36. L. Z. McArthur and B. G. Resko, "The Portrayal of Men and Women in American Television Commercials," *Journal of Social Psychology*, 97 (1975), pp. 209–220.*

37. N. I. Katzman, "Television Soap Operas: What's Been Going on Anyway?," *Public Opinion Quarterly*, 36 (1972), pp. 200–212.*

38. J. R. Dominick, "Crime and Law Enforcement in Prime-Time Television," *Public Opinion Quarterly*, 37 (1973), pp. 241–250.*

39. M. L. DeFleur, "Occupational Roles as Portrayed on Television," *Public Opinion Quarterly*, 28 (1964), pp. 57–74.*

40. George Gerbner and Larry Gross, *Violence Profile No. 6*, Mimeo (December 1974), p. 5.

41. Ibid., pp. 38–39.

42. George Gerbner and Larry Gross "Living with Television: The Violence Profile," *Journal of Communication*, 26 (1976), pp. 173–199.

43. Ibid., pp. 186–187.

44. M. T. O'Keefe, "The Anti-Smoking Commercials: A Study of Television's Impact on Behavior," *Public Opinion Quarterly*, 35 (1971), pp. 242–248.*

45. N. Vidmar and M. Rokeach, "Archie Bunker's Bigotry: A Study in Selective Perception and Exposure," *Journal of Communication*, 24 (1974), pp. 36–47.*

46. R. A. Bauer, "The Obstinate Audience: The Influence Process from the Point of View of Social Communication," in Schramm and Roberts, op. cit., pp. 326–346.*

47. Charles R. Wright, *Mass Communication*, 2nd ed. (New York: Random House, 1975), p. 85.

48. See studies by S. Ward in *Television and Social Behavior, Vol. 4, Television in Day-to-Day Life: Patterns of Use*, E. A. Rubinstein, G. A. Comstock, and J. P. Murray, eds. (Washington, D.C.: Government Printing Office, 1972)*
Also see: S. Ward, D. B. Wackman, R. Faber, and G. S. Lesser, *Effects of Television Advertising on Consumer Socialization*, (Cambridge, Mass.: Marketing Science Institute, 1974).

49. T. D. Cook, H. Appleton, R. Conner, A. Shaffer, G. Tamkin, and S. J. Weber, *Sesame Street Revisited: A Study in Evaluation Research* (New York: Russell Sage Foundation, 97 (1975), pp. 209–220.*

50. R. W. Poulos, "Television's Prosocial Effects: A Positive Look at the Medium," *Journal of Social Issues*, 97 (1975), pp. 209–220.*

51. Several of these studies can be found in G. A. Comstock and E. A. Rubinstein, eds. *Television and Social Behavior, Vol. 3, Television and Adolescent Aggressiveness* (Washington, D.C., Government Printing Office, 1972).*

52. Douglas Cater and Stephen Strickland, *TV Violence and the Child* (New York: Russell Sage Foundation, 1975), p. 1.*

53. Ibid., p. 2.

54. Ibid., pp. 80–81.

55. Ibid., p. 126.

56. Gerbner and Gross, op. cit., p. 43.

57. Alvin Toffler, *Future Shock* (New York: Random House, 1970).

*Many of the research studies cited in this chapter can be found in abstracted form in George Comstock's *Television and Human Behavior: The Key Studies* (Santa Monica, Calif. Rand Corporation, 1975). For the convenience of our readers we have identified with an asterisk those studies covered in Comstock.

Broadcasting, Critics, and Public Interest

9

American broadcasting operates as a private profit making industry which is subject to certain government controls. The broadcast industry has problems that are shared by no other American industry: broadcasting is the only business in which the owners are expected, and often required, to put the public interest ahead of profit. Unfortunately, profitmaking and public interest are not always congenial concepts.

Although everyone is clear about what constitutes profit, not everyone can define the term, public interest. Congress, through the Communications Act of 1934, has indicated that public interest means that broadcasters should encourage free speech, permit discussion of controversial issues, take responsibility for their own programming, and serve their local communities. The extent to which broadcasters should do this has never been defined. Many feel that this term should encompass much more. Some believe that programming in the public interest should exceed the mere entertainment level by being useful, enlightening, or uplifting. Others believe that public interest means hiring more minority groups and portraying them in a more realistic manner in broadcast programming.

Whatever the idea of public interest, broadcasters believe that it will cost them money. They argue that programs that go beyond entertainment have few viewers and lose money. They point out that it takes money, and staff to seek

225

out controversial ideas, to produce local programming, and to train minority employees. Most of the arguments between the broadcasters and the critics end in stalemate. The broadcasters blame the critics for having little business sense and the critics blame the broadcasters for being profit-hungry. As with many issues, the truth probably lies somewhere in-between.

We will concentrate basically on three types of problems in this chapter: the first involves politics and government, the second examines mass or popular culture and its relationship to traditional culture, and the final issue is that of media images or how people would like to see themselves portrayed in broadcast programs. The following section examines the critics of broadcasting along with some of the issues with which they are concerned.

THE CRITICS: WHO ARE THEY?

All critics have somewhat the same purpose in reacting to the broadcast industry; that is, they hope to improve the quality of programming. Critics have approached the critical process from all perspectives. Some have written personal reactions to the industry; some have done considerable research into the historical and economic development of the industry, while still others have conducted experimental research. The writings and conclusions of these critics have varied greatly. Some critics believe that the broadcast industry is basically sound and needs few changes, while others believe that the entire structure must change. Those who favor extensive change have not always had creative solutions; as with most problems, they are easier to state than to solve.

One group of critics that devotes itself to a study of radio and television is composed of members of college and university faculties throughout the country. Although many of these people are on mass communication faculties, there are also many sociologists, political scientists, and economists who also write about broadcasting. These critics probably do the most in-depth investigating of and reporting about the broadcast industry. Unfortunately, since this writing is often highly scholarly or technical, it is never read by the general public. Many members of the broadcast industry feel that academic critics live in an "ivory tower" and are unable to understand the realities of the "real world." These critics are certainly not regarded as part of the broadcast establishment.

Critics who write regularly or who freelance for newspapers and magazines comprise the second group. The *New York Times*, for example, carries regular articles about broadcasting. Most of the popular writing about broadcasting, however, is limited to information about radio and television programming and stars; there is little writing about how the industry works or how it affects society.

Politicians have also jumped into the critical arena. Richard M. Nixon and Spiro Agnew often criticized television for its liberal bias. Long after they resigned, they continued to blame television and other news media for being responsible for ending their political careers. The Democrats have also not been happy with news coverage: Kennedy, Johnson, and Carter have all been critical of media news coverage. Because the media have been so essential to twentieth century politics and politicians, many of the politicians have been particularly critical; in fact, some have even attempted to suppress those media that treated them unkindly.

During the late sixties and early seventies, citizen's groups began organizing to see if they could improve broadcasting. Most of these groups were another variation of the consumer groups that were appearing throughout the country. Some of the citizen's groups set up a permanent organization with the idea of improving broadcasting in general; other groups were more task-oriented.

Many of the short-term groups were very successful. A group in Jackson, Mississippi caused a television station to lose its license because it was not meeting the needs of its black viewers. Another group in New York City challenged the right of WNCN, a radio station, to change its format from classical to rock when the station was purchased by a new owner. Their actions caused the new owners to resell the station to another company that agreed to retain the station's classical format. Other groups, particularly minority and women's groups, have worked behind the scenes with station management to bring about improved hiring practices and to encourage minority and women's programming.

There are also reform groups that have permanent organizations. Action for Children's Television (ACT) was formed in 1968 to improve children's programming and to eliminate commercials from children's programming. Although they have not been able to eliminate commercials, they have succeeded in reducing the number of commercial minutes on children's programs.

The United Church of Christ organized its Office of Communication in 1957 and has since provided assistance to citizens who want to improve local radio and television stations. This group played an important role in helping the citizen's group to win its case against the television station in Mississippi.

The National Citizens Committee for Broadcasting (NCCB) is one of the most influential groups. Based in Washington, this group works for citizen's rights and publishes *Access*, a bimonthly magazine of criticism of industry practices and regulation. NCCB also has a lobby group in Washington.

More specialized media groups include the National Black Media Coalition, the National Latino Media Coalition and the Task Force on Broadcast Media, which is part of the National Organization for Women.

The main goal of all of these groups is to improve the industry through action rather than through speculative writing. These groups not only see the problems in the industry but have very specific ideas about improvements. Although the emergence of the citizen's groups does not please broadcasters, many of the groups have been successful and there will probably be many more formed in the future.

THE ISSUES

News

If the broadcast industry were expected only to provide entertainment programming there would probably not be so much criticism of and apprehension over the industry's power. Because the industry provides news, documentary, and public affairs programming, however, the critics are more apprehensive. Two questions are commonly asked of broadcast journalism: 1) is broadcast news going beyond the news function and creating news as well as covering it? and 2) to what extent does broadcast news distort the facts? To answer these questions we must attempt to define news.

Everyone would agree that a tornado, an assassination, or a war is news. However, all people might not agree that a demonstration, a press conference or a bicentennial celebration is also news. Daniel J. Boorstin, a historian, distinguishes between news and non-news or what he calls pseudo-events. Boorstin says that pseudo-events are not spontaneous; someone plans them or incites them and they are planned primarily for the purpose of being reported. The most important question regarding a pseudo-event, he says, is not "Is it real?" but "Is it newsworthy?"[1] Sometimes a pseudo-event is planned by the person who wants news coverage. For example, the President of the United States may call a press conference to inform reporters about a new domestic policy. Other times the reporters go out and create news by interviewing people who are "newsworthy."

News coverage of pseudo-events is not necessarily bad. Many investigative and interpretative stories result from reporters looking for news. The problem with pseudo-events comes when they are created by people for the sole purpose of getting their name or organization into the news. At both the 1968 and 1972 political conventions many demonstrators "staged" their demonstrations in order to get maximum television coverage. During the 1972 Republican Convention in Miami a group of veterans demanded entry to the convention hotel. Later in an interview they explained that they did not want to get into the hotel; they wanted television cameras to record their being turned away.

Demonstrators are not the only ones to have used the media for their own purposes. People all over the world have realized that whatever is covered by the news media, particularly by television, gains importance. Before the United States and Cuba agreed on a strategy for deterring hijackers, several persons periodically hijacked airplanes to Cuba, often in order to get personal publicity in the nation's media. When the Symbionese Liberation Army kidnapped Patricia Hearst they not only used the media for publicity for the group, they also used it to communicate their demands to the Hearst family. As one writer remarked, "However futile the result, for a few weeks, the SLA, the world's smallest army (maximum complement estimated at twelve souls), commanded the world's largest information machine at will."[2]

Other people are even more blatent in their use of the news media. Evel Knievel, for example, gets considerable news coverage and is well recognized for his ability to manipulate the news media. He believes, in fact, that in another twenty years or so he will be so well known that he will be able to run for the presidency.

In the late 1970s, the problem of terrorists manipulating the media became so serious that CBS News issued guidelines for covering terrorist and hostage stories. The guidelines stated that unless terrorist demands were free from political rhetoric, they should be paraphrased and presented by newspersons rather than by the terrorists. CBS News also said that, except under compelling circumstances, there should be no live coverage of terrorists or kidnappers and that such stories should not be given so much time on the newscast that other important stories are omitted.[3]

Although these guidelines may help to control media manipulation, the fact remains that such stories are news and they cannot be completely ignored, even when news organizations know that the persons involved have the goal of controlling the media for their own political platforms. It is also bad business to neglect stories. If ABC refuses to cover a demonstration that is later shown on CBS and NBC, ABC could lose in ratings and, consequently, in advertisers. News, like entertainment, must be profitable.

Both radio and television news face the problem of filling a set period of time every day regardless of the quantity and quality of news stories. Unlike newspapers that can add or delete pages depending on the length or number of stories, broadcast news is expected to fill the time that has been allotted to it. The evening news shows, for example, are a half-hour long every night. Regardless of the immensity or scarcity of news events which have occurred during the day, this news must be stretched or condensed to fit the half-hour. This very act of expanding and condensing stories introduces some bias into broadcast news.

Television news has another problem that is unique to news operations. In order to cover a story, the station or network must send out a crew of technicians rather than a single reporter. This crew goes out with film or video tape, audio equipment, and lights. Because these crews cannot move quickly or easily, news producers, especially on the national level, prefer stories that can be scheduled in advance rather than those that occur spontaneously. The networks are also more likely to cover stories in cities in which their own crews are stationed rather than stories that occur in out-of-the-way places.

Television news also seeks out the visual and the sensational. When producers select stories, they decide on those which have the most action and look the most interesting. For example, television news will linger over scenes of battles, but it will just briefly show the visually dull negotiations. This practice obviously introduces bias into television news. However, the fact that television news is highly visual is also in its favor. Because of television news many of us see unusual places and events that we would most likely never see in person. From Bombay to Beirut—a panorama of international events is presented to us in our own living rooms.

Corporate Ownership of Broadcasting

The corporate ownership of broadcast property has raised at least two issues of public interest. One issue deals with conflict of interest and the other deals with corporate misuse of media.

Many radio and television stations and networks are owned by giant corporations and conglomerates. Because these huge companies own a wide variety of companies in addition to their broadcast properties, the question is raised whether networks and stations can run news operations that might conflict with corporate goals. For example, in the mid-1970s, the record industry suffered a series of payola scandals, some of which involved Columbia Records, which is owned by CBS. Did the CBS radio and television networks and stations treat this story as just another story or did they deemphasize it? RCA, which owns NBC, receives substantial revenues from government contracts involving the Department of Defense. They also sell electronic parts internationally to industries and governments. If a news event occurs that involves one of the RCA's industrial partners or defense interests, does NBC treat it as it treats other news? Although there is no evidence of corporation manipulation of news, the potential for abuse is obvious.

Some critics also claim that the large corporations use the networks to promote corporate values. Since corporations are the only organizations large and rich enough to afford national advertising rates, they have considerable power over network television. It does not seem likely, for example, that a network is going to do a hard-hitting documentary on automobile pollution when some of its largest advertisers are automobile manufacturers.

Some critics also claim that corporations use television to improve their corporate image. John Kenneth Galbraith, an economist, claims that when a corporation is accused of pollution, of destroying natural resources, or of endangering the public safety, the corporation immediately embarks on an advertising campaign to show the company's devotion to the environment, conservation, and public safety. In other words, the company never solves the problem. Not only is the advertising campaign cheaper, it becomes a substitute for a solution.[4]

Political Candidates

American political campaigns have been greatly affected by radio and television. With the advent of television it was possible for the first time in history for the voice and the image of the candidate to reach every American home. Americans who might not have been interested in politics before could no longer avoid the campaign—the candidates appeared between and sometimes in, favorite programs. Because of the candidates' involvement with the entertainment media, it became apparent that the candidates themselves might become "personalities" or "stars" in the voters minds rather than men and women concerned with serious political issues. However, once television was established as part of political campaigning, candidates were convinced that it had a greater potential for good than for harm.

Advertising agencies and media specialists became part of the American campaign scene in 1952 when Dwight D. Eisenhower hired Batten, Barton, Durstine, and Osborn (BBDO), a major advertising agency, to help plan his campaign. BBDO, in fact, also helped Richard Nixon by arranging and buying time for his Checker's speech.[5] Kennedy, Johnson, Humphrey, McGovern, Ford, and Carter have all used advertising agencies—sometimes depending on them only for commercials, other times consulting them for a much broader campaign strategy.

After advertising agencies began handling political accounts, critics began to complain that candidates were being sold to the public in the same way as breakfast cereal. They said that when the emphasis shifted to the candidate's image and personality, political issues were forgotten. They also pointed out that when an advertising agency built an image for a candidate it also had to control that image for if the candidate acted spontaneously it could easily ruin a carefully created illusion. Thus, an agency-controlled candidate would not be free to talk to people directly—every aspect of the campaign would be rehearsed and staged.

An extreme of what an agency could do occurred in California in the sixties when a Senator decided to seek reelection even though he had undergone brain surgery, was partially paralyzed, and could barely walk or talk. He announced that he would be a candidate in a 42-second film that was so skillfully edited that there was no indication of his disability. Whether the candidate could have won through agency efforts will never be known since he died before the primary.[6] The whole incident, however, raises serious questions about manufacturing images for political candidates.

In a national campaign an agency is certain to use television since it is the best way to reach so many people. Also the public is so accustomed to seeing candidates on television that a prime-time appearance gives the candiate both additional credibility and legitimacy in the voters' eyes.

Unfortunately, not all candidates are equal on television since some are visually more appealing than others. Many critics believe, for example, that Kennedy's victory over Nixon in 1960 was partially due to the fact that Kennedy looked better on television. Nixon later learned how to use television to his advantage by hiring a media specialist, but it was not until 1968 that he regained his political position. Conceivably, the political parties could eliminate potential candidates simply because they do not have the "right" look and sound for the broadcast media.

Another objection that critics have to media campaigns is the great cost—especially for television. Only candidates who are wealthy or who can amass funds can afford media campaigns. At the presidential level, the party and the government will pay much of the costs for the candidate. However, at the state and local level the winning candidate is often the person who has enough money to invest in a media campaign.

Because commercial time is so expensive, politicians try to appear on the news as much as possible. Not only is the news free, it also has greater credibility than paid time. Candidates go to great lengths to attract reporters. The campaign manager prepares news releases, detailed schedules of where the candidate will be and often arranges for food and alcohol for those who follow the "campaign trail." In some cases a candidate may hire photographers or film crews and make his or her own photographs or film available to local stations. When a candidate is shown touring the local slums, the photographer is there because the campaign manager arranged it. Candidates are also not adverse to news manipulation in order to get maximum coverage. They create pseudo-events, such as frequent press conferences and mud slinging bouts with their opponents. They engage in stunts that are designed to attract maximum news coverage, such as walking across their state. The press releases may be far from accurate—especially when they estimate the number of people who attended the latest political rally. A good deal of effort is spent in creating situations that will get maximum news coverage.

There is a good deal of news value in a political campaign; in fact, in a Presidential election year the campaign may be the most important news item of all. It would take a wise news staff to always be able to distinguish between genuine news and pseudo news. However television news is more inclined to cover the nonessential than any other news medium. Candidates virtually monopolize the airwaves in an election year and more than one American has been happy to return to toothpaste commercials and everyday political battles after the election is over.

A candidate who makes all decisions based on advice of a media specialist is not a good, or even a typical, candidate. A media specialist would probably advise a candidate against taking a stand on controversial issues, yet many candidates are willing to take strong positions on issues. Although a media specialist might suggest only a media campaign, many candidates prefer to travel across the country to meet and talk with the people. Probably the greater majority of candidates aim for a well-balanced campaign in which they use all of the media as well as make personal appearances. The candidate to be suspicious of is the one who avoids personal appearances and who relies solely on television to convey his or her image.

Mass Culture and High Culture

One frequent objection to mass media is that they deal so seldom with serious cultural topics such as art, classical music, and literature. Instead the media specialize in popular entertainment that is mass produced and simple enough to be easily understood by everyone. Although all mass media provide mass entertainment, television reaches so many people and consumes so much time that it is held to be the main purveyor of mass culture; that is, the average person's view of the world and the kind of entertainment that represents it. Those who oppose mass culture generally oppose the level of television programming.

There are arguments for and against mass culture. Proponents contend that it is democratic in that everyone can both afford and understand it. They also believe that mass culture serves a useful function in society by giving viewers and listeners a chance to relax and enjoy themselves without expending great mental effort since it is unintellectual in nature. Some people, they argue, do not want to be uplifted and enlightened all the time—they are often content to be purely diverted or amused.

Some media writers have suggested that television might play a role in helping to preserve a so-called high culture by presenting such traditional cultural events as ballets and concerts. When television concentrates on mass culture, it leaves the other media free to develop specialized programming and audiences. For example, radio has become more specialized since television removed its mass audience. Because television exists, radio is forced to develop special formats. This programming ranges from classical music to progressive music; programming that was not widely available before television. These writers also point out that film has become more artistic and deals with more mature themes since the advent of television.

Opponents of mass culture argue that those who are involved in creating it are too money oriented. They fear that serious artists are beguiled by mass culture because it pays more for artists' efforts. They also argue that stations and networks are so interested in making profits that they ignore audiences of 10 or 15 million who are interested in high culture and cater to audiences of 30 or 40 million who prefer mass culture.

Another argument against mass culture is that it deals with trivia and, although trivia may be diverting, it is not very fulfilling. Even the producers of television programs would probably agree that soap operas, game shows, and police stories are not very uplifting. However, they point out that trivia is an inevitable part of a fifteen hour programming schedule. Trivia, they claim, is essential since a classical series, such as the production of all the Shakespearean plays, could be aired in a single week of prime-time programming.

Another argument against mass culture is that it makes its audience spectators rather than participants. This argument is difficult to prove or disprove. Mass culture and leisure time have developed almost simultaneously. If we were to ask people what they did before television, the answer would almost certainly be that they worked longer hours. We can only speculate what people would do without television. Although they might join baseball teams or choirs, it is just as likely that they would return to more radio listening and movie going, both of which call for equally passive audiences.

It is certainly a mistake to say that all mass culture is alike. Some of its offerings are sophisticated, entertaining, and deal with comtemporary themes. Other offerings are mindless and tasteless. Since mass culture is already firmly entrenched as part of American life, the main argument should probably not be whether it should remain, but rather how the bad can be improved and how the good can become even better.

Media Images

During the past ten years many groups whose primary interest was not in broadcasting have become engaged in vigorous criticism of broadcasters. Although these groups are very diverse, including women, black people, Indians, and Mexican-Americans, they have one thing in common: they object to the way in which they are portrayed in television programming.

Black people were the first group to organize and protest. Their objection came in 1952 when the National Association for the Advancement of Colored People (NAACP) condemned the television version of "Amos 'n Andy" as being racist. Organized black protest against broadcasters was not to be heard again until the late sixties. Then black people began to protest that they were either not portrayed at all or that, when they were shown, it was in an unrealistic way. They believed that black characters should be developed in their own right and that these characters should reflect black lifestyles; it was no longer sufficient to put black people into roles that anyone could play. There was also protest that programming never showed black families. It wasn't until the 1970s when Norman Lear created "Good Times" and "The Jeffersons" that black families were regularly seen on prime-time television. Critics note that there are still many areas of black programming that need improvement. Black people are seldom the subject of serious dramatic treatment. Also black news coverage and black participation in news shows as reporters and anchorpersons is still far from adequate.

While black protest came largely in the sixties, women's protest has been very much of the seventies. Women are also concerned both about their lack of media exposure and how they are portrayed on television. For example, the 1975–76 television season opened with female leads in only 13 percent of the prime-time shows. Males had leads in 63 percent of the programming and the remaining 24 percent was general family programming with no identifiable lead.

This lack of exposure also exists in commercials. In a recent study by the Screen Actors Guild, the researchers discovered that of all performers in TV commercials, 32 percent were women and 68 percent were men. When women did appear in commercials, they were more likely to be shown on-camera. Men captured 93 percent of the off-camera speaking roles and 71 percent of the off-camera singing roles.[7]

As well as objecting to their relative obscurity, many women have also objected to the way in which they have been portrayed. They object to being locked into the traditional roles of housewife, secretary, teacher, and mother and want to be shown as doctors, pilots, and breadwinners as well. Perhaps no role arouses so much hostility among feminists as that of the woman as a sexual object, particularly when her body and appearance are exploited to sell a product.

As well as objecting to being portrayed in limited, traditional roles, many women object to the television ideal of a woman whose only concerns are dirty laundry and dishes. Contrary to the philosophy of many television commercials, women seem to resent being made to feel guilty about having spots on their glassware or rings around their husbands' collars.

Women and black people are not the only ones who have objected to the way they are represented. Italians have protested their portrayal as members of the Mafia. Indians complain that movies and television programs about cowboys and Indians show them as wily and treacherous and a threat to more "civilized" people. Other critics have pointed out that the protesting groups are not the only groups who are stereotyped. The Bunker family is not your typical American family nor does the TV cop resemble most law enforcement officers. Families and policemen, however, have not joined the ranks of the protesters.

The groups who have protested about their image are not protesting an occasional program with an occasional stereotype. They believe that when a medium defines its women as sex objects, its blacks as lazy, its Italians as criminals, and its Indians as losers, it presents problems for the entire society. Not only does the society begin to believe the portrayals, it also causes identity problems for the group in question. A black adult remembered that when he was growing up, he and his brothers and sisters used to listen to "Amos 'n Andy" every week with the greatest of pleasure. Then he realized that "they" were supposed to be "us." Those groups who are protesting their media images are asking that the media portray them as they see themselves; that the "they" and the "us" become one.

Any group that criticizes television does not have an easy task. For every group that has been able to bring about change, there have been several other groups that have failed. Some groups have had to go to the courts—an expensive and lengthy process. On the other hand, many broadcasters have been responsive to the public when the public makes its interests known. When this kind of response is made, broadcasters are ready to work in the public interest.

NOTES

1. Daniel J. Boorstin "From News-Gathering to News-Making: A Flood of Pseudo-Events," *The Process and Effects of Mass Communication*, rev. ed., Wilbur Schramm and Donald F. Robers, (eds.,) (Urbana: University of Illinois Press, 1971) pp. 119–120.
2. Martin Barrett, ed., *Moments of Truth*, (New York: Thomas Y. Crowell, 1975) p. 143.
3. *Broadcasting*, April 18, 1977, p. 65.
4. John Kenneth Galbraith, *Economics and the Public Purpose* (Boston: Houghton Mifflin, 1973) p. 158.
5. Dan Nimmo, *The Political Persuaders* (Englewood Cliffs, N.J.: Prentice-Hall, 1970) p. 112.
6. Ibid., pp. 141–142.
7. *Media Report to Women*, March 1, 1975, p. 6.

Agencies of Regulation 10

THE FCC AND THE PUBLIC

In 1964 three petitioners, the United Church of Christ, the Rev. L. T. Smith, and Mr. Aaron Henry, requested that the FCC not renew the license of WLBT-TV, owned by Lamar Life, in Jackson, Mississippi. The parties claimed that WLBT had a long history of discriminatory practices toward the black community in Jackson. Not only did the station refuse black people the right to use its facilities, the station also systematically promoted segregationist views and denied the right of anyone to present opposing views.

Although the FCC denied the petitioners official standing, it did take their claims regarding programming seriously. The commission gave the station a one-year probationary license and ordered the station to stop its discriminatory practices.

The petitioners did not consider the one year license period a satisfactory solution and so they appealed the FCC decision to the United States Court of Appeals. The Court ruled that the petitioners had the right to official standing and that their claims against the station were serious enough to warrant a complete hearing. The FCC held the hearing and again decided in favor of the station and renewed its license with no special conditions.

The people who were involved in the case were outraged at the FCC's decision. They maintained that just because the station had been "good" during its probationary year, it should not be forgiven for its past programming practices. To make matters worse, during the hearing, the FCC refused to hear some of the witnesses against the station.

In order to understand this conflict involving the FCC, let us look at some of the station's practices during the license period in question:

WLBT regularly carried programs and spots about the White Citizen's Council, which maintained that the Communists were behind the Civil Right's Movement.

Although 47 percent of the people living within the station's coverage area were black, they were almost completely unrepresented in the station's programming.

WLBT regularly interrupted pro-integration programming with a sign that said "Sorry—cable trouble."

The station frequently used the terms "nigger" and "negra."

Before each presentation of national news on the "Today" show a local announcer would say: "What you are about to see is an example of biased, managed Northern news. Be sure to stay tuned at 7:25 to hear your local newscasts."

When a black political candidate tried to buy time for his political campaign, the station manager told the candidate that if he persisted his body might be found floating in the local river.

In view of these examples it seems incredible that the FCC could renew a license for a station that was so obviously *not* operating in the public interest. Nevertheless, even though it was not a unanimous decision, the FCC still renewed the station's license. Thus, the only recourse for the petitioners was to go back to the Court of Appeals which again overruled the FCC decision. Finally, after years of hearings and appeals, the FCC was directed by the Court to deny renewal of WLBT's license. The FCC had no choice but to comply.

The WLBT case was one of the most important cases in broadcast regulation in that it established the right of ordinary citizens to request that a station's license be denied. The case set a precedent that has granted numerous individuals and citizen's groups the right to be heard in regard to station licenses.

On the other hand, the case graphically illustrates the shortcomings and limited vision of the FCC. In the following section we will discuss the make-up of the FCC, what it can and cannot do, and some of the reasons why it is so often inefficient and ineffective.

CREATION OF THE FCC

Although the FCC was not the first federal agency designed to regulate broadcasting (FRC, 1929–1934), it was the first commission which had regulatory control over broadcasting and wire communication. Much of the legal philosophy that gave rise to the FCC was developed when Congress created the FRC. In fact, many of the provisions in the Radio Act of 1927 were transfered into the Communications Act of 1934, which established the FCC. For this reason, it is appropriate to review some of the ideas that went into the creation of the FRC.

When Congress was considering a new radio commission, industry representatives, government officials, and educators urged Congress to establish an effective method to protect both the listener and the broadcaster. As Secretary of Commerce Hoover said, "The ether is a public medium, and its use must be for public benefit."[2] Hoover continued by observing:

> [The main] consideration in the radio field is, and always will be, the great body of the listening public, millions in number, countrywide in distribution. There is no proper line of conflict between the broadcaster and the listener. . . Their interests are mutual, for without the one the other could not exist.[3]

Hoover's declaration became the philosophical basis for radio regulation. Let us review the three points that permit the government to regulate radio. They are: 1.Radio is a public medium;   2.There are not enough radio channels for everyone to have a channel;   3.The government must regulate radio waves in the interest of the public and the broadcaster.

Thus, the Radio Act of 1927 set out to protect both the private interests of broadcasters and the more public interest of listeners, but there was no suggestion that the existing system needed to be changed. Basically the Radio Act was to decide which few broadcasters could stay on the air. The private, profit-motivated system of broadcasting continued on the same path it had begun before governmental intervention.

Later during 1933 President Roosevelt, who was dissatisfied with the existing system of radio regulation, called for an interdepartmental study of communications to determine if there was a more effective method for regulating electrical communication in the United States. The resulting study group recommended that a new agency be formed with power to regulate wire communication, which was then under the Interstate Commerce Commission; radio communication, which was controlled by the FRC; and other aspects of electrical communication, which were under the jurisdiction of the President.[4]

As a result of the committee's report and Congressional hearings, the FRC was abolished in 1934 and replaced by the FCC with expanded powers to regulate all interstate wire and radio communication in the United States. In addition, the FCC was created as a permanent body whereas the FRC had been a temporary agency. Although the new commission's jurisdiction had been enlarged, its mandate remained one of protecting the private interests of business within the commission's view of the "public interest".

AUTHORITY FOR CREATING FCC

When Congress wanted to create an agency to regulate broadcasting it looked to the Constitution for guidance. The authority to regulate radio and wire communication was given to Congress in the Commerce Clause of the Constitution, which states, "The Congress shall have the Power . . . to regulate Commerce with foreign Nations, and among the several States . . . ."[5] In the judgment of Congress, broadcasting and other forms of radio communication were commerce within the scope of the Constitution. Furthermore, Congress felt that broadcasting was an interstate activity since many signals cross state lines.

To make certain no conflicts with the states arose, Congress gave the FCC authority to regulate only interstate and foreign wire and radio communication, but without extending the FCC's powers to communication within states. Parenthetically, the FCC was given the authority to regulate all broadcast stations including those that do not appear to cross state lines because no station can say with certainty that its signal will not cross a state line, and many broadcast signals cross state lines and broadcasting is regulated as a class. In addition, when Congress directed the FCC to regulate "wire and radio" communication, it gave the commission authority to regulate long distance telephone communication, telegraph companies, and specialized services such as citizen band, amateur, and taxi radio.

While the FCC has wide authority to regulate business communication, it cannot regulate governmental use of radio communications. This means that the FCC cannot intervene in the activities of the military nor can it regulate the communication activities of other branches of government. However, the military and other governmental agencies that use radio frequencies are not free to wander over the radio spectrum at will. Government users of radio have regulations and statutes that limit their use of radio waves.

"THE PUBLIC INTEREST, CONVENIENCE, AND NECESSITY"

The Communications Act of 1934, which created the FCC, directs it to regulate many aspects of radio and wire communication in quite specific terms. However, Congress did not always wish to be so detailed and so the FCC was given the general mandate of regulating in "the public interest, convenience, or necessity." This mandate gives the FCC wide latitude within which to use its discretion and applies to many areas of FCC jurisdiction. For example, the FCC may write rules and regulations to implement the intent of the Communications Act if the "public interest, convenience, and necessity" will be served. In addition, the FCC must award, revoke, and renew licenses only if it can show that the "public interest, convenience, and necessity" is aided by its decision.

However, the public interest mandate appeared too general to at least two groups of individuals. In fact, these groups were so concerned that Congress had given the FCC unrestrained authority to act arbitrarily that they asked the courts for a ruling on the constitutionality of the "public interest, convenience, and necessity" mandate. These two companies, Pottsville Broadcasting Company and Allentown Broadcasting Corporation, were told by the United States Supreme Court that the "public interest" was as concrete a mandate as the complicated factors of radio permitted.[6,7] Thus, the Supreme Court upheld the FCC's use of the public interest mandate as its authority to regulate.

STRUCTURE OF RADIO LAW

Congress established the FCC as an independent commission along the lines of such agencies as the Interstate Commerce Commission and the Federal Trade Commission. An independent commission is a separate entity, "independent" of the other three branches of government. The independent commissions form a fourth branch of government to regulate, creatively and effectively, one particular aspect of business such as communications. (As we shall see later this concept works well in theory, but not so well in reality).

To function as a regulator the FCC must have the scope of its authority stated explicitly, which is the role of the Communications Act of 1934. This Act is divided into six sections, also called subchapters or titles.[8] The first section of the law states the general provisions and scope of the Communications Act. In this section are the reasons for radio law, definitions of important terms that appear throughout the law, and the organization of the FCC. The second section deals with common carrier regulation such as telephones, telegraph, and microwaves. The third title, of more interest to students of broadcasting, deals with radio. In legal terms, "radio" refers to radio and television since both use radio waves. This section contains the provisions that deal with the formation of Corporation for Public Broadcasting. In fact the legislation forming CPB is to be found here. (See Figure 10–1.)

The fourth and fifth titles of the Communications Act deal with fines or penalties and with procedures and methods, that the FCC uses to carry out its assigned duties. the sixth section deals with miscellaneous matters such as the war powers of the President over electrical communications.

THE FCC AS LEGISLATOR AND JUDGE

Since Congress could not possibly have foreseen all the problems that might arise in radio, the responsibility of writing specific rules and regulations consistent with the Communications Act was left to the FCC. Just as the Communications Act derives its authority from the Constitution of the United States, FCC rules and regulations derive their authority from the Communications Act. And just as provisions in the Communications Act must be consistent with the Constitution, so must provisions in the FCC rules and regulations be consistent with the Communications Act. As Figure 10–2 shows, FCC rules and regulations are subordinate to the Communications Act. But where the FCC has jurisdiction, its rules and regulations take precedence over laws passed by states. That is, the FCC has authority over the interstate aspects of radio communication and states may not intrude into the FCC's domain.

The Communications Act prescribes penalities for violators of either FCC rules and regulations or the Communications Act itself. The penalities are consistent with the importance Congress ascribed to the Communications Act and FCC regulations. A violator of the Communications Act may be fined up to

SCOPE OF FCC AUTHORITY

According to the Communications Act of 1934, the FCC has the authority to regulate the following areas consistent with the public interest:

1. Devices that can transmit radio energy
2. The sale of devices that can transmit radio waves
3. Classify radio stations
4. Prescribe the nature of service provided by stations
5. Assign bands of frequencies to different types of radio services
6. Set the location of transmitters
7. The kind of equipment stations use
8. Create specific regulations consistent with the Communications Act
9. Conduct studies of radio
10. Set the geographic region or area a station may serve
11. Create special rules to control stations engaged in network broadcasting
12. Create specific regulations on keeping station logs, and the type of signals stations may use
13. Set license qualifications for people operating transmitters
14. Designate call letters
15. Set times when stations must air call letters
16. Regulate the construction and color of transmitter towers.
17. Grant licenses
18. Require UHF tuners on television sets

Source: Communications Act of 1934 amended through January 1969.

Title I
General provisions
A. Purpose
B. Definitions
C. Qualifications of
   Commissioners
D. Organization

Title II
Provisions of Wire
A. Licenses
B. FCC Powers
C. Sanctions

Title III
Provisions of
Radio
A. Powers
B. Licenses
C. Procedures
D. Sanctions
E. Corporation
   for Public
   Broadcasting

Title IV
Procedures
A. Appeals
B. Jurisdiction
C. Hearings

Title V
Penal
Provisions

Title VI
Miscellaneous

Figure 10–1. Details of the Communications Act. Source: Communications Act of 1934 Amended to January 1969.

DISTINCTION BETWEEN COMMON CARRIERS AND BROADCASTING

The Communications Act of 1934 distinguishes between broadcasting and all other forms of radio and wire communication by specifically noting that broadcasting does not come under the common carrier provisions of the law. Broadcasting, says the law, is the "Dissemination of radio communications intended to be received by the public" [§3(4)(0)]. Common carriers usually hold local monopolies over the business in which they are engaged. Thus there is only one telephone company in a city or perhaps a state; only one electric power company in an area; and only one water company. In all of these cases the companies give up competition and in return their rates and the places where they can run their services are regulated by public service commissions.

Congress did not want broadcasting to fall into this kind of monopoly situation, but preferred that many stations in a market would compete with each other. Through competition the government hoped that stations would keep their rates reasonable and their programs high quality. Congress did not wish to have the FCC setting program formats, nor did it wish to have the FCC regulating rates.

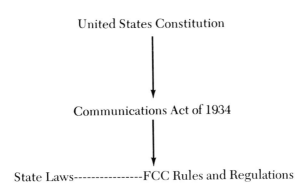

Figure 10–2. Legislative line of authority over radio. All legal authority derives from the United States Constitution as the founding document of the United States. The Communications Act derives its authority from the Constitution and FCC Rules and Regulations derive their authority from the Communications Act. State laws are passed by respective governments. It should be noted that not all state laws come under the jurisdiction of FCC Rules and Regulations.

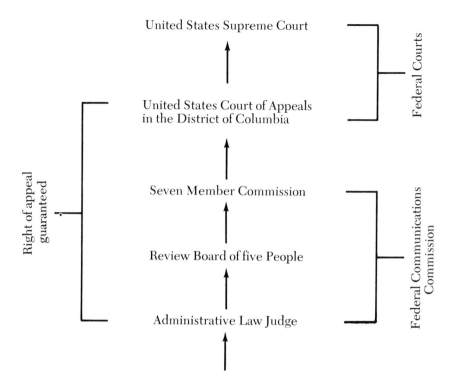

Figure 10–3. Review of FCC decisions. Source: § 402 of the Communications Act of 1934.

$10,000, or may be imprisoned for as long as one year, or both for the first conviction. A second violation may lead to a two-year prison term and a $10,000 fine. Violators of FCC rules and regulations may only be fined $500.[9] There is no provision for a prison term.

Not only did Congress authorize the FCC to function as a legislator, it directed the commission to function as a judicial body; that is, it must review, award, revoke, and renew licenses to use wire and wireless communication devices. In this regard, the FCC must examine the qualifications of applicants to determine if they are qualified to operate a broadcasting station. In its review of applicants, the FCC must use the Communications Act and its own rules and regulations as its basis for judgment.

Licenses are often granted by the staff of the FCC, but if applicants are dissatisfied with the decision they receive, they may appeal through the FCC and the Courts. Within the FCC an applicant may appeal first to an administrative law judge. This judge will rule on legal points and will render a decision. However, if the applicant remains dissatisfied, he or she may appeal to a Review Board composed of five senior FCC employees and, from there, to the seven member commission. (See Figure 10–3.)

The applicant may, further, appeal to the federal courts.[10] If the appeal regards a license issued by the FCC, then the appeal would be heard by the Federal Court of Appeals for the District of Columbia. Appeal to the Court of Appeals will always result in a hearing. If an individual is still unhappy with the decision rendered by the Court of Appeals, then appeal to the United States Supreme Court is the next step. However, the Supreme Court can choose not to hear the appeal. These safeguards are built into the regulatory process so that the FCC may not be the sole arbiter in these matters.

ORGANIZATION OF THE FCC

The FCC has two types of employees: at the highest level are seven commissioners appointed by the President with consent of the Senate. Below the commissioners is the commission staff. This staff is composed of lawyers, engineers, technical personnel, secretaries, and other people required to maintain the Commission. The entire agency is composed of approximately 1900 individuals located in Washington and other cities.

FCC OFFICES

The FCC maintains twenty-four field offices. These offices, located all over the nation, provide testing places for those who wish to take any of the FCC's license tests, and they provide headquarters for the field engineering staff who monitor the performance of stations. These offices are located in the following cities:

Boston, Mass.	Portland, Oregon
New York, New York	Seattle, Washington
Philadelphia, Pennsylvania	Denver, Colorado
Baltimore, Maryland	St. Paul, Minnesota
Norfolk, Virginia	Kansas City, Missouri
Atlanta, Georgia	Chicago, Illinois
Miami, Florida	Detroit, Michigan
New Orleans, Louisiana	Buffalo, New York
Houston, Texas	Honolulu, Hawaii
Dallas, Texas	San Juan, Puerto Rico
Los Angeles, California	Anchorage, Alaska
San Francisco, California	Washington, D.C.

Source: *Federal Communications Commission: Directory of Organization and Personnel*, (Washington, D.C.: National Association of Broadcasters, 1974), pp. 11, 12.

Although the commissioners have the authority to hire the staff, they are bound by civil service laws and provisions of the Communications Act in their hiring practices.

Many staff-level people enter the agency and remain there for much of their working life. Thus the civil service staff is more stable than the commissioners, who are appointed for seven-year terms and who sometimes resign before the expiration of their term. Most proceedings begin with the staff, and many decisions are made without reaching the Commission, making the work of the staff very important.

Commissioners

Qualifications. The commissioners must meet certain qualifications. They must be American citizens who have no financial interest in the manufacture or sale of radio equipment, in businesses involved in communication by wire or radio, in companies providing wire or radio communication, or in any company owning stocks or bonds in a communication company. Furthermore, commissioners may not be engaged in any work or business other than their job as a commissioner.[11]

Tenure. The Communications Act authorized the President to appoint seven commissioners in 1934 with terms varying from one to seven years so that a vacancy occurred each year beginning in 1935. Succeeding commissioners have had seven-year terms, thereby maintaining annual vacancies. The law provides that if a commissioner resigns his or her position before the expiration of the seven-year term, a new appointee may be selected to serve out the unexpired portion of the term.[12] A commissioner's salary, because of a 1975 law, has a built-in cost of living adjustment that automatically adjusts the salary annually to conform to the cost of living index. When the law was passed a commissioner was receiving $38,000 and the chairperson was receiving a salary of $40,000.

Appointments. Since a commissioner is appointed by the President few, if any, commissioners have received a nomination to the FCC without either knowing or working for a presidential candidate or without having close ties with an influential senator. When selecting a new appointee, the President has often consulted members of Congress whom he respects or whose support he needs. Some have suggested that a new President's first appointment has tended to be someone who has received strong Presidential favor; the second appointee usually has been a favorite of the opposition party; and succeeding candidates have tended to be individuals who would alienate no one.

No matter how a President selects commissioners, the Communications Act prohibits the President from placing more than four commissioners of any one party on the FCC at one time. Even with the limitation on party affiliation, a President's power is great because it is possible for him to nominate individuals from the opposition party who favor his views. This power is better understood when one notes how many commissioners recent presidents have appointed. Kennedy nominated four commissioners to the FCC. Later President Johnson selected two new commissioners, and during his years in the White House President Nixon selected eight commissioners. President Ford appointed two commissioners in 1976. It should be noted that each year a commissioner's term expires and the President may reappoint the same commissioner or a new commissioner. Johnson could have appointed at least five new commissioners, but chose to reappoint many of those already on the FCC.

Duties.   The commissioners have authority to expend funds allocated to the FCC for studies related to radio or wire communication, to pay salaries, to purchase equipment, to pay rent on buildings the FCC uses, to conduct hearings on licenses, and to create rules and regulations. The commissioner designated as the chairperson by the President also functions as the chief executive officer for the agency. In this capacity the chairperson has an office, Office of the Executive Director, which assists in planning and directing duties of the FCC. Figure 10–4 shows the arrangement of the various bureaus, offices, and staffs as they relate to the chairperson and other commissioners.

To assist in the execution of their duties, each commissioner may appoint a personal staff composed of a legal assistant, an engineering assistant, and a secretary. Since this administrative staff comes and goes with a commissioner, it does not come under the civil service laws. (see §4(f)(2))

In addition to other duties, the Commission was directed by Congress to prepare annual reports that are to be forwarded to Congress for its review. Congress was specific in prescribing the contents of the annual reports, which are to include: information that would be valuable in answering questions about the regulation of interstate and foreign communication; information that would help Congress assess the work of the FCC; statements about the funds spent by the FCC; recommendations on the need for additional funds. Besides issuing an annual report, Congress directed the FCC not only to make all its records public but also to publish the records in a way that would serve the public interest.[13]

OPERATION OF THE FCC

The FCC as Legislator

As noted earlier, the FCC issues rules and regulations from time to time to implement the intent of the Communications Act. The terms "rules" and "regulations" are used interchangeably. In fact, in *Black's Law Dictionary* the word rule is used in defining regulation and vice versa. The title of the document containing the FCC's guidelines is called "Rules and Regulations." Thus the two may be thought of as meaning the same thing.

Congress imparted power to the FCC to act as the arm of Congress without specific authorization for every rule and regulation. When the FCC creates a new law it demonstrates its legal force even though Congress may choose not to

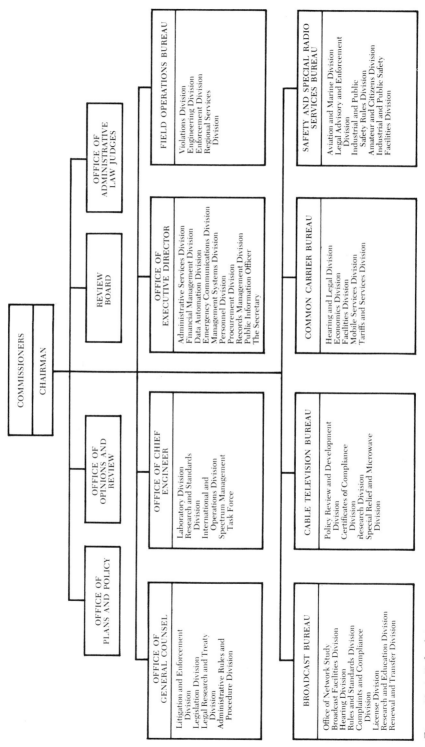

Figure 10-4. Federal Communications Commission. Source: U.S. Government Manual 1975/1976 (Washington: General Services Administration, 1975).

take specific action regarding the rule. In its legislative role, the FCC is to write regulations that would set technical standards for the industry, govern the FCC's own behavior, and serve as the standard in settling disputes.

When the FCC wishes to create a new regulation, it first issues a proposed rule that functions as a trial balloon to see how the industry and citizen groups will react. If the proposed regulation raises protests from interested groups then the FCC conducts public hearings to determine public sentiment. The hearings may result in amendments to the proposed regulation; the proposed rule may be abandoned; or it may become a regulation without change. Whatever the results, a dissatisfied individual or group may appeal to the courts.

The FCC has the power to write regulations that classify stations in ways which would clarify their operation. The FCC has classified some stations as clear channel stations, others as community stations, and still others as regional stations. Each classification limits a station's operations. For example, many community stations can remain on the air only during daylight hours.

In addition to creating rules governing the performance of a station, the FCC was authorized to establish requirements for operators of stations. In this task the FCC has created a number of classes of operators and tests, which applicants for each class must take. The FCC has further written rules that specify what classes of operators a station must employ.

The FCC as Licensor

The most important power of the FCC is its licensing power because it is through this means that the FCC awards and revokes licenses to operate radio equipment. The FCC's licensing power becomes more significant when one realizes that the maximum term of a license, by order of Congress, is only three years. The FCC is free to grant licenses for shorter periods if it feels the public interest will be served.[14] So great is the concern of Congress that broadcasters not have permanent control of a radio channel that each applicant must sign a waiver (Sec. 304) that acknowledges that the license is valid only for the term issued by the FCC and that the licensee has no ownership rights to the radio channel. At the end of the license term the government is free to refrain from renewing the license if the public interest would not be served by renewal. The purpose of the waiver is to clarify that the government, as trustee for the public, owns the radio channels and that the licensee is only borrowing the channel from the government to use in the public interest.

Qualifications

To receive a license the applicant must fulfill the requirements of the Communications Act and FCC rules and regulations. In determining eligibility the FCC must examine the applicant's qualifications in the following areas:

1. Citizenship.   Licenses will not be awarded to aliens or to companies in which alien ownership or control exceeds one-fifth.[15]

2. Legal Qualifications.   No license is to be given to an applicant who has been convicted of a violation of the antitrust laws.[16]
3. Financial Qualifications.   An applicant must show that he or she has the necessary financial assets to set up the station and keep it on the air while it is building sales revenues. The applicant must be able to purchase the necessary equipment and maintain it for a reasonable period of time. The exact amount of time is dependent upon the applicant's estimate of the time needed to build the station into a paying enterprise.[17]
4. Technical Qualifications.   The applicant must be able to show that he or she has the necessary engineering qualifications to operate the station within FCC requirements. This means that the applicant must employ people with the necessary FCC operator licenses.[18]
5. Character Qualifications.   This aspect is usually based in part upon the honesty of comments made on the application and in part upon any criminal convictions the applicant may have.[19]
6. The Program Proposal.   Of great importance to the FCC is the applicant's proposal for programming the station. In this regard the FCC looks at the amount of news, sports, entertainment, agricultural, public affairs, religious, educational, and instructional programming the applicant plans to offer. While the FCC has no exact rules on the amount of time that should be allocated to each area, it does look at how the applicant assessed local needs and proposed to serve those needs.[20]

Securing the License

To secure a license one must file application forms with the FCC indicating that all of the requirements in the Communications Act and FCC rules and regulations have been met. Once this is done the applicant must fulfill certain procedures required by law. First, the applicant must publish the fact that he or she wishes to secure a broadcasting license in newspapers or other local media in the area in which the station will be constructed.[21] By this method the government hopes to discover if other qualified applicants wish to apply for the same channel.

Mutually Exclusive Applications

In the event that no other applicant appears, the FCC may award the license to the original applicant if all of the FCC's requirements have been met. Frequently, however, a second applicant may wish to apply for the same facilities and when this "mutually exclusive" situation occurs, the FCC must conduct a comparative public hearing to decide which applicant is more qualified.[22]

The second major area the FCC considers in the competitive situation is programming. In this regard the FCC attempts to determine which applicant will offer the most local programs, which will offer the most live programs, and which will program the least commercial matter.[23,24]

Fees for Licenses

For the privilege of engaging in broadcasting, one must pay the FCC three different types of fees—filing fees, grant fees, and annual fees. Each of these fees is graduated on the basis of the size and type of station one wishes to operate. The filing fee is paid to the FCC at the time an applicant requests a license and only assures that the FCC will examine the application. It in no way commits the FCC to grant a license to the applicant. The filing fee ranges from $50 to $10,000 depending on the size of market and type of license requested. The lower fee would be for very small AM station while the larger fee would be for a VHF television station in a large market.

After the FCC has taken whatever adminstrative action is necessary and is ready to award the license, the applicant must pay a grant fee. The grant fee covers some of the costs the FCC incurs in providing the license to operate. It is, in effect, the admission price to regular broadcasting. Grant fees range from $340 to $67,500 and, once again, depend upon the size of market and type of service requested.

Finally, the FCC charges stations an annual fee, which is based upon the rates the station charges to advertisers. Like the other two fees the annual fee is intended to defray some of the FCC's operation expenses, and all of the fees are keyed to the amount of revenue the station might be expected to receive.[25] However, as a result of a court case, the FCC's fee schedule was declared illegal and in early 1977 the FCC requested the assistance of Congress in creating a new schedule. As a result, fees were not being collected as of this writing and the future of fees was uncertain.

The FCC, over the years, has come to require specific performance in several areas of programming such as political use of broadcasting, fairness, and personal attack. Each of these areas are briefly mentioned below and are more fully developed as current issues of broadcast regulation in Chapter 11.

Equal Time.   A broadcaster is not required to accept advertising for political candidates, but if the station does carry any advertising, it must afford equal opportunities to all candidates for the same office. This provision stipulates that each candidate be permitted to purchase equal amounts of time for equal amounts of money.[26] If candidate Jones purchases ten thirty-second spots for $15.00 each, then candidate Smith must be permitted to purchase ten thirty-second spots for $15.00 each. Both candidates must be sold the time for the lowest rate card price. If Smith does not have enough money to buy all ten spots, the station does not have to donate the time that the candidate cannot afford.

Not only must each candidate be able to buy the same amounts of time for the same price, but they have the opportunity to secure equal quality time. When Jones buys a ten minute prime-time spot, Smith must be able to buy the same. The quality, length, and cost of the time offered to each candidate must be equal.

Fairness Doctrine.   The Fairness Doctrine is the FCC's statement, made first in 1949[27] and restated in 1964[28] and 1974,[29] requiring stations to be fair or balanced in their treatment of important controversial issues.   The Fairness Doctrine permits editorializing by the licensee, but it orders station owners to be careful in seeing that the overall treatment of controversial issues be balanced so that listeners may have the opportunity to hear most shades of opinion. This Doctrine is invoked when an issue is (1) controversial and (2) of public importance. Under the Fairness Doctrine the station need not balance equal amounts of time devoted to the liberal and conservative viewpoints, but it must use its discretion in being fair.

Programming Statements.   From time to time the FCC writes policy statements on its view of responsible programming such as the Blue Book, which was published in 1946.[30] In 1960 the FCC followed up with a much shorter statement of its views on programming. In this statement the FCC listed fourteen areas which it said were the major elements in determining if the station's programming was in the public interest. They were: 1. local self expression; 2. use of local talent; 3. children's programs; 4. religious programs; 5. educational programs; 6. public affairs programs; 7. editorialization; 8. political broadcasts; 9. agricultural programs; 10. news programs; 11. weather and market reports; 12. sports; 13. minority programs; 14. entertainment.[31] The FCC pointed out that the list was not all inclusive and that it might change from time to time.

By 1971 the FCC believed that programming proposals should be judged upon what the local community wanted and issued a statement on how stations should ascertain the interests of the community.[32] The Ascertainment Primer, as it was called, directed stations to: consult with community leaders and members of the public, evaluate the material collected, and show how programming would serve the needs revealed by the ascertainment survey.

Logs

As proof that the station is both on the air and programming as it should be, each station must maintain program and engineering logs which record all aspects of station operation. According to the FCC regulations [§73.670] the program log must indicate whether a program is sustaining—programs not paid for—or commercial; when the program was aired, and when commercial and public service messages are aired. In addition the type of program must be noted in line with the fourteen types of programs listed in the Blue Book. Stations must also indicate if the program was live, recorded, or network and when station call letters and location were aired.

Besides the program log, the station must maintain the engineering log, which records the frequency on which the transmitter is operating and which indicates the technical measures that show the power with which the station is operating. Other entries include notes in which the operator certifies that the tower lights are operating correctly and registers anything unusual such as a power failure.

Sanctions

To enforce its rules and regulations and the Communications Act the FCC has several sanctions which may be imposed upon stations. The most severe is the revocation of a license authorized in §312(a) of the Communications Act, but the FCC rarely uses this power because it is so harsh. A related power is refusal to renew a license upon its expiration. This power, of course, has the same

LICENSE RENEWAL

Broadcasters have long desired new laws which would make their broadcast licenses more secure. The present law permits a broadcaster to hold a license for three years. At the end of the three year term the broadcaster must apply for a renewal license, which, if granted, would authorize the broadcaster to use the radio waves for another three years. However, the present law permits interested parties to apply for the channel an existing broadcaster is using. If the application of the new party appears better than the proposal for the incumbent, then the FCC is free to award a license to the new applicant and not renew the license of the incumbent.

Broadcasters have gone on record as desiring a five year license and one that can only be challenged when the incumbent has clearly failed to fulfill the conditions of the license. Consequently, broadcasters have been asking the Congress to amend the Communications Act to incorporate their requests. During the ninety-fourth Congress (1975–1976) dozens of bills were pending before both houses of Congress that would give broadcasters all or part of what they wanted in renewal relief.

Most bills differed only in the term of a license or in the conditions under which a license may be challenged. The bills ranged from retaining the present three year term to permitting a five year license term. Some bills would retain the present right to challenge an incumbent, while others would make it virtually impossible for challengers to oppose incumbents. Although many bills were introduced, it is probable that Congress will take no immediate action.

This is a case where Congressional inaction works to the benefit of citizens. Almost all bills would make it more difficult to have a license revoked, either because of the long license term or because of the new legal protection of incumbents.

Source: "Status of Major Legislation in the 44th Congress," *Access* February 9, 1976 (#27), p. 17

impact as revoking a license because the holder of the licensee is not permitted to broadcast after the license lapses.

A somewhat less severe measure taken by the FCC is to renew licenses for a shorter period than the usual three years. This serves as a kind of probation during which the licensee has the opportunity to prove to the FCC that it is willing to improve its performance to merit a full term license.[33]

Before the FCC imposes such sanctions against a station it generally calls a hearing on the station's license. In fact, a licensee has a right to a hearing before its license is terminated or shortened and, because of the seriousness of these actions, licensees generally demand a hearing if the FCC fails to set one. If the licensee does not like the results of the FCC's hearing, it may appeal the decision to the courts.

To provide the FCC with additional though less severe penalties, Congress incorporated a provision for Cease and Desist Orders into the Communications Act [§503(b)]. Through this power the FCC can formally order a station to stop a practice that the Commission has found to be legally unacceptable. However, before the Cease and Desist Order can be issued, the FCC must send the station a Show Cause Order asking why the Cease and Desist Order should not be issued.

In addition to the Cease and Desist Order, the same section of the law provides for fines and forfeitures. Fines differ from forfeitures in that fines result from a conviction (fines have already been discussed.) A forfeiture, on the other hand, may follow a Cease and Desist Order. Forfeitures may range to $1,000 per day to a maximum of $10,000 for multiple violations. The forfeiture, because of the small size of the fine, serves as only a minimal legal reminder to the station.

The final and lowest power of the FCC, a letter of inquiry to a station, has no legal force and sometimes has been called "the raised eyebrow." Broadcasters have come to think of letters of inquiry as a hint that worse things are to come and they should change their ways. Sometimes the FCC sends open letters to one or more stations as a method of informing the entire broadcast industry of its thinking. This informal power has often been used in place of more serious action.

CRITICISM OF THE FCC

Probably every major group concerned with broadcasting—broadcasters, citizen groups, and individuals—has at one time criticized the FCC. Fred Friendly, a former vice-president of the Columbia Broadcasting System and later a professor at Columbia University, once called the FCC "a leaning tower of jello" because of the FCC's inability to take a firm stand on any issue.[34]

However harsh the criticism may sound it has been echoed in other words many times. Even FCC commissioners have criticized their own agency.

Former Commissioner Nicholas Johnson often criticized the agency through dissents to majority opinions, through appearances on television and radio, and in books and journal articles. When the FCC was asked to approve a merger between the International Telephone and Telegraph Company (ITT) and ABC, which would have created the largest communications company in the world, Johnson found evidence that ITT officials were misleading the FCC during the hearing. Additionally, there was evidence that ITT was trying to influence *The New York Times* to print inaccurate stories favorable to ITT. Regardless of the evidence, the FCC approved the merger. This led Johnson to accuse the commission of making "a mockery of the public responsibility of a regulatory commission that is perhaps unparalleled in the history of the American administrative process."[35]

Frequently Johnson accused the FCC of being lax in its enforcement of the public interest. So displeased was Johnson with the climate at the FCC that he often took his cause to the public via television appearances, magazine articles, and books. Johnson believed that the FCC was blinded to the needs and interests of the public by the intense lobbying of the broadcast and cable industries and hoped that the public would exercise its own lobbying force on the FCC to balance that of the powerful broadcast and cable industries.

One recurring criticism from both broadcasters and citizens has been that the FCC takes too long to resolve issues. When the agency first contemplated charging a fee to applicants for radio and wire licenses in 1941, it acted because of pressure from Congress and the public. The FCC considered several fee proposals, but due in part to changing congressional pressure it did not adopt a fee schedule until 1963; this schedule has since been tested in court. Similarly, the FCC spent three and one half years contemplating how to handle the color television question. The FCC began considering the question of cross ownership of radio, television, and newspaper properties during the 1930s and 1940s—an issue that was not resolved until the 1970s. Finally, the FCC took five years to decide which band of frequencies FM broadcasters should have.

Citizen groups and individuals have often felt that the FCC was unwilling to admit members of the public to hearings—a suspicion that has often been well founded. In fact until recent years, the FCC has generally prevented citizen groups from being admitted to hearings. The court case involving the United Church of Christ, discussed at the beginning of this chapter, changed this when the Church appealed to the courts, asking that it be considered a party in interest in the WLBT hearing.

One of the complaints from broadcasters has been that the FCC exceeds its authority as authorized by the Communications Act. When the Radio Act was created, broadcasters wanted the new agency to regulate only the technical aspects of broadcasting and to remain out of programming matters. When the FCC has made nontechnical decisions, broadcasters have complained that the First Amendment rights of the broadcaster has been violated. The federal courts have agreed with the FCC in more than half of the cases.

The FCC's Problems

Although critics have been severe in their criticisms of the FCC, some of the problems have been beyond the FCC's control. While Congress has called it an independent agency, the FCC has been harassed with a variety of problems associated with being too dependent on other branches of government. Often its budget has been too small to accomplish the tasks assigned to it and, because of limited funds, the agency has sometimes been unable to hire the best qualified personnel.

Budget has not been the only problem. Since the commissioners are appointed by the president and approved by the Senate, it is possible that some appointees will be placed on the agency for partisan reasons, thereby reducing the technical expertise of the FCC. And while it is performing its assigned duties, the FCC is continuously exposed to the threat of congressional investigation, presidential influence, and industry pressure.

OTHER AGENCIES CONCERNED WITH BROADCASTING

The FCC is only one of several federal and state agencies concerned with regulating various aspects of broadcasting. Other agencies regulate taxation, defamation, and a variety of other aspects of the broadcast enterprise. These agencies are discussed briefly in the following sections.

Federal Trade Commission

Except for the FCC, the FTC is the agency most concerned with the day-to-day activities of broadcasters. The FTC has congressional authorization to function in two distinct areas—advertising and antitrust. Although the agency maintains a Bureau of Competition for antitrust cases, the FTC's major concern with broadcasting at present is in the area of advertising.

Congress created the FTC in 1914 to assist in the prosecution of monopoly and antitrust cases under the Sherman Antitrust Act of 1890 and the Clayton Act of 1914. Since the Department of Justice had an antitrust division that performed some of the same functions, the FTC did not see its role solely as an agency concerned with monopoly. During the 1930s the FTC decided to get into the consumer protection area and in 1938 Congress amended the FTC Act to include a new clause concerning "unfair methods of competition in commerce" and stated that "It shall be unlawful for any person . . . to disseminate . . . any false advertisement."[36] This amendment came shortly after the Supreme Court handed down its ruling in the Marmola case suggesting that Congress disagreed with the court and wanted the FTC's jurisdiction to include advertising.

Although the FTC had a new mandate from Congress, its actions have not always been of the most aggressive sort. Before 1970 much of the agency's activities were limited to relatively trivial inquiries involving small or medium size businesses, but the actions of the FTC seldom involved the major industries in the United States. Like the FCC, the FTC has often been exceedingly slow about getting its actions concluded. Perhaps the classic case involved Carter's Little Liver Pills. In 1943 the FTC began a drive through its own organization and the federal courts to have the word "liver" removed from the name of the product. In 1959, sixteen years later, the FTC won its case.[37] Despite its slowness, the FTC has disposed of many actions against a variety of businesses. By 1964 the FTC had received over 12,000 agreements from advertisers to halt practices that the FTC felt were not in the public interest. Most of these agreements were from small- and medium-sized businesses. (See Figure 10-5.)

Critics were not satisfied with the work of the FTC. Ralph Nader, the well known consumer advocate, instituted a long-range study of the FTC that examined every aspect of the agency's activities and wrote an extensive report on his findings, which was entered into the *Congressional Record*. Much of what Nader found confirmed the critic's opinions. His group found that the agency took long periods of time to handle legal proceedings, many of which were inconsequential. A 1970 study commissioned by President Nixon confirmed the findings of Nader. It said, "The agency has been preoccupied with technical labeling and advertising practices of the most inconsequential sort."[38] As a result, the FTC was reorganized into a more consumer-oriented organization.

Reorganized FTC.   Until 1970, consumer protection had been under the Bureau of Deceptive Practices, but with the reorganization of the FTC the consumer protection area was placed under the Bureau of Consumer Protection, established to process complaints about consumer products. This branch has tried to inform the public of its role in finding and prosecuting organizations that unfairly use the consumer by supplying information sheets to the mass media regarding cases the FTC is handling or wishes to consider. The Bureau also supplies information to its regional offices, which may be acquired by interested citizens for the asking.

Interestingly, this reorganization of the FTC to a consumer-oriented agency came during the Consumer Era when national attention was directed to the plight of the consumer. Thus the FTC, which was created during the progressive era when government felt pressure to be more responsive to small business, was reorganized during the consumer movement to be responsive to the consumer. As a partial result of the latest revision, the FTC has examined all of the ten largest businesses in the country for various misleading or fraudulent advertising. For example, the FTC has examined Coca Cola, Hi-C fruit drinks, and ITT Continental Baking Company.

Corrective Powers of the FTC.   The FTC has five weapons against companies that engage in false advertising, however, not all of the five powers are legally binding. The FTC's first device is a "letter of compliance," in which an ad-

258

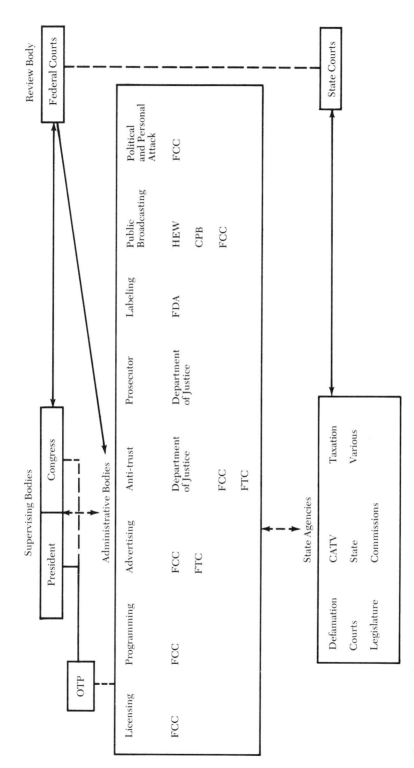

Figure 10–5. Regulatory agencies and interrelationships.

vertiser agrees to refrain from continuing certain practices. This is an informal, low cost procedure that does not have the force of law since the FTC has not proved that the company was engaging in an illegal practice. The second method available to the FTC is a "stipulation," which is a formal agreement from the company in which it agrees to stop the practices that the FTC *has found* to be misleading. Both of these procedures permit the FTC to go to court later if the company fails to abide by the agreement.

The third power, a "consent order," is a formal complaint handed down by the FTC. The advertiser who agrees to the consent order does not admit guilt—also true in the first two agreements—but he or she consents to refrain from engaging in the questionable practice.

The fourth power open to the FTC is the only legally binding power. It is a "cease and desist order" in which the FTC, after formal hearings, directs an advertiser to cease and desist from the misleading practice. The order does not go into effect for 60 days and is appealable to a federal court, but if the advertiser does not appeal he is obliged to obey the order.

The final power—an extralegal device—is publicity. The FTC has the authority to publicize its orders and complaints so that an informed public can carefully select its products on the basis of the findings of the FTC and other bodies employed by the FTC.

The first three of the FTC's powers have the inherent problem that industry can readily fail to comply with the procedure since compliance is purely voluntary. The fourth power has the obvious limitation that it can be appealed to a federal court and, as such, can be delayed for a long time by an advertiser. Using delaying tactics, advertisers are able to exploit all of the effectiveness of an ad campaign and then discard it before the FTC is even able to get a legal injunction against the campaign.

Many of the complaints the FTC receives come from business competitors or private citizens, but recently the FTC has been receiving scripts of all commercials carried on the major networks within seven days after the commercial first goes on the air. It is then possible for the FTC itself to evaluate the commercial for deceptive or misleading practices and to inform the networks of problems it forsees. Generally the networks have voluntarily complied with the FTC's findings.

Corrective Advertising.   A new device the FTC has been using recently to correct misleading advertising has been called corrective advertising. Under this new procedure the FTC has been requiring advertisers to correct the misleading information they inserted into previous commercials. Although it does not come under one of the traditional five powers of the FTC, this procedure has been effective in correcting misrepresentations. An example of corrective advertisement appeared in a Profile Bread commercial. The FTC directed the manufacturer to insert the following statement into the ad:

I'd like to clear up any misunderstandings you may have about Profile Bread from its advertising or even its name. Does Profile have fewer calories than other breads? No, Profile has about the same per ounce as other breads. To be exact Profile has 7 fewer calories per slice. That's because it's sliced thinner. But eating Profile will not cause you to lose weight. A reduction of 7 calories is insignificant.[39]

The message was carried by the ITT Continental Baking Company in twenty-five percent of its advertising for one year in response to an FTC order.

New Powers.   Prior to 1975 the FTC was severely limited in what it could do because every action had to be taken on a case-by-case basis. The FTC could not issue general regulations that would set standards by which an industry would be regulated. Then President Ford signed a new bill into law authorizing the FTC to write general regulations.

Department of Justice

While the FTC is an independent commission not under the direct control of either the President or Congress, the Department of Justice, headed by the Attorney General, is one of the departments of the Executive branch of government under the direct control of the President. Thus the Department's philosophy is, to a large extent, directed by the President in office.

One of the powers of the Department of Justice, through its Antitrust Division, is to enforce the Sherman Antitrust Act and other antitrust laws. In this capacity, the Department of Justice has worked closely with the Federal Communications Commission and the Federal Trade Commission. During the 1940's, James Laurence Fly, as chairman of the Federal Communications Commission, conducted a study of the national radio networks, Columbia Broadcasting System and National Broadcasting System. After two years of hearings and research, the Commission compiled a report that recommended that the National Broadcasting System divest itself of one of the two national networks it operated. NBC operated the Blue network, which carried most of the sustaining programming and the Red network, which carried most of its commercial programs. Both networks served the same communities giving NBC a near monopoly in the communities it served. The report also suggested that the Columbia Broadcasting System be required to rewrite its network-affiliate contract. This change was suggested because the CBS contract gave the network virtual control over local stations. When the Commission completed its study, it gave the Department of Justice the report and it was the Department that fought the case against NBC and CBS through the courts to the Supreme Court, which ruled in favor of the Department of Justice. In this case, the Department of Justice handled the complicated task of arguing the case before federal courts after the Commission had compiled the basic evidence. Many years later in the 1960s, when the Commission was contemplating the merger between the International Telephone and Telegraph Company and the American Broadcasting Company, it was the Department of Justice that filed a protest with the Commission holding that the merger would create a corporation that would be in clear violation of the antitrust laws. Although the Commission approved the merger the Justice Department took the case to court, but before the courts decided the case International Telephone and Telegraph dissolved the merger.

The Department of Justice has often encouraged the Commission in its antitrust proceedings. For example, the Department has repeatedly encouraged the Commission to enforce its one-to-a-customer rule, which would force broadcasters to divest themselves of all but one broadcast property in a given market. But the Department of Justice has not limited itself to influencing the Commission or to fighting the Commission's cases.

The Department itself fought cases against the *Kansas City Star*, the *Lorain Journal*, and Associated Press. Each of these firms had violated the antitrust laws by trying to damage the business interests of a competitor. Thus the Department of Justice has an extensive history of fighting important antitrust cases both on its own and for the FCC.

In addition to prosecuting antitrust cases the Department of Justice is bound to serve as the District Attorney for either the Federal Communications Commission or the FTC in cases involving their respective activities. The Communications Act and the Federal Trade Commission Act prevent either of the commissions from prosecuting their own cases and instruct the Department of Justice, on request from the commissions, to handle the cases in court. Although members of either commission may advise the Department of Justice and may attend the trial, lawyers for the agencies may not argue the cases.

Food and Drug Administration

While the FTC concentrates on advertising claims, the Food and Drug Administration devotes its attention to packaging and labeling of food and drug products. This division of control between the FTC and the Food and Drug Administration is not clearly defined by law since it is more a fact of agreement between the two agencies. Because of this division of authority, the FDA does not directly regulate broadcast stations, however, broadcasters are responsible for violations of FDA regulations and the FTC may prosecute stations who advertise products banned by the FDA.

Congress

The agencies mentioned above are either the product of Congressional legislation or are a branch of the Executive. Thus these agencies report to either the President, or Congress, or both. Congress does not exercise any enforcement powers in handling the problems of regulating the complex broadcast establishment, but it does have many legislative powers.

Congress has the power to affect the actions of most governmental agencies by its appropriations of funds used to operate various agencies. Each year both the FTC and the FCC must file reports with the Congress concerning how they spent funds for the preceeding year and they must also request funds for the forthcoming year. Generally, hearings are conducted to determine if the proposed budget will meet with Congressional approval.

Congressional powers extend beyond control over the budget—Congress must either confirm or reject appointments to both commissions as it sees fit. In the Senate the Commerce Committee is the body responsible for recommending new legislation that covers broadcasting or its allied field, advertising. From time to time this committee, and its appropriate subcommittees, calls hearings to recommend new laws. These new laws may be intended to extend or curb the FCC's power in areas in which senators have particular interests. In the House of Representatives a similar committee, the Committee on Interstate and Foreign Commerce, is concerned with the actions of the FCC and the FTC. In addition, Congress has occasionally appointed special committees to examine particular aspects of the FCC.

The Executive Branch

As already noted, the President has direct control over the Department of Justice and its activities in matters of antitrust and the District Attorney. But the President's powers extend beyond the Department of Justice. The President nominates commissioners to the FTC and the FCC and disburses funds to these two agencies through the Office of Management and Budget.

In addition to the direct legal controls, the President lobbies for issues through the Office of Telecommunications Policy (OTP). In addition, the OTP may conduct studies into more effective uses of radio waves and it may appear before the FCC to argue issues of interest to the President. A more concrete power of the OTP is its authority to prepare proposed bills for Congress on matters related to broadcasting—Congress is free to accept or reject these proposed bills, but they are an effective way for the President to inform Congress of his wishes. OTP also directs the assignment of radio channels used by the government. The sharing of governmental channels is coordinated through the Interdepartmental Radio Advisory Committee, which was formed in 1922. OTP was formed in 1970 and was being phased out in 1977. Its task was given to the Office of Telecommunications in the Commerce Department.

Courts

The federal courts have been directed by the Communications Act to review actions of the FCC at the request of the FCC, a concerned member of the broadcast establishment, or of the public. The same provisions exist for the FTC in the FTC Act. The courts serve as the final arbiter in issues related to the regulation of broadcasting. Judicial review has permitted the courts to act on procedures of the FCC, to elements of the Communications Act, and to FCC programming policies.

Although the courts cannot institute hearings on their own, they have had considerable effect on broadcast regulation. Some critics have suggested that this review power has caused the FCC to create procedures that are as inflexible as those of the courts. Whatever the advantages or disadvantages to having the courts review the regulatory problems of broadcasters, Congress has shown no inclination to curb the courts in their investigations of the commission. In fact, when a court pointed out to a broadcaster that Congress had failed to give the courts the right to review a particular area, Congress, which reviewed the opinion, immediately took action to correct the oversight.[40]

AGENCIES INDIRECTLY CONCERNED WITH BROADCASTING

The above mentioned agencies form the major group of administrative bodies concerned with the direction of broadcasting in the United States, but there are other organizations involved in the total process. The Department of Health, Education and Welfare has been directed by Congress to disburse funds for the construction of public broadcast facilities. Working with Health Education and Welfare is the Corporation for Public Broadcasting, which directs and funds the national public radio and television networks operating on a noncommercial basis. Although the Corporation for Public Broadcasting is not a branch of the government, it is largely funded by the government and operates as a quasi-governmental body.

State Agencies Concerned with Broadcasting

Certain aspects of the regulation of broadcasting have been assigned to the states. State legislatures have the authority to write laws governing defamation over the air—as well as through print and spoken means. A number of states have laws governing these areas. Interpretation of the defamation laws is left to state courts.

Since the coming of cable television, a number of states have set up cable television commissions intended to assure that local cable television stations fulfill certain standards established by the state. Generally, to set up business in a locality, a cable system must have a permit from the municipality in which it will operate, it must be licensed by the state cable television commission (where one exists), and it must meet certain provisions set down by the FCC, which has determined that it has an obligation to regulate the cable television business.

SELF-REGULATION

Self-regulation is the voluntary regulation that an industry imposes on itself; it is in no way legally binding. In the broadcast industry, the most widely followed form of self-regulation has been set by the National Association of

BIG DECISIONS

No, question is too small for the network. The big issue of the 1975–76 season at CBS was whether Cher Bono's navel should be displayed. Although her naval had been seen on CBS in the past, her new show was scheduled for the Family Viewing Hour and CBS executives were not certain that such a sight was appropriate for children. The question was finally resolved: her navel could be exposed but her dresses were to be more modest.

Broadcasters (NAB), which has set programming and advertising standards for radio and television in documents called the Radio Code and the Television Code. Networks, stations, and suppliers of programming material can decide whether or not they want to subscribe to the Codes. If they do subscribe, they are obligated to follow the regulations set forth in the Codes. If they violate any of these regulations, their right to call themselves Code subscribers can be withdrawn by the NAB.

There are basically two reasons why an industry may decide to establish self-regulation. The first reason is that it is good public relations. For example, the movie rating system, which is an example of self-regulation, helps people to decide if they want to see a particular movie. By rating a movie as "PG", "R" or "X" the movie industry warns parents that the film might not be suitable for children. The second reason for self-regulation is that if an industry regulates itself, the government will not intervene—an arrangement the industry prefers.

Enforcement of the Code

The responsibility for the administration of both Codes lies with the Code Authority Director and staff. They are responsible for reviewing programming and advertising, for screening complaints, and for informing subscribers about charges if the subscriber is in violation of the Code.

The Code Authority staff monitors networks, radio, and television stations to make certain that they comply with the Code. Since the networks provide the bulk of television programming, on-the-air network programming is monitored by the Code Authority staff in New York, Washington, and Los Angeles. If requested, the Code Authority will also screen television programs prior to the time they are broadcast. In 1974, approximately 740 hours of network programming were monitored.

Radio and television stations are monitored for their compliance with Code advertising procedures. Monitoring covers such areas as the number of commercials and the number of program interruptions. During 1974, 70,000 television and 45,000 radio broadcast hours were monitored.[41]

If a subscriber violates the Code the case goes before the Code Board. After the Board hears the case, it make recommendations as to what should be done. The final decision rests with either the Television Board of Directors or the Radio Board of Directors, both of which have the power to revoke a station's subscription.

Code Provisions

In the radio code there is a section pertaining to news. It advises stations to use reliable news sources, to present factual and objective news, and to place advertising in such a way that it is clearly distinguished from news. Editorials and commentaries are also to be clearly separated.

The Radio Code is very general about its expectations for program content. The Code says that the broadcaster should be responsive to the community, should advance education and culture, should show responsibility toward children, and so on. In advertising the Code's standards are more specific: it deals with the presentation of advertising, the products that should not be advertised such as hard liquor, the advertising of medical products, the amount of time that can be devoted to commercials, and guidelines regarding contests, premiums, and offers.

The Television Code has sections that deal with news, editorials, and political broadcasts, which are quite similar to the Radio Code. In addition, the code exhorts the broadcasters to seek out and serve the needs of their particular communities.

The Television Code has provisions that deal with program responsibilities. It states that acts of violence must only appear in a responsible context and programs must show the effects of violence on both the victims and perpetrators. Narcotic addiction, drugs, liquor, and smoking are to be deemphasized. In addition obsenity, profanity, and indecency are prohibited.

MISSING HORROR

In James Caan's death scene in "The Godfather," gunmen appear at a highway toll booth and blast at Caan through the window of his car. He staggers out onto the road and is about to be hurled back by another blast. In the television version, the shots came, but Caan's chest does not erupt into a fountain of blood. The horrifying scene— Caan arched back, blood pouring from his wounds, an underworld St. Sebastian—is missing.

Source: David Black, "How the Gosh Darn Networks Edit the Heck Out of Movies," *The New York Times*, January 26, 1973.

BLEMISHED VIEW

Persons with acne should not be depicted as social outcasts nor should their condition be presented in a negative manner (e.g., "Yiick, pimples"). Emphasis on close-up shots or graphic descriptions of pimples or blackheads are believed unacceptable. Additionally, reiteration of words such as "pimples" or "blackheads" should be avoided. Some Code subscribers, because of taste considerations, do not accept these words and prefer in their place "blemishes."

Source: "Taste is Major Issue in Acne Commercials" (Washington, D.C.: NAB, Oct. 67 RITUCN).

The Television Code opposes detailed treatment of hypnosis and prohibits the use of extremely short messages during a program such as "eat popcorn." Any professional advice, diagnosis, and treatment must be in conformity with the law and recognized professional standards. The Code is more flexible in its treatment of the occult and numerology.

The Code maintains that marriage, the family, and other important human relationships should be treated with sensitivity. Sensitivity is also required in portraying persons where race, sex, creed, religion, color, or ethnic origin is involved. The Code forbids rigged contests in which individuals win by dishonest means. In general programming, broadcasters are warned to make clear distinctions between fact and fiction.

OTHER FORMS OF SELF-REGULATION

The Code is only one form of self-regulation found in the broadcast industry. Other forms of self-regulation not covered by the Code are developed by individual stations, networks, and advertisers. All of these groups differ because of different management policies and community standards.

Some stations, particularly in radio, follow the Code but have additional policies that apply to their particular station. Others are not Code subscribers and instead determine all of their own policies. Still other stations follow the code without being subscribers.

The three commercial television networks have divisions or departments that decide on the suitability of broadcast material. They all operate along similar lines and are responsible for reviewing entertainment programs at all stages from script to final production. In addition, the department screens outside films that are rented or purchased by the network.

One of the most interesting forms of self-regulation comes indirectly from the advertiser. Advertisers are anxious to appeal to as many people as possible, so they are likely to associate with what they see as prevailing American attitudes and to avoid controversial topics. Other advertisers are anxious to convey the proper image for their product and will issue advertising guidelines.

Whatever form they may take, codes and other self-regulation methods have the common purpose of protecting the station, advertiser, or network from public criticism and from legal encounters. For the most part the various codes have been successful in their intent.

Broadcasting, because of the nature of the enterprise, is perhaps more regulated than any other industry. At the federal level one agency exists solely to regulate electrical communication, but many other federal agencies are concerned with broadcasting. At the state level cable is often regulated. In addition, states regulate broadcast defamation and state courts determine the amount of damages. Even local governments are involved in the regulation since they control taxation and are in charge of granting franchises to cable operators.

NOTES

1. *Office of Communication of the United Church of Christ* v. *Federal Communications Commission*, 359 F. 2d 994 (D.C. Cir., 1966).
2. Fourth National Radio Conference, *Proceedings and Recommendations for Regulation of Radio* (Washington, D.C., November 9–11, 1925), p. 6.
3. Ibid.
4. Walter B. Emery, *Broadcasting and Government* (East Lansing; Michigan State University Press, 1971), p. 33.
5. U.S. Constitution, Article I, Section 8.
6. *FCC* v. *Pottsville Broadcasting Company*, 309 US 134 (1940).
7. *FCC* v. *Allentown Broadcasting Corporation*, 349 US 358 (1955).
8. Citations of the Communications Act in this chapter refer to the law as it appeared in Pike and Fisher *Radio Regulation* updated through 1975.
9. Ibid., §501 and §502.
10. Ibid., §402.
11. Ibid., §4.
12. Ibid.
13. Ibid., §5.
14. Ibid., §307 (b).
15. Ibid., §310 (a).
16. Ibid., §308 (b).
17. Ibid.
18. Ibid.
19. Ibid.

20. *Report and Statement of Policy re: Commission en banc Programming Inquiry*, 25 Fed. Reg. 7291 (1960).

21. Communications Act, op. cit., §309.

22. *Pottsville*, op. cit., Allen T. Simmons, 11 FCC 1160, 1947. *Public Service Responsibility of Broadcast Licensees* (Washington, D.C.: FCC, 1946).

23. Ibid., §73.670.

24. *Kentucky Broadcasting Corp.*, 12 FCC 282 (1947).

25. FCC Rules & Regulations, §1.1101.

26. *Communications Act*, op. cit., §315.

27. *In the Matter of Editorializing by Broadcast Licensees*, 13 FCC 1256 (1949).

28. *Applicability of the Fairness Doctrine in the Handling of Controversial Issues of Public Importance*, 29 *Fed. Reg.* 10415 (1964).

29. FCC, "Fairness Doctrine & Public Interest Standards: Handling Issues of Public Importance," 1974.

30. *Applicability*, **op. cit.**

31. *Report and Statement of Policy re: Commission en banc Programming Inquiry*, 25 Fed. Reg. 7291 (1960).

32. *Federal Communications Commission Primer on Part 1, Section IV-A and IV-B of Application Forms Concerning Ascertainment of Community Problems and Broadcast Matter To Deal With Those Problems*, 27 FCC 2d 650 (1971).

33. *Communications Act*, op. cit., §307 (d).

34. Quoted in Harold L. Nelson and Dwight L. Teeter, Jr., *Law of Mass Communications: Freedom and Control of Print and Broadcast Media* (Mineola, New York: Foundation Press, 1969), p. 553.

35. Leonard Zeidenberg, "Seven Years and Five Months: A Look Back at the Tenure of Nick Johnson," *Broadcasting* (December 10, 1973), p. 26.

36. Subcommittee on Communications Staff, *Cable Television: Promise Versus Regulatory Performance* (Washington, D.C.: Government Printing Office, 1976).

37. *Federal Trade Commission v. Raladam Co.*, 258 US 483 (1931).

38. 52 Stat. 111 (1938).

39. *Carter Products Co.* v. *Federal Trade Commission*, 361 US 884 (1959).

40. Reported in Nelson, et. al., op. cit., p. 521.

41. "Advertising: Mea Culpa, Sort Of," *Newsweek* (September 27, 1971), p. 98.

42. *National Broadcasting Co., Inc., et al.* v. *United States et al.* 319 US 190 (1943).

43. *Kansas City Star* v. *United States*, 240 F 2d 643, (1957).

44. *Lorain Journal Co.* v. *United States*, 342 US 143 (1951).

45. *Communications Act* op. cit., §402 (b).

46. Letter from Stockton Helffrich, Code Authority Director, February 7, 1975.

Issues in Broadcast Regulation

REGULATION AND THE FIRST AMENDMENT

The FCC and other federal agencies regulate the activities of broadcasters and cablecasters. No equivalent organization regulates newspapers, magazines, billboards, and books. In fact, early in the evolution of American law, a jury decision clarified the point that government must exercise care if it intervenes in the newspaper world.[1] Journalists and prominent individuals in the United States were concerned over the repressive power that European governments had long exercised over their publishers and hoped that America would not be forced into a similar situation.

An early case involving John Peter Zenger, a newspaper publisher, demonstrated the importance of free expression by proving that truth was a defense against a libel charge.[2] In this case, an edition of his paper had criticized a governmental action. From this small beginning, American laws guaranteed an ever-increasing amount of freedom of speech until finally the First Amendment, which was incorporated into the Constitution in 1791, prohibited government from enacting any laws infringing upon an individual's right to publish and speak. The First Amendment made it impossible to legislate any of the editorial decisions that might confront a newspaper publisher. The government was thus restrained from creating a federal newspaper commission or similar entity.

It appears contradictory, then, that the federal government created a federal agency to regulate the activities of broadcasting. After all, broadcasters are engaged in an activity that involves speech and the First Amendment protects an individual's right to say what he or she wishes. Thus, there appears to be a conflict between the FCC's involvement in broadcasting and the freedom that newspaper publishers enjoy.

But the conflict is resolved, to some extent, when one realizes that newspaper publishers were never confronted with the interference and chaos that broadcasters experienced prior to the creation of the FRC in 1927. An unlimited number of people can publish newspapers without interfering with any other publisher. But only a limited number of stations can broadcast before they begin to interfere with other stations' broadcasts. Wallace H. White, Jr., a congressman from Maine, observed that it is as essential to schedule use of radio frequencies as it is to schedule trains.[3] Although White's statement was made in 1922, it was not until 1927 that appropriate legislation was passed.

Later, at the fourth radio conference in 1925, Hoover observed that there were two parties using the air waves whose rights needed to be protected: the broadcaster and the public. It was, said Hoover, the public's right that should be protected.[4] Thus, the listener should be protected against unnecessary interference, noise, and confusion on the air. The listener must be protected against the chaos of conflicting broadcasters who would make it impossible for any listener to receive an intelligible program.

From Hoover's statement evolved the notion that the air waves were the property of the public and had to be protected for the public. Thus, Hoover argued new legislation would enhance rather than violate the First Amendment rights of the listener. Of course, Hoover and others of his era were not unaware of the rights of the broadcasters. To protect broadcasters, they urged government not to create laws that would permit a federal agency to regulate the business matters of a station. Protective legislation, Hoover said, would benefit all.

The specific authority invoked for radio regulation, once the First Amendment problem was solved, derived from the Constitution—specifically the Commerce Clause (Article 1, § 8), which directs the federal government to regulate interstate and foreign commerce. Since radio waves often cross state lines, radio is considered interstate commerce. The Radio Act of 1927, which was later incorporated into the Communications Act of 1934, grew from this reasoning.

Under the Radio Act of 1927, the federal government selected the most qualified applicants for broadcast licenses and awarded them a limited number of licenses to operate in the "public interest." The government had the authority to police the air waves for offending stations so that listeners might hear diverse programs. To secure the right to use a radio transmitter, one must acquire a license for a temporary period during which the holder is authorized to broadcast. The same is true under the Communications Act of 1934. A broadcasting license is much like a driver's license. The government holds the

SUPREME COURT ON GAG ORDERS

Gag orders imposed against the news media by a court may well violate the constitutional rights of the news media. This 1976 Supreme Court decision gave the news media much more latitude in covering trials. A gag order is a restriction on coverage of pre-trial or trial information by the news media. These orders are issued by a judge who feels that a defendant's right to a fair trial will be affected by media coverage.

Thus, there were two conflictng constitutional rights involved in the Supreme Court's decision: the news media's right to freely print and speak as guaranteed in the First Amendment and a defendant's right to a fair trial guaranteed in the Sixth Amendment. Some judges have felt that people who become jurors may be unfairly influenced by exposure to pre-trial coverage.

In its decision the Supreme Court held that while there may be circumstances when a gag order is necessary, they are very rare. Indeed some of the Justices felt that there probably was no event so serious as to require a gag order. Although the decision did not absolutely forbid all gag orders, it did make the issuing of such orders much more difficult. The decision was welcomed by many members of the news media as one that would make their job of reporting news much easier.

Source: "Highest Court Loosens Gags on Trial News," *Broadcasting* July 5, 1976, p. 24.

roads as public property for all Americans. As long as one uses the roads properly, one's license will continue to be renewed. The license holder may go wherever he wishes and may use the roads in any way that is within the limits of the law, but he does not own the roads. Radio is the same. A radio station may secure a license and may use the radio waves as it wishes as long as it does not violate the relevant laws. But the radio station does not own the radio waves; they remain the property of the public and are merely loaned to a licensee.

The licensing system provides the government with a method for insuring that only those who will make the best possible use of the radio waves have access to them. It is the intent of the government to be certain that every member of the public is served with some form of programming and that radio does not serve only a few.

With this concern for public benefit in the use of the air waves in mind, the FCC has created certain regulations to guide it in evaluating the performance of licensees. Some of those guidelines are discussed in the following sections of this chapter.

HISTORY OF THE FAIRNESS DOCTRINE

The Fairness Doctrine, one of the FCC's oldest principles, requires radio and television stations to present both sides of controversial issues. Although the doctrine was formally written into regulation in 1949, the precedents for the regulation go back to 1928 when the FRC denied a license to Great Lakes Broadcasting Company because it would not offer balanced programming.[5] In a decision of its own the FCC reaffirmed the need for balance in a 1938 case.[6] But the 1941 the FCC decided that a licensee could not engage in editorializing, a decision that was at least partially motivated by the war and concern for divisive opinions.[7]

Then, as the second world war came to an end, the FCC began informing stations that they must make positive efforts to treat controversial issues with balance and a citizens group even got a commitment from station WHKC agreeing to a policy on controversial issues that did not discriminate against any particular group.[8] A year later the FCC went even further by expressing the view that unpopular issues should be dealt with.[9] These decisions were the ground work for the Fairness Doctrine, which was written in 1949. (See Figure 11-1.)

Probably the single most important element of the 1949 fairness statement was that it reversed the 1941 anti-editorial decision and permitted broadcasters to engage in editorializing. The right to editorialize, however, did not release broadcasters from their obligation to present balanced programming.

Some of the major provisions of the Fairness Doctrine are:

1. In a democracy, informed public opinion is necessary, therefore, the news media must cover the vital public issues of the day, that is, licensees have an obligation to inform.
2. The public has a right to be informed.
3. Because there is not enough time for everybody, licensees must pick and choose among those who wish to use the air. This does not mean that the licensee has the right to exclude views contrary to its own.
4. A general policy of refusing time to people with opposing views is unacceptable.
5. Two guidelines were established to aid the broadcaster in deciding whether to allot time to a spokesperson for an issue: has the viewpoint of the person requesting time already been adequately covered; and is there a better spokesperson for the view?
6. The Commission held that editorializing, in and of itself, would not necessarily make the station unbalanced in its programming.[10]

The Fairness Doctrine placed the FCC on record as supporting balanced programming when involving controversial issues of public import. The state-

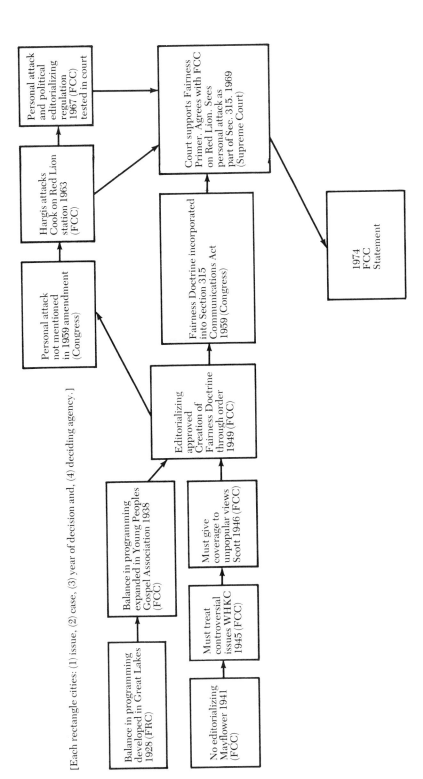

[Each rectangle cities: (1) issue, (2) case, (3) year of decision and, (4) deciding agency.]

Figure 11-1. The evolution of four doctrines: fairness, equal opportunity, editorializing, and personal attack.

273

ment tended to be general and did not give the FCC strong enforcement powers, a problem that bothered Frieda Hennock, one of the commissioners.

Yet the Fairness Doctrine was later to receive support from both the Congress, and the Supreme Court. In 1959 Congress amended §315 of the Communications Act of 1934 to include the Fairness Doctrine. Then ten years later the Supreme Court, in reviewing the Red Lion case, held that the Fairness Doctrine was a principle consistent with the Communications Act and the Constitution. Two branches of government had given their seal of approval to the doctrine as it then existed. However, the Supreme Court left open the option of later review of the Fairness Doctrine. In 1972, a federal court exercised that option and directed the FCC to reexamine the Fairness Doctrine to determine if it was still needed. The resulting report was made public in 1974.[11]

Expanded Fairness Rules

The first major statement made by the FCC after 1949 regarding the Fairness Doctrine came in 1964 when the FCC issued a lengthy Fairness Primer to clarify questions that might have arisen.[12] This statement authorized any member of the public who wished to complain about a station's failure to abide by the doctrine to forward to the FCC a letter requesting its cooperation. The Commission wanted the letter to contain: (1) the name of the station involved; (2) the issue involved; (3) the date and the time the program in question was carried; (4) the basis upon which the station's presentation was one sided; (5) whether the station afforded reply time.[13] Thus individuals who wish to secure some correction through the Fairness Doctrine must do some groundwork first.

In addition, the 1964 statement listed several areas in which the Fairness Doctrine was applicable. These included: (a) civil rights; (b) political spot advertisements not involving a candidate; (c) "Reports to the People" by politicians who held elected office; (d) local controversial issues; and, (e) national controversial issues.[14]

Ten years after it released the 1964 Fairness Primer, the FCC issued another major document regarding fairness.[15] This report was the result of a 1972 Court of Appeals decision instructing the FCC to reexamine the doctrine to see if changes were needed.[16] After hearings, the FCC concluded that much of the doctrine was still needed and served a valuable function.

In the 1974 statement, the FCC reminded the broadcast industry that the Fairness Doctrine was created to encourage robust discussion and that the FCC was concerned with the reasonableness of a station in handling controversial matters. The FCC used the statement to clarify its meaning of "controversial issues of public importance," the conditions that invoke the doctrine. Public importance could be assessed by the significance ascribed to an issue by elected officials and by the amount of coverage the news media gave the matter. The FCC felt that the amount of public debate stimulated by an issue would be an indication of how controversial it was.

TABLE 11–1   Conditions of Three FCC Policies: Fairness, Personal Attack, and Equal Opportunities

	Fairness Doctrine	Personal Attack	Equal Opportunities
Jurisdiction	Controversial issues	Individuals	Political candidates
Condition invoking provision	A. Important public issue B. Controversial issue	Individual who has been defamed	Use of station by legally qualified candidate
Relief granted	Station's discretion in balancing discussion of issue	Free reply time	Equal paid time
Quality of relief	Some time of station's choosing	Equal class and quality of time	Equal quality; equal arrangement of time
Cost	Free	Free	Lowest rate card cost
Statutory or other authority	§315 of Communications Act	FCC 1964 and 1974 Statements	§315 of Communications Act

The FCC went on to explain procedures to be followed by the licensee and by individuals involved in handling an issue. Stations, the FCC said, would be judged on their overall performance. The station must exercise diligent effort to give time to the opposing side, and the burden of finding the opposing view was on the licensee. Viewers or listeners wishing to make a fairness complaint must submit evidence indicating how they decided the station was unfair.[17]

Finally, the FCC restated the principle of the Zapple Doctrine. Named after Nicholas Zapple, a Congressional lawyer who had been instrumental in getting the FCC to create the new regulation, the Zapple Doctrine applies the equal opportunities provisions of Section 315 to supporters of political candidates.[18] (See Table 11–1.)

The Fairness Doctrine—Some Problems.   Over the years, many people have criticized the Fairness Doctrine as a violation of broadcasters' First Amendment rights of free speech. This view was voiced by Julian Goodman in a speech at Ithaca College in September 1976. Goodman said that many broadcast journalists are unwilling to present controversial issues, thinking that the FCC might reprove them. The Fairness Doctrine, Goodman said, prevented broadcast journalists from enjoying the freedoms that newspaper journalists have. It stifles the expression of opinion. Goodman urged repeal of the Doctrine and promised much more thorough news reporting would result.

Congress has not been unaware of the cries for repeal, and a number of bills have been introduced into both the House and the Senate, but to date no action has been taken.

Enforcement of the Fairness Doctrine

Editorializing.   In the Fairness Doctrine the FCC took the postion that editorializing was not bad or good in and of itself. In fact, the FCC held that prohibiting editorializing would not be desirable. As long as the licensee presents a fair and balanced view of controversial issues, no action would be taken to prevent editorializing.

How, then, has this policy been enforced? Perhaps the "Selling of the Pentagon" case reflects typical FCC response when it refused to take any action at all because it foresaw First Amendment problems.[19] After CBS carried a documentary on Pentagon advertising that was critical of the practice, a Congressman wrote to the FCC suggesting that it do something about the biased point of view taken by the network. In a reply to Representative Harley O. Staggers, the FCC indicated that it was unwilling to prosecute CBS because it believed that the editorial judgements of a network should be honored in the absence of a clear and compelling indication that the broadcaster had deliberately tried to misrepresent the issues.[20]

The FCC believed it was very important that the broadcaster have a policy requiring honesty of its news staff and fairness in the presentation of news items. But FCC control over the content of news or editorials would be a violation of its authority. The FCC held that it "[could] not and should not dictate the particular response to thousands of journalistic circumstances."[21] As a result, the FCC refused to review the decisions made by CBS. That, they held, must remain the responsibility of the licensee.

Editorial Advertising.   While the FCC has applied the Fairness Doctrine to the content of programs, only occasionally has it applied the doctrine to advertising. An exception occurred in 1967 in the Banziff case.[22] In this case the FCC found that cigarette advertising was such a national issue that it merited the application of the Fairness Doctrine. The FCC pointed out that it had no intention of applying the doctrine to other products.

Consistent with this position was the FCC refusal to consider a 1970 fairness complaint directed against automobile advertising. In a case brought by the Friends of the Earth against WNBC in New York, the FCC refused to take action, holding that the problems of automobile use—air pollution arising from the car's emissions and deaths resulting from accidents—were of such a nature that the FCC could not rule on them.[23] A court, however, instructed the FCC to reconsider the case and held that the Fairness Doctrine might, indeed apply.

The FCC has refused to consider complaints against commercials that are intended only to advertise a product without overt editorializing. Since networks have a policy prohibiting advertisements of an argumentative or editorial nature, they restrict the whole practice of advertising. The Business Executives' Move for Vietnam Peace (BEM) was unhappy with the networks' policies and tried to get the FCC and the courts to find the network's policy illegal. Neither the FCC nor the United States Supreme Court was inclined to reverse the networks' policies.

The Future of the Fairness Doctrine

Although the Fairness Doctrine has been accepted by both the United States Supreme Court and the Congress as a sound legal principle, many have been attacking the doctrine. For example, former Senator Sam Ervin has officially questioned the doctrine. In addition, Senators Proxmire, Pastore, Hruska, and Representatives Drinan, Thone, and Macdonald have all introduced bills that would eliminate or modify the Fairness Doctrine. The Proxmire bill would simply delete Section 315 from the Communications Act. This is the provision that covers fairness and political broadcasting.

A bill submitted by Pastore and Macdonald would remove the equal opportunities provisions for presidential and vice-presidential candidates. All of these bills were introduced during the ninety-fourth Congress and, while they have not yet been passed, they do reflect the feelings of some important members of Congress. Whether the Fairness Doctrine will survive the present attack is uncertain; however, the day may soon arrive when the doctrine is abolished.

MONOPOLY AND BROADCASTING

From the time the antitrust laws were enacted in the late 1800s, many Americans have had a fear of large corporations. First the large oil companies were broken up, then government went on to prosecute other industries including the tobacco companies. That same fear extended to the broadcast industry.

The courts have supported the FCC when it prosecuted cases against companies that were engaged in practices that tended to restrain trade. One of the first cases involved NBC and CBS.[24] NBC owned two networks—the Red and the Blue—as a result of agreements it had made with AT&T back in the 1920s (see Chapter 2). CBS, on the other hand, had contracts with its affiliates that gave it the right to sell all the commercial time on the station it wished without consulting the affiliates. In return for giving up control over the station's time, the affiliates received sustaining or free programs during all of the hours the network could not sell. The affiliates were free to take or reject the time as they chose.

The Supreme Court, on the request of the Department of Justice and the FCC, ruled that both agreements were unacceptable. Although the case involved business arrangements that tended to restrain trade, the court principally considered the First Amendment and "public interest, convenience, and necessity" problems. The court held that the networks had not been deprived of their freedom to speak by the new regulations and that the FCC's "public interest" mandate was a sound directive for the decision it made.

As a result of this decision NBC had to sell one of its networks. It chose to sell the Blue network, which was purchased by Edward Noble and renamed

American Broadcasting Company (ABC). Thus, NBC was reduced to one network. The same ruling forced CBS to revise its network-affiliate contract in such a way that control over its time was returned to the station.[25]

The FCC did little in the area of antitrust or restraint of trade until the 1960s when the case of WHDH—owned by the Boston *Herald Traveler*—arose.[26] The Herald Traveler company owned a newspaper and radio and television stations in Boston. In a 1969 decision the FCC revoked the license of WHDH-TV on the grounds that it was unacceptable for one company to own so many communication properties in one city. (In this case there was a second issue—*ex parte* or off the record meetings between the president of the Herald Traveler and FCC commissioners.) The WHDH case was the first incident involving what has become known as the "one-to-a-customer" rule. This rule is only one of several FCC regulations intended to encourage diversity in the field of broadcasting.

FCC Rules Designed to Promote Diversity

One-to-a-Customer Rule.   At present, the most controversial FCC regulation regarding diversity is the one-to-a-customer rule, which had it first test in the 1975 *Washington Star* case.[27] A wealthy Texas banker, Joe L. Allbritton, wished to purchase WMAL-AM-FM-TV in addition to the *Washington Star*—all in Washington, D.C.

Such a purchase would violate the FCC's one-to-customer rule, which prohibits a single owner from purchasing broadcast and newspaper properties in a single market. The rule also prevents the purchase of radio and television properties in the same market.[28] During December of 1975, the FCC granted Allbritton the authority to purchase the radio and televisions stations. He had already purchased the newspaper.

The FCC agreed to the sale because it felt that Washington needed two newspapers and it appeared that the *Washington Star* would fold without the financial support the broadcast stations could provide. But the FCC granted Allbritton's request on the condition that he sell the radio and television stations within a specified period of time and retain only the newspaper. In addition, Allbritton would have to sell a radio and television station he had purchased in Lynchburg, Virginia.[29]

In the Allbritton case, the one-to-a-customer rule was applied to a company that wished to purchase broadcast in addition to print properties in a single large market, but the FCC has also applied the rule to individuals who already owned both broadcast and print properties. During late January 1975, the FCC ordered owners of media in sixteen small markets to sell some of their holdings. These were newspaper-radio, newspaper-television, or radio-television owners in small markets who had created a "media monopoly," in the Commission's view.[30] The FCC, exhibiting no willingness to tackle media monopolies in the large markets, confined its application of the one-to-a-customer rule to small ones. The decision affected stations and newspapers in places like Albany, Georgia; Mason City, Iowa; and DuBois, Pennsylvania.[31]

Yet in large markets there are newspaper-broadcast owners like the *New York Daily News*, which owns WPIX-TV. Each national television network owns television and radio stations in the same city. In 1977 a court of appeals directed the FCC to establish a policy that would break up cross-ownerships in all markets. The FCC has indicated that it will appeal the decision, thus the outcome is uncertain at this writing.

Seven-Seven-Seven Rule.   The seven-seven-seven rule permits a single owner to hold up to seven AM, seven FM, and seven television stations in the nation. (Obviously, all of these stations may not be held in a single market.) The number of VHF television stations the owner may hold is limited to five. A single owner may have five VHF and two UHF, or seven UHF, or any other combination of UHF and VHF stations so long as the total does not exceed seven and the total VHF's does not exceed five.[32]

Duopoly Rule.   The duopoly rule prevents an owner from possessing more than one station of a particular class in a single market. For example, a broadcaster may own only one AM station in any one market; the same applies to FM and television stations. Under this rule, it would be impossible for an individual or corporation to possess more than one television station in New York City.[33]

Networks and Anti-trust.   Recently there have been many objections to the networks and their domination over local television schedules. Most television stations either subscribe to a network, receive syndicated programs that were once on a network, or both. Westinghouse Broadcasting Company has complained that it does not have enough time to program its own shows and has asked the FCC for action. The FCC has held a hearing but has formulated no new rules.

On another front, the Justice Department has filed a suit against the three networks, saying that they have a monopoly over prime-time programs. In late 1976, the Justice Department and NBC reached an agreement which would end the law suit and limit the amount of programming NBC could produce for its own use during the ten years after the agreement was signed. But NBC was unwlling to sign the agreement unless ABC and CBS would also sign. Neither network expressed any willingness to join NBC and it appears that the suit may continue for several years.

Regulation of Socially Harmful Broadcasting

Obscene and Indecent Material. One of the most difficult problems confronting the FCC and other administrative agencies is the problem of defining what is obscene and indecent and making sure that these definitions do not conflict with the First Amendment. The United States Code prohibits broadcasters from carrying anything that is obscene, indecent, or profane on the air (18 USC § 1464). But the wording of this section does not define obscenity, indecency, or profanity.

In the Roth case of 1957, the Supreme Court attempted to provide some guidance for determining if a work is obscene.[34] The important elements that resulted from the case were the Court's six criteria for evaluating obscenity. "The standard for judging obscenity, adequate to withstand the charge of constitutional infirmity," is whether the work is obscene [1] to the average person, [2] when applying contemporary community standards, [3] if obscenity is the dominant theme of the material, [4] if the work taken as a whole is obscene [5] when it appeals to prurient interest.[35] In addition, the work must be utterly without redeeming social value.

During 1973 and 1974 the Supreme Court evolved a new standard for obsenity. The important case was *Miller* v. *California* (1973) in which the Supreme Court spelled out three elements in deciding if a work was obscene.[36] The three tests are as follows: (1) The court must find that to the average person the work appeals to prurient interest. In this test the "community standards" must be local rather than national standards; (2) The sexual content of the work must be depicted in a patently offensive way as defined in local state law; and, (3) the work must lack serious literary, artistic, political, or scientific value.[37] The *Miller* standard replaced the old *Roth*.

FCC Regulation of Obscene or Indecent Material

One of the FCC's first cases involving obscene or indecent material involved Charlie Walker, a disc jockey who worked for WDKD in Kingstree, South Carolina. According to the FCC, Walker had used off-color and smutty language on the air for a period of eight years. Because of the Walker broadcasts and other reasons, the FCC denied WDKD's application for a renewed license in 1962.[38]

In 1972 and 1973 "topless" radio became popular. These were radio programs in which a host interviewed callers about their sexual hangups and often went into explicit details. As a result of many listener complaints, the FCC fined WGLD-FM in Illinois $2,000 for the sex talk shows it carried in March of 1973.[39] The NAB added provisions to its code to prevent topless radio, and stations across the country ceased carrying these shows. The topless radio fad promptly died.

In 1977 the FCC's authority to prevent the broadcast of offensive material was called into question by a court of appeals. WBAI, a radio station in New York City, had broadcast record by George Carlin dealing with "seven dirty words." The FCC ruled that WBAI could not broadcast such material during times that children might listen to the station; however, WBAI appealed to the courts, which reversed the FCC. The FCC did not understand the First Amendment, said the court, when it ordered WBAI not to air Carlin's record during certain time periods. While this case does not deal directly with topless radio, it does point out that courts are viewing the First Amendment quite strictly.

Just as broadcasters must obey certain requirements with reference to obscenity, so must cablecasters abide by specific FCC regulations. On local origination channels—those channels on which the cable system carries its own locally produced or syndicated programs—cable operators must abide by regulations which prevent them from carrying any broadcast that is profane, obscene, or indecent. This means that they can neither produce obscene material nor can they permit others to cablecast obscene material.[40]

On channels set aside for public, educational, and governmental use—called access channels—the cable operator may also censor that which is obscene, profane, or indecent.[41] The cable operator must not permit access channels to be used for advertising or for carrying information regarding lotteries or political candidates.[42]

Program Regulation

Some broadcasting regulations are based on the social effects of programming. Perhaps the clearest example of this was the congressional action in 1972 prohibiting broadcasters from carrying cigarette advertising.[43] The grounds for this decision were numerous studies that had found cigarette smoking to be harmful to the health.

Using the same reasoning, the FCC (1971) issued a notice declaring that song lyrics that tended to promote the use of illegal drugs were unacceptable for broadcast.[44] The Commission held that broadcast station owners had an obligation to check song lyrics to make certain that they did not violate the established standards. Nicholas Johnson, one of the commissioners, emphatically protested the majority decision, saying that "it was an attempt by a group of establishmentarians to determine what youth can say and hear.[45]

One month later, the commissioners issued a second statement defending their first notice. They said that the decision was based upon the sound principle that licensees had a responsibility to control the contents of broadcasts.

Children's Programming.   One of the FCC's concerns has been to protect children from programming containing scenes of excessive violence or sex. Congress shared the same concern, and during the early 1970s it conducted studies into the effects of such programming upon children. These studies suggested that there was certainly a relationship between viewing violent programming and committing acts of violence.[46] On the basis of those studies, Congress ordered the FCC to take some positive action to eliminate excessive violence from television.

Richard Wiley, then chairman of the FCC, saying that any regulation would be a clear violation of the First Amendment, met with the heads of the three national networks in an attempt to get their cooperation for his strategy of self-regulation. The networks agreed to make the first hour of prime time—8:00 to 9:00 p.m. in the Eastern and Pacific zones and 7:00 and 8:00 p.m. in the other time zones—a family viewing period. The networks consented to reduce the amount of violence and sex shown to a level acceptable for family viewing. In addition, the NAB added provisions to extend the family viewing period through the hour preceeding the networks' family hour. The two hour period following the news each evening would thus be devoted to family viewing.

On the occasional evening they carried a potentially offensive program during the family hour, the networks agreed to broadcast viewer advisories. Advisories would also be used during later hour programming that might disturb a large number of people in the audience. For these programs, the networks would forward notices to television magazines so that they might print advisories.

These voluntary decisions by the networks and the NAB constituted self-regulation with government serving as a catalyst. But industry acted under the threat of FCC regulation or congressional action. Interestingly, a number of organizations and people, including Norman Lear, Writers Guild, Screen Actors Guild, and the Directors Guild, sued the three networks, the NAB, and the FCC because they felt that their right of free speech was abridged by an agreement between the networks, the FCC, and the NAB. At this writing a district court opinion agreed with the writers, but the FCC, NAB, and the networks are appealing the case.

FAILURES OF THE FCC

The FCC, as the agency that has been charged with overseeing the broadcast industry, has been examined by Congress a number of times. In fact, the FCC has been under investigation or faced the possibility of investigation by Congress almost every year since it was created.[47] Other agencies and even its own members have scrutinized the FCC. Congress has found many problems, and at least one FCC commissioner feels that the FCC has rarely been effective.[48]

Failure of FCC to Effect Diversity of Control in Broadcast Industry

Perhaps one of the areas in which the FCC has been most ineffective in regulating broadcasting is in diversity—breaking up large group and corporate ownership. In 1967, the FCC was confronted with the decision to approve or reject a merger between ABC and International Telegraph and Telephone (ITT). Had the merger been completed, ABC-ITT would have been the largest communications corporation in the world. Not only that but, according to Nicholas Johnson, the company was engaging in several questionable practices in order to persuade the FCC to approve the merger.[49]

Although the Department of Justice opposed the merger, the FCC approved the arrangement. The agreement was later called off, but the FCC had gone on record as approving an arrangement that involved questionable dealings. Only three of the seven commissioners had opposed the move.

Even the FCC's one-to-a-customer rule had difficulties from 1968 to 1975. In 1968, the FCC proposed a new rule that would encourage diversity in ownership in a market. The rule was adopted in 1970, but it was modified in 1971 (see earlier part of this chapter). Little was done to enforce the rule until 1974, and then only under intense pressure from the Department of Justice. The FCC's final decision did little more than preserve the status quo.

As a result of the pressure and public hearings, the FCC decided (1975) to force sixteen small markets to break up their media monopolies. That action is still pending. Also, in 1975 the FCC partially waived the one-to-a-customer rule by permitting Joe Allbritton to buy both radio and television stations in addition to a newspaper in a single market.

A citizens group, National Citizens Committee for Broadcasting (NCCB), believed that the FCC's one-to-a-customer rule did not go far enough. NCCB wanted the rule to be applied to all cross-ownership arrangements, regardless of market size. They also demanded that existing cross-ownerships be broken up. To get the regulation changed, NCCB appealed to the United States Court of Appeals in Washington, D.C. In 1977, the Court agreed with NCCB's argument and directed the FCC to revise its regulations accordingly. The Court of Appeals decision is being appealed, so the final outcome rests with the United States Supreme Court.[50]

Ineffective Enforcement of Decisions

Not only has the FCC been slow in effecting change, it has often been inconsistent in its creation and enforcement of regulations. For example during the 1940s the FCC created what became known as the "Blue Book." The Blue Book was written because the FCC felt it had a responsibility to review a broadcast station's performance in the areas of programming and commercial policy. In fact Paul A. Porter, then chairperson of the FCC, said in 1945 that the FCC would review how the program promises made by stations were met in their programming.[51]

The Blue Book was created to elucidate how the FCC handled its responsibilities. The book was a compilation of situations and cases showing how the FCC had handled various applications. It covered a variety of issues including (1) competing applications, (2) hearing procedure, (3) how station promises were fulfilled in programming, (4) aspects of "the public interest" as interpreted by the FCC, and (5) commercial policy.[52] But the FCC procedures and principles were never followed largely because the broadcast industry protested so vigorously.

Ten years later, when the broadcast industry was plagued by the quiz scandals of the late 1950s and when everyone was trying to make *ex parte* contacts at the FCC, Jack Gould writing for *The New York Times* felt that it was time to bring the Blue Book back and begin enforcing the hearing and programming standards stated in the Blue Book.

Indecision in FCC Action

FCC indecision, another recurring problem, probably reaches its most refined form in the cable television area where the FCC has changed its rules and regulations no fewer than three times (see Chapter 1). At first the FCC held that it had no regulatory authority over cable, but by 1962 it had found limited authority by regulating microwave companies that supply television programs to cable systems. The first and second cable Report and Orders in 1965 and 1966 were used by the FCC to assert extensive and repressive control over cable. Finally, in 1972, the FCC became less restrictive in its handling of cable television.

Ties of Commissioners to the Industry

A problem at the FCC has been *ex parte* contacts between the broadcast industry and FCC officials. An *ex parte* contact occurs when a representative of a company under investigation meets with the FCC official in charge of the investigation in a private, off-the-record setting. Although the private meeting might not always lead to a favorable vote from the official, the possibility of influencing a decision exists.

During the 1950s, the problem was so great that the period has often been called the "Whorehouse Era"—a period when the FCC arranged actions rather than judged the facts.[53] The off-the-record meetings, no matter what their intent, raised questions about the objective environment in which regulation was taking place. During this period lawyers hoped to get commissioners to vote favorably for their clients by offering the commissioner a gift or favor. Favorable decisions were traded for gifts.

The problem of *ex parte* was apparent in the WHDH case when the FCC revoked the station's license in part because an earlier chairperson of the FCC had had off-the-record contact with an executive at WHDH. The WHDH case is only one of the *ex parte* cases. Another involved commissioner Richard A. Mack and a Florida applicant for a station. When the record of Mack's involvement with the Florida station became public, he resigned under pressure.[54]

At least two studies have shown that large numbers of commissioners enter the communications industry or communications law practice after leaving the FCC. Few of the commissioners came from the communications industry, so it would appear that they had used the FCC as a stepping stone to the industry they had regulated. This, of course, raises questions about the public spirit of these people.

Only a few commissioners have actively worked for the public concern. James L. Fly fought the monopoly problems in the broadcast industry in the 1940s. During the late 1940s and early 1950s, Frieda B. Hennock worked for educational television allocations in opposition to the commercial interests. In the 1960s Newton Minow fought for more serious broadcast programming, and Nicholas Johnson was in the forefront of fighting for consumer interests. Yet these four commissioners represent only a small fraction of those who served the FCC.

Political Intervention

Although the FCC was designed to be free of other governmental pressures in the execution of its duties, the freedom which it has is more of an illusion than a reality. In the writing of the Communications Act of 1934, Congress retained the power to approve or reject the annual budgets of the FCC, to amend the Communications Act, and to review the decision and rules of the FCC. Congress gave the President both the right to appoint commissioners and to disburse funds to the agency and, as ordered by the Constitution, Congress gave the courts the right to review every action of the FCC. These powers give the three branches of government great control over the daily actions of the FCC. (See Figure 11–2.)

In addition to the legal forces, there are intense political forces trying to influence the FCC. The broadcast industry, through its rich and powerful trade

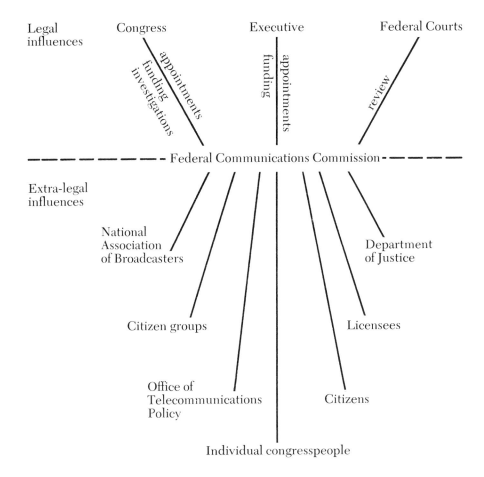

Figure 11–2. The supercharged political environment in which the Federal Communications Commission operates. Each of these groups has an interest in influencing FCC actions.

lobby association, the NAB, urges the FCC to make decisions favorable to the broadcast industry. Citizens groups frequently demand that the FCC listen to their protests. Individual congressmen may, at the urging of their constituents, call commissioners to "suggest" changes in policy.

Because of the intense political pressures, the FCC not only must conform to the law, but it must also balance favorable and unfavorable political forces.[55] Only by maintaining this balance can the FCC have some semblance of freedom of choice.

PROPOSALS FOR IMPROVING THE FCC

Numerous methods for reforming the FCC have been advanced, each with merits. Some of these proposals are discussed briefly in the following sections.

Insulation from Political Influence

As has been noted above, the FCC comes under considerable political influence from the Congress and the Executive. If the agency is to work effectively, it should be given freedom from excessive external intervention so that it need not fear the anger of a Congress or a President. This, some feel, can be accomplished by lengthening the term for commissioners, including, perhaps, life tenure on the FCC as for judges in the courts.[56]

Separate Functions

Dividing the legislative and judicial roles of the FCC between two agencies might solve some of the agency's problems. That way the new agency responsible for enforcing the regulations would not have the power to modify regulations for its convenience.[57]

License by Lottery

Most applicants who apply to the FCC for a license have met the minimum qualifications for holding a license since the first action of the FCC is to weed out those who fall short of minimum requirements. The qualifications and proposals of the applicants for a channel are usually very similar. Consequently, the awarding of the license becomes an exercise in looking for minute details that may distinguish one applicant from another. Such a process necessarily gives much work to lawyers, but may prove of little overall benefit to the viewing and listening audience.

Because applicants do not differ significantly, Richard Wiley, then chairperson of the FCC suggested in a speech before the NAB in 1976 that licenses be awarded on the basis of lottery. Thus when several applicants who meet the minimum qualifications for holding a license apply for the same channel, the winning applicant's name would be drawn at random or would be chosen by computer. Although this process lacks the apparent precision of the more traditional method of conducting hearings on the qualifications of applicants, it is clearly faster and cheaper. Of course, no one can be sure that it is better for the consumer of the mass media.

Such a revolutionary procedure probably will never receive Congressional support—and it may not even have serious support from Wiley who proposed it—but it does reflect the problems the FCC faces when trying to decide among a group of nearly equal applicants.

Citizen Participation

One author properly observed that "without the sustained interest of a majority of the voters, the public interest is neglected and a regulatory agency is ripe for capture by the regulated groups.[58] Washington is a political city where laws and regulations are created in an environment of intense political competition. Lobbying is just as common on Capital Hill and before the Executive as it is before the FCC. Much of the regulatory chaos results from this lobbying—or at least from an unwillingness to admit its existance.

Because of the nature of the regulatory environment, the most promising reform may come from the active involvement of citizen groups like the National Citizens Committee for Broadcasting (NCCB). Like the NAB, which lobbies for the interests of broadcasters, NCCB lobbies for the interests of citizens. These competing forces must eventually force the FCC to begin balancing the demands of citizens against those of broadcasters.

LAW OF EFFECTIVE REFORM

Citizen groups must follow certain procedures if they wish to get effective action from the FCC. To help people who have little experience in appealing to the FCC, Nicholas Johnson has created what he calls the "law of effective reform." According to this principle, there are three steps that one must complete. They are:

1. State the facts in the situation that provide the basis for the complaint. These facts must be carefully and accurately spelled out.
2. Cite the appropriate legal principle that provides for relief. This includes FCC rules and regulations, appropriate statutes, court cases, and constitutional provisions.
3. Clearly spell out the remedy or correction desired: a fine, revocation of a license, or a change in programming.

Source: Nicholas Johnson: *How to Talk Back to Your Television Set* (Boston: Little, Brown and Company, 1969), p. 202.

NOTES

1. Edwin Emery, Philip H. Ault, and Warren K. Agee *Introduction to Mass Communication*, 3rd ed. (New York: Dodd, Mead and Company, 1971), pp. 38, 99.
2. Ibid.
3. Walter B. Emery, *Broadcasting and Government* (East Lansing; Michigan State University Press, 1971), p. 27.
4. Ibid., pp. 28, 29.
5. Great Lakes Broadcasting Company, Fed. Radio Comm., D. 4900 (1928).
6. Young People's Association for the Propagation of the Gospel, 6 FCC 178 (1938).
7. Mayflower Broadcasting Corporation, 8 FCC 333 (1941).
8. United Broadcasting Company, 10 FCC 515, 5 RR 799 (1945).
9. In re Petition of Robert Harold Scott for Revocation of Licenses of Radio Stations KQW, KPO and KFRC, 11 FCC 372 (1946).
10. In the Matter of Editorializing by Broadcast Licensees, 13 FCC §246 (1949).
11. *Red Lion Broadcasting Co.*, v. *FCC*, 395 US 367 (1967).
12. Applicability of the Fairness Doctrine in the Handling of Controversial Issues of Public Importance, 29 Fed. Reg. 10415 (1964).
13. Ibid.
14. Ibid.
15. Fairness Doctrine and Public Interest Standards—Handling of Public Issues (1974).
16. Ibid.
17. Ibid.
18. Ibid.
19. In re Complaint Concerning the CBS Program "The Selling of the Pentagon," 30 FCC 2d 150 (1971).
20. Ibid.
21. Ibid.
22. Letter from Federal Communications Commission to Television Station WCBS-TV 8 FCC 2d 381 (1967).
23. *Friends of the Earth* v. *FCC*, 449 F.2d 1164 (D.C. Cir.) (1971).
24. *National Broadcasting Company*, v. *United States* 319 US 190 (1943).
25. Ibid.
26. Sterling Quinlan, *The Hundred Million Dollar Lunch* (Chicago: J. Phillip O'Hara, Inc., 1974), pp. 111–116.
27. "Allbritton gets his Deal for Washington," *Broadcasting* (December 22, 1975), pp. 19, 20.
28. Ibid.
29. Ibid.
30. "FCC at last Defines Policy on Broadcast and Newspaper Crossownership," *Broadcasting* (February 3, 1975), p. 23.
31. Ibid.
32. FCC, *38th Annual Report/Fiscal Year 1972* (Washington: Government Printing Office), p. 42.
33. Ibid.
34. *Roth* v. *United States* 354 US 476 (1956).
35. Ibid., 354 US 477.

36. *Miller* v. *United States* 413 US 25 (1974).

37. Ibid.

38. Palmetto Broadcasting Company, 33 FCC 250 (1962).

39. 41 FCC 2d 919 (1973).

40. 47 CFR 76.215.

41. 47 CFR 76.251.

42. Ibid.

43. Frank J. Kahn, *Documents of American Broadcasting* (New York: Appleton-Century-Crofts, 1973), p. 434.

44. Licensee Responsibility to Review Records Before Their Broadcast 28 FCC 2d 409 (1971).

45. Ibid.

46. Report on the Broadcast of Violent, Indecent and Obscene Material (Washington, D.C.: FCC, 1975), pp. 1–3.

47. Walter B. Emery, *Broadcasting and Government* (East Lansing: Michigan State University Press, 1971), p. 396.

48. Ibid.

49. Nicholas Johnson, *How to Talk Back to Your Television Set* (Boston: Little, Brown, 1969), pp. 49–59.

50. "Government Widens Attack on Newspaper, Broadcasting Crossownership," *Broadcasting*, January 7, 1973), p. 16.

51. Freedom of Information Center, *FCC's "Blue Book" (1946)* (Columbia, Missouri, December 1962), p. 1.

52. Ibid.

53. Quinlan, op. cit., pp. 1–14.

54. Ibid., pp. 5, 6.

55. Erik Barnouw, *A Tower in Babel* (New York: Oxford University Press, 1966), p. 251.

56. Erwin Krasnow and Lawrence D. Longley, *The Politics of Broadcast Regulation* (New York: St. Martin's Press, 1973), p. 9.

57. "Wiley Offers New Order for Licensing," *Broadcasting* (March 29, 1976), p. 24.

58. Marver H. Bernstein, *Regulating Business by Independent Commission* (Princeton, N.J.: Princeton University Press, 1966), p. 285.

Alternate Technologies, New Directions

12

A glass fiber no bigger than a human hair is now carrying television programs from antennas on top of a New York skyscraper down thirty-four floors to control equipment owned by a company named Teleprompter. Teleprompter's use of glass fibers, called optical fibers, is the first regular, practical use made of fibers for carrying television communications. The new system, put into operation on July 8, 1976, worked so well that Teleprompter executives predicted that by the end of the 1970s fibers would be in regular use.[1]

Fibers use light instead of electricity for communication, replacing wires with glass fibers as the medium for conducting signals from one place to another. Engineers consider fiber communication the most important advance in electronics since the invention of the transistor in the 1950s. One of the major advantages of fibers is their ability to carry many signals on a single strand. In fact the Teleprompter fiber, which is ninety microns in diameter, can carry 167 television channels. (A micron is one millionth of a meter.) Another important advantage of fibers is that they are potentially less expensive than coaxial cable for carrying television programs (see page 32 for a discussion of cables). This is true partly because the fiber is made from glass, which is cheaper than wire. More importantly, however, fibers require repeater amplifiers (actually lasars) every one and one half miles, whereas coaxial cables require about three amplifiers per mile. These amplifiers keep television picture levels high so that subscribers may see sharper pictures.

The popularity of the broadcast media has inevitably stimulated many to try to provide additional services through new technologies like fibers. For example, there simply have not been enough television stations to serve everyone with the desired quantity of television programs. Therefore, enterprising individuals began constructing cable systems capable of bringing television to rural areas and small cities that had little in the way of television service. Cable eventually began serving cities that had a number of television stations with special television services. But cable was only one of the new technologies. Other recent innovations include video disk, video tape machines for the home, projection television sets, optical fibers, and satellites.

Television and radio depend upon technology; upon the inventions of engineers and scientists concerned with electronics. The tremendous growth of these media are just as dependent now on new technology as they were in their infancy. Now there are not only color television sets but the potential to create stereo television sets. Perhaps three dimensional sets will be commonplace in

SATELLITES FOR COMMERCIAL COMMUNICATION

The first satellite set into orbit for commercial purposes was the Early Bird, in April 1965. This satellite had the capability to carry 240 two-way telephone calls or one television signal, and proved that satellites could make a profit. It later became part of an international network of satellites called Intelsat. The Early Bird satellite was owned by Communications Satellite Corporation (COMSAT). COMSAT joined with other countries and companies and formed the International Telecommunications Satellite Consortium (Intelsat) in 1964. This new consortium intended to make satellite communications available to member companies and nations.

Some of the most recent satellites sent up by Intelsat allow for some 6250 telephone conversations and two television programs to be carried simultaneously. These international satellites have been used by television networks to send news and documentary information from all over the world to the networks' headquarters in New York. Shortly after the close of the Vietnam war, one television network used satellites to bring the latest news about the war and its aftermath to American viewers.

Satellites could be used to link computers connect television stations to the network headquarters with which they are affiliated, and to facilitate long distance telephone conversations.

Source: *Satellite Communications Reference Data Handbook* (Springfield, Vas National Technical Information Service, 1972) pp. 1–5 to 1–11.

A Communications satellite can be used for long distance transmission of television pictures and information. (COMSAT.)

the future. The direction that technology, and the economic factors that control this technology, takes will determine the future of television and radio.

In the next few pages we will examine some of the new technologies—those that have come along recently and others that are still in the developmental stages—that hold great promise for the nation and the world. We will discuss how cable television and satellites changed the complexion of broadcasting and how other technologies might change the whole media environment in the coming years.

SATELLITES FOR EDUCATION AND SPECIAL USES

Not all satellites are used by large corporations and governmental agencies. In fact, several groups have been using satellites for educational and amateur purposes. The first satellite intended for amateur radio operators was Orbiting Satellite Carrying Amateur Radio-I (OSCAR-I), launched on December 12, 1961. Since then, six more amateur satellites have been launched. Some 100 amateur radio stations in sixteen countries have used the OSCAR satellites for communications. The satellites cost about $100,000 each and the ground eqiupment can be acquired for about $1000.

In the Pacific basin, PEACESAT makes it possible to exchange medical information, agricultural data, and news among the many islands between Hawaii and New Zealand. The project was initiated by the University of Hawaii and the Wellington Polytechnic Institute in New Zealand. The ground stations for this satellite system have been built for prices ranging between $5000 and $25,000, using readily available components. They use a satellite sent up by the United States on a no cost basis.

These two examples show that satellites may be constructed and used at a relatively low cost and that they provide great promise for the application of satellites in educational uses.

Source: "Communications Satellites: Now You Can Have Them Too," *Access* 33 (May 3, 1976), pp. 6, 7.

CABLE TELEVISION

Early Development of Cable Television

The first of the new technologies, perhaps one of the most promising, is cable television. While broadcast television can provide only a limited number of television signals in a market, cable television has the capacity to deliver up to one hundred television signals to a home receiver.[2] This abundance could provide channels catering to such diverse areas as education, sports, old movies, and business.

The first cable systems were not so ambitious in their intentions, they only hoped to deliver signals from television stations to remote areas not served by regular television stations. These young cable systems grew because the FCC was not able to authorize television stations to every community that desired them. Some of the early systems only picked up one to four television signals with regular antennas and connected viewers homes with these signals.

Probably the first cable system was located in Mahanoy City, Pennsylvania and was started in 1948.[3] About the same time that Mahanoy City got its cable system—then called community antenna television (CATV) systems—other communities in California, Oregon, and Pennsylvania were also building their own systems. The new systems came into being because television could not be picked up from the air locally: Mahanoy City, for instance, was surrounded by mountains that blocked the signals.

The Mahanoy City system was started by an employee of the Pennsylvania Power and Light Company who was involved with a local appliance store that sold television sets. The new system, constructed to encourage demand for television sets, was built by placing television antennas on a nearby mountain to pick up signals from Philadelphia. To get the signal from the mountaintop to subscriber homes, the new operator strung wires from tree to tree down the mountain. By June of 1948 the operator had 727 subscribers.[4]

Most of the early systems were started in much the same way by local residents who wanted to encourage sale of televisions. These systems became known as "Mom and Pop" operations because of their local nature and small size. By the end of the television freeze in 1952, there were more than seventy cable systems and more than 14,000 subscribers.[5] Because all cable systems served small and medium sized towns that did not have access to broadcast television signals, no one seemed too concerned about the newly developing industry. The federal government refused to regulate it and large industry did not invest in cable because it did not think it could make sufficient profits, but things would change.

Cable Becomes Competitive.   In 1962, the complexion of the cable industry changed dramatically when Mission Cable was build in San Diego, California.[6] This was the first time a cable operator had dared to enter a city that had extensive television service. Many questions were raised about cable television's competition with broadcasting and the ability of a cable system to raise enough money to construct as large a system as would be needed in San Diego. San Diego became a test city for determining if cable could effectively compete with existing television stations.

Residents, who could already receive four television signals, were being asked by Mission Cable to subscribe to its service and receive television pictures from a cable rather than out of the air. It was apparent to the management of Mission Cable that the cable would have to offer more than signals from the four local stations if the company was to survive. When Mission Cable was fully operational it provided the following services to residents of San Diego: signals from the four local stations, local programming from three network stations in Los Angeles, programming from the independent television stations in Los Angeles, and programming originated by the cable company. This assured subscribers that they would receive everything that residents of Los Angeles had, in addition to local programming. The new offerings were sufficient to attract subscribers, and by late 1975 Mission Cable had about 113,000 making it the largest single cable system in the United States.[7]

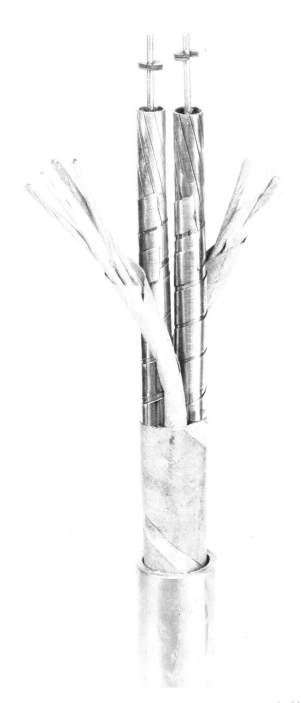

Coaxial cable has become an important part of the telephone, television, and cable television industries in the United States. (Culver Pictures.)

As one might expect, broadcasters were not happy with the new developments in cable television and they petitioned the FCC to write restrictive rules
that would hamper its growth. The NAB engaged in an advertising campaign to
inform the public of the problems with cable television and the dangers of its
competition with broadcast television. Broadcasters were clearly fearful that
their economic position might be damaged. Although cable has had its problems with broadcasters and others, it has increased its subscriber lists every
year. By 1976, cable systems existed in many large cities and over 15 percent of
all television homes in the nation were wired for cable.[8]

Technical Features of Cable

Cable systems today are somewhat more complex than they were in 1950, but
they are still comprised of the same basic elements. There is an antenna system
to pick up television signals; a headend, or building where the signals are put in
a form to be sent to the home; and a distribution system connecting these
signals with the homes.

Antenna and Headend.   In many cable systems, the antennas are much like
those that home owners place on their rooftops. These antennas are usually
mounted on a tall tower, which is located on a nearby hill.[9] By mounting the
antennas as high as possible, the cable operator can pick up television stations
from great distances. Sometimes the cable operator wants to pick up television
stations from greater distances than are possible using nearby antennas. Then
an antenna is erected near the distant stations and microwave transmitters are
used to send the signals to the cable system headend.

The headend receives the televisions signals and uses complex electronic
equipment to amplify and send the televsion signals into the cable that runs to
every subscriber's home. Many cable systems also originate their own programming and have facilities in the headend building for creating television programs.[10] These programs range in sophistication from full news shows to instruments that print time and weather information on the television screen.
Besides the television signals, some cable systems also provide signals from
nearby FM stations so that people may listen to music through their cable.

Distribution Systems.   The television and radio signals that leave the headend
on the distribution cable are combined so that one can carry many television
and radio signals. Many systems have the capacity to carry twenty or more television signals in addition to radio programming.[11] This cable, which connects
the headend with the subscriber television sets, is a coaxial cable. Like electric
or telephone wires, cable television wires must be suspended on poles above
the ground, or buried. Usually cable companies pay telephone and electric
companies rental fee for hanging the cable on poles. This is a "per pole" charge
that is paid each year. Thus, the cable company pays for each pole it uses.

The complex equipment at the headend is usually not strong enough to
send signals that will reach all the way to the end of the cable. Special repeater
amplifiers are therefore inserted into the cable at intervals to increase the

strength of the signal. These amplifiers are capable of amplifying all of the television and radio signals that come from the headend of the cable system.

The final step in the cable system is a short section of coaxial cable that runs from the main cable to the subscriber's home. This final section, called a drop, extends to the room or rooms in which the subscriber has television or radio sets.[12]

New Technical Features

Like other aspects of the electronic media, cable television has developed some new innovations. One is greatly increased channel capacity; present technology can provide up to one hundred channels.[13] All of these channels could be picked up on television sets that have a converter designed to pick up extra channels outside the usual twelve VHF. Although no one hundred channel system exists at present, a forty-two channel system is being used in San Jose, California.[14]

Satellites now supplement cable television by providing pay television signals to cable systems that wish to connect with a pay cable network through satellite interconnection. (Pay cable is discussed more fully later in this chapter.) A pay cable company in, New York, for example, purchases motion pictures and sports programs that are transmitted to a satellite above the United States. The satellite, in turn, transmits the pay programs back to earth where they are received by special ground equipment. The pay programs are then sent to cable television systems, which in turn sell the right to view the pay programs to subscribers.

Since a single satellite covers about one-third of the world, one company using a single satellite can sell its pay television programs to a large number of ca-

---

VIDEO ENVIRONMENT

Homes and living rooms are now being designed with television and the other aspects of the media world in mind. Video cassettes, video disks, and projection television are taken into account in the design of a new home or room. Some carry the media experience to the extreme, with chairs, tables, and lights all arranged in such a way as to take advantage of projection films and television.

It is even possible to purchase for about $25,000 a system that will project an image of a golf course. Just in front of the screen is a place to practice one's golf. When the ball hits the screen, special sensors determine the direction and speed of the ball and project it down the projected golf course to the point where the ball would land. With this new device it is no longer necessary to leave one's home to play golf, with the added advantage of no more lost balls.

ble systems. Thus, a single satellite used by a pay cable company can provide television programs to the entire United States as well as other countries in the western hemisphere. One company, Home Box Office (HBO), is already using a satellite to send its pay television programs to subscribing cable companies.

Just as pay television companies use satellites, commercial broadcast networks like CBS and NBC could use satellites to interconnect the stations that carry their programs. At present the commercial networks are not making use of such potential, instead they are interconnecting stations by using cable and microwave eqiupment owned by telephone companies.

Another possible use of satellites that has only been partially realized is direct broadcasting to homes, schools, and special interest organizations. Home users and others must have receiving antennas outfitted to pick up the satellite signals, but with the specialized equipment every home in the nation could receive signals from a single satellite. Such broadcasting would make the present form of broadcast television networks obsolete and could revolutionize television broadcasting. One possible consequence could be the creation of a few satellite stations that would supply all television in the nation, abolishing the need for local stations.

A technical innovation that has great promise for television communications is the fibers, as discussed earlier. The small strands of glass fibers that use light instead of electricity have the potential of greatly increasing the number of channels of communications available to the cable subscriber. Since one small strand of fiber can carry many more signals that a coaxial cable that is three-quarters of an inch thick, fibers can supply the nation's communication needs without taking up much space.

Equally important, fibers can carry all the forms of communications that cables do. One fiber strand can carry television and radio programs, computer data, police and fire information, and picture telephone conversations.

Economics of Cable Television

Cable television came into being because people wanted more programs. As the number of television stations increased, the demand for programs and the sale of television sets increased. Cable merely capitalized upon this demand by extending service to areas lacking adequate television service. Cable, consequently, depended upon the fact that many people had already invested in expensive television receivers. In this sense, broadcast television had already created the market, and cable was a "parasitic" service benefiting from the fact that television stations had induced consumers to purchase costly sets.

The earliest cable systems came into being solely to supplement broadcast television by taking service to areas not reached by many existing stations. But as service expanded, television station owners began demanding that the FCC take some action to protect existing stations.[15] In 1962, the FCC exercised limited jurisdiction over cable, but it was not until 1966 that the FCC expanded its authority to all cable systems. The 1966 ruling required cable systems to carry all local television stations. It also stated that if the cable system brought in a distant signal that duplicated a local station's signal, the cable system could not carry the duplicated program the same day it was carried on the local station.[16] This protected broadcast stations, but it hampered the development of cable systems.

Since these early systems provided only redistribution of existing television signals, they had no advertising revenue. They were supported by monthly subscription fees and an initial connection charge paid by set owners to be connected to the cable system. Both of these sources of revenue still exist, and at present the average subscription fee is about six dollars per month and the connection fee can go as high as one hundred dollars with the average being approximately twenty dollars.[17]

More recently, cable systems have sold advertising to increase revenues. They have sold time on a channel used to carry local programming. At least 200 systems accept advertising and they charge from $5 to $200 per minute.[28] For 1975 this advertising revenue amounted to about $3.1 million. This is only a small amount when compared to commercial television advertising revenues amounting to several billion dollars per year, but the amount of advertising revenue available to cable television has been increasing.

Another source of support for cable television is pay cable. These pay channels require the subscriber to pay a fee for watching movies and sports events not available on regular television. The programs are shown, as in a theater, without any commercial interruptions. By 1976 approximately 100 cable systems had some form of pay cable with about 273,000 subscribers.[19] Home Box Office, (HBO) was the first company to offer a national pay cable service, commencing its operation on September 30, 1975.[20]

The Promise of Cable

Cable television has subscribers in cities with and without broadcast television. It became successful primarily because it promised two things to subscribers: better quality pictures and more programs from which to choose. Broadcast television has often been bothered by "ghosts" or double pictures on the screen, by poor color, and by pictures that roll. Cable television eliminates all of these technical problems and sends the viewer a distortion-free picture.

Although cable television can offer many channels, the average is about ten.[21] Most present systems are capable of offering three national commercial networks, the public television network, and several independent television stations. Recent innovations in cable have shown that it can fill many needs besides relaying television station signals to the home. Some other uses of cable include local origination channels that offer some or all of the following services: time and weather dials that are continuously read by a television camera; news channels that print the latest news on the screen; local live channels providing news, entertainment, sports, and public affairs; and access channels.[22]

The last category, access channels, differs from other services offered by cable facilities in that it is programming generated by the public, by government, and by education and is carried on separate channels. The FCC has defined four classes of access channels: *public access* channels intended for any private citizen who has something to say; *government access* channels intended for use by local governmental bodies for informing the public about what is happening in government; *education access* for educational and instructional purposes; and *paid access* channels that may be used by anyone who wishes to pay for special time to carry programs of his or her choosing.

Current FCC rules require that cable systems operating with more than 3500 subscribers must provide channel capacity for the four classes of access. To fulfill the requirements of the rule, cable systems constructed after 1972 must include at least one extra channel specially designated for access programming. When the cable system was built before 1972, the year the regulation was written, the cable owner need not add extra channels to fulfill the access requirements. The old systems are permitted to accommodate access programming on cable channels that also carry network programming.

When a cable system provides time for access use it may not censor the content of the program unless it violates some law. In addition, FCC rules and regulations (§76.251) say that users of free access channels may not advertise any product or service. Neither may they use the channels to promote a lottery or to air any obscene or indecent material. The same rules apply to the leased channels, except that they may advertise.

In some cable systems these four classifications of access are combined on one channel, while others allocate three or more different channels. Amherst Cablevision outside Buffalo, New York provides all three of the access channels, but it goes a step farther by actually covering town meetings in their entirety on its government access channel.

The foregoing services are one-way programs, that is, the cable operator sends television pictures to the viewer's home, but there is no opportunity for the viewer to respond to the cable system or to others on the cable. Some systems are experimenting with different uses of two-way cables. In fact, the FCC requires that all new cable systems have the capacity to handle two-way programs.[23]

If two-way television is ever fully utilized, cable systems will be providing many nonbroadcast services. With some conversion equipment to send signals back to the headend of the cable system or to any other point, the subscriber could request anything desired. Students at home could contact their library and have information shown to them over a special cable channel. Stores could use a cable channel to record credit card purchases and get bank clearance or they could provide electronic catalogue services to the home. Individuals might confirm doctor and dentist appointments through a two-way system.

Indeed virtually everything in the worlds of business and education could be done by cable, but while the promise is there, the reality seems far away. Cablecasters, like their counterparts in broadcasting, have been far more preoccupied with acquiring new subscribers to improve their profits than they have been with developing new and better services for their viewers.

However, some of these services could be sold to generate additional income for the cable system. For example, the subscriber could be charged for the conversion equipment connected to the home television set; physicians and dentists could be charged a rental for connecting their appointment service to the cable system. Of course, before all of these new services can be offered by the cable systems, the systems must increase the number of channels they carry so that the new services will not interfere with the broadcast signals they are already providing.

Pay Cable

By 1972 cable television was providing pay cable. For the most part the early years of cable television were dominated by the passive reception of a television signal from a station at some distance and the relaying of the picture to the viewer's home, but pay cable began to change cable's role to that of an active producer of television. Interestingly, the first experiments with pay television were done with broadcast television. However, the broadcast experiments were not nearly so successful as the later cable tests. HBO was one of the first companies to offer subscription movies and sports when it began operation in 1972.[24]

But how does pay cable work? Subscribers to a cable system have the option of adding the pay cable channel for an extra fee. The extra channel, when it is offered, is carried on the same cable as the basic service channels, but the cable operator makes it impossible for a home television set to pick up the picture unless the owner pays for the service. There are three ways that a cable system can prevent unauthorized people from receiving the signal. One method is to place the pay program on a channel that is outside the twelve VHF and seventy UHF channels a television set is capable of receiving. But this method is not very secure because it is possible to purchase special converters that will tune in the pay channel; therefore, many cable systems have gone to a line trap or a scrambler.

The line trap is a small device placed in the cable drop that goes from the main cable to the subscriber's home and prevents the pay channel from passing down the cable to the subscriber's set. When a cable system uses a scrambler, it mixes up the television picture at the headend and sends this mixed up signal to the subscriber. In those homes where the subscriber pays the extra fee, a descrambler is provided so that the subscriber may see a clear picture.

The rental that a pay cable subscriber must pay may be either a flat monthly charge that covers all viewing or it may be a per use charge covering only the programs a subscriber chooses to watch. Pay cable has been able to attract viewers because it offers first run motion pictures and sports not carried on commercial television and there are no advertising interruptions.

It is apparent from the foregoing discussion that the pay channel complements commercial television. However, commercial broadcasters oppose pay channels because they fear that they will syphon off all of the desirable sports shows and movies before the commercial operators have an opportunity to use them. Many broadcasters feel that pay cable will acquire leases on the best movies before the networks have an opportunity to show them, and others believe that within a few years pay cable may well have more money to spend on program material than the networks. The fears that broadcasters have expressed appear unfounded since one of the criticisms of broadcasting has been that it is unable to carry all of the programming the public demands. Consequently, with pay channel there should be enough programming for everybody.[25]

Pay channels are appearing all across the nation as is evidenced by HBO service to communities in the Northeast, the South, and the West. Optical Systems, another pay cable operator, serves California cable systems, and other companies provide pay television in states such as Ohio, Texas, and Florida. Extra service for the subscriber and added income for the cable operator have made subscription television a success and trebled income of organizations like HBO in the first eight months of 1974.[26]

This success led HBO to announce a plan in 1975 to establish a national pay television network using the two ground connections it already had and satellites to send programs to all parts of the nation. The new system could provide programs to cable systems in at least twenty-one states including California, New York, Oregon, Texas, Florida, and Pennsylvania, and has about one million potential subscribers. Although the present system can provide signals to only twenty-one states because there are only a limited number of ground stations for picking up the signal from the satellite link, the satellite beams television signals to all parts of the nation. Undoubtedly, when HBO finds sufficient additional cable systems willing to subscribe, other ground stations will be constructed or leased to receive the pay programming. If HBO's system, which was implemented on September 30, 1975, is successful, other pay cable networks will surely be formed in the years ahead and commercial networks will find themselves competing with subscription networks that have no commercials or station breaks.[27]

Until 1977, FCC regulations made it somewhat difficult for pay television services to acquire all of the programming they might want because the regulations permitted the pay operator to show only movies that were made less than three or more than ten years ago. Although the rule benefited broadcasters, during 1976 and 1977 the FCC began softening it. However, just as the FCC thought it had a solution, an appeal to the courts went against the FCC. The court said that the FCC had not shown any need for pay cable rules. The effect of the decision was to abolish all pay cable rules. As with other decisions, the FCC is currently appealing the court's ruling.

In addition, the FCC restricts the sports events a pay cable service may provide. In the cast of recurring events like the Olympic games, the cable system may not carry the event if it has been carried over broadcast television during any season in the past five years. If a sport like baseball is carried over broadcast television, the amount of commercial coverage given the game is used to reduce the amount of coverage a pay cable operator may devote to the game.

In January 1976, the staff of the Committee on Interstate and Foreign Commerce in the House of Representatives released its highly critical study of the FCC's method of regulating cable television. The report suggested that Congress pass laws to force the FCC to take a new approach to cable regulation.

It further said that the FCC had made a mistake in regulating television, which led to a less than satisfactory regulatory scheme for cable. The FCC relied too heavily on "one-way, mass message, and supported by advertising" television. The report also noted that the FCC had too often been pressured by the broadcast industry to regulate in favor of broadcasters.

As a result of its findings, the Committee suggested that several principles should guide FCC regulations:

1. Although cable has traditionally been regulated as a supplementary service to broadcast television, it should be regulated in its own right.
2. Cable should be allowed to grow and bring important new services to the communities it services.
3. Cable television should be available in rural parts of the nation. This meant that rural cable legislation should be created to carry cable to rural areas as had been done with rural electricity laws.
4. Limitations should not be imposed upon cable just for the protection of broadcasters.
5. Copyright laws, which did not apply to cable in 1976, should be expanded so that cable operators would pay their share of copyright fees.
6. The government should determine which aspects of cable are interstate in nature and regulate only those elements, leaving to state and local authorities the regulation of all other parts of cable.
7. When possible, matters regarding cable development should be left to marketplace forces and to experimentation.
8. Federal regulation should be permitted only when there is "clear and compelling" evidence that regulation is needed.[28]

THE FUTURE

Technology advances rapidly in the broadcast and cable fields. First television, then cable, color, video disk, and optical fiber were created. But many innovations that were developed some time ago are still not available in any great quantity. For example, effective two-way communication using cable television has been feasible for some time, but is available on only a few systems. The inhibiting factor—the element that slows development—has certainly not been a lack of new inventions or improved technology, but rather economics. Cable television has not developed as far or as rapidly as it might, largely because television broadcasters have felt that their economic position would be damaged by the new medium. This concern of broadcasters led them to urge the FCC to create regulations to inhibit the development of cable television, regulations that were undoubtedly somewhat successful in their intent.

Each technological advance that threatens an entrenched industry must fight an uphill battle before it can be fully utilized. Indeed, it is the friction that arises between new innovations and established business interests that has prevented cablecasting from developing further. The tendency of the FCC to protect entrenched business has not helped the development of new industries either.

Where television, radio, cable, and their allied technologies will go in the future is largely dependent upon the success of the three waring parties: the FCC, established businesses, and the growing new technologies. It is interesting, however, to look at some of the options that may be available to telecommunications users in the future.

FM Pictures

FM radio may well benefit from a new technology that makes use of its ability to carry subcarriers (see Chapter 1, p. 16). Engineers have found that they can transmit pictures by slow scan facsimile, without overloading the capacity of an

One of the new television games is one in which the golfer sees a course in front of the tee. Sensors pick up the direction and force of the golf ball as it hits the screen and show the player where the ball would have gone. (Golf-O-Tron, Inc.)

FM subcarrier. Facsimile is a process of transmitting still pictures, such as a copy of a page or a still photograph using television scanning techniques. The picture is sent very slowly to conserve on radio frequencies. Although the process is slow—it takes about a minute to build up a picture—this FM facsimile process has great promise. FM stations could send airline schedules, stock market reports, and many other kinds of information to subscribers just as background music services are now sent to subscribing businesses.

Cable. Perhaps the least expansive view of the future is to expect that cable communications will grow from a service to fifteen percent of the nation to a service to nearly all. The major consequence of such a trend would be to make available to all Americans the services presently available to cable subscribers only. This would mean that subscribers could choose among more television programs than are available on broadcast television. It would probably also mean that most Americans would have access to some form of commercial-free pay programming. And, as cable developed, there would be available more and more nonbroadcast services.

An important by-product of such growth would be the probable demise of broadcast television stations. Since all or most of the television viewers would be connected to a cable system, there would be no need for television stations to broadcast; in fact, where cable is popular, people have given up their antennas in favor of the cable. Television stations, then, could opt for connecting their signals directly to cable systems or going out of business.

The abundant number of channels available on cable may completely restructure the nature of television programming, just as the advent of television forced a change in the nature of radio programming. Perhaps television programs would become more specialized, with whole channels devoted to the interests of the young or the old. Undoubtedly, the abundance of television channels would provide a much greater outlet for individual producers, educators, and government officials.

Satellites. A fully developed satellite system could provide the nation with a different set of options. Large libraries could be set up in several parts of the nation with extensive files of films, video tapes, slides, and audio tapes. From these vast resources, a satellite might beam instructional programming into schools throughout the United States, so that students even in remote areas could have access to the finest historical, scientific, and artistic materials. Also, important lectures, debates, and political events could be made available live to schools for enrichment purposes. Satellites could give rise to a national system of education.

In the same way, a satellite system could bring all Americans important cultural and political events as they are happening. One could see concerts, dramas, speeches, and even fairs readily on special channels allocated to cultural and informational programming. These special events would not interfere with entertainment broadcasting because of the abundance of channels.

Of course, the present networks could beam their programming to all Americans by connecting to a satellite. This beam would bypass local stations, and networks would become, in effect, super-stations. Such super-station networks would probably lead to the demise, or at least the massive reorganization, of local stations.

Fibers.   The advantages of fibers result from combining them with other technologies. The capacity of fibers to carry information is so great that they can simultaneously serve television broadcasting and many other forms of media. While fibers may be cheaper than wire communication, converting from wires to fibers will require a tremendous investment.

A gigantic network of fibers connecting homes, governmental institutions, and businesses could be created. The present telephone system is such a network, but fibers greatly increase the amount of information that could flow from point to point. A fiber system could send entertainment and informational programming to homes, in addition to nonbroadcast services like picture telephones and computer interconnections.

Because of the giant capacity of a fiber network, people could transact all of their business from home. Thus, business people could transact business from home, indeed, meetings could be set up with all participants sitting at individual consoles. Every conceivable service that could be offered by traditional cable systems could be provide by a fiber system. With a fiber system, one could communicate with computers, friends, and neighbors; fibers could be our telephone system, our cable system, our radio service, our political forum, and our place of business. The need to travel from place to place by automobile, train, or plane would be reduced. Perhaps such a national fiber system could help cope with the energy problems that arise from the vast consumption of oil used in transporting people from place to place.

The communications satellite fits into this scheme by providing connections across great distances where it is impossible or difficult to use ground links. For example, a satellite could interconnect an American fiber system with a European system by relaying information across the Atlantic. In a similar way, satellites could be used to serve other parts of the world that are separated by oceans or large empty deserts.

But there are some real problems that need to be resolved before such a massive new system is constructed. For example, who would own the fiber network: the government, a quasi-governmental institution composed of government and private industry, a large private corporation, or the telephone companies that now exist? Would the company(ies) that owned the fiber system provide all of the services themselves or would they rent out portions of the fiber system to cable companies, television networks, and local telephone companies?

For individual citizens an even greater question is raised: that of privacy. What methods would be established to protect one's privacy when using the fiber system? Without strict new laws fiber-tapping could reveal much confidential information about a person's life.

Although the precise form of future electronic communication is unclear, it seems reasonable to say that many more channels of entertainment and information will be available to most Americans. Entrenched business interests will continue to try to protect the present form of telecommunications in the interest of their profit and loss picture. At present, television is fighting the cable interests that threaten television broadcast stations; during the 1950s, radio opposed the advance of television. But while entrenched business interests will always fight to protect the status quo, the development of telecommunications to date indicates that some form of new technology will undoubtedly emerge.

How the new technologies are developed may well be dependent upon the alignment of powerful economic forces. The newspaper industry gave up its fight with the new technology of radio largely because many newspapers owned radio stations and were unwilling to enforce the news embargo against their own stations. In many cases the entrenched economic powers of newspapers became the new economic power of radio. Radio networks became the owners of new television networks and many radio stations were the owners of early television stations.

Meanwhile, the powerful networks were showing no real interest in FM radio and, consequently, a long time elapsed before FM was to achieve a sound economic position. Of course, many AM and television stations now own FM stations, therefore the economic interests of the older media are the same as that of FM.

A similar situation is occurring in cable television, with many broadcasters holding interests in cable systems. Although the FCC discourages such cross-ownership, it does exist and will undoubtedly aid cable in future developments.

As in the past, it seems likely that powerful economic interests will at first oppose the use of new technologies, and then will invest in them. With new investments will come the desire to fully develop the potential of the new medium, and the earlier resistance will give way. What is not certain is which of the new technologies will be the first to attract the attention of large media investors and thus be developed most rapidly.

NOTES

1. Les Brown, "TV's Use of Fiber Transmission Begins," *New York Times* (July 9, 1976), pp. A-1, A-12.
2. *Cable Television in New York* (Albany: New York Conference of Mayors and Municipal Officers, no date), p.4.
3. Staff Report, Subcommittee on Communications, U. S. House of Representatives, *Cable Television: Promise versus Regulatory Performance* (Washington, D.C.: Government Printing Office, 1976), p.9. Although there is not universal agreement on the location and the date of the first cable system, the Mahanoy City case appears to be the first.
4. Ibid.
5. Ibid., p. 11.
6. Sloan Commission on Cable Comunications, *On the Cable: The Television of Abundance* (New York: McGraw-Hill, 1971), p. 24.

7. *Cable Sourcebook 1976* (Washington, D.C.: Broadcasting Publications, 1976), pp. 5, 40.

8. Staff Report, op. cit., p. 17.

9. *Technology of Cable Television* (Washington, D.C.: Cable Television Information Center, 1972), pp. 8, 12.

10. Ibid.

11. Ibid., p. 9.

12. Ibid., p. 10.

13. *Technology of Cable Television*, op. cit., p. 4.

14. Ibid.

15. Staff Report, op. cit., pp. 1–12.

16. *Information Bulletin #18: Cable Television* (Washington, D.C.: FCC, February 1976), p. 2.

17. Ibid., p. 1.

18. Ibid.

19. *Cable Sourcebook 1976*, op. cit., p. 5.

20. Ibid.

21. *Information Bulletin #18*, op. cit., p. 1.

22. *Cable Data* (Washington, D.C.: Cable Television Information Center, 1972), pp. 5–12.

23. Ibid., pp. 12, 13.

24. *Cable Sourcebook 1974* (Washington, D.C.: Broadcasting Publications, 1974), p. 5.

25. See the Sloan Commission study for an analysis of program types that could be carried on cable television.

26. "Pay Cable's Horizons Expand even Farther,"*Broadcasting* (June 2, 1975), pp. 25, 26.

27. *Cable Sourcebook 1976*, op. cit., p. 5.

28. *Cable Television: Promise versus Regulatory Performance* (Washington, D.C.: Government Printing Office, 1976).

Index

A

ABC *see* American Broadcasting Company
AC *see* alternating current
Access 227
Access channels 299, 300
ACT *see* Action for Children's Television
Action for Children's Television (ACT) 160, 161, 227
"Adams Chronicles, The" 174, 177
ADI *see* Areas of dominant interest
"Adventures of Helen and Mary" 74
Advertisers
    program ownership 141
Advertising
    and the broadcaster 152–154
    and program content 162
    and program ownership 141
    commercial chaos 154
    commercials 153
    complaints about 161–162
    decline in radio 93, 94
    editorial 276
    first used to support radio 58–60
    increase in commercials 154
    influence on programming 162–163
    integration with programs 152
    medium for 154
    money spent for 151
    problems of 160–162
    self-regulation 266–267
    regulations and guidelines about 153
    research in 163
    role in mass media industries 150–152
    role of 149–150, 160–161
Advertising agencies 157–159
Affiliates *see* network affiliates
Agnew, Spiro 227
"Aldrich Family, The" 109
Alexander Bill 51
Alexanderson, Ernest 46, 54
Allentown Broadcasting Corp. 240
"All in the Family" 116, 143, 201, 218
All Radio Methodology Study (ARMS) 204, 205

Alternating current 2, 3
Alternator 45, 46, 52
    General Electric and 52
AM *see* amplitude modulation and
    modulation
"America in the Air" 82
American Broadcasting Company 114,
    115, 117, 129
    enters television networking 80,
    108, 109
    formation of 87–90
    profit of 130
American Marconi Wireless Telegraph
    Company 43, 52
American Newspaper Publishers Associa-
    tion 79
American Society of Composers, Authors,
    and Publishers (ASCAP) 78, 139
American Telephone and Telegraph Com-
    pany 60
    buys audion 49
    engages in networking 60–63
    first advertisers on WEAF 59
    partners to RCA 52
"Amos and Andy" 83, 93, 96, 109, 207,
    234
Ampex
    video tape machine and 112, 113
Amplitude 7
Amplitude modulation 6, 10–15
    antenna for 13, 14
    broadcast band 11
    federal classifications 13
    range of signal 11–15
    range of sounds carried 10, 11
    size of channel 10
Andrew W. Mellon Foundation 117
Arbitron
    designation of market areas 187–
    188
    use of diaries 193, 196–197
Areas of dominant interest (ADI) 187–
    188
ARMS *see* All Radio Methodology Study
Armstrong, Edwin
    develops FM 90–92
    invents superheterodyne circuit 54
ASCAP *see* American Society of
    Composers, Authors and
    Publishers
Aspect ratio 21, 22
Associated Press 40, 79
Associated Press of New York (APNY) 40
Atlantic-Richfield Co. 177
Atlantic (trans-) cable 39, 40

Atmospheric noise 15
AT&T *see* American Telephone and
    Telegraph Company
Attenuation 7, 8
Attitude change 218
Audiences
    obstinate 218
    black people 212
    discussion of messages 218
    for soap operas 213
    hours watched 212
    older adults 213
    urban poor 212–213
Audimeter 190–193, 202
Audion 46–49
Average rating 200

B

"Back Home Hour" 74
Baldwin, T. F. 211–212
Bartering 157
Batten, Barton, Durstine, and Osborn
    (BBDO) 111, 231
Bauer, R. A. 218
Baird, John L. 103
Ball, Lucille 109
"Beacon Hill" 184–185
Bell, Alexander Graham 40, 41
Bell Laboratories 96, 103
Benny, Jack 75, 93
"The Beverly Hillbillies" 115
Bell Telephone Company 41
"The Big Surprise" 114
Billboard 138
"Bionic Woman" 117
Black people
    appearance in commercials 216
    portrayal in programming 216, 234
    programs as reinforcement of preju-
    dice 218
    viewing preferences 212
Black weeks, in ratings 193
Block, Martin 77
"Blondie" 83
BMI *see* Broadcast Music, Inc.
Boorstin, Daniel J. 228
Bower, Robert T. 215
Branly, Edouard 42
Brant Rock, Massachusetts
    voice transmissions from 54
BRC *see* Broadcast Rating Council
British Marconi 42
Broadcast bands
    federal assignments of 11, 16

Broadcasting
    advertising support and   152
    as a business   146, 163, 225–226
    definition   1
    voices, music, and   10, 11
Broadcast Music, Inc.   78, 139
Broadcast ownership   122–124
    changes in ownership patterns   146
    conglomerate ownership   125–127
    cross-media ownership   125, 278, 279
    failure of diversification   128, 282, 283
    limits on ownership   278, 279
    market areas   122, 124, 186–188
    multiple ownership   124–125
    single ownership   124
Broadcast Rating Council (BRC)   204, 205
Buchanan, Eleanor Johnson   111
Bullard, Admiral   52
Bureau of Competition   257
Bureau of Consumer Protection   257
Burns and Allen   75
Businessmen's Move for Vietnam Peace   276

C

Cable television (CATV)   35, 36
    access   299, 300
    early development   293–298
    economics of   298, 299
    future of   299–301, 303, 304, 305
    pay cable   299, 301
    regulation of   300–303
    technical features of   296, 297
Campbell-Swinton, A. A.   96
Cantor, M. G.   211
Carlin, George   280
Carnegie Commission on Educational Television   169, 182, 210
Carnegie Foundation   169, 174
Carpentier, Georges   57
Cantril, Hadley   207
Carter, Jimmy   227
Carter's Little Liver Pills   257
Caruso, Enrico   54
Camera, television
    intensity of beam   22, 23
    light sensitive plate   22
    Mosaic   22, 23
    target   22, 23
CATV   see cable television
CBS   see Columbia Broadcasting System

Cease and desist order   254
Ceasar, Sid   109
Chain broadcasting regulations   87–90
Channel capacity   297, 300
Channels
    class I, II, III, IV   13, 14
    size of FM   16
    television   25–28
    television, use of   25–28
"Charlie McCarthy—Edgar Bergen"   93
Chayfsky, Paddy   110
"Cheyenne"   114
Children
    effects of commercials on   218
    program preferences of   212
Children's programs
    as models of social skills   218
    improvement of   227
    removal of commercials from   160–161, 227
    writers and producers of   211
Children's Television Workshop   172–173, 177–178
Circuit   2
Circulation areas   188–189
"Cisco Kid"   109
Citizens groups   146, 227
Citizenship, of licensee   247
Classical radio   94
Clark, P.   214–215
Clayton Act of 1914   256
Clear channels
    class I and II   13
    power of   13
Clerk-Maxwell, James   41
"Climax"   105
Coats, George A.   63
Coaxial cable   32
Code, by wire   1
Codes, radio and television   264–266
Coherer receiver   42, 46
"Colt 45"   114
Coincidental telephone interview   196
Columbia Broadcasting Company (CBS)   31, 63, 79, 80, 93, 129
    as corporate owner   127, 129
    color experiments   103–105
    coverage of racial issues   216
    develops the image orthicon   100
    enters television networking   108, 109
    ownership of media property   127
    profit   130
    rewrites network-affiliate contract   86–90

Columbia Phonograph Broadcasting System 63
Columbia Phonograph Company 63
Commerce clause 239, 270
Commissioners
    appointment of 245–246
    assistants 247
    duties of 247
    qualifications of 246, 247
    employment of 246
    holdings of 246
    resignation of 246
Committee on Interstate and Foreign Commerce (House) 72
Committee on Nationwide Television Audience Measurement (CONTRAM) 204
Communications Act of 1934 72, 106, 114, 128, 139, 165–166, 225, 239–250, 270
    penalities provisions 253, 254
Communism, fear of 111, 112
COMSAT 291
Congress
    investigations of ratings 203–204
    oversight duties 261, 262
Conrad, Frank
    experiments with 8XK, KDKA 56
    Harding-Cox Election aired 56
Consent order 259
CONTRAM see Committee on Nationwide Television Audience Measurement
Coolidge, Calvin 65, 207
Copyright 77
Corinthian Broadcasting Corporation 126
Corporate ownership of broadcasting 125–127, 129, 230
Corporate underwriting see public broadcasting
Corporation for Public Broadcasting (CPB) 169–172, 263
Corrective advertising 162, 259–260
Cost per thousand (CPM) 154, 190
"Counterattack" 111
Courts 262, 263
Coverage of stations 11–15, 16, 17
CPB see Corporation for Public Broadcasting
CPM see cost per thousand
Critics, of broadcasting 226–227
Crosby, Bing 75
Cumulative ratings (CUME) 200
Cycle 4

D

DC see direct current
"Death Valley Days" 75
De Fleur, M. L. 216, 217
de Forest, Lee 46–49, 53–54
    and audion 46–49
    and triode 53–54
De Forest Wireless Company 46
"Deintermix" 107, 108
Demographics 185–186, 201–202
Dempsey, Jack 57
Department of Commerce 64
Department of Health, Education, and Welfare (HEW) 168, 263
Department of Justice, duties 260, 261
Depression
    effects on radio 73–77
    see also Great Depression
Designated Market Areas (DMAs) 187
Diaries
    accuracy of 213
    in audience research 193–196
"Dick Van Dyke" 115
Direct current 2
Disc jockey 77, 78
Disney, Walt 109
Distribution systems, cable 296
DMA see Designated Market Areas
"Doctor I.Q." 83
"Double or Nothing" 83
Drive time 156, 203
Dumont Television Network 89
Duopoly Rule 279
Dun and Bradstreet 126

E

East Pittsburg, and KDKA 56
Editorial advertising 276
Editorializing 276
Educational radio
    growth of 165–166
    program formats 171
    see also public broadcasting
Educational Television and Radio Center (ETRC) 168
Educational Television Facilities Act 168–169
EHF see extremely high frequency
8XK see KDKA
Eisenhower, Dwight D. 231
Electrical impulses see waves, radio
Electricity 2
Electromagnetic spectrum 8, 9

"Electromagnetic Waves in Air and Their Reflection" 42
Electron beam   *see* camera, television
Electronic monitoring, in audience research 190
Epilepsy, and television 219
Epstein, Edward Jay 211
Equal opportunities   *see* equal time
Equal time, for political candidates 251
Ether 41
Everson, George 96
Executive Branch 262
Ex parte 278, 284
Extremely high frequency 8

F

Fairness Doctrine 211, 252, 274–277
Family Hour 217, 281, 282
Farnsworth, Philo 96
FCC   *see* Federal Communications Commission
Federal Communications Commission
    allocation of noncommercial channels and educational broadcasting 101, 102, 167–168
    and color television 103–105
    and commercials 153, 160–161
    and FM 90–92
    and industry 284
    and networks 88–90
    authority of 240–245
    criticism of 161, 254, 255, 256–287
    duties of 240–245, 247, 248, 249–251, 286
    formation of 237–245
    license by lottery 286, 287
    organization of 245–247
    politics and 285, 286
    regulation by 101–108
Federal Radio Act of 1927 65, 67, 71–72, 165
Federal Radio Commission (FRC) 6, 7, 71–72
Federal Trade Commission (FTC) 240
    corrective advertising 259, 260
    false and misleading advertising 162, 256
    formation of 256
    investigation of ratings 203
    powers of over advertising 153, 257, 258, 259
    problems of antitrust 255, 256
Fees, for licenses 251
Fessenden, Reginald 45, 46, 54

Fibber McGee and Molly 75
Fiber communications 290, 306, 307
Field, Cyrus 40
Film responds to television 109, 110
"Fireside Chats" 76, 77
First Amendment and broadcasting 255, 269, 276, 279
"First Line of Defense" 82
Fleming, John 46
FM   *see* frequency modulation
    see also modulation
FM pictures 304, 305
Food and Drug Administration 261
Ford Foundation 168, 176
Fourth network
    in commercial broadcasting 132–133
    in public broadcasting 170, 182
Frame 21, 24
Frankfurter, Felix 72
Freeze, Television 100–103
Frequency 3, 24
Frequency modulation 7, 15–19, 90
Friendly, Fred 111, 254
Fringe time 156
FTC   *see* Federal Trade Commission
Future Shock 221

G

Galbraith, John Kenneth 230
Game and quiz shows 144–145
G.E.   *see* General Electric
General Electric (G. E.)
    and NBC 61, 62
    and RCA 52, 53
Generator 2
Gerbner, George 217, 220, 221
Godfrey, Arthur 93, 109
"The Goldbergs" 109
Golden Age of Radio 92–94
Goldmark, Peter 103
Goldsmith, A. N. 56
Goodman, Julian 275
"Goodyear Television Playhouse" 110
Gorrell, Leslie 96
Gray, Elisha 40
Great Debates 109
Great Depression 73–77
Great Lakes Broadcasting Co. 272
"Green Acres" 115
"Green Hornet" 83
Gross, Larry 217, 220, 221
"Gunsmoke" 115, 201–202

H

Halberstam, David   129, 210
Haley, Alex   117
Hamilton Music Store   57
"Happy Days"   117, 141
Harding-Cox Election aired   56
Havas (France)   40
"Hawaiian Eye"   115
"Hawaii Five-O"   117
HBO   *see* Home Box Office
Headend   296
Hearst Corporation   126
Hearst, William Randolph   40
Hennock, Frieda   101, 102, 274, 284
Henry, Joseph   41
Herald-Traveler   278
Hertz   4
Hertz, Henrich   41, 42
Hetrodyne circuit   54
HF   *see* high frequency
High Culture   232–233
High frequency   8, 9
Hilgemeir, Edward   114
Home Box Office (HBO)   35, 299, 301–303
Hookup charge   298, 299
Hoover, Herbert   60, 65, 238, 270
Hope, Bob   75, 93
Hotel Baltimore   79
Households using television rating (HUT)   199
HUT   *see* households using television rating

I

Iconoscope   100
"I Love Lucy"   109
Image Orthicon   25, 100
Image size   22
Indecent materials   280
Independent stations   132, 140
Industrial Revolution   38
Ionosphere   4, 5, 6, 7
Instantaneous rating   200
Institute of Radio Engineers   90
Intercity Company   64
Interdepartmental Radio Advisory Committee   262
Interference, among stations   57
International News Service   79
International Radio Telephone Company and RCA   52
International Telephone and Telegraph Company
    and ABC   255, 282

Interstate Commerce Commission   72
Ives, Herbert   103

J

Jarvis, Al   77
JCET   *see* Joint Committee on Educational Television
Joint Committee on Educational Television (JCET)   167–168
Jingles, use in advertising   160
Johnson, Lyndon B.   246
    criticism of news coverage   227
    role in establishing public broadcasting   169
    study of decision not to seek reelection   215
Johnson, Nicholas   255, 281, 284
Judson, Arthur   63

K

Kaltenborn, H. V.   81
Kansas City Star   261
KDKA   56, 57, 60
Kennedy, John F.   109, 115, 227–231, 246
Kennedy, Robert   116
KGW   61
KiloHertz   4
Kinescope   24, 26
    see also pick-up tubes; cameras, television
King, Martin Luther   116
"Kojak"   117, 143
KPO   61
"Kraft Television Playhouse"   110
KYW   60

L

Lang, Gladys Engle   210–211, 215–216
Lang, Kurt   210–211, 215–216
"Laverne and Shirley"   117
Lazarsfeld, Paul F.   208
Lear, Norman   113, 116, 132, 234, 282
Lemert, J. B.   215
Letter of compliance   257
Lewis, C.   211–212
Licenses
    by lottery   286
    challenges to   227
    mutually exclusive   250, 251
    penalities for violating law   241–245
    procuring of   250

qualifications of   249, 250
Light   8
"Lights Out"   109
Little, D. G.   56
Local (Class IV) channels   13, 14
Lodge, Sir Oliver   43
Logs   252
London Times   51
"Lone Ranger, The"   75
Lorain Journal   261
Low frequency   8, 9

M

Mack, Richard A.   284
Macy, John W.   171
Mahanoy City, Pa.   294
"Make Believe Ballroom"   77
"The Man From U.N.C.L.E."   115
"Mannix"   117
Manning, Willard G.   210
Marconi, Guglielmo   42–46
Markle Foundation, money for public
    broadcasting   174
Market areas   122, 124, 135, 186–188
Marmola   256
"Mary Hartman, Mary Hartman"   132
"Mary Tyler Moore"   116, 117
Mass culture   232–233
MBS   *see* Mutual Broadcasting System
McArthur Day Parade   210–211
McCarthy, Joe   111
McGowan, Jack J.   210
Media   208, 212, 215
Media buyers   159
Media research   163, 220–222
Medium frequency   4, 8, 9
MegaHertz   4
Merton, Robert K.   208
"Message of Israel"   75
MF   *see* medium frequency
Metropolitan Opera Company   54
Microphones   84, 85
Microwave relays   32–34
Middle of the road   77, 94
Miller v. *California*   280
Minow, Newton   284
Mission Cable   294, 295
"Mission Impossible"   115
Mobil Oil   178
Modulation   9–11
    AM   10–11
    FM   15
    TV   27–30
"Mom and Pop" cable   294, 295

"Monitor"   93
Monopoly   277–279
Monthly fees   298, 299
MOR programming *see* radio and mid-
    dle of the road
Morse, Samuel F. B.   38–40
    see also telegraph
Mosiac   23
Motion, illusion of   20
"Motorola Playhouse"   110
"Mr. District Attorney"   83
Multiplex   92
Murrow, Edward R.   82, 112
Mutual Broadcasting System (MBS)   63,
    77, 78, 80, 86, 129
    complains to the FCC   87–90
Mutually exclusive applications   250, 251

N

NAACP   *see* National Association for the
    Advancement of Colored People
NAB   *see*   National   Association   of
    Broadcasters
NAEB   *see* National Association of
    Educational Broadcasters
Nally, Edward, J.   56
Nantuckey Island, and Marconi   43
National Association for the Advancement
    of Colored People (NAACP)   234
National   Association   of   Broad-
    casters (NAB)   78, 115, 263, 280
    codes   263–266
    enforcement of codes   264, 265
    establishment of Broadcast Rating
        Council   204
    guidelines for commercials 153–
        154, 161, 265
    provisions of code   265, 266
    ratings methodology studies 204–
        205
National Association of Educational
    Broadcasters (NAEB)   167
National Black Media Coalition   227
National Broadcasting Company (NBC)
    80, 93, 129
    coverage of racial issues   216
    enters television networking 108,
        109
    formed   61–63
    hiring of correspondents   211
    profits   130
    sells Blue Network   86–90, 278
National   Citizens   Committee   for
    Broadcasting (NCCB)   227, 283

National Educational Television (NET) 168–169
National Endowment for the Arts   172
National Endowment for the Humanities   172, 177
National Latino Media Coalition   227
National Organization of Women (NOW)   227
National Public Radio (NPR)   169, 179, 180
National Radio Conferences   65
National Television System Committee   31, 96, 104
National Wireless Association   51
Nature   96
NBC   *see* National Broadcasting Company
NCCB   *see* National Citizens Committee for Broadcasting
Networks
    anti-trust   279
    broadcast standards   133
    business of   86–90
    engineering   133
    external structure   129–132
    fourth network   132–133
    international structure of   133–134
    management   133
    network affiliate contract   88, 131
    network affiliates   129, 130–131
    networks and advertisers   129–130
    origin of   61–63, 100
    production   133
    programming   133
    sales   133
    secondary affiliates   130
    self-regulation   266
    service to affiliates   130–131
    traffic   133
News
    and sensationalism   229
    believability of medium   214
    bias in   216, 227
    conflicting research about   214–215
    constructed image of events   210–211, 215–216
    coverage of racial images   216
    creation of   228–229
    distortion of facts   228–229
    economic influence on   211
    guidelines for covering terrorists   229
    influence on ratings   229
    manipulation of news media   228–229

    policy of networks   211
    preference for medium   214–215
    psuedo-events   228
    violence in   115, 116
News Services   40
"The New York Philharmonic Orchestra"   93
New York Times   226
Nielson, A. C.   187, 190–196
Nipkow, Paul   94, 95
Nixon, Richard M.   109, 227, 247
    Checker's speech   231
    objections to public broadcasting   170
Noble, Edward   277
Noll, Roger, G.   210
NOW   *see* National Organization of Women
NPR   *see* National Public Radio

O

Obstinate audience   218
Obscenity   279, 280, 281
Office of Telecommunications Policy (OTP)   262
Off-network   *see* syndication
One-to-a-customer rule   278
Opinion leaders   218
Optical fibers   290
Oscillation   3, 4
Oswald, Lee Harvey   116
Owen, Bruce   210
Owned-and-operated stations (O&Os)   124, 130, 131

P

Paley, William S.   63
Paramount, and ABC   108
Pastore, John O.   115, 219–220
Pay cable   301–303
Payola   139
PBS   *see* Public Broadcasting System
PEACESAT   293
Peck, Merton J.   210
Personal interviews, in audience research   198
Persistence of vision   20, 21
"Petticoat Junction"   115
Philco   90
Pick-up tube   22–25
    phosphorus dots   22, 25
Picture tube   23–25
Pilots   *see* programming, television

Plumbicon   25
Political candidates   230–232
Pottsville Broadcasting Company   240
Preece, Sir William   42
Press-Radio War   78–81
Prime time   156
Program proposal of licensee   250
Program requirements, of FCC   252
Program preferences   212–215
Program rating   199–200
Programs   77, 109, 110
    and attitude changes   218
    and ratings   146, 200–202
    appearance of women and
        minorities   146
    affiliate viewing of programs   142–
        143
    attracting audiences for advertisers
        135
    changes in programming   145
    children's programming   145, 281,
        282
    diversity of   201
    dramatic and comedy shows   73, 74
    during depression   73–77
    feature films   143
    game and quiz shows   144
    ideal audience for   135
    importance of market size   135
    influenced by advertisers   162–163
    local productions   140
    mini-series   143
    network programming   141
    news   144
    pilots   142
    portrayal of occupational roles   216–
        217
    program costs   140, 141–142
    program sources   140
    purpose of   135
    radio   77, 79–86
    regulation of   281, 282
    religious programs   145
    reruns   142
    selection process   142–143
    soap operas   145
    specials   144
    sports   144
    syndication companies   140–141
    variety shows   144
Progressive radio   94
Pseudo-events   144, 228
Public broadcasting
    diversity of programming   180
    establishment of   169

    funding   171–172, 173, 174–178,
        181–182
    local station production   177, 178–
        179
    pressure from commercial
        broadcasters   182
    vulnerability to political pressures
        181
Public Broadcasting Act of 1967   169, 171
Public Broadcasting Financing Act of
    1975   182
Public Broadcasting System (PBS)
    establishment of   169
    management of station program
        cooperative   176–177
    power struggle with CPB   170–171
    underwriting office   178
"Public interest, convenience, and
    necessity"   65, 72, 238–240
Public notice, of intent to procure
    license   250
Public television   170, 174–176
Pulse, Inc.   198

Q

Qualifications, of license   249, 250
Quantum theory   4
Queensboro Corporation   59
Quiz program scandals   113. 114

R

Radio Act of 1912   64, 270
Radio Act of 1927   65, 67, 71
Radio
    advertising and programming   136
    market size and programming   136
    MOR   77, 94, 136
    Top-40   77, 94, 136
    types of programming   94, 136–139
Radio Code   264
Radio Corporation of America (RCA)   31,
    57
    color television experiments   96,
        103–105
    experiments in television   96, 97
    develops video tape machine   112,
        113
    flaws   61
    formed   52
    forms NBC   61
    frequency modulation experiments
        90–92
    partners   52, 53, 60, 61

"Radio Group" 61
Radio waves, location on spectrum 8, 9
RCA *see* Radio Corporation of America
Rand Corporation, study of media
    concentration 129
    cross-media ownership 210
Rates, advertising 156
Rate cards 156, 191
Ratings 146, 185–205
    data for 187–188
    importance of 146, 185–186, 205
    monitoring of 203–205
    reporting results 199–200
    use in radio 202–203
Recall interview 196
Record communication 39
"Red Channels: The Report of Communist
    Influence in Radio and Televi-
    sion" 111
Regional (class III) channels 13
Red Lion 274
Red Scares 111, 112
"Red Skeleton Show, The" 105
Regional networks, educational 179
Reis, Philip 40, 41
Republic, S. S. 43
Reruns *see* programs
Research 163, 210–222
Research methods 208–210
"Rip-and-read" newscast 94
Robinson, J. P. 214
Rockefeller Foundation
    money for public broadcasting and
    174
Roosevelt, Franklin D. 72, 76, 77, 88,
    96, 238
"Roots" 117
Roper study of viewer preference 214–
    215
Roth 280
Ruby, John 116
Ruggels, L 214–215
Russo-Japanese War 51

S

Sampling, in audience research 189
Sanctions 241, 244, 253, 254
Sarnoff, David 54, 56, 72, 90
Satellite links 35
Satellites 305, 306
Scan, of electronic beam 24
Scanning 24, 96
Scatter propagation 34, 35

Scheduling strategies for programming
    200–201
Screen Actors Guild 234, 282
Secretary of Commerce 64
Self-regulation 263–267
"Selling of the Pentagon" 276
Senate, hearings on violence 220
Serling, Rod 110
"Sesame Street" 218
"Service to the Front" 82
Senlecq, M. 96
Seven-seven-seven rule 122, 279. *See
    also* broadcast ownership
"77 Sunset Strip" 115
Sex talk shows 280
Sexual stereotyping 216
Share of audience rating 199
Shepard, John III 60
"Sherlock Holmes" 75
Sherman Anti-trust Act 256
SHF *see* super high frequency
Short wave 36
"Shower of Stars" 105
Shutter speed 21
SIA *see* audimeter
Silverman, Fred 203
"Six Million Dollar Man" 117
"Sixth Report and Order" 101
"$64,000 Question" 114
Smith, Kate 75, 207
Soap operas 213, 214, 216
Soviet Union 111
Splawn, W. W. 72
Sponsored programs 155
Sports broadcasting 57
Spot commercials 155
Standard Rate and Data Service 156
Staggers, Harley O. 276
Station Program Cooperative (SPC)
    176–178
Station representatives 159–160
Stations 98
    broadcast standards 134
    engineering 10–30
    structure of 128, 129–132
    management 133
    production 134
    programming 133
    range of Am 11–15
    range of FM 16, 17
    sales 134
    television 19–30, 98
    traffic 134
Stefani (Italy) 40

Stemple, Herbert   114
Stereophonic (FM)   16
"The Streets of San Francisco"   117
Stipulation   259
"Studio One"   110
"Sugar Foot"   114
Sullivan, Ed   109
Sunday, Billy   74
Super high frequency (SHF)   8, 9
Supreme Court   89
Surgeon-General, Study of Television Violence and Agression   115, 219–220
"Suspense"   109
Sustaining programs   155
"S.W.A.T."   117
Sweep Weeks, in ratings   193, 196
Synchronizing impulses   23
Syndication companies   140–141

T

"Talent Scouts"   109
Target   22, 23
Teenagers, program preferences of   212
Telegraph   39
"Telephone Group"   61
Telephone interviews, in audience research   196, 198
Telephone, invention of   40, 41
Television   19–30
    aspect ratio   21
    brightness (intensity)   23
    camera   22, 23
    channels   25
    color   30, 103–105
    definition   19
    early experiments   94–97
    educational   101–103
    freeze   30, 31, 98, 100–103
    image size   22
    light sensitive plate   22
    line system   20
    networks established   100
    persistence of vision   20, 21
    picture quality   19, 20
    resolution of picture   20
    scanning   24
    system   31
    transmission   25–29
    see also modulation
Television and Growing Up: The Impact of Television Violence   220
Teleprompter   290

Thomas, Lowell   81
Titanic, S. S.   43, 44, 54
"Toast of the Town"   109
"Today"   109, 237
Toffler, Alvin   221
Toll broadcasting   see advertising
Top-40/contemporary   77, 94, 137–139
"Topless" radio   280
Tradeout   157
Trans-Radio Press   79
Translators   36
Triode   47, 48, 54
Truman, Harry   109, 111
"Twenty-One"   114

U

UHF   see ultra high frequency
"The Untouchables"   115
"Unicontrolled" receiver   56
Ultra high frequency   8, 9
    FCC and   26, 101–103
    growth of   105–108
United Church of Christ
    Office of Communication of   227, 236
United Independent Broadcasters   63
United Press   79
U. S. Office of Education
    funding to Children's Television Workshop   173, 177
    participation on JCET   167
United States Court of Appeals   125
"Upstairs, Downstairs"   174, 178

V

Vail, Alfred   39
Very high frequency   8, 9, 26, 98, 101–103
Very low frequency   8, 9
VHF   see very high frequency
Video tape   112, 113
Vidicon   25
Vietnam   116
Violence Profile   217, 221
Violence, television
    and adults   220
    and aggression   218–220
    and children   218–220
    as a reflection of society   219
    as essential to plot and conflict   211–212
    as revealing information about society   217

JCET study   167–168
study of Surgeon General   115, 219–220
trends in programming   114–116, 217
VLF   *see* very low frequency
Volume   *see* amplitude

W

Wavelength   4, 7
Walker, Charlie   280
"War of the Worlds"   82
"Warner Brothers Presents"   109
Washington Star   278
Watson, Thomas A.   41
Waves   4–8, 14, 15
WBAI   280
WBAY   59
WBLS-FM   125
WCBS (WCBW)   108
WDKD   280
WEAF   59, 60, 61
Western Electric   46
    partner in RCA   52
Western Union   40
Westinghouse   127
    partner in RCA   52, 61
WGLD-FM   280
WGN   58, 61
WGY   60
WHDH-TV   278, 284
Whig National Convention, telegraphed   39
White, Wallace H. Jr.   270
WHKC   272
Whorehouse era   284
Wiley, Richard   281
Wilson, Woodrow   51
Wireless   1, 38
    invention of   41–43
    maritime uses of   43, 44
    military uses of   51
Wireless Ship Act   49, 64
Wireless Speciality Apparatus Company, partner in RCA   52–53

Wireless Telegraph and Signal Company (British Marconi)   42
Wire relays   32
WITF-TV   173
WJZ   60, 61
WLBT-TV   236, 255
WLS   58
WLW   86
WMAL-AM-FM-TV   278
WMCA-AM   125
WNAC   60
WNBC (WNBT)   108, 227
WNCN   227
WNET   169
WNEW   77
Wolff (Germany)   40
Women, portrayal on television   216, 234–235
Wometco Enterprizes, Inc.   126
WOR   86
World War I   56
    all nongovernment stations closed   51
World War II   79–86
    freeze on licensing   98
    radio during   79–86
World's Fair (1939)   96
WTMJ   92, 96
W2XMN   90
WXYZ   86

X

X-rays   8

Y

Young, Owen, D.   52
    forms RCA   52, 53
"Your Show of Shows"   109

Z

Zapple Doctrine   275
Zenith Radio Decision   65
Zenger, John Peter   269
Zworykin, Valdimir, inventor of kinescope   24, 26, 96, 97, 100